The Paradoxes of Peacebuilding Post-9/11

This book is published in cooperation with the North-South Institute, an international development research centre based in Ottawa, Canada (www.nsi-ins.ca).

Edited by Stephen Baranyi

The Paradoxes of Peacebuilding Post-9/11

STANFORD SECURITY STUDIES
an Imprint of Stanford University Press
Stanford, California

Published in the USA by Stanford University Press, Stanford, California.

ISBN 978-0-8047-6090-4

CIP data for this book is available at the Library of Congress.

To all those who persist in working for sustainable peace
rather than
being captivated by the latest newsworthy crisis

Contents

Preface

Roy Culpeper and Brazão Mazula

Shortly after the tragic events of 11 September 2001, the International Development Research Centre (IDRC) convened a dialogue with partners to reflect on where the enterprise of postwar peacebuilding was heading. At a pivotal meeting in late 2002, many partners, especially from the South, expressed profound concerns about the enduring gaps between the dreams of liberation and transformation associated with peacebuilding in societies like El Salvador, Palestine, and South Africa, and the grim realities of fragile peace, violence, and enduring injustice on the ground. Others, particularly from the North, worried about the possibility that the enterprises of peacebuilding, and of protecting those most vulnerable to grave human rights violations, were being subordinated to geopolitical interests, as seemed to be happening in Afghanistan.

The What Kind of Peace Is Possible (WKOP) project grew out of that initial dialogue. It was a novel attempt to create space (particularly) for Southern researchers and practitioners to put their stamp on mostly Northern debates. It was an attempt to help Southern analysts ground their arguments in solid research and in an ongoing dialogue with stakeholders – especially women, the poor, and excluded identity groups – whose voices were often sidelined by conventional assessments of peacebuilding. WKOP also aimed to influence peacebuilding practices in each society and, modestly, at the UN. Finally, it aimed to do all this through partnerships between six Southern civil society institutions and three Northern research centres – all listed in the section on Contributors.

This book brings together some of the outputs from this collective effort. The introduction sets out the issues and situates them within broader debates. Nine case studies examine particular experiences in depth. A concluding chapter compares the cases and synthesizes key conclusions. Each of these texts was submitted to extensive peer review through the WKOP project. Most were validated in the author's own society.

It has been a challenge, a pleasure, and an honour to be associated with the WKOP project for three years. For an organization like the Centre for the Study of Democracy and Development (CEDE) in Mozambique, the project required tremendous effort at every step, from the design stage through policy engagement and the delivery of final outputs. Yet the WKOP project enabled us to deepen our research at the nexus of peacebuilding and local development, reach out to new actors at the national level and in several municipalities, and share our experiences in important international forums. As part of the collective monitoring and evaluation process, other Southern partners also remarked that this collaboration helped them to broaden their research – for example, on the gender dimensions of peace-building – and strengthen their ability to feed evidence-based conclusions into policy processes. For the North-South Institute (NSI), coordinating such an ambitious undertaking also brought many challenges, including that of providing sufficient support for Southern institutes while delivering on many other responsibilities. WKOP has also been a profound learning experience for NSI, since it has influenced both the content of our analyses and our way of working with partners.

As chief executives of our respective centres, each of us has only been able to modestly engage with this project. This gives us a privileged position from which to view its results, some of which are captured in this book. From our standpoint as insider-outsiders, three outcomes of this complex process are especially noteworthy.

First, the combined results of these case studies and the overarching pieces underscore the urgency of addressing two major trends in contemporary international affairs. The first is the enduring gap between short-term peacebuilding measures and the long-term changes required to prevent the recurrence of armed conflict. This trend is at the core of the new UN Peacebuilding Commission's mandate. The second is the drift away from relatively successful multilateral peacebuilding based on negotiated agree-ments towards more unilateral but far less successful stabilization opera-tions, as in Iraq today. This second trend is not receiving the attention it deserves, including in Canada, where the current government seems bent on justifying errors in countries like Afghanistan. This book is a sober re-minder about the long-term consequences of stabilization operations.

Second, the case studies shed light on the nuances and possibilities inher-ent in particular experiences. The studies on Guatemala and Mozambique challenge mainstream assessments of peacebuilding in those countries by arguing that, while peacebuilding has been relatively successful, it remains fragile, though it could be deepened through greater creativity and pressure on the part of specific local, national, and international actors. The study on Haiti offers an original interpretation in that it shows how even an unpromising stabilization operation can be turned around through a combination of principled leadership and political inclusion. The two studies on the Palestinian Territories, including an original study on disarmament, demobilization, and reintegration (DDR), provide new insight into the missed opportunities for change presented by the election of Hamas in January 2006. Their pessimistic conclusions about current Israeli stabilization efforts are perhaps less original, but no less important, in practical terms.

Third, the chapters in this book are only some of the outputs from the WKOP project. In each country partners also produced policy briefs with action-oriented recommendations for key actors, particularly at the national level. We invite readers to look at those policy briefs on the North-South Institute's website. In most countries partners also worked with the media to generate broader public debate on these issues. In some contexts recommendations were picked up by governments and, more often, by civil society coalitions. Even in Sri Lanka, partners can take some credit for keeping recommendations for deeper institutional reforms on the public agenda at a time when most actors were understandably focused on preventing renewed warfare. This is entirely consistent with the main conclusion of the WKOP project – namely, that without profound reforms over longer time frames, supported by broader national constituencies, peace is unlikely to be sustained. Building those constituencies is clearly a challenge everywhere.

We trust that some readers will find the inspiration, and concrete ideas, needed to nurture such constituencies for sustainable peacebuilding in their own society and beyond. And we hope that others might begin to understand why neither peace nor stability can be imposed from the outside through the barrel of a gun.

Acknowledgments

All edited books are a collective endeavour, but this one involved a large number of colleagues who deserve acknowledgment. I thank all the authors for their perseverance in conducting original research, writing, editing, and adhering to a common framework, despite the difficult conditions most faced in their respective societies. Thanks are due to our institutional partners in each country and to the numerous practitioners whose input made the research so rich. Warm thanks go to my North-South Institute colleagues, particularly Kristiana Powell, Jennifer Salahub, Lois Ross, Diane Guevremont, Ann Weston, and Roy Culpeper, for their support over the life of the WKOP project.

Our funders – the International Development Research Centre, the Canadian International Development Agency, the Ford Foundation, and the Norwegian Agency for Development Cooperation – deserve credit for their unflagging support. I am especially grateful for the engagement of IDRC colleague Pamela Scholey, who bridged the gap that usually separates funders from researchers by co-authoring a chapter in this book.

Thanks to Emily Andrew, other UBC Press colleagues, and three anonymous reviewers for their generous contributions to this publication. While the authors accept primary responsibility for any remaining omissions or errors, we are grateful to all those who put their energies into making this work possible.

Acronyms

ADERAM	Asosyasyon pou Develòpman Economik Rivyè Blanch [Association for Rivière Blanche Economic Development] (Haiti)
ANBP	Afghanistan's New Beginnings Programme
ANN	Alianza Nueva Nación [New Nation Alliance] (Guatemala)
ASECs	Assemblées de la section communale [communal section assemblies] (Haiti)
CASECs	Conseil d'administration des sections communales [communal section administrative councils] (Haiti)
CCI	Cadre de coopération intérimaire [Interim Cooperation Framework] (Haiti)
CDC	community development council (Afghanistan)
CEDE	Centro de Estudios de Democracia e Desenvolvimento [Centre for the Study of Democracy and Development] (Mozambique)
CEP	Conseil électorale provisiore [Provisionary Electoral Council] (Haiti)
CFA	ceasefire agreement (Sri Lanka)
CIDA	Canadian International Development Agency
CNG	Conseil national de gouvernement [National Council of Government] (Haiti)
COCODES	Consejo Comunitario de Desarrollo [Community Development Council] (Guatemala)
CODEDES	Consejo Departamental de Desarrollo [Departmental Development Council] (Guatemala)
COMUDES	Consejo Comunitario de Desarrollo [Municipal Development Council] (Guatemala)

CONADES	Consejo Nacional de Desarrollo [National Development Council] (Guatemala)
COREDES	Consejo Regional de Desarrollo [Regional Development Council] (Guatemala)
CSOs	civil society organizations
DAC	Development Assistance Committee
DDR	disarmament, demobilization, and reintegration
ECHA	Executive Committee on Humanitarian Affairs (United Nations)
EGP	Ejército Guerrillero de los Pobres [Guerrilla Army of the Poor] (Guatemala)
FADH	Forces armées d'Haïti (Haitian Armed Forces)
FAR	Fuerzas Armadas Rebeldes [Rebel Armed Forces] (Guatemala)
FCA	Fondo de Compensación Municipal [Municipal Compensation Fund] (Mozambique)
FGT	Fundación Guillermo Toriello [Guillermo Toriello Foundation] (Guatemala)
FLACSO	Facultad Latinoamericana de Ciencias Sociales (Latin-American Faculty of Social Sciences)
FMLM	Farabundo Martí National Liberation Front (El Salvador)
FPs	facilitating partners (Afghanistan)
FRELIMO	Frente de Libertação de Moçambique [Mozambican Liberation Front]
FRG	Guatemalan Republican Front (Frente Republicano Guatemalteco)
GPPAC	Global Partnership for the Prevention of Armed Conflict
ICISS	International Commission on Intervention and State Sovereignty
ICRW	International Center for Research on Women
IDRC	International Development Research Centre
IFIs	international financial institutions
IPA	International Peace Academy
ISAF	International Security Assistance Force (Afghanistan)
ISGA	Interim Self-Governing Authority (Sri Lanka)
JVP	Janatha Vimukthi Peramuna [Sinhalese nationalist party] (Sri Lanka)
LICUS	Low-Income Countries under Stress (World Bank initiative)
LTTE	Liberation Tigers of Tamil Eelam [Tamil Tigers] (Sri Lanka)

MAE	Ministério de Administração Estatal [Ministry of State Administration] (Mozambique)
MICAH	Mission internationale civile d'appuien Haïti [International Civilian Support Mission in Haiti]
MINUGUA	Misión de Verificación de las Naciones Unidas en Guatemala [United Nations Verification Mission in Guatemala]
MINUSTAH	Mission des Nations Unies pour la stabilisation de Haïti [United Nations Stabilization Mission in Haiti]
MRRD	Ministry for Rural Rehabilitation and Development (Afghanistan)
NATO	North Atlantic Treaty Organization
NSI	North-South Institute
NSP	National Solidarity Program (Afghanistan)
OAS	Organization of American States
ODA	official development assistance
OECD	Organisation for Economic Co-operation and Development
OEF	Operation Enduring Freedom (Afghanistan)
OPL	Organisation politique Lavalas (Haiti)
ORPA	Organización Revolucionaria del Pueblo en Armas [Revolutionary Organization of the People in Arms] (Guatemala)
PA	Palestinian Authority
PA	People's Alliance party (Sri Lanka)
PACs	Patrullas de autodefensa civil [civil defense patrols] (Guatemala)
PAN	Plan por el Adelantamiento Nacional [National Advancement Party] (Guatemala)
PARPA	Plano de Acção para a Redução de Pobreza Absoluta [Action Plan for the Reduction of Absolute Poverty] (Mozambique)
PBC	Peacebuilding Commission (UN)
PDPA	People's Democratic Party of Afghanistan
PGT	Partido Guatemalteco de los Trabajadores [Guatemalan Communist Party]
PIJ	Palestinian Islamic Jihad
PLC	Palestinian Legislative Council
PLO	Palestinian Liberation Organization
PMA	policía militar ambulante [mobile military police] (Guatemala)
PPD	Participacion y Democracia (Program for Participation and Democracy)

PRSP	poverty reduction strategy paper
PRTs	provincial reconstruction teams (Afghanistan)
PSR	Palestinian Center for Policy and Survey Research
PSS	Palestinian security sector
RENAMO	Resistência Nacional Moçambicana [Mozambican National Resistance]
R2P	responsibility to protect
SAP	structural adjustment program
SEPAZ	Secretaría de la Paz [Peace Secretariat] (Guatemala)
SIRHN	Subcommittee for Immediate Humanitarian and Rehabilitation Needs (Sri Lanka)
TNA	Tamil National Alliance (Sri Lanka)
UNCTAD	United Nations Conference on Trade and Development
UNDP	United Nations Development Program
UNF	United National Front (Sri Lanka)
UNFAO	United Nations Food and Agriculture Association
UNSC	United Nations Security Council
UNSCR	United Nations Security Council Resolution
UPFA	United People's Freedom Alliance (Sri Lanka)
URNG	Unidad Nacional Revolucionaria Guatemalteca [Guatemalan National Revolutionary Unity]
USAID	United States Agency for International Development
VAT	value-added tax
WKOP	What Kind of Peace Is Possible

The Paradoxes of Peacebuilding Post-9/11

1

Introduction: What Kind of Peace Is Possible in the Post-9/11 Era?

Stephen Baranyi

What change will peace bring us? What is to be expected from this peace?

> – John Paul Lederach, 1999 echoing stakeholder voices

Women's perspectives tend to privilege the notion of a "just" peace, as defined from the perspective of the discriminated and disempowered.

> – Rita Manchanda, 2001

If people are denied the fruits of peace – such as shelter, education, health care and employment – sustainable peace will be much harder to achieve.

> – Jan Egeland, 2004

In September 2005, diplomats met in a special general assembly of the United Nations (UN) to review the implementation of the Millennium Declaration. On matters related to rebuilding societies after wars, speakers stressed the need for increased investment in peacebuilding and enhanced UN capacities to coordinate such efforts. Some states stressed the importance of renewing efforts to transform the attitudes and institutions that generate armed violence. Others drew the links between sustainable peacebuilding, respect for human rights, equitable development, and the prevention of armed conflicts.

In the end, member states and UN officials agreed to establish a peacebuilding commission to coordinate international efforts overall and in priority countries. They agreed to establish a voluntary fund for peacebuilding to stabilize financing for such efforts and a peacebuilding support office in the UN Secretariat. Though the outcome document also included general statements on conflict prevention and the responsibility to protect (R2P), it avoided making any operational connections between those issues and new UN mechanisms to enhance postwar peacebuilding.

The broad support for the creation of the Peacebuilding Commission and related mechanisms reflected the recognition that it is in most states' interest to strengthen international efforts to rebuild societies damaged by war. It represented a qualified vote of confidence for UN leadership in this domain, and it was a clear reminder that UN agencies must work better with others – including host governments and civil society organizations, regional bodies, and international financial institutions – to secure peace. But this and the much more cautious reaction to R2P also reflected widespread disquiet about controversial unilateral military interventions, particularly in Iraq, and dissatisfaction with the international community's inability to consolidate peace in societies as diverse as Haiti and the Palestinian Occupied Territories.

Is it true that many postwar peacebuilding efforts are failing to deliver on the goal of sustainable peace? Why is it so difficult to parlay short-term measures – like the disarmament, demobilization, and reintegration (DDR) of combatants – into the longer-term transformations required to sustain peace and prevent war? Has the trend towards international military intervention affected the sustainability of peacebuilding efforts? What combination of local, national, and international strategies can bridge enduring peacebuilding deficits? In brief, what kind of peace is possible in the post-9/11 era?

These are the questions that a group of researcher-practitioners has been grappling with since 2003 in the What Kind of Peace is Possible (WKOP) project. Through WKOP we have conducted research and engaged stakeholders in dialogue on the difficulties/possibilities for sustainable peacebuilding in six contexts. Guatemalan and Mozambican partners have led this work in their countries, two cases in which relative success can already be observed over the long term. Haitian partners led the work in a country where failed peacebuilding spawned a new international intervention in 2004, the outcomes of which are still uncertain. Afghan, Palestinian, and Sri Lankan partners led this work in their countries/territories, where quite distinct peace efforts have all but collapsed. Norwegian partners led original research on DDR in Afghanistan and Guatemala, while a Palestinian-Canadian duo conducted similar research in the Palestinian Territories.

This book focuses on three aspects of postwar peacebuilding: DDR, democratic governance, and economic development. Many other aspects – from infrastructure rehabilitation to truth and justice – are also important, but we selected these dimensions because they seem central to the end goal of sustainability. For reasons that will be explained in this chapter, our research has also focused on peacebuilding at the national and local levels, with a particular concern for national agency and social inclusion.

This chapter is a revised version of the paper that guided the group's case studies. It reviews global policy debates on peacebuilding and related issues, such as fragile states. It delves into debates on the democratic governance and economic dimensions of peacebuilding, and it glances at the literature on DDR. It previews the nine case studies in *The Paradoxes of Peacebuilding Post-911* and highlights a set of propositions that informed our research. The chapter ends by suggesting that, despite the fallout from 11 September 2001, there may, in some contexts, still be significant space for sustainable peacebuilding. National and international stakeholders committed to sustainable peace could form more effective coalitions to push for deeper changes in those societies. This somewhat open-ended introduction should be read in tandem with the concluding chapter, which ends on a more sober note regarding what kind of peace is possible post-9/11.

Peacebuilding since 1989

Drawing on distinctions made by analysts of UN peace operations, we divide the evolution of peacebuilding since the end of the Cold War into three types: "second-generation" multidimensional peacebuilding tied mostly to negotiated peace agreements in the early 1990s; more robust but still multilateral "third-generation" peace operations that increased in the late 1990s; and more forceful, sometimes unilateral, "fourth-generation" interventions since 9/11.[1] These generations have overlapped, several types coexist today, and movement from one to another has not necessarily yielded better outcomes. Before exploring this last observation in more depth, let us elaborate on the trend itself.

The collapse of the Soviet Union and the end of the Cold War generated much optimism about the possibilities for resolving wars that had been fuelled by the East-West rivalry. Against that backdrop, from the late 1980s to the mid-1990s a series of ambitious peace operations were carried out in Namibia, Nicaragua, El Salvador, Mozambique, Cambodia, Angola, Guatemala, and Bosnia. Despite their differences, these operations had certain common characteristics. Most derived their mandates from internationally mediated negotiations between national parties. Peace agreements were verified by multilateral peacekeeping and civilian observer missions. They involved coordinated reconstruction encompassing the DDR of ex-combatants, the voluntary resettlement of refugees and internally displaced persons, demining, institutional reforms to promote human rights and democratic governance, and (sometimes) truth and reconciliation processes. In keeping with the triumph of the West in the great contest of the Cold War, peacebuilding also included macroeconomic and fiscal reforms to establish a market-oriented environment conducive to reconstruction.

The policy rationale underpinning this first type of post-Cold War peace operations – dubbed "second-generation peace operations" because their multidimensional mandates and capabilities went far beyond classical Cold War UN peacekeeping – was codified in key multilateral documents such as the UN Secretary-General's 1992 *Agenda for Peace* and the 1997 Organisation for Economic Co-operation and Development (OECD) Development Assistance Committee (DAC) *Guidelines on Conflict, Peace and Development Co-operation.* Scholars such as Roland Paris (1997, 2004) have convincingly argued that this rationale could be described as "liberal peacebuilding" because it rested on classical liberal assumptions about the benefits of multiparty democracy, free markets, and international cooperation as solutions to problems of violent conflict.

Although the UN and the Northern donors grouped in the DAC assumed that the international community had key roles to play in peace processes, they recognized that these processes would only be successful if they were owned by national actors over the long run. While this approach tended to focus on the challenge of "bridging the relief-to-development" gap in the initial postwar years, there was a belief that peace could only be sustained through a transformation of the institutions and attitudes that had fuelled war. It was acknowledged that peace could only be consolidated through reforms to the markets, political, security, and other institutions, as well as the worldviews of key actors in war-torn societies.

Despite the apparent successes of this type of post-Cold War peace operations, by the mid-1990s there was an emerging belief that negotiated solutions might not be possible in some contexts and that military intervention may be required. The establishment of a safe haven for Kurds in Northern Iraq and the 1994 intervention in Haiti were precursors to this trend. In turn, the failure of national authorities and the international community to protect civilians from massive human rights violations in Bosnia and Rwanda spurred a profound rethinking of what is required to protect people and to promote peace. By the time violence escalated in East Timor and Kosovo in early 1999, some governments and multilateral organizations were ready to deploy forces to protect civilians. Those efforts were dubbed "third-generation peace operations," or "peace enforcement operations," because they involved the use of force in ways that departed significantly from the classical UN peacekeeping norm of consent. The tools of liberal peacebuilding were used to reactivate the economy and to nurture democratic institutions, with the difference that state-like entities were also being built in Timor-Leste and Kosovo.

The US-led invasion of Afghanistan, shortly after the terrorist attacks on 9/11, was an extension of this trend towards forceful intervention, but it was distinct in several respects. That intervention was justified on the grounds of self-defence. Moreover, it was only endorsed by the UN Security Council and justified on humanitarian grounds after the fact. The US-led intervention in Iraq two years later was initially justified as pre-emptive self-defence and was never fully sanctioned by the UN Security Council. In Afghanistan the invading forces allowed the UN and the new national authorities to lead in rebuilding the country and forging longer-term governance arrangements. In Iraq the occupying powers remained in almost complete control of public life until their partial handover to the Interim Government in June 2004. One could characterize the interventions in Afghanistan and, especially, in Iraq as a new phase of much more forceful, unilateral military interventions and attempts to build peace under conditions of continued warfare. One could use the label "fourth-generation peace operations" to characterize these experiences, though the occupation of Iraq should probably not be associated with the concept of peace at all. These new operations coexist with efforts that belong to earlier phases – such as the UN Mission in Sudan (which fits the second-generation mould) and the African Union Mission in Sudan (which fits the third-generation model).

In sum, since 1989 there has been an increase in the use of force, external leadership, and unilateralism, and a decrease in negotiated peace processes, national ownership, and multilateralism in peacebuilding efforts. It is tempting for those concerned about fourth-generation interventions to look back on the 1990s as the golden age of peacebuilding. Yet it is important to develop a less romantic view of second-generation operations. Three patterns are important in this regard. First, many of those operations brought wars to an end but some did not secure even that minimal aim: for example, Angola returned to war despite major peacemaking, peacekeeping, and peacebuilding efforts. Second, even cases in which wars have been terminated, it has proven difficult to implement the reforms many see as necessary for sustainable peacebuilding. Third, negotiated peacekeeping and peacebuilding did not provide answers to the challenge of protection from massive human rights violations. The preview of peacebuilding in Palestine illustrates the limitations of second-generation efforts (see Box 1).[2]

Parallel to the evolution of peacebuilding in practice, several literatures emerged that analyzed those experiences. In the mid-1990s, several comparative studies concluded that what distinguished cases of successful war termination (like El Salvador) from cases of failure (like Angola) was the level of international engagement as well as the presence or absence of "spoilers" – namely, powerful actors opposed to peacebuilding on the ground (e.g., Hampson 1996). These studies were followed by larger quantitative and comparative studies. One of the most comprehensive studies, coordinated by the International Peace Academy (IPA), concluded that two basic categories of factors shape outcomes: (1) characteristics of the implementation environment on the ground, especially the character of spoilers, spoils, and the policies of neighbouring states; and (2) the approaches of international actors (namely, their strategies, resource commitments, and incentives, particularly their security interests). The IPA study suggested that the

Box 1
Peacebuilding in the Palestinian Territories

The 1993 and 1995 Oslo Peace Accords initially brought significant peace dividends to Palestinians and Israelis:

- Israel withdrew from parts of the occupied territories and Palestinians curtailed their attacks on Israeli targets.
- The Palestinian Liberation Organization (PLO) returned to establish the Palestinian Authority, including holding elections for the Legislative Council.
- The economy grew at an average of 5 percent per year (1995-2000).

Yet flaws in the accords and in their implementation sowed the seeds of failure:

- The executive branch and the PLO old guard maintained control over power, resisted demands for accountability to the Legislative Council and the judiciary, and put off demands to incorporate opposition movements through local elections.
- The interim nature of the peace agreements, and their tendency to privilege the short-term security priorities of Israel and the PLO old guard, converged to undermine human rights and democratic development over the longer term.
- The international community was unable to deploy peacekeepers due to opposition by the government of Israel and US support for that position.
- This was the background to the second Intifada in 2000. Renewed violence and reoccupation drove the economy into recession, narrowed democratic spaces, and fuelled the popularity of Hamas and other nationalist forces.

The phased local elections that began in December 2004, and the first free and fair Legislative Council elections in January 2006, brought Hamas into democratic politics. The unilateral Israeli disengagement from the Gaza Strip and initial signals by the Olmert government also suggested that there might be new hope for peace.

According to the case study by the Palestinian Center for Policy and Survey Research: "Little progress is possible without solid international intervention. Yet successful Palestinian peacebuilding is more likely a mission impossible for the international community of the Cold War and post 9/11 era."

likelihood of success – defined in terms of war termination – was greatest where an enabling environment on the ground converged with the vital security interests of external actors and led the latter to commit significant military and financial assets to peace operations. This research also led the authors to conclude that international actors should give priority to measures like DDR and security sector reform in the short run and, secondarily, to human rights protection and reconciliation, if they want to lay foundations for lasting peace (Stedman, Rothchild, and Cousens 2002).

These studies have made enormous contributions to our understanding of peacebuilding. They have unpacked the interplay between certain conditions on the ground and international engagement with regard to shaping degrees of success or failure. They have yielded pointed policy recommendations for international actors.

Yet there are striking limits to this literature. First, it rests on short-term, minimalist criteria for success – namely, war termination that outlasts the departure of most international actors and the holding of one or two elections. This raises the question of whether these benchmarks are satisfactory to national stakeholders and whether they are sufficient to prevent the recurrence of armed conflict over the long run. Second, this literature tends to paint a simplistic picture of national actors. It enriches our understanding of spoilers and their reliance on spoils like diamonds, but it provides few insights into the strategies of national actors on the other sides of the equation: the reformist politicians, socially conscious businesspersons, or community-based organizations crucial to the construction of peace in certain contexts. Third, by downplaying the positive agency of national actors, this literature sheds little light on policy options for national forces or the transnational alliances that could foster durable peace. Finally, this literature is dominated by Northern scholars. This does not invalidate its intellectual merits, but it does raise questions of perspective, of whether analysts living closer to the front lines might provide fresh insights into issues like the agency of national actors and criteria for assessing peacebuilding over the long run.

Other literatures are beginning to fill these gaps. A strand of thinking rooted in Johan Galtung's seminal distinction between "positive and negative peace" suggests that peace processes that do not address the deep causes of conflict will often lead to the recurrence of violence over the long run. John Paul Lederach, for example, has cogently argued that the ultimate goal of peacebuilding should be "sustainable reconciliation" – namely, broadly based, self-regenerating social processes that address the proximate and underlying causes of enmity. Time is a crucial dimension: peacebuilding should link action on immediate priorities (like ceasefires and DDR) with action on institutional change during the first decade and with longer-term structural and attitudinal transformation over the course of one or more generations. The prospects for building sustainable reconciliation are also enhanced by linking the engagement of top-level leaders such as political authorities, middle-level leaders such as religious officials, and grassroots-level institutions represented by community leaders. It is by linking these levels of society through "peace infrastructures" that the recurrence of violent conflict can be prevented. This requires integrated approaches: "a multiplicity of roles ... multiple levels of activity ... diverse strategies and approaches, each with a distinctive contribution to make" (Lederach 1997, 152; see also Rupesinghe 1995; Galtung 1969).

A literature review by Alejandro Bendaña has documented Southern contributions to this line of thought. It notes the work of African analysts such as Laurie Nathan (2001) and Yash Tandon (1999), who have cogently argued that international peacebuilding efforts have paid too little attention to the structural causes of violence within African societies or to the international drivers of conflict, such as trade liberalization and market-oriented structural adjustment. Similarly, in 2000 a group of prominent Central American analysts concluded that crucial reforms – particularly in the realms of economic, social, and agrarian policy – tended to drop off peacebuilding agendas due to the convergence of national elites' and international agencies' other priorities. South Asian analysts, such as Jayadeva Uyangoda, have also made compelling arguments about the need for more attention to the structural underpinnings of and solutions to armed violence (Bendaña 2003; Saldomando 2002; Uyangoda and Perera 2003).

Bendaña stresses the coincidence between these perspectives and feminist approaches, given the latter's emphasis on just peace and social transformation. A seminal study by the International Center for Research on Women (ICRW) confirms that there have been dramatic advances at the interface of gender and peace work (Strickland and Duvvury 2003). After decades of activism and scholarship on the experiences of women as victims of war and agents of peace, many Northern governments and multilateral agencies began to enshrine commitments to gender mainstreaming in their peacebuilding and conflict prevention policies in the late 1990s. This culminated in the adoption of UN Security Council Resolution (UNSCR) 1325 on women, peace, and security in 2000, committing the UN and member states to implementing gender-sensitive approaches to peacemaking, peacekeeping, peacebuilding, and conflict prevention. Reports on its implementation have concluded that much has been done to follow up on UNSCR 1325. This includes increased participation by women in official peace negotiations and implementation processes; the adoption of new international norms; enhanced gender training for peace observers; and the prosecution of those guilty of rights violations against women in certain countries.

Much remains to be done to implement the agenda of resolution 1325. Yet, as noted by ICRW, there has been even less movement on the broader agenda of transformation. That agenda includes addressing power, its unequal distribution across social divides, and the consequences of these imbalances for peace. It includes transforming national political institutions to enable women and men to negotiate their interests in peaceful ways based on respect for universal human rights. It includes contesting the prevalence of masculine identities that emphasize domination and working to replace them with identities more open to negotiation. Yet, despite solid arguments by feminist activists that sustainable peace also requires a more permanent transformation of social norms around violence, gender, and power, this broader agenda has received little attention in intergovernmental forums and in most peace processes.

This may be partly due to the fact that this broader agenda raises questions about what is possible and how one might forge transformative coalitions in concrete situations. Indeed, a striking pattern in this literature is the poverty of debate between minimalists (who prioritize measures to secure war termination) and maximalists (who argue that deeper transformations are necessary to consolidate peace and to prevent the recurrence of war). Minimalists tend to downplay long-term challenges, while maximalists have not looked carefully enough at the obstacles facing the broader agenda of transformation (or even at the concrete options available for advancing that agenda in different contexts).

One aim of the WKOP project has been to bridge these perspectives and to prod the peacebuilding community to move beyond unproductive min/max dichotomies. The preview of the case study on Guatemala provides a glimpse into the possibilities of bridging polar perspectives in this debate (see Box 2).[3] The propositions presented at the end of this chapter offer a set of conceptual bridges between minimalist and maximalist views.

Conflict Prevention, R2P, and Fragile States

From the mid-1990s onward, three new streams of policy thinking emerged, drawing on but also challenging the international discourse on postwar peacebuiding. Starting with the Carnegie Commission's seminal report on the Prevention of Deadly Conflict, influential international actors began to advocate a "shift from a culture of reaction to a culture of prevention." The rationale behind this effort was that the international community could not afford to wait for massive human rights violations or wars to exact their toll before engaging in peacemaking and peacebuilding. In order to save lives and to use scarce resources more efficiently, diplomacy (or "operational prevention") and reforms (or "structural prevention") should be initiated before conflicts escalate into massive violence (Carnegie Commission 1997).

Box 2
The "Relative Success" of Peacebuilding in Guatemala

Peacebuilding has brought enormous benefits to this Central American country since the final peace accords were signed in December 1996. These include:

- War termination and the demobilization of about 25,000 ex-armed forces and 1,000 guerrilla ex-combatants.
- A consolidation of democratic electoral processes and new laws to decrease the exclusion of indigenous peoples.
- Advances in decentralization through revived development councils.

Yet key peace accord commitments have not been implemented:

- Successive legislatures have failed to pass peace accord laws in key areas (e.g., fiscal reform and the regularization of indigenous peoples' lands).
- Minimal tax reforms were not implemented, and public expenditures have not been redistributed from security to social priorities such as health and education.
- Decentralization remains limited in practice. Increased participation by women and indigenous peoples has not yet led to their influence on major local decisions.

This mixed record is due to a number of factors:

- The peace accords and their partial implementation were due to the converging strategies of reformist elites in government, guerrilla leaders, civil society organizations (CSOs), and the international community led by the UN. It was also due to the temporary disorganization of domestic conservative networks.
- The latter – elements in Congress and the judiciary, parts of the domestic corporate sector, and former members of the civil defence patrols – regrouped to resist the implementation of the more far-reaching peace-building commitments.

The peace process could still lead to sustainable peace if the government follows up on its legislation codifying key peace commitments by:

- Renewing efforts to raise taxation levels and generate the national resources needed to finance pending commitments in areas like rural development.
- Supporting efforts by development councils to contribute to peace-building by nurturing their capacities for participatory engagement in public policy at both local and national levels.

Development councils and CSOs could formulate clearer strategies to secure the implementation of pending peace accords. The international community could continue supporting agents of change in the government, the councils, and the CSOs who contribute to these measures and to the agenda of sustainable peacebuilding.

This new thinking was reflected in the 1997 OECD DAC Guidelines and even more so in its 2001 Supplement, but it was also codified in key multilateral statements, such as the Miyazaki Initiative of the G8, the United Nations Millennium Declaration, and the UN Secretary-General's (2001) *Prevention of Armed Conflict*. These all contained commitments to adopt diplomatic and other measures to prevent the escalation of conflicts into wars. Some also advocated the use of multilaterally sanctioned force, where necessary, to protect vulnerable populations from grave human rights violations. All reiterated commitments to rebuild societies after wars, to address the structural underpinnings of conflict, and, thereby, to prevent the recurrence of armed violence.

These commitments were followed up with practical measures to strengthen the early warning and preventive diplomacy capacities of multilateral institutions and to mainstream conflict prevention in the programming of official development agencies (Schnabel and Carment 2004). The Global Partnership for the Prevention of Armed Conflict (GPPAC) brought together many of the NGOs and other civil society actors that also took up this banner (GPPAC 2005).

From the outset, work on conflict prevention was intimately linked to debates on humanitarian intervention. That debate has ancient roots, but it was revived by the tragedies in Rwanda and Bosnia in the 1990s. Widespread frustration over the inability of the UN, regional organizations, and great powers to protect victims from genocide and ethnic cleansing led some to call for the development of new international norms and capacities for humanitarian intervention. In 1999, important precedents were set when the North Atlantic Treaty Organization (NATO) intervened to stop ethnic cleansing in Kosovo and when Australia led a multinational force to stop another genocide in East Timor. The peacebuilding efforts that followed these interventions are quintessential "third-generation" peace operations.

The international divisions over intervention in Kosovo reflected the enduring difficulties of instituting new norms and protection capacities through the UN. In response, the Canadian government and other actors convened the International Commission on Intervention and State Sovereignty (ICISS) to bridge the gulf between those advocating humanitarian intervention and those defending the sanctity of state sovereignty. In late 2001, the ICISS released *The Responsibility to Protect* report, recognizing that sovereignty includes the responsibility of states to protect their citizens from massive human rights violations such as genocide and ethnic cleansing. When states fail to live up to this duty, the international community has a responsibility to protect populations at risk. R2P includes the responsibility to react militarily, in a proportionate manner, when all other options have been exhausted. It includes the obligation to seek and obtain authorization by the UN Security Council to demonstrate "right intention" and reasonable prospects of success. R2P also encompasses the responsibility to help rebuild societies affected by war in ways that address the causes of conflict as well as the responsibility to prevent the escalation of conflict into armed violence. Indeed, "Prevention is the single most important dimension of the responsibility to protect" (ICISS 2001, xi).

The ICISS report suffered from being released shortly after the 11 September 2001 tragedy. As a result, its recommendations were ignored by decision makers in the United States as they became consumed with the counterattack against al Qaeda and its Afghan hosts, with the broader "War on Terror," and with the hunt for weapons of mass destruction in Iraq. After the occupation of Iraq, many other governments and publics became even more suspicious of any doctrine that could be used to justify ill-conceived Northern-led military interventions. This unfortunate historical link is one reason why it has been so difficult to obtain broad support for R2P in the UN.[4]

While 9/11 and its aftermath overshadowed the R2P effort, the role that the Afghan state played in harbouring al Qaeda galvanized international interest in the phenomena of failed/weak/fragile or crisis states. That shift was driven by events in the United States. A year after 9/11, the Bush administration tabled a national security strategy identifying failed states as a major security threat. It outlined a strategy to combat terrorism and the emergence of power vacuums that could be exploited by transnational terrorist networks. The document framed regime change and nation building as essential complements to the doctrine of pre-emptive defence (President of the United States 2002). Since then, the Bush administration has taken many initiatives to address the problem of failed states both in particular countries and globally.

Official development assistance (ODA) agencies were already grappling with problems of state fragility when this cause was taken up by the Bush administration. ODA debates were driven by peacebuilding and conflict prevention units concerned about their agencies' apparent embrace of the aid effectiveness agenda. Indeed, the drive to enhance ODA and debt relief for countries that showed the will and capacity to use resources effectively – the so-called "good performers" on the development stage – raised profound questions about what to do with the "poor performers." Throughout the 1990s, peacebuilding units had advocated that donors should not simply cut ODA or increase their humanitarian aid in countries drifting towards collapse. They had championed the view that "working around conflict" was morally and politically undesirable since it could fuel humanitarian crises, aggravate governance challenges, and spur the regionalization of conflicts (Uvin 2002). Renewed interest in fragile states provided fresh justifications for investing in poor performers despite the logic of aid effectiveness.

Since 9/11, development agencies have elaborated on this rationale through the OECD Development Assistance Committee Fragile States Group and the World Bank's Low-Income Countries Under Stress (LICUS) initiative. Through the DAC, they have drafted "Principles of Good International Engagement in Fragile States," stipulating that donors should share and fine-tune ongoing analysis in such contexts, maintain activities in support of the poor (e.g., social service delivery), promote change by supporting reformers inside and outside the state, strengthen donor coordination, and promote policy coherence (OECD DAC/DCD 2005; see also World Bank 2002). These principles are being tested in several fragile states, including Haiti.

These processes have been informed by a stream of analyses that emerged in the mid-1990s (major contributors include Gross 1996; Mallaby 2002; Rotberg 2002; Ignatieff 2003; and Chesterman, Ignatieff, and Thakur 2005). This literature unpacked the continuum of state failure, ranging from "failed states" that are unable to provide the most basic public goods to most of their citizens to "capable states" that provide these services and more to their citizens. It suggested that many states in the developing world fall between these extremes and may be termed "fragile" states. The literature catalogued the causes of failure, from the legacy of colonialism to the impacts of the Cold War, the poor policy choices of some developing country governments, inequitable financial regimes, and so on. It identified international policy options ranging from preventive diplomacy to developmental approaches. Many of these analyses converged around the need to promote better governance – or state building – in fragile states. For some, this means focusing on establishing the rule of law and democratic governance; for others, it should also include promoting socioeconomic reforms to help ensure the basic rights of citizens to adequate livelihoods, public health, and so on.

Post-intervention stabilization efforts in Afghanistan, Haiti, and Iraq are testing grounds for fourth-generation peace operations and approaches in fragile states. One problem is that the strategic interests of major Western powers – and not R2P criteria like massive human rights violations – drove decisions to intervene in these cases. Another is that initial peacebuilding efforts have been marred by ongoing warfare. Iraq is the high-profile case in this regard, yet peacebuilding in Afghanistan and Haiti is also compromised by continued violence, de facto collaboration with paramilitary leaders responsible for past human rights violations, and the difficulties of consolidating democratic and participatory development processes (ICG 2004b) The preview of the study on Haiti (see Box 3) illustrates the complexities of fourth-generation peacebuilding today.[5]

In sum, the debates on conflict prevention, R2P, and state fragility have usefully broadened international agendas beyond postwar peacebuilding to address issues of human rights violations, conflict, and vulnerability at earlier stages. The most visionary policy prescriptions, such as the ICISS and UN High-Level Panel reports, advocate an integrated approach to these problems, from immediate diplomatic responses to the carefully circumscribed use of force and longer-term support for governance and socioeconomic reforms. Some policy prescriptions place considerable emphasis on strengthening national change agents. The events of 9/11 have certainly pushed issues of state fragility up the international agenda in a way that proponents of R2P can only envy.

Yet, in practice, these discourses have three major flaws that are related to the challenges of sustainable peacebuilding. First, there has been uneven follow-up on the comprehensive agenda, particularly on R2P and fragile states. Champions of R2P, such as the Government of Canada, have focused on advancing norms to govern the use of force and only began to reconnect this with the prevention and rebuilding pillars after much (difficult) dialogue with NGOs. Some Western governments' practical responses also betray a bias towards military intervention and much less interest in programming for long-term conflict prevention and sustainable peacebuilding (except perhaps on a narrow range of governance initiatives). Sustaining senior officials' interest in less fashionable aspects of prevention and peacebuilding – such as reforms to promote the inclusion of the poor and gender equality – is proving to be difficult in the new "whole-of-government" environment. The United States is clearly the extreme case here, but others (such as Canada) are also falling into these patterns in disturbing ways.[6]

Second, the complex links between R2P, the discourse on fragile states, and the selective use of force by Western powers have deeply undermined Western credibility. The unilateral intervention against Iraq and the use of the failed state label to describe a repressive but hardly weak state (dismantled by external intervention) has had a negative impact on the R2P and fragile states debates. The West's unwillingness or inability to respond adequately to the resurgence of massive violence in Israel and Palestine has also undermined its credibility. The Canadian government's justification for the 2004 intervention in Haiti, without open debate from an R2P perspective, has also damaged the R2P campaign – particularly in Latin America and the Caribbean.

Box 3
Haiti: Peacebuilding in a Fragile State

The first peacebuilding effort in Haiti began in 1994, with the return of the elected president through an international military intervention. The return of President Jean-Bertrand Aristide and the support he enjoyed opened the door to many reforms, including:

- The dismantling of the Haitian armed forces and the establishment of a national civilian police.
- The establishment of a multiparty political system and the widening of spaces for the free expression of different political options.
- The reduction of tariffs and the privatization of many public enterprises.
- Efforts to promote decentralized local development.

Yet a decade later, the state, its social supports, and international backing had all but evaporated. The failures of peacebuilding included:

- The subordination of state institutions – such as the Electoral Council, the judiciary, and the police – to the goal of keeping President Aristide in power.
- The near collapse of the economy due to the contradictory mix of market-oriented and populist reforms that failed either to generate growth or to reduce poverty.
- A profound fiscal crisis and the withdrawal of most external financial assistance.
- The resurgence of widespread human rights violations.

In February 2004, the United States, France, and Canada coordinated a military intervention that sealed President Aristide's removal from power. The Multilateral Intervention Force was soon replaced by the UN Stabilization Mission in Haiti (MINUSTAH). Since then, the situation has been characterized by ambiguous trends:

- The elaboration of an interim cooperation framework and its partial implementation with the inflow of sizeable international assistance.
- Attempts to reform security agencies in the context of escalating violence, crime, and human rights violations, particularly in late 2004.
- Attempts to revive promising local development efforts across the country.
- National and local elections in early 2006, bringing to office a reformist president and considerable diversity in the National Assembly and in the municipalities.

Time will tell whether Haitians and the international community use this opening to forge a more consensual approach to peacebuilding and to democratic development.

Third, even more than postwar peacebuilding, these debates are dominated by Northern officials and analysts. The number of sophisticated Southern interlocutors on conflict prevention and R2P has grown in recent years,
particularly in Africa (given the urgency of these issues on that continent).
Yet, especially on fragile states, debates and policy initiatives are still driven
by Northern governments and are informed by North-based analysts. As
with the work on peacebuilding, this does not invalidate these discourses,
but it does raise questions about what Southern interlocutors might contribute to these debates (e.g., with regard to understanding the possibilities
for positive Southern agency in counteracting very real problems, such as
genocide and different states of fragility).

Democratic Governance and Its Local Dimensions

From the outset of the post-Cold War years, there was a widespread belief
that democratic governance was a key component of peacebuilding. In some
war-affected societies, this was driven by opposition parties that had fought
for access to state power or for a new social compact between elites and
other citizens (Wood 2001). In others, this was driven by actors who viewed
multiparty parliamentary systems, independent electoral commissions, and
judiciaries and human rights ombudspersons as essential for the peaceful
management of differences (Reilly, Harris, and Lund 1998). International
commitments to nurture democratic institutions were codified in policy
statements by the UN, the OECD DAC, and key regional organizations.
Numerous official and NGO cooperation programs were initiated in this
domain. Other aspects of governance, such as accountability and transparency, also received considerable attention, especially from the international
financial institutions. Yet democratic governance has continued to move
up international agendas in recent years, fuelled in ambiguous ways by post-
9/11 preoccupations with the War on Terror.

These trends have also connected with a growing interest in democratic
governance at the local level. Local democratization is seen by some as being critical to the success of peacebuilding since local participation and accountability seem essential if a culture of peace is to take root beyond capital
cities. However, experience suggests that local democratization can not only
bring gains but also aggravate conflicts. Enabling national policies and programs are crucial to maximizing peacebuilding benefits. Enabling initiatives include devolving decision-making authority and taxation powers to
back up the decentralization of responsibilities for the delivery of public
goods. Building the capacity of local institutions to manage services, nurture participation, resolve local conflicts, and negotiate relations with higher
authorities is also essential. Programming in this area requires ongoing
conflict-sensitive analysis of local actors, needs, and contexts (Bush 2004;
Suhrke and Strand 2005).

A rich literature that assesses the results of democratization efforts in post-war contexts is beginning to accumulate. In his seminal work on this issue, Paris (1997, 2004) cogently argues that the hasty promotion of elections and superficial institutional changes can actually destabilize fragile peace processes, particularly when combined with economic liberalization. At the sectoral level, an eight-country study by the Netherlands Institute for International Relations concluded that international democracy assistance tends to cluster around a limited menu of electoral and human rights assistance, that short-term projects tend to proliferate at the expense of institution building, and that, despite a growth of governance assistance budgets, international funding falls dramatically short of what is required for long-term democratic development. The preference for technical assistance projects has also prevented donors from addressing political obstacles at the national level (de Zeeuw 2004).

Other studies have looked at these dynamics at the local level. Based on a comparison of experiences in Bosnia, the Palestinian Occupied Territories, and the Philippines, Kenneth Bush stresses the importance of local champions, institutional capacities (including the capacity to engage civil society organizations), supportive national policies (such as real fiscal decentralization), and international assistance for local democratization to take root in postwar contexts. Above all, he emphasizes the importance of having realistic time frames because peacebuilding "takes a long, long time" (Bush 2004, 24).

Focusing on the politics of local peacebuilding, Woodward (2002b, 22) recently concluded that, "in all cases for which there are field studies, decentralization programs were donor-driven." Donors often have conflicting agendas – ranging from limiting the power of the state to reducing public expenditures to broadening democratic participation. National and local stakeholders also have mixed motives for supporting or resisting decentralization. Some national leaders use decentralization to undercut the political bases of their rivals, while others use it and privatization to accumulate state assets at bargain-basement prices. Some national leaders will resist decentralization because they fear the collapse of the unitary state or the loss of power (and revenues) to local rivals. The level to which power and funds are decentralized is often contested.

Carrie Manning (2003) offers a framework for thinking about local-level peacebuilding that emphasizes the importance of the state across national territories, beyond the capital; the interaction of different levels of government, and different stakeholders, through these levels; and the "myriad negotiations" that shape peace on the ground. Within this framework, Manning divides challenges to local peacebuilding into two categories. Centrally driven obstacles include national leaders who try to recoup ground lost in peace negotiations by treating local spaces as reserve domains of power (e.g., extreme nationalist Serb parties in Bosnia); vague peace agreements; major actors who want to control territory in order to extract resources and make money (e.g., UNITA in Angola). Locally generated obstacles include local officials who stand to lose office, revenues, or impunity from reforms (this in contexts where there are often few livelihood alternatives). Yet, borrowing an insight from the recent scholarship on federalism, Manning concludes that the need to negotiate peacebuilding among actors at different levels also opens up important possibilities to foster more sustainable peace outcomes.

In Sri Lanka a group of researchers recently explored how devolution could open spaces for advancing rights and self-determination at the local level. They conclude that this would require further devolution of mandates and resources to local-level administrators, something that, historically, has been resisted by bureaucrats from all ethnic communities. Without romanticizing local spaces, they document rich experiences of community-level conflict resolution, multicultural coexistence, and development cooperation. Strengthening these experiences requires state reform and project interventions. "If project interventions are to be part of a peace agenda that includes substantive democracy by strengthening local capacities," they argue, "more attention would have to be given to the analysis of local politics and local knowledge" (Mayer, Rajasingham-Senenayake, and Thangarajah 2003, 8). State reform should include complementary strengthening of local and national capacities to deliver public goods and accountability to various constituencies.

The preview of the study on peacebuilding in Mozambique (see Box 4),[7] written by colleagues at the Centro de Estudios de Democracia e Desenvolvimento, provides a sense of how these dynamics are unfolding in a relatively promising environment for peacebuilding.

In sum, over the past fifteen years, the policy and scholarly sides of the peacebuilding community have accumulated considerable knowledge about democratic governance in postwar contexts. The belief that democratic development is central to peacebuilding has become entrenched, yet there is a clearer awareness of the dilemmas and difficulties that this entails. There is much more caution about imposing superficially liberal institutions through hasty elections, and there is a clearer understanding of the need to develop long-term, context-specific democratic development strategies. However, research suggests that donor assistance in this domain remains non-strategic, short-term, and under-resourced.

Moreover, despite some work on national institutions, there is a need for greater comparative analysis of the types of national strategies, institutional innovations, and national political coalitions that are conducive to sustainable democratic development.

Box 4

Democratization, Decentralization, and Peacebuilding in Mozambique

Peacebuilding has brought enormous benefits since the war ended in 1992:

- Three free and fair national elections have been held. The national elections in November 2004 did not generate serious incidents of violence.
- Two rounds of local elections have also occurred.

Yet certain trends could undermine peace:

- Power remains concentrated in the hands of the central government and the ruling party. The eruption of violence after the 1999 national elections, in a region with a strong RENAMO presence, highlights the links between the concentration of political power and the fragility of peace.
- The limited character of decentralization reflects and aggravates these trends. Only thirty-three of 151 cities and major towns have been included in the process. The centre remains reluctant to devolve significant fiscal powers (to tax and spend) to municipalities. Decentralization has been a top-down process controlled by the central state, especially in municipalities where the opposition is strong. According to the Mayor of Nacala: "In one word there isn't decentralization because control ... by central government remains strong and that doesn't give the municipalities the tools to work efficiently."
- Though women play important roles in Mozambican public life (e.g., through their high level of representation in the National Assembly), men continue to hold the levers of power nationally and in most municipalities.

Nonetheless, there are important opportunities emerging to advance democratic development, including at the local level:

- The World Bank worked with the Government of Mozambique to develop a decentralization strategy and to conclude a letter of sector policy in 2006. Other donors have supported decentralization efforts, with different degrees of commitment to deepening their democratic and peacebuilding aspects.
- The new National Association of Municipalities presents an opportunity for local leaders and civil society organizations, including women's organizations, to engage the government in a process to deepen democratic decentralization.

A major change in recent years has involved the broadening of peace-building to include local-level actors as key players. There is an emerging consensus that local engagement should include efforts to strengthen the capacities of municipal governments and CSOs for democratic governance, while fostering national frameworks that enable decentralization. There is a growing understanding of the political obstacles to decentralized govern-ance, including the mixed agendas of donors and of different national ac-tors. What is required is a much greater understanding of the "politics of the possible" – namely, the types of local innovations that are possible in different contexts and the political coalitions that could sustain successful strategies over the long term.

Socioeconomic Development and Its Local Dimensions

In the late 1990s, there was a revival of the old debate on the relationship between armed conflict and socioeconomic development. There is broad consensus on the inverse relationship between level of economic develop-ment and proneness to armed conflict. The poorer the society, the greater the likelihood that it will experience armed conflict. Yet there is little con-sensus on the relationship between conflict and the variable of socioeconomic inequality. Drawing on large data sets, some analysts conclude that poverty and inequality lead to armed conflict where there is strong "horizontal in-equality" (i.e., overlap between socioeconomic inequalities and ethnic, class, or geographic identities that provide bases for rebellion) (Fearon and Laitin 2003). Drawing on case studies, others suggest that the strategies and ca-pacities of state elites, versus those of opposition leaders, also mediate the links between socioeconomic conditions and war (Daudelin 2002).

One strand of this debate has become known as the "greed and grievance debate." Seminal works reconceptualize contemporary wars as struggles for power and profit rather than as struggles over causes like social justice (Berdal and Malone 2000). They argue that the key to ending these wars involves, for example, denying spoilers such as UNITA in Angola access to the rev-enues from diamond extraction, while enhancing incentives for them to lay down their arms and to comply with peace agreements. Outcomes of this work include the development of new multilateral regimes to regulate the revenues from extractive industries such as diamonds and oil. Yet re-cent studies have yielded more nuanced analyses of the interplay between greed and grievance. For example, Ballentine and Sherman (2003) show how economic incentives combine with socioeconomic or political exclu-sion to fuel contemporary wars. Therefore, they conclude, the international community should continue to tighten belligerents' access to natural re-source revenues, while also promoting inclusive governance and socioeco-nomic reforms that increase incentives for belligerents to lay down their arms for good.

Paul Collier and his World Bank colleagues bring these insights together in a report on civil wars and development policy. They argue that four measures are central to preventing armed conflict: (1) tightening international governance of natural resource revenues; (2) increasing aid and targeting it towards extremely poor countries at risk; (3) improving the sequencing of postwar aid by scaling it up gradually and sustaining it over longer periods of time; and (4) using international forces to lay the foundations for peace. They suggested that national actors should: (1) give priority to infrastructure rehabilitation, social investment, and macroeconomic growth, in that order; and (2) reduce military spending, pursue security sector reform, and promote genuine democratic governance (Collier et al. 2003). Although this work has attracted many followers in governmental circles, it is being criticized by others on several grounds. First, respected analysts have carefully reviewed this research and concluded that some of its arguments rest on problematic coding, deceptively small sample sizes, and other shaky methodological foundations (Suhrke, Villanger, and Woodward 2004).

Second, Collier's work does not do justice to the accumulated knowledge on how donors actually act in postwar situations. It does not acknowledge the tendency for externally sponsored macroeconomic and fiscal policies to undermine rather than to reinforce peacebuilding processes. As the chief UN mediator in the peace talks in El Salvador in the early 1990s, Alvaro de Soto had observed how the peace accords he helped broker between the government and the insurgents were undermined by a structural adjustment program (SAP) negotiated between the government and the international financial institutions (IFIs). For example, the fiscal austerity measures in the SAP weakened the government's ability to finance key commitments in the peace accords, such as the creation of a new civil police (de Soto and del Castillo 1995). In the late 1990s, James Boyce and Susan Woodward looked at a larger number of cases to see whether the international community had learned from de Soto's critique. They observe that some donors had enhanced their ability to support national institutions and actors that are crucial to peacebuilding and to deny assistance to spoilers. Yet they conclude that, despite these advances, the IFIs and some other donors had difficulties abandoning their commitments to economic orthodoxy, even in postwar settings. Donors still tend to privilege measures to purchase short-term stability over equitable growth. They also spend too much on the services of external agencies and too little on strengthening national capacities for peace (Boyce 2002; Woodward 2002a).

These findings converge with a study on peacebuilding programming conducted by the original Utstein countries – Germany, the Netherlands, Norway, and the United Kingdom. That study concludes that, despite many advances in recent years, peacebuilding programming in those countries suffers from a "major strategic deficit" (Smith 2003, 10). It is based on short-term planning, inadequate consultation with national stakeholders, poor integration of governance and socioeconomic interventions, inadequate coordination among donors, as well as poor monitoring and evaluation. Indeed, "despite this considerable effort in evaluating peacebuilding activities ... there is no basis for drawing wider conclusions about ... what works and what does not in [Utstein-4] peacebuilding" (50). This finding, by four of the most active bilateral donors, suggests that greater changes are needed to improve donor practices than those recommended by the World Bank.

A third limitation of this literature is that it also tends to focus on international actors and their policy options. When it does look at national actors, it tends to emphasize spoilers at the expense of institutions and leaders that anchor or could anchor effective conflict prevention. As a literature review commissioned by the War-Torn Societies Project some years ago concludes: "Discussions are primarily led by external actors and Western scholars. Subsequent recommendations are directed at international organizations involved in post-conflict countries rather than at the domestic actors of reconstruction ... The focus of attention should thus shift to domestic actors and involve them in research on – and design of – locally accepted solutions" (Carbonnier 1998, 64).

There are exceptions to this tendency, including the work of the War-Torn Societies Project. Collier's 2003 report certainly includes recommendations for national governments. Yet there is also a storehouse of work on the economic dimensions of peacebuilding being generated in the South. For example, a consortium of Guatemalan organizations joined forces to produce the first independent assessment of the Land Fund, an institution crucial to the implementation of the land and rural development policy commitments in the peace accords. That study looks at the interplay between national institutions and international donors, and it includes policy recommendations that have since been taken up by both sets of actors (CONGCOOP and CNOC 2002). Similarly, Sri Lankan researchers have produced illuminating analyses of the tension between the previous administration's economic and peace policies. One such study includes pointed recommendations for what the new national government and donors could do to harmonize economic policies and peacebuilding – by placing greater emphasis on equitable growth in the south of Sri Lanka and on institutional capacity-building in the north and east (Kelegama 2004a).

Southern analysts are also generating insights into the contributions of local actors to economic reconstruction. For instance, a group of Sri Lankan and German scholars has examined the ways in which subnational spaces can become arenas for non-discriminatory approaches to reconstruction – in the rehabilitation of agricultural production or educational services, for example – that could lay the foundations for sustainable peace. However, for this to work, local, national, and international agencies will have to conduct conflict impact assessment more systematically and design conflict-sensitive development interventions to avoid dividing communities further (Mayer, Rajasingham-Senenayake, and Thangarajah 2003). In Guatemala, La Facultad Latinoamericana de Ciencias Sociales (FLACSO) recently published a study documenting the highly uneven capacity of local governments and indigenous peoples' organizations to administer municipal lands. Based on that finding, this research highlights the potentially negative impacts of decentralizing the administration of lands without investing much more in strengthening the capacities of local actors to manage those assets in conflict-sensitive ways (Thillet and FLACSO Guatemala 2003).

The preview of the case study on Afghanistan (see Box 5),[8] shows how these patterns manifest themselves in a particularly challenging setting. In sum, over the past fifteen years, renewed debate at the interface of socio-economic development and peacebuilding has generated considerable insight. The international community has learned about the pitfalls of orthodox approaches to economic liberalization in postwar contexts. At the policy level, more clarity has emerged about the need to balance measures to secure macroeconomic stability and growth, with measures to restore social services and to lay the foundations for equitable development. Much is also being learned about how to generate more inclusive socio-economic development in rural areas and at the local level beyond large cities – through enabling national legislation and institutional reforms, by building the capacity of smaller municipal governments in areas like transparent taxation and fiscal management, and by nurturing the economic potential of communities. Yet our case studies suggest that practice still lags far behind policy learning and that there is room for much bolder innovation on the ground.

DDR, Spoilers, and Agents of Change

DDR is another area in which there is a pressing need for bolder innovation. The three chapters on the demobilization and reintegration of combatants offer a compelling analysis of the policy literature on DDR and spoilers. They remind us of the accumulated insights into the factors that shape the success of DDR programs:

- contextual factors such as the nature of the armed conflict
- the character of armed actors themselves
- the nature of the DDR programs deployed to deal with combatants.

They observe that the most prominent contributions to this literature, for example by Stedman, place more emphasis on the urgency of disarming

---

Box 5
Peacebuilding, Rural Development, and War in Afghanistan

The international intervention against the Taliban government in October 2001, and the implementation of the Bonn Agreement since, have brought benefits to Afghanistan:

- Complex processes of constitutional reform and democratic consultation led to relatively free presidential and parliamentary elections in 2004-05.
- Over 3 million refugees have returned, reconstruction has begun in many provinces, and there have been important initiatives in the area of women's rights.

The high-priority National Solidarity Program (NSP) was initiated by the Ministry for Rural Rehabilitation and Development (MRRD) in 2003 to foster rural development and to improve relations between the central state and rural communities.

- By January 2006, almost 10,000 of Afghanistan's 20,000 villages had been reached through small NSP projects in areas such as public health.
- To be eligible for an NSP grant, communities must elect a Community Development Council (CDC) and include women as well as men. The experience of local participation has been positive for many communities.
- Though the NSP appears to be popular, the sustainability of NSP projects is questionable. Evidence from thirty communities suggests that consultation with stakeholders is inadequate and that the needs of women and the poor remain marginal to major decisions. Moreover, many community-level projects lack connections to each other or to other rural development programs.

At the macro level:

- The war between Taliban and al Qaeda forces and US-led coalition forces continues in the southern and eastern provinces.
- The central state remains weak and unable to deliver basic public goods.
- Rural development, a key to peacebuilding in a country where 70 percent of the population lives in rural areas, remains incipient – outside the opium economy.

What could be done to change these dynamics?

- The government and the international community could harmonize their practices with the goal of sustainable peacebuilding. They could channel more investment into national institutions, socioeconomic development, and rural development.
- This could include providing longer-term funding to the NSP to ensure its sustainability. MRRD, facilitating partners, and development councils

could strengthen their capacities to apply good practices of development –
including finding more effective ways of nurturing participation by
women.

It could also include fostering real dialogue with Taliban leaders.

---

and demobilizing combatants to prevent their emergence as spoilers and
less on the need for sustainable reintegration. They note the emergence of a
counterpoint to this line of analysis, particularly from UN agencies and
their NGO associates, advocating more developmental approaches, more
support for community-based DDR, and more emphasis on strengthening
national institutions' ability to complete reintegration over the long run.

Still, all three chapters fault mainstream and developmental approaches
to DDR for not sufficiently considering the potential of ex-combatants as
agents of change. In particular, they suggest that the tendency to demonize
combatants – due to their human rights violations or their potential to
undermine peacebuilding – has blinded us to the possibility that some of
these movements, the individuals in them, and the communities in which
they are embedded, might actually contribute to peace implementation.

The case studies explore this possibility in three societies – Afghanistan,
Guatemala, and Palestine. In each case, they start with careful analyses of
the characteristics of different armed actors and their historical links to conflict and peace processes. In each case, they conclude that there is untapped
potential to bring certain ex-combatant groups more fully into peacebuilding
processes as agents of change. However, in the case of Palestine, the authors
conclude that this is unlikely given the current convergence of powerful
national, regional, and international actors' strategies around the War on
Terror.

Conclusion

This chapter introduces the question of what kind of peace is possible in the
post-9/11 era by reviewing major debates related to postwar peacebuilding
and more specific literatures on the challenges of democratic governance,
economic development, and the demobilization of ex-combatants in postwar contexts. Through this review, I craft a critique of dominant approaches
and highlight alternatives emerging from the margins of the field, including the South. The following propositions capture the hunches that guide
the more grounded exploration of these issues as presented in the case studies offered in this book.

Proposition 1: It is fair to assess postwar peacebuilding efforts in the first ten years primarily according to whether they have helped end wars. Yet it is important to assess longer-term peacebuilding efforts according to whether they are addressing the causes of conflict and are leading to sustainable peacebuilding.

Proposition 2: Multidimensional peacebuilding has contributed much to ending several wars since 1989. Yet a major limitation of these efforts is that few have paved the way for the deeper reforms required to sustain peace beyond the initial decade of peacebuilding.

Proposition 3: The termination of these wars was due to a convergence of the interests of key domestic stakeholders with those of major international actors. Yet it has been difficult to forge the transnational coalitions required to underpin more profound changes – such as deepening democratic practices at the local level – over the long term.

Proposition 4: Multidimensional peacebuilding provides a framework for nurturing transnational coalitions – or peace infrastructures – linking agents of change from the local to the national and international levels. Yet stakeholders should invest much more to build the domestic base of these coalitions and to deliver the institutional reforms required to extend their life well beyond the departure of major international actors.

Proposition 5: From the standpoint of sustainable peacebuilding, the outcomes of third- and especially fourth-generation peacebuilding efforts are even more problematic than are those of second-generation operations. This is partly due to the mixed international motives that have tended to drive such operations, despite the ideals of the R2P discourse. It is also due to the unpromising national and local circumstances one tends to find in situations in which key stakeholders are excluded by warfare and/or by limited negotiations.

Proposition 6: Even in such situations, peacebuilding can move towards a more solid footing by engaging a broader range of stakeholders, including leaders of the poor, women, or ethnic groups that have been excluded from transitional arrangements. Addressing these groups' legitimate political, socioeconomic, and/or cultural demands through reforms could help reposition peacebuilding efforts. Decisive movement towards the use of force as a last resort, based on the rule of law, is also a necessary ingredient for recovering ground lost during contested interventions.

Proposition 7: Despite the belief that democratization is essential to peace-building, the achievements of these processes have been quite limited in many postwar contexts (e.g., with regard to the participation of women, the poor, and indigenous peoples in decision making, particularly at the local level beyond capital cities).

Proposition 8: There are many entry points for democratic development in postwar contexts. These include fostering national legal and institutional reforms, strengthening municipal governments' capacities for participatory policy making, and building the capacities of historically excluded stakeholders to influence policy processes.

Proposition 9: Economic and social policies for sustainable peacebuilding continue to attract too little attention and investment. Macroeconomic orthodoxy still tends to trump creative public policy for inclusive development. Official development assistance tends to focus on immediate postwar priorities and invests too little in strengthening national and local capacities for conflict-sensitive development over the long term. National governments are failing to deliver enabling policies such as fiscal decentralization and rural development. Community-level projects remain poorly linked to broader strategies.

As such, economic and social policies/programs in postwar settings still fall short of yielding the outcomes necessary to sustain peace and to prevent the recurrence of conflict.

Proposition 10: In some societies there are spaces for much more innovative, conflict-sensitive economic and social policies/programs, such as harmonizing macroeconomic policies with the goals of sustainable peacebuilding, investing much greater resources in strengthening the capacities of national and local governments, and linking community-based projects with strategies for more inclusive rural and urban development. Politically, it is essential to nurture broader coalitions of reformers in order to advance such approaches for the generational time frames required to consolidate peace.

Proposition 11: Despite successes and innovations in the disarmament, demobilization, and reintegration of ex-combatants in some contexts, these programs still tend to suffer from an over-emphasis on military instruments, an under-emphasis on long-term socioeconomic and political reintegration, and an insufficient consideration of ex-combatants as potential agents of peacebuilding.

Proposition 12: DDR programs could be enhanced by starting with more careful analyses of different armed groups, drawing them and their communities (not just senior commanders) into peacebuilding processes where possible and linking these to strategies to deepen governance and socioeconomic reforms over the long run.

This chapter also presents some findings from the case studies. The previews already presented dealt with cases in which peacebuilding has occurred in one form or another for at least five years. The preview of the Sri Lankan case (see Box 6),[9] illustrates the challenges of sustainable peacebuilding in a process that has relapsed into open warfare.

The propositions put forth in this chapter were initially offered to the WKOP team to provoke reflection and to guide their case studies. Researchers picked up on those most relevant to their cases. They use a common methodology, beginning with a review of the literature on peacebuilding in their society. This secondary research is complemented by analyses of primary documents, aggregate data such as opinion polls, key informant interviews, and participant observation at the national and local levels. Each study then examines implementation patterns in selected areas of governance, economic reconstruction, or DDR, weaving gender and social analysis into the assessment. All case studies have been revised on the basis of peer reviews as well as validation meetings with local, national, and international stakeholders.

The concluding chapter revisits the propositions offered here by comparing the case studies in a more systematic manner than I have done. In particular, it returns to the core question of the book – what kind of peace is possible in the post-9/11 era? – with more definitive yet more pessimistic conclusions than those suggested in this introduction.

Box 6
War and Peace in Sri Lanka

Even before the peace talks between the government and the Liberation Tigers of Tamil Eelam (LTTE) reached a deadlock in early 2003, several obstacles had emerged that made sustained progress difficult:

- The LTTE leadership had shown little sensitivity to other stakeholders' demands that any devolution of power to the north and east be conditional on a democratization of LTTE practices.
- The United National Front (UNF) government was unable to respond positively to LTTE proposals for interim arrangements that would have tested a model of regional autonomy within the framework of a unitary state.
- The UNF government's position was weakened by its orthodox market-oriented economic policies, which failed to distribute the peace dividend to the north and east or to the rural poor in the south.

In 2004 and 2005 this led to the election of new governments. Since then the following occurred:

- Two governments have had even less margin to return to the negotiation table, partly due to the influence of Sinhalese nationalist elements in their coalitions.
- Despite mediation efforts by the Norwegian government, the LTTE has felt sidelined by other international actors due to the global War on Terror.
- The LTTE has also split along regional lines and has repeatedly violated the 2002 ceasefire agreement (CFA).
- Notwithstanding the creation of the Civil Society Sub-Committee on Peace and Reconciliation, civil society has remained marginal to the peace talks.

These dynamics, the pressure they have put on the CFA, and the destruction caused by the tsunami in December 2004 have made it difficult to keep creative options for transformative peacebuilding on the agenda.

Though national key actors' energies are currently focused on waging war, the case studies in this book suggest that, at some point, they will have to return to negotiations. At that time, a deeper transformation will have to be on the agenda.

2

Peace in Guatemala: Settling for What Seems Possible or Aiming for What Is Desirable

Gabriel Aguilera Peralta

The peace process in Guatemala has received considerable attention in terms of its historical background, the war (1960-96), and the peace negotiations (1991-96). The process of compliance with the Guatemalan Peace Accords has been less studied. We might say that we have good analyses of the experience of peacemaking but not of the experience of peacebuilding.[1]

As noted in the introductory chapter, peacebuilding analysis raises the problems of establishing both appropriate benchmarks for assessing success or failure and appropriate time frames for passing judgments. Minimalists believe that success should be assessed against the implementation of short-term objectives like democratic elections; maximalists propose that a successful peace process is one that deals with and resolves the structural causes that gave rise to armed conflict. In this view, achieving long-term objectives requires lengthy periods of time, some authors suggesting that an entire generation is needed (i.e., nearly twenty-five years). Thus, the maximalist point of view coincides with the goal of long-term peacebuilding, which seeks to prevent conflict through transformations that eliminate the main causes of wars.

In their conception and in their design, the Guatemalan Peace Accords are entirely maximalist. That is also the official position adopted by the Guatemalan state and political parties. It is in the academic realm, based on analyses of actual implementation processes, that minimalist positions have been put forth (Pásara 2003).

This chapter examines peacebuilding dynamics in Guatemala, taking into account the tension between minimalist and maximalist analyses. It attempts to determine whether compliance with the Guatemalan Peace Accords has contributed to democratic governance and whether economic policy has contributed to their sustainability. Within the universe of assumptions of change implied in a maximalist approach, I have selected the issues of decentralization, strengthening participation, local governments, and, running through these, the empowerment of women and indigenous peoples.

Given the relevance that variables such as human rights and militarism have had in the past with regard to characterizing the situation in Guatemala, we should pause to consider whether decentralization and local government actually define peace in this state. My answer is perhaps not, but they point to long-term potential and thus help to clarify the debate between minimalists and maximalists.

In practice, human rights and demilitarization are central variables; however, given advances in both areas and the significant number of organizations and projects that follow, it would be hard to say anything new on these topics.[2] In other words, it would seem that sustainability of the peace process does not depend on human rights or on the military's adapting to a democratic society since these goals have basically been achieved. But sustainability may well depend on the extent to which peace commitments are diffused throughout all levels of Guatemalan society and on the intensity with which people's everyday lives are transformed, especially the lives of women and indigenous peoples.

These ideas imply that sustainable peace is linked to issues of governance, which is understood as the interaction between government and the governed with regard to social demands and the capacity (and will) to satisfy them. This also reflects on the legitimacy of government as a result of good governance (Oriols Prats 2000). I should also add that good governance includes the capacity to democratically engage with conflict processes (ibid.).

To a considerable extent, the capacity of the state to react appropriately to the demands of its citizens is determined by the availability of fiscal resources. Thus, the importance of economic policies that accompany a discourse like the one I am examining. Although the economic dimensions of peace constitute a specific topic of inquiry (which is why I do not attempt an in-depth review), I only touch on the issue as required for this particular study.

I focus particularly on decentralization – a crucial element of the peace commitments – because I believe that this is what may hold the key to sustainability. I take decentralization to mean "an interconnected process of state reform through which decision-making capacities and resources are transferred from the central government to sub-national, municipal or local institutions" (Rosende 2002, 53).

I also focus on the Urban and Rural Development Councils, those singular entities that have the potential to link local governance, shared development, and sustainable peace. My fieldwork consisted in monitoring a number of councils at the departmental and municipal levels, although not to a statistically valid degree. This has made it possible to understand how the Guatemalan Peace Accords operate and are received at the local level. I also consulted extensively with actors within women's and indigenous peoples' organizations.

This chapter's hypothesis may be stated as follows: whereas the maximalist expectations cannot be justified by what the peace process has accomplished to date, their potential should not be discounted. The peace process has been developing norms and institutions that could make these expectations feasible in the near future. Furthermore, the peace objectives will multiply as the process of decentralization and state reform takes a deeper and stronger hold.

Anatomy of the Guatemalan Peace Accords and Levels of Compliance

Of all the Latin American conflicts, the internal war in Guatemala was one of the longest and most costly with regard to loss of human lives. The conflict lasted thirty-six years, between 1960 and 1996, and it is estimated that some 200,000 persons died. At least four hundred rural communities were destroyed, and by 1982 over one million persons had either been displaced or become refugees – a figure that, for the 1980s, amounts to one Guatemalan in seven.

This confrontation stretched out through various governments and insurgent organizations – which, towards the end, had come together in the Guatemalan National Revolutionary Unity (URNG)[3] – and was waged without observing international humanitarian law. Consequently, massive and grave human rights violations occurred during the conflict. In the last decade and a half of the twentieth century, international changes generated by the end of the Cold War and the Esquipulas process in Central America opened windows of opportunity for dialogue and negotiation that concluded the regional conflict and the internal wars in Nicaragua and El Salvador and that began the peace process in Guatemala.

The early contacts between the government and the URNG took place in 1987; negotiations began in 1991 and concluded in 1996, proceeding through the first four governments of the country's democratic transition. From 1994 on, conversations were facilitated by a representative of the secretary-general of the United Nations, and the commitments reached were monitored by an entity of that international body.

The process produced thirteen accords, nine of which were substantive (or of the so-called "long agenda"), five of which were operational (or of the so-called "short agenda"), and one of which – a summary – was ad hoc. Box 1 lists the accords (Colegio de Abogados y Notarios 1996).

Analysis of the accords should distinguish between content and implementation. Their content is noteworthy in that, as a whole, these understandings of peace in Guatemala surpass other experiences in the Western hemisphere in terms of both depth and breadth. In addition to dealing with the necessary concrete phenomena needed to end the war, these accords

Box 1
Guatemalan Peace Accords

Accord	*Status*
Procedural accord for the search for peace through political means (26 April 1991).	Operational. Establishes the negotiation format.
General thematic agenda accord (26 April 1991).	Operational. Agenda.
Framework accord on democrat-ization through political means, known as the Querétaro Accord (25 July 1991).	Substantive. Defines the democratic project and accepts a negotiated political solution.
Framework accord for the renewal of negotiations between the Government of Guatemala and the Guatemalan National Revo-lutionary Unity (10 January 1994).	Operational. Establishes a new format and agenda. Sets up the Civil Society Assembly and calls for United Nations mediation.
Global accord on Human Rights (29 March 1994).	Substantive. Commitments on human rights and United Nations verification.
Accord for the resettlement of populations uprooted by the armed conflict (27 June 1994).	Substantive. Strategy and guarantees for reintegration and resettlement of population displaced by the war.
Accord for the establishment of the Commission for Historic Clarification of the human rights violations and the acts of violence that have caused suffering to the Guatemalan population, known as the Commission for Historic Clarification (23 June 1994).	Substantive. Creates the Truth Commission.
Accord on the identity and rights of indigenous peoples (13 March 1995).	Substantive. Recognizes the rights of indigenous peoples, confronts discrimination, and establishes parity commissions between indigenous peoples and the state for follow-through.

Accord on socioeconomic aspects and the agrarian situation (6 May 1996).	Substantive. Commitments for democratization, social development and participation, modernization of the state, fiscal reform, and reform in agriculture. Establishes parity commissions for follow-through.
Accord on strengthening civilian power and on the role of the army in a democratic society (19 September 1996).	Substantive. State reform, participation of women, reconversion of the army and the police, and dissolution of the Civil Defence Patrols and other paramilitary corps.
Accord on constitutional and electoral reform (7 December 1996).	Substantive-operational. Calls for specific constitutional reforms and changes to the Electoral Law considered necessary for compliance with commitments set up in other accords.
Accord on incorporation of the URNG to the legal regime (12 December 1996).	Operational. Framework for the disarmament and reincorporation of the URNG.
Accord on the schedule for the implementation and verification of the Guatemalan Peace Accords (29 December 1996).	Operational. Four-year schedule for compliance with the commitments.
Accord for Firm and Lasting Peace (29 December 1996).	Substantive. Summarizes all of the accords.

Source: Colegio de Abogados y Notarios (1996).

include a series of reform proposals that encompass political, economic, social, and cultural relations in Guatemala. They go so far as to attempt to resolve problems that originated in the nation's early history (e.g., issues involving inter-ethnic relations). There is the assumption that Guatemala is a strong, demilitarized state with a sound fiscal capacity that furthers development and growth.

In terms of gender issues, it should be noted that the "Women's Sector" was organized within the Civil Society Assembly, the gathering of social sectors that developed a parallel debate on the contents of the peace talks and generated suggested inputs for the accords as they were being discussed.

Many of these suggestions were incorporated in the final documents, including item 29 of the Schedule Accord, which established the National Forum of Women (see Box 2).

Box 2
Agreements on Gender Included in the Guatemalan Peace Accords

Issue	*Commitment*
Socioeconomic and agrarian situation	Guarantee to implement equality of opportunity in educational and training programs; equal access to housing by eliminating obstacles and impediments that affect women in terms of rent, credit, and construction; national health programs for women; the rights of women to work, organize, and participate.
Resettlement of uprooted populations	Eliminate all forms of de facto or legal discrimination of women in terms of access to land, housing, credit, and participation in development projects. A gender focus will become part of all government policy, programs, and activities.
Identity and rights of indigenous peoples	Recognizes the specific vulnerability and defenceless-ness of indigenous women in the face of discrimination as women and as indigenous persons. Calls for legislation that makes sexual harassment a crime and for additional penalties when the victim is indigenous. Establishes the Indigenous Women's Defence Centre.
Strengthening of civilian power	Strengthen opportunities for the participation of women in politics. Establishes the development of informational campaigns and educational programs that promote the rights of women to participate in politics at all levels, with equal opportunities and free of discrimination. Calls on social and political organizations to adopt policies that encourage the participation of women. Calls for respect, encouragement, and legalization of women's organizations in both rural and urban areas. Establishes that opportunities for women's participation – both on an individual or organized level – be guaranteed in all forms of political power.

Source: MINUGUA (1997, 2004a).

The follow-through on the accords included the UN Verification Mission in Guatemala (MINUGUA)[4] and the Peace Accords Accompaniment Commission, which was made up of representatives from government, the URNG, civil society, and MINUGUA. Additionally, a network of parity commissions – with indigenous peoples and state representatives – and non-parity commissions was set up to promote the fulfillment of specific commitments. The Peace Secretariat (SEPAZ) was set up by the government to oversee overall governmental compliance with the accords. Civil society was organized into numerous verification and support entities, which included the so-called "departmental working tables," or provincial commissions.

In order to further appreciate the far-reaching nature of the negotiations, it should be kept in mind that the process consolidated gradually and was opposed by certain civilian and military groups. I refer to these groups as "spoilers." The main reasons for their opposition had to do with the belief that unnecessary concessions were being made to the militarily inferior insurgents and/or disagreements with regard to the reforms that were being negotiated.

It is not easy to evaluate the level of compliance with the peace accords as this would require systematizing the objectives, projected outcomes, components, and ranked results of the hundreds of derivative obligations. The original Schedule Agreement was an attempt to resolve this complex situation by condensing the political obligations into some three hundred commitments to be fulfilled within a four-year period. In retrospect, it seems amazing that anyone believed it was possible to accomplish a transformation of those dimensions within such a short period of time.

As part of its mandate, MINUGUA issued regular reports on the overall situation of the accords, the specific human rights situation, and other noteworthy issues. The Accompaniment Commission also issued reports when and if members were able to reach a consensus. For their part, numerous civil society groups issued their own views on compliance. The strong level of interest and influence that the international community maintained in the process has also been noteworthy.

Four key variables can be considered central to an overall assessment of implementation: (1) the political will of governments, (2) the dynamics within civil society and the broader population's sense of ownership of the accords, (3) the support of the international community, and (4) the availability of economic resources. We also need to distinguish between operational and substantive commitments.

The two operational commitments on procedures and agenda were met without major problems. The operational commitment on demobilization and reinsertion was probably the one that was best implemented: the URNG gave up its weapons and demobilized in a process that was supervised by

188 UN blue beret observers. The insurgents reintegrated into civilian life, set up foundations and think tanks, and formed a political party that made significant strides in the two elections following the peace agreement.

It should also be noted that security guarantees have been observed and that there have been no acts of violence against demobilized insurgents. Among the shortcomings of the process is the fact that projects designed to ensure the sustainability of the programs were not fully implemented. As will be explained in Chapter 8 of this book on DDR in Guatemala, the overall assessment of those processes is positive, although the last component can be considered incomplete.

The Schedule Agreement must be regarded with a different set of criteria. The assessment carried out by MINUGUA and the Accompaniment Commission at the end of the first four-year period determined that there had been partial compliance. Some commitments had been fully implemented; others were still in process; and a third block had not been met at all. During this process, it became evident that the fulfillment of some commitments generated new ones of a follow-through nature, and these have been deemed second-generation commitments. In 2000, the Accompaniment Commission established a new schedule for what remained to be done and assigned a new four-year period in which to do it (Comisión de acompañamiento 2000).

The government was responsible for fulfilling 170 of the 179 commitments set forth in the original Schedule Agreement. MINUGUA estimated that by the end of 1999 only 63 of these had been entirely fulfilled while 103 remained to be completed. At the end of 2000 the Accompaniment Commission assessed that 63 obligations were pending and that 56 second-generation commitments had been added to the list. The second Schedule included a total of 119 obligations to be implemented by the end of 2005.

The accord on constitutional reforms, which deals with substantive issues, is operational. It has not been fulfilled, but this is due to the defeat of the constitutional referendum *(Consulta Popular)*, which called for voter approval of the changes and which was held on 16 May 1999.

In terms of the substantive content of the accords, the four variables mentioned above can be applied in the following manner:

1 *Governmental political will* is a decisive variable because most of the obligations in the accords pertain to the executive branch. The three administrations that have held office since the peace agreements were signed – namely, Álvaro Arzú (1996-99), Alfonso Portillo (2000-3), and Oscar Berger (2004-8) – all made public commitments to comply with the peace agreements and took measures to incorporate them as part of their policies. While advances could be noted under all three administrations,

what has not yet been achieved is the will to adopt politically costly decisions and to eventually confront powerful interest groups.

2   Indeed, several commitments were seen to be at odds with the interests of *economically powerful groups* that have traditionally held the state captive. These spoilers actively opposed the peace process through legal and political means, by influencing public opinion, and even through violence. Partly because of that sector's control of the mass media, in Guatemala *the population* did not take full ownership of the peace process. Various polls indicate an unsatisfactory level of familiarity with the accords, although there appears to be a general trend in support of the idea of peace (Molketin 2001). Most citizens do not appear to have incorporated the peace agenda into their daily concerns. On the bright side, *numerous civil society actors* have been actively and deeply engaged with the accords.

3   The *international community* maintained an active interest in the process. Beyond the Consultative Group meetings, most international actors raised compliance issues in their bilateral relationship. Depending on the space allowed by the host government, many diplomatic representatives and international bodies became quite influential. However, with time, the level of support began to diminish. MINUGUA's mandate, initially set to end in 2000, finally came to a close in December 2004.

4   The estimated cost and the *availability of economic resources* are also factors in implementing the accords. In order to achieve social development and to comply with the public expenditure goals required by the peace commitments, the aim was to reach a steady 6 percent growth rate by 1999. The goals set forth in the accords were meant to increase expenditures on health, education, public safety, and the judiciary by 50 percent by the year 2000, as compared to the benchmark year of 1995. Another goal was to steadily reduce the budget of the Ministry of Defence, bringing it down to 0.66 percent of GDP by the turn of the century.[5]

The logic behind these plans held that economic and social reforms, including fiscal reform, would result in economic growth and social development. However, as shown in Figure 1 on GDP growth, several basic assumptions proved to be wrong. First, despite increases in the late 1990s, growth slowed down in the new millennium.

A similar problem arose in the matter of taxation. The assumption that the national government would cover its share of the costs of peace was premised on the fiscal reforms codified in the Socio-Economic Accord. The goal was to increase the tax burden to 12 percent of GDP, a modest goal when compared to average tax rates in the Americas. The accord stipulated that a process leading to a fiscal pact should be convened. After numerous

Figure 1

GDP growth in Guatemala, 1996-2006

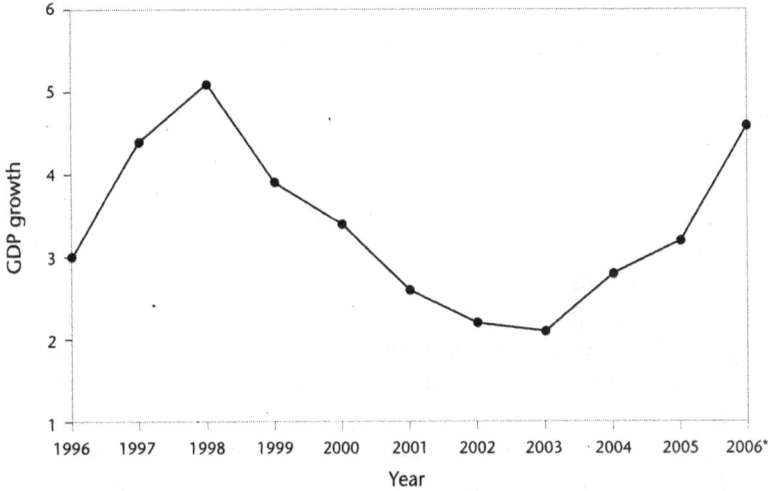

* Estimated.
Source: Comisión Económica para América Latina y el Caribe (2007).

delays, this process was initiated in early 2000, and it generated an impressive body of agreements to increase the government's tax income. Yet, in early 2001, the new government and parts of the business elite rejected it (Gamboa and Trentavizi 2001).

After the failure to reach consensus, the state implemented its own taxation policy in 2001, taking on board many recommendations from the Fiscal Pact. As a result of these reforms, tax income in 2002 was the highest ever recorded, at a modest 10.6 percent. However, confrontations and legal challenges from sectors of the business elite resulted in a reduction to 10.2 percent by 2004 and to a continuously diminishing rate (Banco de Guatemala 2006).

All of this raises a question as to the real cost of carrying out the peace commitments. In the 1996 Schedule Agreement, the government estimated costs at US$2.312 billion. At the first Consultative Group meeting held in Brussels in 1997, the amounts pledged by individual countries and multilaterals met this estimate (Gobierno de Guatemala 1997). Additional pledges were added after the Special Consultative Group for the Reconstruction of Central America was convened, following the destruction unleashed by tropical storm Mitch. By the end of 2001, the total amount of funds from signed agreements and in projects that were already under way came to US$3.214 billion (Inter-American Development Bank 2002). As well, the third Consultative Group meeting, held in Washington in 2002, reviewed the peace process and pledged additional support in the amount of US$1.296 billion (Gobierno 2003).

Even though the pledges of financial support surpassed the original estimated needs, in practice, the real amounts were smaller, and, for reasons that include Guatemala's technical difficulties with regard to project design and its lack of counterpart funds, actual disbursements were even smaller. Thus, the state was unable to put together the national resources that the Peace Portfolio required.

Another important area of the peace process involves the Legislative Peace Agenda, which entails the approval of legal measures required to put the Guatemalan Peace Accords into practice. This agenda has moved forward only haltingly. Between 1966 and 2004, fourteen laws were approved; yet, by the end of 2004, it was estimated that thirteen key new laws were still pending.

The slowness of the Legislative Peace Agenda has had an adverse effect on the implementation of the accords as, ten years after they were signed, nearly 50 percent of the legislation essential to their realization is still pending. This does not include the pending constitutional reforms.

Peace in Local Spaces: The Development Councils

President Berger's understanding of moving the peace process to the local level involves working with the Urban and Rural Development Councils.

The Development Councils originated in the processes of state decentralization that began in the 1970s. In the aftermath of the 1976 earthquake, working within the concept of development planning, a series of policies were enacted to set up the so-called "development poles" – intermediate urban centres in which the means of production were concentrated – and to reorient public investment and the growth of infrastructure along territorial lines (Gálvez 2002). The main criteria were to promote efficiency rather than to foster social development. Moreover, during the war, part of that structure was incorporated into the counter-insurgency strategy, with the aim being population control (Aguilera 1988).

Decentralization came to the forefront during the transition to democracy as part of democracy building and as an attempt to foster social development. The Urban and Rural Development Councils were institutionalized when they were included in the 1985 Constitution and were charged with formulating development policy along territorial lines. The Constitution also mandated that the councils be allocated the necessary fiscal resources with which to do this (*Constitución Política de la República de Guatemala* 2001).

The role of the councils has since been spelled out in specific legislation: "The system of development councils is the principal means of participation

for the Mayan, Xinca, Garífuna and non-Indigenous population to participate in the conduct of public affairs in the democratic process of planning
development, taking into account the principles of national unity and of
Guatemala as a pluricultural and multilingual nation" (*Ley de los Consejos de
Desarrollo Urbano y Rural* 2002). The basic structure of the councils is as
follows:

Name	*Jurisdiction*
• National Council (CONADES)[6]	National, the highest level
• Regional Council (COREDES)[7]	Region that comprises a group of departments
• Departmental Council (CODEDES)[8]	A single department
• Municipal Council (COMUDES)[9]	A single *municipio* within a department
	Community Council (COCODES)[10]
	A community within a *municipio*

Both state and civil society representatives participate in the councils,
although the make-up may vary depending on the level of participation.
The key actors are shown in Box 3.

Box 3
Key Actors in the Development Councils

THE STATE	CIVIL SOCIETY
The Executive	*Groups representing the grassroots, women, indigenous peoples, and intellectuals*
The Presidency, Ministry of Finance, Planning and Programming Secretariat, Executive Coordination Secretariat, and Presidential Secretariat for Women.	Representatives of indigenous peoples, cooperatives, peasant organizations, workers organizations, non-governmental development organizations, organizations of women, the University of San Carlos, and private universities.
Municipal government	*Business sector*
Mayors represent municipal governments.	Associations of agricultural, retail, financial, and industrial enterprise. Associations of small- and medium-sized businesses in manufacturing and services.

As mentioned above, at every level the councils are mandated to formulate development policy and territorial organization; formulate and monitor plans, programs, and projects; review, monitor, and propose public investment in their areas; supervise the performance of public officials; and promote the participation of women and indigenous peoples.

The councils were promoted during the first government of the democratic transition (1985-90); however, in practice, they were only set up at the departmental level. This is because adversaries of the project went to court and managed to block the municipal and community councils, arguing that they violated municipal autonomy. The issue was taken up in the Guatemalan Peace Accords, and the legal hurdles were resolved through reforms enacted in 2002.

The new legal adjustments mean that the councils now have the potential to become spaces for interaction between government and civil society as well as for social actors to participate in the conduct of public affairs at the level that most relates to their everyday lives. The new strategy for the ongoing peace process aims to give the councils the additional role of monitoring and promoting compliance with the accords.

Our researchers carried out individual and group discussions with representatives of women's and indigenous peoples' organizations.[11] We also analyzed the results generated by the joint project conducted by Programa Participacion y Democracia (PPD)[12] and the Guatemala office of the Latin-American Faculty of Social Sciences (FLACSO).[13] This project sought not only to help the councils and their participants adapt to the new legislation but also to understand the extent to which the peace directives were known and were being applied at the local level. It also carried out specific research on the participation of women and indigenous peoples. The WKOP project worked with the same sample of municipal and departmental councils.[14] Because of the small number of cases in the total universe – it is estimated that as many as 323 COMUDES and two thousand COCODES may be functioning or in the process of starting up – our sample became a pilot project whose function was to begin to look at the dynamics of the councils.

Three specific issues – accreditation, regulations, and committees – drew our attention. To begin with accreditation, even though legislation gives civil society access to the councils, this is not automatic. Among conditions that must be met are raising awareness, organizing, capacity building, and legalizing representation. The first condition means disseminating information on the nature and role of the councils and on the importance of participation. Issues of organization and legalization are complicated by civil society fragmentation, which, once overcome, allows for capacity building and the development of support mechanisms for delegates.

Capacity building for women requires special attention. When women manage to overcome the inherent difficulties facing civil society access to the council, they are likely to face patriarchal prejudice, which tends to be accentuated in rural areas. A series of practical difficulties became evident. Some council meetings that started at the end of the workday would become night sessions, and this was a problem for peasant representatives who often travelled long distances in order to attend the meeting. For women, this meant additional difficulty from husbands and family members who would ask, "Who is going to prepare dinner if you go to the meeting?"

Some new delegates feared that they were not up to exercising their representation. They would ask questions like: "What am I going to report to my *compañeros* when I am not even allowed a turn to speak at the meetings?"

With regard to regulations, although developing them would appear to be a routine administrative process, it is, in fact, highly political because it refers to how a council will actually function. What must be kept in mind is that the councils are meant to exercise decentralization at its fullest, and government representatives must learn to share the decision-making spaces with civil society. Because regulations encompass the rules of the game, issues such as empowering the weaker sectors need to be elucidated.

In practice it has been hard for COMUDES to overcome the authoritarian tradition of the country's political culture, which regards mayors as sort of "little presidents." Some mayors – or governors, for that matter, in the case of departmental councils – proceed under the assumption that the councils function to gather opinions and to discuss accountability but that they are the ones to make decisions.

With regard to committees, we found that working committees are central to the exercise of power in the councils. How committees are organized, what issues they take up, and how they actually work are indicators of how far a particular council has moved towards a culture of democracy and whether or not there is real participation. Power plays develop in as many fields as there are committees and, in general, through three types of players: government officials (e.g., a mayor, a representative of the municipal council, or a governor), the diverse representatives of civil society (e.g., indigenous representatives, women's leaders, and business members), and state agencies (e.g., the Presidential Planning Secretariat through its departmental technical units, the Executive Secretariat of this agency, and departmental delegations from the different ministries).

Furthermore, we should keep in mind that civil society cannot be assumed to be homogeneous. Local business-sector delegates may wield greater influence and stronger technical capacity – and get along better with government officials – than delegates from peasant, indigenous peoples' groups or women's groups.

While in certain committees (e.g., a project or budget committee) technical capacity is necessary in order to play any kind of significant role, in other areas links to the grassroots may prove essential (e.g., in the case of conflict resolution and some types of security issues). A certain level of technical capacity is necessary if one is to wield any significant influence in the councils, and this is precisely because their role is to conduct public affairs as an extention of decentralization policies. Popular-sector representatives can meet this requirement to some extent through capacity building and training, but it would appear that professional advisors are still needed to shore up their role in the councils.

Several problems have been detected during the first two years of the new legislation on development councils. These include the following:

Political problems
- failure of state and municipal authorities to accept the role of civil society representation
- numeric disparity between state representation and civil society representation in CODEDES.

Technical problems
- unfamiliarity with council legislation and lack of capacity to work within the framework
- absence of regulations and operational mechanisms, such as working committees
- insufficient planning and work plans
- difficulty accrediting civil society representation and insufficiently prepared delegates
- lack of communication between civil society entities acting in the same spaces
- insufficient community involvement in the work of the councils.[15]

Several factors limit the participation of women in the councils: "illiteracy is a front line factor, along with lack of organization and *machismo*. Indigenous Peoples and women's presence is timid and barely visible ... we need to take a more leading role. This is even worse in the COCODES and COMUDES."[16]

Councils are not sufficiently familiar with the peace commitments, nor are they prepared to take on functions delegated to them within the new peace framework, such as promoting dialogue and conflict resolution. In fact, the Guatemalan Peace Accords are barely present in the daily workings of the councils.

Furthermore, as one interviewee noted, political parties have been known to manipulate the councils, and COMUDES face many limitations in trying to carry out their work:

Municipal governments, especially those belonging to the party in power, try to impose sympathetic Municipal Councils, going so far as to leave out members from the previous council. The new makeup minimizes and excludes the previous composition of the council and participation of the Community Councils.

Obstacles have been set up to the democratic development of Community Development Councils. Many municipalities refuse to register COCODES formed by community initiative, or demand that they be legally notarized. Practically none of the municipalities have accepted Community Development Councils set up according to the customs and traditions of Indigenous Peoples even though this is clearly established in the law. (SERJUS 2005)

The problems that hamper councils can be summarized as follows:

- There is no policy debate, and attention tends to focus on infrastructure projects.
- Sometimes funds assigned to CODEDES are used for projects that were not approved in the council system.
- Civil society representation is absent at the national level because the seats are allotted to representatives of the regional councils.
- The national planning system, which should involve the councils, has not been set up.
- Development planning should be micro-regionalized.
- Third-level COCODES should be set up in municipalities where the population exceeds that of the second-level COCODES.
- Civil society inclusion has not been completed in the majority of CODEDES.
- The national and regional levels of the council system have not been fully implemented.
- Lack of funding makes CODEDES vulnerable, weakening the entire foundation of the council structure.
- Government representation at the various levels of the council structure should have the capacity to negotiate and make commitments.
- Representatives throughout the councils should improve the feedback provided to those they represent (interview with Amilcar Burgos, 2005).

On the other hand, it is possible to note advances generated by the new legislation. These are highlighted by the following excerpts from our interviews:

Indigenous authority is recognized in both the new council legislation and the Municipal Code ... in the everyday movement of things you can see ideological changes in Guatemalan society, so racist and divided, regarding women and Indigenous Peoples (interview with Violeta de Carpio, 2004).

As women, we now dare say things in public ... men and women leaders have been combining experience with informed capacity ... leaders have a broad assortment of knowledge (interview with Teresa Zapeta, 2004).

We have seen some progress during this time, there have been some changes ... We know there has been an opening, and also, some of the legal changes are a result of the Peace Accords. We should be clear on the fact that these changes have opened many spaces, although this is but a step in the process of giving the population [the right] to participate (interview with Tomasa Bulux, 2004).

[Participation] today is more conscientious; people have a vision and proposals ... in the sense that we as women have to be present in this type of decision ... so women are participating. [At the] urban level they say things like "Indians won't let themselves be trampled, women won't let themselves be trampled" ... [this] means a lot, these phrases compare the present with twenty years ago when women couldn't speak, whereas today when women have proposals (interview with Francisco Calí, 2004).

There is also a positive appraisal of women's experience in developing alliances:

We had to develop strategic alliances with other civil society actors such as workers, peasants, NGOs, Chambers of Commerce, in order to raise the visibility of social actors in the council ... we know that our presence in the CODEDE is transitory, but the space for women has been won and will be permanent. They can't take the space away from us, it's there. We have to continue to strengthen the united women's sector in order to eliminate poverty, unemployment, rape and racism and to [fight for] respect for our cultural values, for inclusion and to protect [our] rights, for the [right to] intellectual development, to exercise freedom of expression and, of course, [to] avoid calls to violence and confrontation, [to] build a culture of peace in our daily lives (interview with Aura Lolita Chávez, 2004).

Other advances are also recognized:

There are undeniable advances in the institutional development of the councils, among them the improvement of the normative framework approved in 2002, the practice of strategic planning in COMUDES and CODEDES in the context of validating the strategy to reduce poverty, the experience of micro-planning carried out by certain COCODES, initial experiences with

accountability in some municipalities and the availability of financial resources coming from the VAT [value-added tax] and other sources (interview with Amilcar Burgos, 2005).

All told, a preliminary appraisal appears to indicate that the legislation
and institutions required for implementing the accords' main commitments
on decentralization already exist. While early experience has been problematic in many ways, accomplishments may well be great and future possibilities are no doubt promising.

Lessons Learned and Prospects for the Future

Answering the question of what type of peace is possible in Guatemala requires us to return to the debate between maximalists and minimalists. As
both sides agree that the actual conclusion of the war – as stipulated in the
operational commitments of the Guatemalan Peace Accords – was a success, our discussion bypasses this.

As will be explained in Chapter 8 of this book on DDR in Guatemala,
there are few cases in which the disarmament, demobilization, and reintegration of insurgents have taken place so quickly and efficiently, managing
to maintain a secure environment for the former guerrillas. Yet the two
major problems in this area are (1) the long-term sustainability of support
for the demobilized and (2) the fact that not all actors in the conflict were
covered.

Today, sustainable peace relies on the substantive accords, explained above.
In the maximalist perspective, the depth and complexity of the root causes
of the conflict mean that only comprehensive observance of the commitments can really guarantee peace, lead to broad structural change, and, as a
result, to the gradual emergence of a new country.

Therefore, while time frames and operational mechanisms may be needed,
the maximalist proposal is that the state and society continue to implement the accords, including the "new generation" commitments that arise
along the way, until comprehensive observation is achieved. It is also expected that the international community will continue to support the process. Additionally, maximalists believe that compliance is feasible and that
sluggish observance has been due to lack of political will, financial difficulties, and the actions of spoilers.

The minimalist perspective, on the other hand, questions the very structure of the accords as well as their ambitious mandate. Minimalists do not
believe that social and economic structures that have evolved over a long
period of time can be totally renovated by political mandate. Excessively
ambitious goals may initially unleash great enthusiasm but, ultimately, lead
to frustration and to an erosion of the idea of peace. From this point of

view, because of the conditions in Guatemala, it was never possible to fully implement the substantive content of the accords. Thus, it is thought that efforts at comprehensive compliance should be discontinued and that we should settle for what has been achieved to date. What remains should be considered as regular development agendas – desirable goals that are not constrained by short time frames (Pásara 2003).

With the end of MINUGUA's mandate and of the time frame for the second Schedule Agreement, it is evident that a considerable part of the commitments has not been met (MINUGUA 2004a). Thus, it seems reasonable to doubt whether compliance will be possible.

Nonetheless, the Berger government has again ratified the state's commitment to the accords and has proposed a new plan. In practice, these plans change the original strategy of the accords as the general mapping of commitments will probably be left by the wayside. The new plan is to concentrate follow-up on a smaller group of commitments, those that represent the core of the agreements. The thinking appears to be that the same limited resources that hampered reaching compliance on schedule could nonetheless be effective if concentrated in a more demarcated field. A central element of the new strategy has been to legislate the basis for the long-term implementation of the accords. The Framework Law for the Guatemalan Peace Accords was passed by Congress in August 2005 on the basis of a consensual proposal that, over two years, was negotiated between civil society and the state.

The new legislation recognizes the Guatemalan Peace Accords as state commitments, and it sets up the National Council for Compliance with the Peace Accords with representatives from political parties, the state, and civil society. One new element in the structure is the so-called Coordination for Social Participation and Consultation Committee, which is composed of civil society representatives who are in support of compliance. Another is the inclusion of a UN Development Program representative as a permanent observer.

The new strategy provides for national coverage through a support network that would involve the Urban and Rural Development Councils (Gobierno de Guatemala 2004). The plan also emphasizes that, in this phase, the government will rely on national actors, scaling down the front-line role of the international community. This decision may mean that the government is banking on the national capacity to achieve sustainability. The relaunching of the accords is based on three priorities: (1) dialogue and participation of indigenous peoples, (2) sustainable rural development, and (3) reparations for victims.

In conclusion, the comparative analysis of the minimalist and maximalist perspectives on the Guatemalan peace process tends to confirm the conclusion that it is "fair to assess postwar peacebuilding efforts in the first 10 years primarily according to whether they have helped end wars. Yet it is important to assess long-term peacebuilding efforts, over periods of 10-25 years, according to whether they are addressing the causes of conflict and are leading to sustainable peacebuilding" (Baranyi 2005c, 8).

In addition to what has already been said about the implementation of the operational accords, compliance with their substantive agenda has also made significant advances. Among the most noteworthy of these are the following:

Demilitarization and strengthening of civilian power. The military overflowed its confines during the war and under authoritarianism, influencing the entire state apparatus and expanding into control of civil society. Given these conditions, demilitarization was a central goal of the peace process.

It is fair to say that, in general, this goal has been achieved. The size and budget of the Guatemalan army have been reduced; the institution is in the process of reconverting and is subordinated to civilian power. The military continues to participate in internal security and is mandated by the government to do so.

Recognition of indigenous peoples rights. It would be hard to find another time in Guatemala's history in which the recognition of the identity and rights of indigenous peoples has advanced as much as it has under the peace accords. By establishing the multiethnic, pluricultural, and multilingual character of the nation and recognizing that it is made up of four peoples – three of them indigenous – the accords helped to lay the groundwork for remodelling not only the government apparatus but also the culture of the country.

Nonetheless, there has been a lack of compliance with the specific commitments to implement indigenous rights, and for the most part the country's civic culture is still imbued with racism and discrimination (MINUGUA 2004a). However, change has been unleashed, and that trend continues.

Observance of human rights. The centrality of this point arises from decades of grave human rights violations. Individual and political rights tend to be observed, although some worrisome situations persist,[17] and violations of second- and third-generation rights have yet to be tended to. One major issue is that reparation for victims of the conflict is still in the early stages, although the establishment of the National Reparations Commission in 2004 was a help. Also, deep deterioration of individual security due to the rise of various aspects of organized crime and its penetration into the national police force is adversely affecting democratic governance.

Democracy. Political democracy is fully in force. Transparent and legitimate elections have taken place and there is separation of powers and the rule of law. Since the democratic transition and the 1985 Constitution predate the accords, these advances are not solely due to the peace process; however, peace has no doubt strengthened democracy. Of particular importance is the strengthening of local spaces for democratic action due to the work of the Urban and Rural Development Councils.

Economic reform. The agreements have linked the possibility for the consolidation of democracy and social reform, and they have taken on an economic dimension, especially through fiscal reform. While the spoilers' opposition to tax increases have made this objective impossible to achieve at present, nonetheless the need for this change has been placed on the national agenda.

The Guatemalan Peace Accords have also given rise to significant advances in terms of gender rights. On this issue, it should be kept in mind that there is no specific accord on women's rights because they were treated as a transversal issue referred to in various accords and commitments. Of particular relevance was the creation of the National Women's Forum, the Secretariat for Women, and the Office for the Defence of the Indigenous Women as well as the participation of women in the Urban and Rural Councils.

Despite these accomplishments, it is necessary to reflect from a feminist perspective on whether or not the peace process has introduced significant change on gender issues. Peace negotiations were carried out mainly by men, while women's groups concerned with gender issues had only partial influence on the process. Given these conditions, we can venture the hypothesis that the interests, positions, experiences, and visions of society from the perspective of women were not central to the negotiations (even though, as we have seen, women's needs and issues were taken into account).

What are the lessons from the Guatemalan experience? Five are particularly noteworthy:

The initial impulse is key. The peace agreement created huge sympathy and expectations both at home and abroad, and these translated into political support, international cooperation, and positive public opinion, all of which left little room for manoeuvres by spoilers.

However, this capital was short-lived. Initial operational success maintained the momentum, but sluggish performance on substantive issues rapidly consumed the early enthusiasm. The country returned to its regular political dynamics, and peace lost its place at the top of everyday concerns. Spoilers recovered their capacity to inflict damage, as evidenced by the defeat of the constitutional referendum and the momentous effects this has had on the legitimacy of the process.

The international community continued to assist the peace process beyond what could have been expected, despite the emergence of other crises, wars, and grave human rights violations around the world. However, even this extended support had to come to an end as external actors and will-power cannot take the place of national resolve. Thus, in the future, the international presence will probably come mostly from normal development cooperation programs.

In retrospect, it seems obvious that better use could have been made of the first and perhaps the second years of the peace process. The lack of political decisiveness on the part of the state and political parties may explain the limited use of this window of opportunity. By 1997, electoral dynamics were superimposed on the peace agenda.

The new government's initial commitment to peace in 2000, the Fiscal Pact, and an ongoing process to reschedule tasks all seemed to indicate that, to a degree, the early positive spirit had been recovered. However, these hopes were short-lived, mainly because an intense political struggle between the government and business sectors carried over into the entire presidential term and made it impossible to establish national spaces of understanding.

In sum, the lesson is that it is necessary to take full advantage of the initial momentum created by the political conclusion of an armed conflict because this momentum is hard to keep alive.

The importance of full involvement of the state and political parties. The Guatemalan Peace Accords constituted an agreement signed by the Executive Branch of government and the guerrilla commanders. Each successive president of Guatemala has, in turn, made public statements defining the accords as state obligations. These accords were not presented to Congress to be made into law. As mentioned above, what did take place in an attempt to comply with some of the commitments was the constitutional referendum, which was defeated by the voters. All of this led to legal difficulties and provided ammunition to spoilers.

Even though the courts supported some measures and Congress passed several specific laws referring to peace commitments, the earlier legalization of the accords would have provided them with lasting force. Furthermore, because the Executive Branch took on the responsibility of negotiating peace and complying with the accords, other branches of government were less involved in their observance. Lack of involvement on the part of other branches of government was corrected in 2005, with the new Framework Law for the Peace Accords, a measure that should have been there in the beginning.

The absence of political parties in the negotiating process was surely an even greater weakness. Although parties expressed support for the negotiations when the peace was signed, the Accompaniment Commission, for example, limited participation to the government and the URNG. During the 2003 election campaign, participating parties agreed to a national shared agenda that ratified their commitment to the accords (UNDP 2003). Furthermore, the new format for the National Peace Council, which was set up in 2006, includes parties with majority representation in Congress. Sustainability of the peace commitments requires strong and steady involvement of political parties.

The importance of broader public ownership. In practice, the accords granted new rights to the population as a whole. However, the long texts were not sufficiently disseminated, and even though most of the people knew about peace and approved it, they were unfamiliar with the content of the Accords. Despite campaigns waged by civil society organizations, MINUGUA, and, to some extent, the government, most of the population was unable to develop a sense of ownership. Moreover, the already complicated texts have undergone successive rescheduling, adding to their complexity. To this we might add that efforts to translate the accords into the language of popular education and into indigenous languages were clearly insufficient.

It is no doubt true that various spaces were set up to foster ownership of the accords, the main ones being the Parity Commissions between the state and representatives of indigenous peoples, the Women's Forum, the departmental discussion tables, and the work of the Accompaniment Commission. Nonetheless, their efforts seem to have reached only specific population groups rather than the broader population.

The importance of adequate financing. In a nutshell, there is no peace without financial resources. Many commitments were not carried out because the government did not have the means to do so. Although international support appeared to be sufficient, actual disbursements did not always meet what had been pledged or were lost because the government failed to provide the required matching funds. Corruption and the failure to achieve fiscal reform were also serious problems. The modest goal of achieving tax income equivalent to 12 percent of GDP was never reached.

All of this meant that successive governments did not have the resources to comply with the peace portfolio and were unable to provide the matching funds required by cooperating international bodies (which meant that part of what could have been available went unused). The seemingly obvious lesson is that actors interested in furthering peace should attend to the financial dimension of the situation as well as to the political dimension. Further, it is necessary to have a certain level of national unity in order to make the requisite fiscal reforms.

The importance of being realistic. This lesson refers to a thread that runs through this chapter. While the Guatemalan Peace Accords conjured up the possibility of a noble outcome inspired by the desire to overcome a history plagued by cruelty, it appears that certain factors were not taken into account. This is the crux of the problem of compliance. It was assumed that when peace was signed all social actors had agreed to a "social pact" that would transcend partisan debate and sectoral conflict. While this was desirable, it was not realistic as post-conflict societies invariably emerge from war deeply divided. What can be realistically expected in the medium term is the national unity that was absent in the first place.

Over the longer run, numerous internal and external factors influence peacebuilding processes, as is postulated by Down's tenet on increasing complexity:

> The more time passes from the conclusion of a peace mission, the more likely it is that any number of other extraneous factors (e.g., business cycles, famines, unusually good or bad weather, the policies of a neighbouring state, the behaviour of the first elected leaders) are actually responsible for what has taken place rather than the technology of the peace mission itself. (Downs and Stedman 2002, 49)

The lesson here is that peace agreements should be ambitious enough to address the causes of conflict, but they should also be realistically framed in accordance with the historic context, the international situation, and the country's geopolitical location. These lessons appear relevant to other cases in which significant success and pending reforms exist side by side (e.g., Mozambique).

Five Axes for the Peace

The present situation in Guatemala points to a phase in which leadership of the peace process should pass from the large international and national actors to state representatives at the regional and local levels and to civil society leadership. Thus, the peace process should move from a debate rooted in national policy to realization through regional, provincial, municipal, and community dynamics.

With the closure of MINUGUA, the accords became a national responsibility, which makes buy-in and participation at the local level all the more important. It also determines the role that institutions like the Human Rights Ombudsman's Office are now called on to play.[18]

Guatemala has a well-developed road map for building a culture of peace and for furthering its socioeconomic development and multicultural character. However, after fifteen years of international support and influence – both during the negotiations and through the first years of implementation – the decision to take advantage of this opportunity rests solely on national political determination. This proposition confirms Baranyi's (2005c, 8) contention that "multi-dimensional peacebuilding provides a framework for nurturing transnational coalitions – or peace infrastructures – linking agents of change from the local to the national and international levels. Yet stakeholders should invest much more to build the domestic base of these coalitions and deliver the institutional reforms required to extend their life beyond the departure of major international actors."

In summary, five strategic axes appear to be crucial to the sustainability of the peace goals. The first axis involves state norms. These include legislating peace institutions and commitments as extensively as possible, including both the long list of bills pending in Congress and possible new options, such as making the National Women's Forum a permanent institution. In this vein, the previously mentioned Framework Law for the Peace Accords is noteworthy.

The second axis involves attempting to root the accords in the dynamics of the development councils. This is positive in that it guarantees continuity. As we have seen above, this process is still not sufficiently in place to allow for an evaluation. But the idea is a good one, and, with adequate attention and support – and given the time for the necessary changes in the prevailing political culture – the councils could strengthen participatory democracy and the observance of peace.

As mentioned above, the third axis entails the greater involvement of political parties in the process of monitoring and providing support for compliance with the accords. The fourth axis involves indigenous peoples' efforts to achieve a truly intercultural country. Their labours are based on the accords precisely because, in their understanding, peace is a process rather than an endpoint; it is "a guide to begin building a democratic country without exclusion or discrimination" (interview with Francisco Calí, 2004). In this view, the insistence on peace is part of the envisioned multicultural, multilingual, and multiethnic nation to which indigenous peoples aspire as well as part of a more gender-equitable society.

The fifth axis is linked to the financial sustainability of the accords' commitments: the unfinished fiscal reform must be retrieved. This is a difficult undertaking because the entrepreneurial sector, which is the dominant force in the politics of the country, still refuses to recognize the right of the government to raise tax revenue. However, without enough economic resources from national sources, it will be impossible to put into practice most of the reforms contained in the accords.

At the end of the day the main question is: who can promote transformative peacebuilding? In Guatemala, some of us believe that it is possible to create a bond between those sectors of the political and intellectual elites who are supporters of sustainable peace, women's and indigenous peoples' leaders, and other civil society leaders who are associated with the development councils. As difficult as it is, the country has no alternative but to fulfill the content of the peace accords over the long run. That insight may also apply (with due regard to important national differences) to the other case of "relative success" studied in this volume – namely, Mozambique.

Acknowledgments
I conducted the research for and wrote this chapter, while Braulia Thillet de Solórzano, Carmen Lucía Pellecer, and Aura Bolaños de Aguilera undertook the fieldwork, with the help of Otilia Lux de Cotí. While I am grateful to them for their participation, I take full responsibility for the content of this chapter.

Decentralization and Sustainable Peacebuilding in Mozambique: Bringing the Elements Together Again

Eduardo J. Sitoe and Carolina Hunguana

Since the signing of the 1992 Rome Peace Accords between the FRELIMO (Mozambican Liberation Front) government and the then-RENAMO (Mozambican National Resistance) guerrilla movement,[1] Mozambique has experienced major political and economic transformations. In economic terms, with the restoration of normalcy in the countryside, the return of millions of refugees and displaced persons, and the influx of foreign direct capital, beginning in 1995, Mozambique has boasted one of the highest macroeconomic growth rates in the sub-Saharan region (with the exception of 2000, when the country was hit by severe floods). Indeed, in the critical area of poverty, Mozambique was able to progress from a mere US$95 per capita GDP in 1995 to US$313 in 2004. In the political domain, the country has made significant inroads towards the entrenchment of peace and democracy, holding three successive national elections in 1994, 1999, and 2004 and two local government elections in 1998 and 2003, all of which were generally regarded as free and fair.

Despite these positive developments in both political and economic spheres, peace dividends in the country are yet to be fully realized by the majority of the Mozambican people. To date, macroeconomic growth rates in the country have not adequately addressed the enduring regional and socioeconomic inequalities. For example, the percentage of Mozambicans living below the line of absolute poverty was only reduced from 70 percent in 1997 to 60 percent in 2005. Moreover, there has been some violence in national and local government elections. Following the second general elections in 1999, more than one hundred persons died due to post-election violence in the northern district of Montepuez. In addition, the government still gives greater priority to administrative deconcentration than it does to political decentralization. This may endanger gains already made by enabling a return to the excessive concentration of power at the central level.

It is within this context that our research takes the perspective that sustainable peacebuilding in Mozambique will depend on the extent to which democratization and political inclusion, on the one hand, and the reduction of poverty and regional imbalances, on the other, will better the lives of ordinary citizens. This assumes that improving the lives of ordinary citizens has the potential to reduce the temptation to use violence to pursue individual or group interests. Thus, the focus of our research is on sustainable peacebuilding as it relates to specific democratic governance interventions and to economic public policy measures. Its specific themes are (1) decentralization and provincial/local governance and (2) fiscal decentralization.

The three critical questions that our research addresses are:

1   How can political, administrative, and fiscal decentralization foster political inclusion and address marginalization, including that of women, particularly in rural areas?
2   How can decentralization be used to reduce poverty and inequality, including gender inequalities as well as regional imbalances?
3   How can deeper and more inclusive decentralization contribute to the prevention of violence and the consolidation of sustainable peace?

In relation to our first theme, decentralization and provincial/local governance, the rationale is that decentralization increases popular participation in decision making because it brings the government closer to the people, while making it both more accessible and more knowledgeable about local conditions as well as more responsive to people's demands. In the case of Mozambique, decentralization can be a tool both to enhance the dimension of political inclusion as well as to address the country's prevalent regional imbalances. As Weimer (2004) adds, decentralization is also a way of consolidating democracy and, at the same time, of institutionalizing a certain form of peace. An increase in the degree of legitimacy and effectiveness of democratic institutions ("consolidation") means, at the same time, an increase in stability and the strengthening of peace, even if we take into account the fact that competition between political forces and parties can generate conflicts.

With regard to our second theme, we take a closer look at the fiscal reform now taking place in Mozambique as part of global public sector reforms. Here, our specific focus is on intergovernmental fiscal relations. Our research develops out of the recognition that the development of an effective intergovernmental fiscal policy, as well as the development of adequate institutions and intergovernmental best practices, is a tool both for good governance and for the reduction of poverty. In the case of war-torn societies such as Mozambique, the design and effective implementation of a sound intergovernmental fiscal system can be a vehicle for establishing political compromises and inclusion. This is because local financial issues currently constitute the principal bottleneck with regard to the decentralization/

municipalization of the country and, thus, have a certain significance on the path towards instituting sustainable peacebuilding.

That being the case, this chapter addresses several of the propositions highlighted in the introductory chapter. It applies the idea that it is important to assess the long-term outcomes of peacebuilding efforts, tests the notion that multidimensional peacebuilding efforts have great difficulties laying the foundations for the deeper reforms required to sustain peace, and asks whether this is due to the challenges of forging the new political coalitions required to underpin more profound changes. It examines these propositions in the areas of democratization and economic development, focusing on decentralization as a vehicle for both of these as well as for sustainable peacebuilding. Finally, it ends by identifying a network of national and international actors, in government and civil society, that could work together to advance the projects of democratic decentralization and sustainable peacebuilding in Mozambique.

This research endeavour relied on a combination of four methods. First, we conducted a systematic review of the national literature on democratization and peacebuilding in the country, looking at the most representative pieces of work produced by "privileged" commentators such as Joseph Hanlon, Bernhard Weimer, Brazão Mazula, and Iraê Baptista Lundin. Second, we conducted in-depth interviews with key informants throughout the country: with officials and citizens both at the municipal/district levels and in Maputo. Third, a series of focus group discussions was set up in the six municipalities that provided much of the empirical ground of our research. Both at the local/community level and with regard to opinion makers and decision makers in Maputo, our research utilized an interactive methodology; and, in each case, guiding questions were set up to structure the interviews according to the theoretical and methodological frame of the WKOP project. Finally, a number of validation meetings comprising round-table debates and seminars were organized to test our preliminary arguments and to fine-tune our conclusions and policy recommendations.

Our research focuses on the municipalities of Nacala and Ilha de Moçambique in the northern province of Nampula; Beira and Dondo in the central province of Sofala; Vilankulo in the southern province of Inhambane; and Maputo. These municipalities provide an illustrative sample of larger and smaller towns, some led by the governing party and some led by the opposition, with one case (Dondo) widely seen as a success story.

Historical Context

In many ways, the recent history of Mozambique is still very much marked by two basic realities. One is the nature of the colonial and fascist regime that prevailed in Portugal and, obviously, in its colonies from 1926 until 1974 and that created in its colonies a highly centralized, authoritarian, repressive state heavily policed by the armed forces. The second is the armed struggle waged by FRELIMO against the Portuguese colonial forces from 1964 until 1974. While the first of these historical stages points to the difficulties that Mozambique faces in its efforts at democratization, the second relates to the difficulties between FRELIMO and its major political opponent, RENAMO. Since 1975, when the country first became independent, FRELIMO has been the party in power. At first it presided over a one-party socialist state and, later, was the ruling party in a pluralized political order, which was established with the first multiparty general elections in 1994. As for RENAMO, its membership consisted primarily of individuals disillusioned with FRELIMO both before and after independence, though Rhodesian security forces and former Portuguese commandos played a critical role in its origin (Vines 1996; Cabrita 2000; Mazula 2002).

In economic terms it is worth noting that Mozambique's colonial political economy may be divided into three different historical phases:

- 1885 to 1926, which was characterized by the predominance of non-Portuguese external capital
- 1926 to 1960, which saw the fascist and nationalist economic policies of Antonio Salazar, whose main goal was to use the colonial possession to accumulate capital for the colonial power
- 1960 to 1973, which was characterized by a deep economic crisis shortly followed by a substantive restructuring of capital that gave rise to a seeming boom in the industrial sector.

It was during the first period of Portuguese domination that the main features of the Mozambican political economy were firmly established. These were to survive well beyond the birth of the new state in 1975 and consisted of (1) a deep economic dependence on foreign capital and (2) Mozambique's role as a service economy in the context of Southern Africa (Mondlane 1969; Munslow 1983; Newitt 1995). Indeed, initially, the colonial economy was only made possible by the recruitment of British and South African investment assisted by the imposition of a harsh forced-labour system.

The main challenges that these rather paradoxical policies posed to the development of the colonial Mozambican economy were far-reaching. First, given both the forced-labour system and the heavy reliance on the service economy, they meant underutilization of the agricultural and agro-industrial potential of the country. Second, they placed a heavy burden on peasant production, which, in fact, was the primary source of labour, thus contributing to the permanent distortion of the rural economy. Additionally, these colonial migration agreements and the constraints imposed on the peasant economy made possible the creation of a huge mass of proletarians who lacked the material conditions for their existence in their country of origin. Later, shortly following the fall of the colonial system, the economy entered into a deep crisis, not least as a result of the massive emigration of skilled labour, including most of the Portuguese settlers who were forced by circumstances to abandon Mozambique even before independence (Wuyts 1980; Castelo-Branco 1994).

Basically, the post-independence political economy of Mozambique can be divided into three distinct phases:

- from 1974 to 1977, which was the transitional period and which was characterized by a deep economic crisis
- from 1977 to 1984, which was the period in which the economy of Mozambique had a socialist focus, with central planning as the prime institutional arrangement for the allocation of resources and management in general
- from 1985 onward, which is the period in which markets were rediscovered and the market economy became a norm.

With the fall of the colonial system, the economy entered a deep crisis, first as a result of the great destruction caused by Portuguese settlers who decided to abandon the newborn state and then by the policies adopted by the FRELIMO government, which saw agriculture as the basis of the economy, with industry as the driving force. Though sound, this policy lacked any tangible precedent in the economic history of Mozambique.

After the third Congress of FRELIMO in February 1977, which transformed it from a liberation movement into a Marxist-Leninist party, a new development strategy was adopted. This strategy was designed to achieve the levels of economic production that existed before the 1973 crisis and, within ten years, to eradicate underdevelopment. In the agrarian sector, the plan envisaged state enterprises and cooperatives; in the industrial sector, the priority was basic industries. The regime's first development undertaking did not succeed for a number of reasons – namely, its heavy dependence on external resources, the bureaucratic allocation of these resources in accordance with the methods of central planning, and, perhaps more significantly, the destruction caused by the war that broke out around 1977 (Castelo-Branco 1995). Indeed, export trade was devastated by the destruction of rural life (through terrorism) and the sabotage of transportation routes, with an annual loss reaching US$250 to US$300 million. This must be added to the loss of transit traffic revenue, particularly due to the diversion of South African cargo, which represented between US$275 to US$300 million a year. If one adds to these figures the cost of the emergency program (which was running at US$300 million a year), the massive destruction of health and education infrastructures, and millions of displaced persons and refugees, the effects of the war become even more evident (UN-ECA 1989; Hanlon 1996).

Governance and Peacebuilding

Context and Policy Challenges

Given the fundamental clash between FRELIMO and RENAMO, the new-born state was immersed in a vicious war from 1976 until 1992. Obviously, the war had an external element to it, with first the Rhodesian security forces and later the military and security apparatus of the South African apartheid regime fighting side-by-side with the RENAMO guerrilla movement. However, it is also true that a considerable number of Mozambicans allied themselves with RENAMO, particularly those who were against the Soviet political style initiated by the first FRELIMO regime, whose goal was to create a highly centralized state.

Regardless of how one judges the war that raged for sixteen years, the extent of bloodshed, starvation, and social dislocation it caused cannot be underestimated. In essence, the war not only destroyed the social fabric of the country but also virtually – step by step – brought the state itself to the point of collapse. Even after the removal of the regional and global dimensions of this war (i.e., the end of apartheid in South Africa, the fall of the Eastern Bloc, and the end of the Cold War), within the country the battling forces were in a military stalemate. It was a war that neither the FRELIMO government nor the RENAMO guerrilla forces could win. Nevertheless, the war would not just fade away, and both protagonists were not prepared to disappear from Mozambique's political map.

However, a very important development was then occurring around the world, which relates to what Samuel Huntington (1991) refers to as the third wave of democratization. The beginning of the 1990s witnessed a rapid spread of democratic politics in Latin America, Eastern Europe, Southeast Asia, and sub-Saharan Africa. In May 1991, Angola, the sister country of Mozambique, had concluded the Bicesse Accords, whose purpose was to end the long civil war in that country and pave the way for the country's first multiparty elections, which were to be held the following year and were to be supervised by the United Nations. As a result, democratic multi-party politics was seen as a solution to the stalemate in Mozambique. It was thought that this would reverse the destruction and provide the protagonists with a non-military means of continuing their political struggle.

Since October 1992, when the Government of Mozambique and the RENAMO guerrilla fighters signed the Rome Peace Treaty, the country has successfully held three general multiparty elections (in 1994, 1999, and 2004, respectively) and two local elections (in 1998 and 2003, respectively). In

December 2004, the country held its third general election. Oddly, President Joaquim Chissano did not run for a third presidential term, even though the 1990 Constitution then in force would have allowed it. Chissano, the FRELIMO leader since the 1986 death of Samora Machel (the country's first president), was replaced by Armando Guebuza, one of Mozambique's war veterans. Interesting developments were also taking place within RENAMO, in particular the spectacular rise in the number of youth leaders to be found in the top ranks of the party. Even though these people had not taken part in the war, they seemed to enjoy a certain respectability within RENAMO.

As RENAMO and its leader, Afonso Dlhakama, lost the election for the third consecutive time – with a relatively poorer result than they had in the previous election – it is difficult to predict what will now happen with the party. However, contrary to expectation, and despite the fact that RENAMO refused to accept the results announced by the electoral bodies, it did not use violence to pursue its interests.[2] After a meeting of the party's national council, the RENAMO leader announced that their actions would be entirely peaceful and would occur within the country's democratic framework. All of this means that Mozambique is indeed experiencing a reasonable level of political stability and that the democratic process seems to be becoming more entrenched year after year.

However, experience has taught us that Mozambique is extremely vulnerable to the outbreak of violence, particularly during electoral periods. This pattern occurs in three phases: (1) an initial phase of violent, though mostly verbal, confrontations between the two major parties as the voting days approach, (2) a relatively peaceful voting period, and (3) a post-election period of violent conflicts with a slow return to normalcy. However, following the December 2004 general elections, it seems that there was a much faster return to normalcy after a post-election period of relative anxiety but no explicit violence.

Thus the key challenge to democratic governance in Mozambique has been resolved by the cohabitation of the major political protagonists. This is neither to trivialize the results of the democratic politics in place nor to suggest the country is a quasi-democracy. Not at all! The point is that the status of Mozambique's democracy must be judged in terms of its significant contribution to the ending of the war, the normalization of politics, and the return to political stability. This also indicates the degree to which – irrespective of the fragility and deficiencies still evident – the democratic process in Mozambique will be maintained. This process, it is hoped, will be maintained not just because politicians will not be tempted to reverse it but also, and primarily, because the wider society would fiercely resist them if they did so.

Given the foregoing analyses, it is also important to bear in mind the fact that FRELIMO and RENAMO are not ordinary political parties; rather, they are parties born out of military organizations, and this is reflected in their internal structure and discipline as well as in their hegemonic drive. Both of these political parties are imbued with a winner-take-all spirit, and very seldom do they seem prepared to cede ground to their rival. To compound the problem, each of these parties commands the allegiance of a sizeable proportion of the population. Though this allegiance may have a regional and ethnic base, the reality is that the main dynamic is between the centre and the periphery. While FRELIMO commands the allegiance of the elite and middle classes, mostly from urban areas and the south of the country, RENAMO commands the allegiance of those who oppose the status quo and sizeable populations from the centre-north of the country.

Another problem results from the fact that these parties have dispersed hundreds of their former military cadres around Mozambique, and these people can (and sometimes are prone to) use their military background to impose their views and interests. This was shown clearly in the violent events in Montepuez and Changara (located in the northern provinces of Cabo Delgado and Tete, respectively) and Inhaminga and Maringué (in the central province of Sofala), which followed the refusal of RENAMO to accept the results of the 1999 second general election. These constitute a warning that sustainable peacebuilding in Mozambique remains a huge task that requires the active intervention of all Mozambicans, regardless of their party affiliation or their ethnic or regional origin.

The establishment of multiparty democracy was the primary tool for the peace settlement and peacemaking in Mozambique. It was also the necessary, though insufficient, condition for peacebuilding in the country. The case of Mozambique is therefore highly relevant to any attempt to understand the aftermath of efforts towards peacebuilding, which bring together local, national, and international actors. Indeed, the case of Mozambique supports our initial propositions – namely, that even negotiated, multidimensional peacebuilding efforts have enormous difficulties moving from immediate postwar reconstruction measures to the deeper reforms required to consolidate sustainable peace. To a certain extent, and because war was effectively ended in that country, Mozambique can be said to be a relative success story. However, the entrenchment of the democratization process with a view to securing sustainable peace is still a tremendous challenge for the country and its people. In this regard, the case of Mozambique has similarities with the case of Guatemala, which is discussed in Chapter 2.

Indeed, by 1994 it had become apparent that, in order to secure fundamental peacebuilding, it would be necessary to establish a political framework characterized by inclusion rather than exclusion (Mazula 2000). Though

FRELIMO was fiercely opposed to the idea of a national unity government, the idea of political inclusion was guaranteed through the initiation of the process of political and administrative decentralization. As then understood, this guarantee ensured the legitimacy of the system and brought all political-al forces and citizens into the governing process as part of a meaningful and long-lasting peacebuilding process (interview with Baptista Lundin in 2004; Mazula 2002).

Decentralization and Provincial/Local Governance

Our research begins with the assumption that decentralization and local democratization are necessary components of peacebuilding and conflict prevention. As noted in Chapter 1, there is an urgent need to "forge the transnational coalitions required to underpin more profound changes – such as deepening democratic practices at the local level – over the long term." Additionally, these "transnational coalitions – or peace infrastructures – [must link] agents of change from the local to the national and international levels."

It was in this context that we designed the key questions that, during our research, we posed to different players in Mozambique. These questions were: (1) How can we make sure that decentralization will encompass polit-ical inclusion and an end to the virtual marginalization of Mozambicans, particularly those living in the rural areas, thus constituting a sound basis for peacebuilding? (2) How do we use the opportunity presented by decen-tralization to address the challenge of poverty reduction as well as that of reducing inequalities and regional imbalances? (3) In the context of a sound system of intergovernmental relations, how do we ensure both efficiency and equity on the one side, and autonomy and participation of the munici-pal authorities, on the other?

According to sources in the Ministry of State Administration (MAE),[3] the original theoretical base of the decentralization process was geared towards strengthening the state through the development of citizenship at the local level. Individuals would no longer be just persons but also citizens partici-pating in the smallest administrative units, which were called municipal-ities. The aim here was to create the state from below. The legislators who led this process intended to reinforce the administrative process in the en-tire country. This was not simply a matter of supporting the concept of de-centralization but, rather, of presenting a policy for strengthening the Mozambican state.

However, defining and implementing the decentralization process was marked by the difficulty of trying to reconcile the different policy options with the existing legal and institutional framework. Law 3/1994 provided for the creation of both urban and rural municipalities. The RENAMO con-tingent in Parliament seized the chance opened by this law to demand that municipalities should coincide with the territory of the existing 128 districts in the country. This would involve extending opportunities to decentralize local governance throughout Mozambique. FRELIMO parliamentarians objected to this proposal on the grounds that it would fracture the governance of the country; they insisted that building national reconciliation and restoring the state were the highest priority. RENAMO parliamentarians then rejected the entire package, arguing that it was unconstitutional.

Next came the adoption of Law 9/1996, which provided for the inclusion of local government in the country's Constitution. Subsequently, Law 2/1997 defined the existing legal framework for local government (*Autarquia* in its Portuguese version). According to Law 2/1997, local government includes both the municipalities (cities and district towns) and villages. There are twenty-three cities and 128 district towns in Mozambique, of which only the former and ten of the district towns were entitled to establish local government structures in 1998. Thus, the existing local governments represent only a tiny fraction of the country's potential number of municipalities.

What happened to the initial notion of decentralization, and why was it so restricted in the decentralization/municipalization process in Mozambique? As Bernhard Weimer points out:

> We have to ask ourselves if the central government is today as well predisposed to decentralize power as before the 1994 general elections that brought about plural politics in the country. It is important to bear in mind that currently there are other interests to be defended, and of course there are also new political challenges.[4]

Thus, in terms of the transfer of power and competences from the central government to municipal authorities, the first question raised relates to the reasoning behind the decentralization process as well as to the choice of the first thirty-three municipalities created in the country. Our interviewees were unanimous in pointing out the usefulness of the decentralization process both for the diffusion of power and for ensuring citizens' participation and social cohesion. However, they also pointed out that all these advantages could only come about if appropriate implementation strategies were put in place and clearly institutionalized. However, not all the actors have a similar view regarding the decentralization process. As already indicated, the first point to be dealt with in reflecting on the process of decentralization/municipalization relates to the government's philosophy of "gradualism." Indeed, Law 2/1997 and Law 11/1997 establish the following:

1   "That the creation of municipalities shall be gradual (out of an initial number of 33 territories) according to the existence of a set of conditions for their creation in other territories ..." (Law 2/1997, Article 5).

However, nowhere in the legislation is it concretely and objectively specified what these conditions amount to, though it is stated that their determination will be confirmed by the country's national Parliament.
2   The same is true with regard to the transfer of power and resources from
the central level to the decentralized territories, where the gradual concept is introduced without further regulation and clarification.

The key point is that, adopting the spirit and the letter of Law 3/1994,
municipalities could effectively have been extended to all districts of the
country, even though only those living in the corresponding capital cities
and villages would have the chance to elect their leaders. On the contrary,
Law 2/1997, with its philosophy of gradualism, meant that, somewhat ar-
bitrarily, only thirty-three municipalities were created in the main capital
cities and ten villages, thus denying a considerable portion of the population the possibility of exercising democratic rights at the local level. Therefore, on a practical level, the possibility of "gradually" – but immediately
and within a clear, transparent, and democratic framework – expanding the
existing municipalities to cover all district capitals (both cities and villages)
would accomplish the aims of political and administrative decentralization
that had been enshrined in both legal documents. As a matter of principle,
this should be the thrust of the national policy document on political and
administrative decentralization.

According to José Elija Gnambe, the national director for municipal development in the MAE, the government has in fact approved a national
policy document for decentralization. It is within this policy document that
the philosophy of gradualism has been developed. The director goes on to
indicate that this document clearly states that the central government has
the exclusive authority to decide whether a specific territory meets the conditions required for it to become a municipality. This policy statement obviously came about because the central government took the initiative to
start the process leading to the creation of new municipalities. According
to the director, it is the prerogative of the central government to decide to
expand the number of existing municipalities.

However, local political actors see this top-down approach as basically
anti-democratic and believe that it runs the risk of invalidating the reasoning behind the decentralization process. Since one of the goals of decentralization is to foster local development and to reduce poverty, it does not
make sense to exclude local communities and leaders from the process of
deciding whether or not a given territorial unit merits being a local government unit. Indeed, according to António Delfim (a RENAMO member of
the Municipal Assembly of Nacala in the northern province of Nampula),
the decentralization process has had a very bad beginning. He claims this is
due precisely to the fact that local communities were not involved in its

design and that the democratization process has not been followed by economic development. There is, then, the perception that decentralization was an obvious case of a mainly top-down approach to democratization. As Delfim pointed out in an interview in 2004:

> Though democracy is being built in the country, it cannot move further without the corresponding democratization of the people. We know from the experience of developed democracies that it is up to the people to cry out for democracy and not the ruling elite. Democratization must be rooted in the populations themselves, but here we, the politicians, are imposing democracy on the people. The international community, the donor community, all interfere in our political affairs.

As a number of other interviewees pointed out, political parties seem to have privatized and manipulated the processes of democratization and decentralization. A FRELIMO member of the Municipal Assembly of Nacala, Buana Ali, also voiced this view. This indicates that such perceptions cut across political affiliations. In this context, it would be interesting to find out whether or not decentralization has allowed for the internal democratization of political parties. There seems to be a perception that the internal operations of political parties have not yet become democratic.

Another point pertains to the simultaneous nature of the devolution and deconcentration processes currently taking place in Mozambique. The decentralization process also has a deconcentration dimension that covers the local organs of the state – namely, provincial governments, district administrations, and administrative posts. Within the group of international donor agents active in the field of decentralization and local governance, there are different approaches to the decentralization process. Indeed, while some donor agents support the process of decentralization and the reasoning behind devolution, others are only ready to foster deconcentration (Soiri 1999). The latter seem to be closest to the dominant view in government circles. Until now, these layers of state administration have been hierarchical and have been dominated by the central government; however, under the new legislation, their range of authority will widen (see Law 8/2003). As well, the National Program for Planning and Financial Decentralization, launched by the central government with the financial assistance of the World Bank, will assist these layers of state administration to develop a decentralized and participatory planning approach and to build financial capacity at the district level.

The approach to decentralization in Mozambique is more a matter of deconcentration and less a matter of genuine political decentralization. This perception was strengthened by the adoption of Law 8/2003, which deals with the organization and function of local state bodies. Law 8/2003 defines a district as the basic planning unit for the development of the country, and it includes a provision for the transfer of funds from the central government to the district level. Thus, what municipalities expected to receive is instead being given to district administrations. This process is being led by officials appointed by the central government, and it has not been legitimated by local communities. This is further complicated in the cases of municipalities that occupy the entire district in which they are located (e.g., Maxixe, Nacala, and Ilha de Moçambique). Why, then, not go back to Law 3/1994 and simply make the district the territorial unit for municipalities with elected leaders? All these legal and conceptual ambiguities regarding decentralization indicate that the central government does not yet have the political will to put in place a serious decentralization process. Perhaps this is because of the possibility of a radical change in the geographic and social base of power in Mozambique. That five out of thirty-three municipalities are now controlled by RENAMO, plus the fact that a number of seats in different municipalities are in the hands of either RENAMO or locally constituted independent groups of citizens, might be partially responsible for this state of affairs.

The crucial problem is that the power of the district authorities is directly linked to the central government, of which they are simply local representatives. This fact obviously means that district authorities differ completely from those who hold local government authority, whose base of legitimacy derives from the local communities who elect them. Thus, Law 8/2003 provides room for deconcentration but not for political and administrative decentralization as envisaged in Law 2/1997. As the coordinator of the program on decentralized planning and financing indicated, the current approach envisages the delegation of authority from the central government to the district authorities but not necessarily for the complete transfer of authority.[5]

So the critical question here is: To what extent will all these measures develop local capacity to allow the municipal, district, and provincial layers of government to deliver essential services with a view to increasing productivity and thus reducing poverty and inequalities in Mozambique? And how will they open spaces for the deepening of the democratization process – through local participation – that, in the end, will constitute a sound basis for sustainable peacebuilding. The point is that, although the district and provincial layers of government can ensure service delivery, will we see the "peace infrastructures" to which Stephen Baranyi (2005c) refers, specifically with respect to the urgent need to deepen democratic practices at the local level? Are those voices, both within the dominant parties and within the municipalities, that demand such participation being clearly articulated and heard?

Our research has shown us that donors are mainly driven by the strategy of reducing poverty by targeting the level closest to the poor – that is, the rural and local levels. Donors are aware of the sensitivity to political decentralization in government circles, and, as a result, they appear inclined to support deconcentration. However, within donor circles there is also a belief that, by fostering deconcentration as a strategy for local empowerment, it might also be possible to develop capacity at the local level and that, later, this could lead to the establishment of sound local governments. In other words, populations used to participating in district forums as part of a deconcentration strategy might well later begin to demand the democratic right to elect their own local leaders.

Such a strategy would ensure effective and efficient local empowerment and service delivery to deal with poverty reduction while also functioning as a democratic laboratory that would ensure political decentralization. The question is, how long would this strategy need to work before it could deliver such results? Would it not make more sense to attempt to bring both decentralization and deconcentration together in order to achieve the twin aims of poverty reduction and political inclusion at the local level? Our research suggests that the latter would be a plausible alternative.

Consider the municipality of Dondo in the province of Sofala, which is politically dominated by RENAMO, the party in control of the municipality of Beira, the third most important city in Mozambique. Yet Dondo has elected a FRELIMO militant as its mayor. While FRELIMO does not have a majority in the municipal assembly, critical decisions in the municipality are usually made by consensus. At a more substantive level, Dondo has developed a set of participatory mechanisms that stretch from the neighbourhood level up to the municipal level. At the bottom of this participatory tree, we find neighbourhood activists who are mainly responsible for civic educational endeavours in health, education, and the environment. We then move up to ward development committees, which are generally composed of twelve members (six men and six women)[6] plus a presiding community leader. These ward committees are responsible for all developmental issues in their respective zones and have quarterly meetings with the municipal council to discuss issues of common concern. At the top of the tree we find the Municipal Consultative Forum, which brings together the ward development committees plus a number of influential local leaders, local entrepreneurs, traditional leaders, religious figures, leaders of political parties, civil society activists, and representatives of the district administration. It appears the municipality of Dondo is becoming the best example in Mozambique of a democratic laboratory. As well, Dondo seems well positioned to target poverty reduction. So, the value of bringing together both democratic decentralization and administrative deconcentration is clearly confirmed by the example set in Dondo.

Given all these features, Dondo is a peculiar case in our sample of municipalities. Through the Consultative Forum, in Dondo it was possible to achieve consensual interparty coexistence as well as a positive relationship among the distinct municipal organs and between them and the local administrative bodies of the state. All of these entities combine forces to benefit the development of the district and the municipality. On the other hand, in the municipalities of Nacala and Ilha de Moçambique, the story is different. The district administration and the municipal authorities are engaged in permanent struggles over power. This scenario is worsened by the fact that, in both municipalities, as well as in Maxixe and Maputo, the municipal territories and those run by the local representatives of the central government are the same. There are no huge differences between the municipalities of Nacala and Ilha de Moçambique, on the one hand, and those of Maxixe and Maputo, on the other, in terms of the difficult relationship between the municipal authorities and the local state bodies, despite the fact that in the former municipalities RENAMO is in power while in the latter FRELIMO is in power. This suggests that the problems are not rooted in partisan politics but, rather, in the difficult coexistence between the local government and the local bodies representing the central authority.

This is one of the problems that, if not properly addressed – specifically through the design of a coherent and well-informed national policy and strategy of democratic decentralization – may hamper the success of peacebuilding in Mozambique. Nevertheless, perceptions of the process of peacebuilding are clearly mixed. Some of the local stakeholders whom we interviewed think that peacebuilding in Mozambique is almost irreversible, given the combination of several measures that were taken since the signing of the Rome Peace Accords (e.g., institutional reforms plus the merit of those who succeeded in keeping the reconciliation process going). A civil society activist, Horacio Ferreira, interviewed in Beira in 2004, explained that peacebuilding in Mozambique had three main ingredients. First, there was the creation of the 1990 multiparty political constitution; second, there was the signing of the Rome Peace Treaty in 1992; and third, the country held successive national and local elections, beginning with the first general multiparty elections in 1994. For this activist, the case of Mozambique clearly differs from those of other countries, such as Angola. According to Ferreira:

> The return to war is not a possibility in Mozambique. People live in peace and all are happy. The former warring parties know for sure that nobody here wants war again in this country. This is a very important point because no war is possible without popular support for it.

This is a very optimistic point of view, given that most other commentators, not to mention the violent events following the elections in Montepuez in 1999 and Moçímboa da Praia in 2005, suggest that a return to violent confrontations cannot entirely be ruled out – certainly not without taking proactive measures to prevent them.

Most tellingly, a number of our key informants indicated that there is a need to be more cautious when it comes to assessing the prospects of sustainable peacebuilding in the country. Archbishop Jaime Gonçalves, the only Mozambican who was part of the team of mediators during the Rome peace process, is one of these people, and he made the following comment:

> The experience of the last 12 years tells us that the institutionalization of democracy in our country is yet to become a force that can guarantee a sustainable peacebuilding in the country. However, a number of things were indeed done, such as the inauguration of multiparty politics, the creation of Parliament ... [T]hese means [sic] that something was accomplished in the direction of peace consolidation. But these 12 years also demonstrate that there are still a number of fragilities that have to be surpassed, one of which relates to the ways in which we organize and conduct elections, be they at national or local levels (interviewed in November 2004).

In fact, the events in Montepuez, following the announcement of the 1999 election results (which involved people from FRELIMO and RENAMO) as well as the violent clashes following the by-election in the municipality of Moçímboa da Praia in May 2005, confirm the foregoing view. On the other hand, our research showed that, in the municipality of Ilha de Moçambique, there is a tendency to replay the interparty conflict between FRELIMO and RENAMO in the relationship between the central government and the local forum. This calls into question the quality of reconciliation, tolerance, and political stability at the local level.

Our research indicates that the way forward is basically fourfold: First, as the experience of the election observation team indicated, in the short-term there is a need for civil society organizations to be more robustly involved in monitoring the governance process, particularly in relation to electoral processes. Second, there is also a need for the newly created National Association of Municipalities to forge alliances with both civil society organizations (particularly those active in the area of lobbying and policy advocacy) and the decentralization donor group in order to press for more profound legal and institutional changes, with a view to deepening the democratic process. Third, civil society organizations and international NGOs working at the community level, specifically those involved in setting up participatory forums at the district level, should encourage local communities to press for more democratic opportunities at the district and provincial levels of government. Fourth, all the entities mentioned above, both individually and through partnerships, should seize the opportunity presented by the priority that the government and the World Bank have given to public sector reform in order to secure what has already been accomplished in decentralization/municipalization.

Economic Policy and Peacebuilding

Context and Policy Challenges

Mozambique has gone a long way to restore normalcy after the sixteen-year civil war that destroyed its social fabric. Certainly, immediately after the peace process, the FRELIMO government put forward a development strategy that was mainly oriented towards alleviating poverty through sustainable economic growth. The major components of this strategy were: (1) the development of human resources, (2) the rehabilitation of basic infrastructure, (3) the restoration of agricultural production, and (4) incentives to private investment. At the sectoral level, its priorities were education, health, rural development, employment, and roads.

As a result of these measures, during the 1990s, Mozambique experienced one of the highest average annual growth rates in the sub-Saharan region. Of course, this was no surprise in a country where economic growth started from scratch. Agricultural production and commerce, which benefited from increased security and a return to the farm fields, drove the average annual growth by an average 8 percent from 1993 to 1997, while privatized manufacturing industry began to play a growing role in the economy.[7] The GDP growth rate was around 1.3 percent in 1995, rising to 6.6 percent in 1996, then to 14.1 percent in 1997 (UNDP 1998). However, in 2002 and 2003, the growth rate fell to 8.2 percent and to 7.9 percent, respectively (UNDP 1998 and 2000b; Instituto Nacional de Estatística 2006). According to the Bank of Mozambique,[8] this downturn was due to the global and regional economic environment following the Iraq War and the Zimbabwe crisis.

Nevertheless, this seemingly sound economic performance has particularly benefited from the growing interest of foreign investors in Mozambique, as seen in the form of megaprojects. The first of these megaprojects was the MOZAL aluminum smelter of Gencor/Billiton, the Industrial Development Corporation of South Africa, Mitsubishi of Japan, and the Government of Mozambique, which amounted to an investment of US$1.3 billion. However, the biggest project is the Maputo Iron and Steel Project, budgeted at US$1.6 billion. In terms of investment, this project is followed by the Maputo Development Corridor, which is estimated at an investment of US$1.4 billion (UNDP 1998). More recently, Sasol Petroleum has been added to this list of billion-dollar projects. The problem with this pattern of economic growth is twofold. First, this massive influx of foreign capital, which is responsible for the positive macroeconomic indicators, barely has an impact on the rural agricultural sector, which provides the basic living

Figure 1

GDP growth in Mozambique, 1995-2004

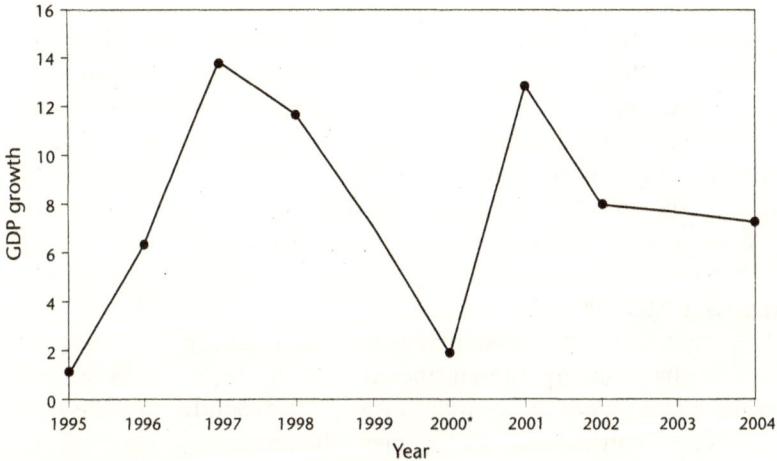

* In 2000, Mozambique was hit by severe floods.
Source: UNDP (1998, 2000b); Instituto Nacional de Estatística [Mozambique] (2006).

conditions of more than 68 percent of the population. Second, the degree of employment generated by the megaprojects is well below that needed even to deal with the surplus labour in urban areas.

Despite these constraints, there is a strong perception, at least in major cities, that the structural adjustment policies are a success history. International financial institutions and other donors praise Mozambique for being able to maintain political stability and to keep a vigorous climate within which liberal economics can flourish. This has led to a situation in which development agendas are concurrently shaped through the interplay of three basic players: the government, bilateral donors, and international financial institutions. Effectively, most local actors are still fragile, poorly organized, and lacking in capital and know-how. Further, given the fact that women in Mozambique represent a sizeable percentage of working adults and, in most cases, lead their families, they are critical with regard to the country's prospects for effective and sustainable development.

Women are the main food producers in Mozambique. They represent 60 percent of the active labour force in the agricultural sector, and that number represents 90 percent of the total female labour force. Due to the war and the migration of men to the mines of South Africa, the majority of women were either single mothers or widows; in either case, they were heads of families. Across Mozambique, 24 percent of families are headed by women.

Most revealingly, in the southern zone of Mozambique (historically the reserve of the labour force for South Africa), this figure is as high as 41 percent (*Noticias*, 9 May 1999).

One relevant aspect of the gender dimension of labour markets in the agricultural sector is that, on average, families led by women, being short-handed, tend to cultivate less land than do those led by men. Female-led families also appear to be more vulnerable than male-led families as they are generally dependent on remittances from family members living in the cities or involved in the South African mining industry. However, a recent study has shown that, though generally vulnerable, female-led families tend to "achieve more with less resources," particularly with regard to the care given to the most vulnerable family members (i.e., children and the elderly) (*Noticias*, 9 May 1999).

It is important to note here that women are most active in the informal sector of the economy. Indeed, the cross-border migration between Mozambique and four of its neighbours – Swaziland, South Africa, Zimbabwe, and Malawi – consists mainly of women who are active in the food, beverage, clothes, and toy industries. This may be a direct consequence of the liberalization process, which led most families to turn to the informal sector in order to avoid starvation. However, in actual terms, it also reveals the extent to which women are increasingly able to break the patriarchal gender relations that, for centuries, have prevailed in Mozambique.

The basic policy and strategy document of the Mozambican government designed to meet some of the key problems confronting the country is the Action Plan for the Reduction of Absolute Poverty (PARPA).[9] The plan arose out of the recognition that Mozambique is one of the poorest countries in the world, with about 60 percent of its population living below the line of absolute poverty.[10] The strategy identifies six key priorities: education, health, agriculture and rural development, infrastructure, good governance, and macroeconomics and financial management. PARPA calls for a 20 percent reduction in the number of Mozambicans living in absolute poverty by 2010. It takes as its base the year 1997, when the incidence of absolute poverty was at 70 percent, and indicates that it should fall to 60 percent by 2005 and to less than 50 percent in 2010. According to the executive director of Confederation of Mozambican Business Associations, taking into account both the PARPA target for 2010 and the projected population growth by that year, 50 percent would amount to 10 million people living in absolute poverty.[11] If one assumes that 60 percent of the current 19 million inhabitants live in absolute poverty (about 12 million people), it is obvious that the PARPA's goal is not very impressive.

Indeed, in the consultation between the government, its key partners, and civil society organizations regarding the preparation of the second PARPA for 2006-10, the issue of regional imbalances and persistent socioeconomic inequalities, particularly affecting marginalized rural communities, has taken centre stage. Civil society organizations like the Poverty Observatory, the G20 (a coalition of over twenty organizations striving for economic justice), and the Mozambican Debt Relief Group are pressing PARPA to shift its priorities from a strong concern with macroeconomic growth to a concern with the redistribution of resources. These groups believe that it is crucial to address the socioeconomic inequalities and regional imbalances that might well fuel violence and, hence, pose a danger to the future stability of the country.

This is why, with regard to peacemaking and peacebuilding, Mozambique has been described as a country of "relative success," a situation that Mazula (2002) refers to as "a paradox of success."[12] Successful peacemaking in Mozambique has resulted from the goodwill of various social segments and strata and their commitment to the country's political stability and peaceful existence. For peacebuilding to be equally successful, there is an urgent need to tackle the pressing issue of poverty reduction as well as the growing gulf between the rich and the poor, with the former enriching themselves at the expense of the latter (Hanlon 1996).

Fiscal Decentralization, Equitable Development, and Peacebuilding

As this research demonstrates, in order to sustain efforts towards national integration and the consolidation of peace, the economic and social dimensions of development as well as the issue of inequalities have to be at the forefront of the national agenda. One of the critical factors we examined in our research relates to what we consider to be the economic dimension of peacebuilding. Here we look at the issue of fiscal decentralization in the context of political decentralization/municipalization conceived as a tool to meet some of the challenges posed by the imbalances and inequalities inherent in the current economic development process.

In the debate on fiscal reform, what appears to be relevant is not whether fiscal responsibilities have been decentralized but, rather, the rationale behind decentralization, its mechanisms, its limits, and its expected results. With regard to financing the existing municipalities, it is plain that, generally speaking, they are unable, on their own, to finance all the responsibilities that have been placed on them. This is particularly evident in the area of social policies (education, health, etc.), where their responsibilities far exceed their capacity to generate revenue. If municipalities are to be transformed into the main service deliverers to communities, how will their limited capacity for revenue generation affect this, particularly in the least developed zones? The other problem is that, currently, municipalities obtain revenue through taxation of urban property, open markets, and so on, all of which are secondary in the global structure of the revenue base. This occurs in a situation in which commercial banks persistently restrict credit.

In an adequate system of decentralization, functions and responsibilities must be accompanied by resources. In order to transfer funds from the central government level to the local level, a system of intergovernmental fiscal relations must be established. Normally, these intergovernmental fiscal relations consist of different types of transfer mechanisms that, at the same time, allow some possibilities for subgovernments to raise their own resources. If we look at Mozambique, we see that this is not the case. Clearly, municipalities have many functions, but they do not have the funds required to ensure their realization.

Therefore, the issue of the sustainability of municipalities is a key problem. The central government is aware of the difficulties municipalities face, and it is expected to provide subsidies to those less capable of revenue generation and management. However, the central government's only support mechanisms are the Municipal Compensation Fund (FCA) and the Local Initiative Investment Fund, which are not able to meet the needs of municipalities. This is why municipalities such as Metangula and Catandica faced huge problems before the November 2003 local elections. In a study of municipalities in Mozambique, Hassan (2002) pointed to the huge difficulties facing these local authorities as a result of deficiencies in fiscal decentralization. The FCA contributed well over 50 percent of the budget of local governments. The latter's potential for investment was about 20 percent, with personnel salaries generally taking up about 45 percent of their budget. Most municipalities showed a clear incapacity to find all the avenues of local revenue generation. So far, no municipality has been able to generate revenues above 40 percent of its budget. Municipalities of medium size (e.g., Pemba, Quelimane, and Mocímboa da Praia) had much better revenue generation than did big municipalities (such as the capital city, Maputo, which reported the worst revenue-generation level, taking into consideration its huge potential) (Hassan 2002, 50).

Considering that 80 percent of national fiscal revenue is drawn from the current municipal territories, and that about 60 percent of the GDP is also generated within these thirty-three municipalities, how can their continued deficit be explained? There seems to be a clear imbalance between what the state takes from the municipalities and what it gives back to them. The 1.5 percent to 3 percent of the central budget that the state provides municipalities through the FCA does not seem to meet their needs. Weimer (2002) indicates that the percentage of FCA transfers for 2002 in relation to the central budget was estimated at just 1 percent, which is basically negligible. Clearly, the state should first completely fulfill its obligation with respect to the percentage of FCA funding given to municipalities, while seriously considering expanding – possibly doubling – this percentage.

On the other hand, municipalities have the right to raise certain incomes. However, the question that can now be posed relates to the real capacity of municipalities to survive and to deliver good and efficient services based on those incomes. Therefore, there is a need to guarantee that the thirty-three municipalities – and those that will be created in the future – do in fact have real access to sources of revenue that can be achieved through the revision of current fiscal policy. Municipalities cannot survive only on the transfer of funds from the central government because these transfers could reinforce fiscal dependency, enabling the state to maintain control over management mechanisms and priorities.

Though the state has an important redistributive function in terms of national wealth, this should not be undertaken at the overt expense of certain municipalities. Taking into account the local productive potential as well as the local potential for wealth generation, municipalities should be given priority as the primary beneficiaries of these resources. Abdul Ilal, an official of German Technical Cooperation, interviewed in 2004, had the following to say in this regard:

> In my capacity as analyst – and not in my capacity as representative of an institution active in providing support to the decentralization process in Mozambique – I think that often we talk about the need for equilibrium, but we do not reach it. The history of regional developments tells us that we are always confronted by inequalities. Some might argue that inequalities can be driving engines for development themselves ... Looking at the different municipalities it is possible to see that a certain number of them will grow faster than the rest because they have already sustainable sources of revenue generation. Given all these factors, I think that the state should redistribute, compensate, search for equilibrium, but must never seek to eliminate, suffocate the capacity of those municipalities that are now making a good contribution.

The mayor of Nacala's point of view is similar:

> In my opinion the central government should give us more chances to raise income because the present system of transfers doesn't work. I think that it will be better to adopt another strategy that gives, to the municipalities, the opportunity to raise, by themselves, some income taking into account their capacity to generate resources in different domains. It will also be necessary to revise the percentage of resources that must go to the municipality and its population. On the other hand, we have some problems with the Ministry of Finance. There are a lot of delays in the transfers. In one word there isn't de-centralization because the control made by the central government remains strong and that doesn't give the municipalities the tools to work efficiently (interview with Manuel José Dos Santos, November 2004).

It is now evident that another issue is the widespread need to find formulas that would guarantee the equitable distribution of national resources and wealth. Most key informants believe that a genuine democratization process and sustainable peacebuilding can only be ensured by the removal of regional imbalances and the asymmetric distribution of resources. As a RENAMO member of the Nacala Municipal Assembly, Pilaure Buana, comments:

> The democratization process can only be consolidated via the decentralization of the economy as well as the state funds. I personally do not understand why it is that the funds earmarked for HIV/AIDS are all concentrated in Maputo City, even though there are people dying in Nampula. The Nampula province provides more funds for VAT, but the province of Gaza has more schools and hospitals. This is not strictly a problem of the FRELIMO party as such, but of those people responsible for leading the process (interviewed in November 2004).

Archbishop Jaime Gonçalves voiced similar concerns:

> The biggest lacuna of the efforts towards entrenching peace in the country is regionalism, a problem that most intellectuals prefer to give ... the name of regional asymmetries. But we have to be very careful not to confuse ideas. There is a danger of equating asymmetries with the idea that we are downgraded, and this sort of perception cannot be a good basis for a sustainable peacebuilding. We have to demonstrate with concrete actions that we are all united and that every region of the country merits respect and all are equally important.

During the round table on fiscal autonomy and the delivery of public services, it was noted that, in the media in Mozambique, there is a basic deficiency with regard to key aspects of the decentralization/municipalization process. There is, therefore, a need to undertake a vigorous and well-planned training and orientation program for those who work in the media, taking into account their importance as public opinion makers. The purpose here is also to increase pressure, through media coverage, on the central authority to address and reverse the existing problems and limitations of the decentralization process. For their part, some who work in the media raised interesting questions related to the real capacity of municipal authorities to provide quality public services, which, in turn, would motivate the populations to take an active part in local politics (e.g., as voters, users, and taxpayers). They raised these questions also bearing in mind the fact that about 50 percent of the national budget is externally funded – and most often with strings attached.

Interestingly, there is a more sustained engagement by civil society organizations in the area that combines equitable development and peacebuilding than there is in the area of political decentralization as such. Therefore, if the National Association of Municipalities took a proactive role in securing a better system of intergovernmental fiscal relations, natural partnerships could be forged with organizations such as the G20, the Mozambique Debt Relief Group, and various organizations for economic justice attached to the Christian Council of Mozambique and the Roman Catholic Church. Most bilateral donors in Mozambique are also keen to address issues of economic justice, particularly within the scope of the UN Millennium Development Goals. Finally, in the context of public sector reform, there are critical areas concerning public finances, good governance, and the prevention of corruption that can be used to press for a much better economic policy – one oriented towards the reduction of regional imbalances and socioeconomic inequalities (a dimension that necessarily includes the issue of fiscal decentralization).

Conclusion

Our research confirms that, in Mozambique, the tasks related to peacemaking have been successfully accomplished but that those related to peacebuilding have not. The way to achieve this ultimate goal must include implementing targeted measures that combine democratic decentralization and equitable economic development. A clearer vision of what is required in order to sustain peace as well as more dynamic cooperation between key national and international actors are what is needed to bring about such reforms.

Political, administrative, and fiscal decentralization process is crucial for the diffusion of power, for ensuring citizen participation and social cohesion, and for addressing the issues of regional imbalances and socioeconomic inequalities. These phenomena are considered to be sound bases for peacebuilding in Mozambique. Indeed, most Mozambicans are eager for more development and are thus unhappy with the perceived deficiencies and slowness that currently characterize this process. Indeed, our research uncovered the widespread perception that the decentralization process that is now under way does not yet clearly express the political will to consolidate democratic governance.

The philosophy of "gradualism," which informs the decentralization process in Mozambique, leaves open a number of key issues, such as its time frame (with regard to limits and points of reference), the clarification of which would enable all stakeholders (particularly civil society actors and the community in general) to follow it, to better understand it, and to have a say in its implementation. The government has so far argued that new municipalities have not been created because it is first necessary to consolidate the existing thirty-three municipalities. However, there is a view that the creation of new municipalities should not be based solely on the criteria of financial sustainability. The process should also involve ensuring that citizens participate in the selection of their leaders and in the management of their territories. Therefore, we suggest that, on a practical level, the realization of Law 3/1994 and Law 2/1997 would result from "gradually" – but expeditiously and within a clear, transparent, and democratic framework – expanding the existing municipalities to cover all district capitals (cities and villages) so as to achieve the aims of political and administrative decentralization. In essence, this would be the thrust of the national policy document on political and administrative decentralization. Because of the potential for equal participation, equity, and social justice that the gender dimension poses in the area of political inclusion and peacebuilding, it is strongly recommended that a gender-sensitive strategy be adopted in the design and implementation of this national policy document.

Our research indicates that strengthening democratic decentralization for peacebuilding would require: (1) that civil society organizations become more robustly involved in monitoring the governance process in the country, particularly in relation to electoral processes (as the experience of the Electoral Observatory indicates); (2) that the newly created National Association of Municipalities forge alliances both with civil society organizations (particularly those active in lobbying and policy advocacy) and with the decentralization donor group to press for more profound legal and institutional changes; (3) that civil society organizations and international NGOs working at the community level (specifically, those involved in setting up participatory forums at the district level) encourage local communities to press for more democratic openings at the district and provincial levels of government; and (4) that all the entities above, both individually and through partnerships, seize the opportunity presented by the priority that the government and its key foreign partners (specifically, the World Bank) accorded to public sector reform in order to strengthen what has already been achieved in decentralization/municipalization.

This emerging but still barely visible network of local, national, and international actors could be a concrete expression of the peace infrastructures that the introductory chapter suggested are necessary to secure deeper reforms and to sustain peace over the long term (Baranyi 2005c). It is particularly important to quickly build such a coalition in Mozambique in order to prevent the country's slide towards greater corruption and centralization of power.

More needs to be done with regard to the adoption of appropriate legal instruments and implementation strategies to ensure the development of an equitable economic environment for peacebuilding. As our research reveals, this is clearly connected with the need to define a consistent system of intergovernmental relations. In the meantime, the state should fulfill its obligations to disburse funds allocated by the FCA and local initiatives mechanisms, while expanding – possibly doubling – the existing amount in order to boost the financial viability of local governments. There is also a need for a thorough revision of current fiscal policy in order to expand the revenue base of municipalities. More important, though, in order to address the issues of regional imbalances and socioeconomic inequalities, there must be a determined shift away from the current stress on macroeconomic growth rates – particularly within the framework of PARPA and other key development policy documents and strategies – and towards issues of equity and socioeconomic justice.

In order for these tasks to be fully realized, a number of measures are required, beginning with a more sustained engagement on the part of civil society organizations at the interface of equitable development and peacebuilding. The National Association of Municipalities must take a proactive role in securing a better system of intergovernmental fiscal relations. Beyond this specific target, civil society organizations active in the area of economic justice should join forces, particularly in the context of state-civil society consultations, in order to define Mozambique's poverty reduction strategy paper (PARPA) so that it reflects policies that specifically address the challenges posed by the economic marginalization of impoverished regions and communities. Finally, all stakeholders identified here should seize the opportunity provided by public-sector reform to press for a much better economic policy – one oriented towards the reduction of regional imbalances and socioeconomic inequalities (which, of course, includes the issue of fiscal decentralization).

Our research also confirms that Dondo is the best example in Mozambique of a democratic laboratory. It is also well positioned to target poverty reduction and thus clearly confirms the desirability of bringing together both democratic decentralization and administrative deconcentration. Dondo is also relevant in view of the belief that leads donors to foster deconcentration as a strategy for local empowerment, the assumption being that creating capacity at the local level could later allow for the establishment of sound local governments. Our critical questioning of this belief leads us to suggest that, if it followed the example of Dondo (i.e., linking both political and administrative decentralization), the country could achieve the aims of poverty reduction and political inclusion through political participation at the local level.

Nevertheless, we should remember that decentralization will not automatically lead to the twin goals of democratic governance and poverty reduction. We must ensure that decentralization is developed within a framework within which priority is given to the principles of participation, transparency, a clear delimitation of responsibilities and competences, as well as a system of self-responsibility. Most of the existing municipalities in Mozambique still suffer from deficiencies in four key areas – sustainability, autonomy, transfer of power and authority, and sound municipal management capacity. Two of their basic problems relate to a limited local capacity to generate revenue and to mobilize adequate human resources. Addressing these shortcomings, as well as promoting best practices, might set us on the best possible path to ensure the entrenchment of peace through political, administrative, and fiscal decentralization.

In a number of these areas – despite obvious and important differences – Mozambique has much to learn from the experience of Guatemala, in particular with regard to defining legal and normative instruments to attain deeper decentralization as well as with regard to designing an institutional framework to attain civil society participation at different levels of governance.

Acknowledgments

This chapter was written for the WKOP project, with funding from IDRC, the Canadian International Development Agency (CIDA), the Ford Foundation, and NORAD. A Portuguese version of this chapter was published as a CEDE working paper in September 2005.

4

Local Governance and Sustainable Peace: The Haitian Case

Hérard Jadotte and Yves-François Pierre

> I have striven not to laugh at human actions, not to weep at
> them, nor to hate them, but to understand them.
>
> – Baruch Spinoza

Since the fall of the Duvalier régime in February 1986, Haiti has experienced a long period of political, social, and economic instability – even though it has not experienced organized warfare as such. In 1991, the Lavalas coalition brought Jean-Bertrand Aristide to power through electoral means, only to be overthrown by the Haitian Armed Forces (Forces armées d'Haïti [FADH]) later that year. In 1994, after many rounds of internationally mediated negotiations with the FADH had failed, the United States spearheaded Operation Restore Democracy. That operation put President Aristide back in office. It was also an important precursor to the "peace enforcement operations," or "third-generation peace operations" described in the introduction to this volume.

Aristide's return to power opened the door to democratic reforms such as the dismantling of the FADH and the establishment of a national civilian police, the reinauguration of free political expression via a multiparty political system, and the privatization of many public enterprises. The country experienced a period of relative calm from 1996 to 2000, during the Préval government. However, President Aristide's return to power in 2001, through a highly contested election, brought economic decline, grave human rights violations (organized by his newly created party, Fanmi Lavalas), and massive street demonstrations on the part of a growing democratic opposition. Fresh mediation efforts by the international community stalled, while an armed movement called the Revolutionary Resistance Front emerged and soon occupied most of the national territory. In February 2004, under pressure from the United States, France, and Canada, President Aristide resigned and left the country under circumstances that remain to be fully clarified.

At the same time, a multilateral intervention force was deployed to stabilize the country. In April 2004, the UN Security Council authorized the deployment of the UN Stabilization Mission in Haiti (MINUSTAH),[1] a more genuinely multilateral effort. Under the umbrella of these international forces, national actors constructed the Consensus of Political Transition, which put a new transitional government in power for a two-year period.[2] The third-generation peacebuilding process that emerged can be seen as the merger of key national and international interests (Hector 2007, 16). By mid-2004, its goals had been broadened from stabilization and the protection of human rights to the more maximalist goal of laying the foundations for democratization and development. The Cadre de coopération intérimaire (CCI), agreed upon by the transitional government and the international community in July 2004, codified a gradualist strategy with maximalist goals (10). This chapter offers a unique case study of a country that has gone through two robust peace operations in ten years. We explore five key questions. First, how, in historical perspective, do we explain the failure of robust peacebuilding from 1994 onwards? Second, what were the key governance and economic dimensions of peacebuilding during that period, and how did local development projects fit into them? Third, what are the initial results of the stabilization operation initiated in 2004? Fourth, what are the prospects for sustainable peacebuilding under the Préval government? Fifth, what could selected local, national, and international participants contribute to make the current peace operation more sustainable?

This chapter is divided into two major sections, each of which focuses on a distinct level of analysis. The first section focuses on the national level and offers a brief analysis of historical efforts to build democracy and to foster development in Haiti. It pays particular attention to the tensions between the "ideal state" codified in the 1987 Constitution and the "real state" practised by successive rulers. This enables us to explain the crises that led to international interventions in 1994 and 2004. The second section grounds this discussion in an analysis of dynamics at the local level. Concretely, in order to analyze the extent to which political and economic processes contributed to sustainable peace at the local level, it examines three community development initiatives and addresses three questions. First, how do the projects contribute to the establishment of democratic governance at the local level? Second, what impact do they have on the economic development of the communities in which they are implemented? Third, how do these projects manage conflicts that could potentially threaten to negate the gains they have made in the areas of governance and development? The final section synthesizes the results of the local studies and presents conclusions and recommendations linked to current peacebuilding challenges in Haiti.

This study is based on a rereading of the secondary literature on peace-building in Haiti – literature written by both Haitian and non-Haitian authors. During visits to the field and to the institutions involved we collected both quantitative and qualitative data. This was done through unstructured interviews with key contacts and local recipient groups who directly and indirectly benefited from the projects. These interviews were supplemented by primary documents and reports.

Three local development projects were selected for this study: one each in Gonaïves, Gros Morne, and Marmelade. All are in the department of Artibonite, a key site of the struggle for democracy in Haiti. Gonaïves is the fifth largest city in the country, and it suffers from widespread and extreme poverty. In September 2004, tropical storm Jeanne destroyed much of the city's infrastructure and productive capacity. In the months following the catastrophe, the city was the focus of many projects aimed at improving conditions and restoring order. Some of the most conflicted neighbourhoods, such as Raboteau and Lòt Bò Kanal, benefited from highly labour-intensive work programs. The project based in Gros Morne is a community development project rooted in local farmer organizations, and it has been in existence for some thirty years. The Marmelade development project, which is less than five years old, is rooted in statutory local governance structures. These projects were chosen because they reflect very different types of community-based development interventions.[3]

Historical Context

Centralization of the Country's Administrative and Financial Management

In Haiti, management and administration have traditionally been characterized by the centralization of state power. Through civil and/or military authorities, local governments have always been dominated by the central government.

From Haiti's independence in 1804 to the fall of the Duvalier dynasty in 1986, there has been a long tradition of centralized management and administration, which is sustained by the marked domination of the state's central power (the seat of national sovereignty) over the other levels of government. After independence, the same practices of exclusion, to which both slaves and emancipated blacks and mulattoes had been subjected by the colonial administration, were maintained by the new leaders of the Haitian government over the newly emancipated Haitian peasantry. Local governments at the department, district, municipal, and commune levels were always dominated by the central government through authorities appointed to head these political and administrative entities. These various governments extracted the greatest possible amount of financial resources on behalf of the central government. Faced with the same domination and marginalization by state power after independence as they had faced before, peasant farmers thrived by setting up local markets, farm work exchange groups, informal rules for farm tenancy, sharecropping, and land acquisition practices.

The creation of, and first elections to, the communal councils (Conseils communaux), which indicated a certain degree of autonomy for the councils, took place around the middle of the nineteenth century as part of the social movement that led to the revolt against the twenty-five-year military dictatorship of President Boyer in 1843. In an effort to counteract the influence of the military leaders, President Rivière Hérard passed a law in 1844 that created a local civil power in the form of the Conseils d'arrondissements. This first attempt at communal autonomy would not last. In 1847, the government of Faustin Soulouque gained control of the communities by directly appointing their representatives.

There were attempts to re-establish power in the communes through laws that delegated them a degree of autonomy in the second half of the nineteenth century, such as the law of 1881, which re-established the election of communal council members and abolished the Conseils d'arrondissements. However, until the end of the Duvalier regime in 1986, successive central governments ensured that the communes were mere extensions of themselves. They did this by appointing military or civil representatives to the various levels of local government. Under the government of François Duvalier, the arrondissement prefects, who were members of a paramilitary force (the Volontaires de la sécurité nationale) and who were directly appointed by the republic's president-for-life, had the task of counterbalancing the power of the military leaders of the arrondissements and departments. The Volontaires occupied various other levels of local power and ensured the central power's control.

What analysts call the "political crisis," or the "unending political transition," dates from 7 February 1986, which marks the end of the long presidential reign of François Duvalier (1957-71) and his son Jean-Claude Duvalier (1971-86), who departed to a golden exile in France. This period corresponds exactly with what Samuel Huntington (1991) refers to as the third wave of democratization.

Political Transitions in Haiti

The abrupt end of the Duvalier regime is symptomatic of the inability of Haiti's traditional political system to institutionalize the passage from one government to another or from one regime to another. With the twentieth century and the American occupation (1915–34), political transitions in Haiti ceased to correspond to the classical model of the nineteenth century

– that of the political leader/warlord who leaves his provincial stronghold to dominate the legislature and the political players in the capital. One of the objectives of the American occupation was to break this model through unifying and centralizing the political arena in Port-au-Prince. Beginning in 1934, the prevailing model for political transitions went through an interregnum in which the administration was the responsibility of the army.

In fact, the post-Duvalier transition started in 1982, with the beginning of a long period of a steady economic stagnation. Haiti had recorded a GDP growth rate that went from 4.75 percent in 1973 to 8.41 percent in 1976. Around 1982, the country began to experience negative GDP growth, from –2.73 percent in 1981 to –3.42 percent in 1982 (Institut Haïtien de statistiques et d'informatique 1999-2007). The regime of Jean-Claude Duvalier was obliged to adopt the "lean" principles of the first structural adjustment programs developed by the World Bank and the International Monetary Fund. To a great extent, this economic crisis was responsible for the fall of the regime, and it helps to explain the specific nature of the long post-Duvalier transition period.

The open transition with the departure of Jean-Claude Duvalier proved to be relatively different. In the international context of 1957, respect for democratic standards was still a privilege of rich countries; the anti-communist non-democracies were "excusable" and benefited from full "indulgence." However, in 1991, after the communist implosion, the application of democratic standards was extended to the poorest of the poor countries. While the preceding transitions seemed to concern only the traditional elites, after 7 February 1991 the political sphere opened to other social categories, owing to the established notion of democracy, which included several key actors from organizations that arose with the new civil society (Hector 1985).

As in previous times, the interregnum was placed under the control of the FADH, which established the national government council (Conseil national de gouvernement [CNG]). This was composed of three members, one of whom was a civilian and two of whom were the highest-ranking military officers. In its first message to the nation, the CNG's objective was to establish all the institutions that constitute the basis of a liberal, just, and democratic society. This objective was confirmed by the fact that it was included in the new Constitution, which was widely adopted by referendum in 1987. The Constitution explicitly defined the new regime as a "liberal, representative and participatory democracy."

The Ideal State: The Constitution of 1987 or the Rejection of Centralization
Developed by a constituent assembly that included various sectors of civil society, union leaders, and representatives of political parties, and widely supported in a referendum after the fall of the Duvaliers in 1986, the 1987 Constitution marked a fundamental reform, previously unknown in the

administration of regional and local powers. It emphasized the democratic self-governance of the communes, which were composed of a number of communal sections, and recognized the existence of departments – the highest level of the three territorial communities, wards, and arrondissements.

The Constitution rejected the domination of the central powers over regional and local powers. It did this by advocating a system of shared powers among the various levels of government, which placed national sovereignty on all citizens rather than on the state. In other words, the people are seen to have natural and inalienable rights, and the state must respect these rights because they existed before those of the state. In addition, in its preamble, the new Constitution states that, through effective decentralization, the people wish to establish a system of government based on fundamental freedoms and respect for human rights, public peace, economic fairness, and the collaboration and participation of the entire population in major decisions affecting national life.

Corresponding to the three territorial communities are assemblies that have legal authority over their operation (see below). At the level of the communal sections, led by communal section managing committees (Conseil d'administration des sections communales [CASECs]), each with three members, the Constitution provides for the election of the communal section assemblies (Assemblées de la section communale [ASECs]). The members of the ASECs are elected through universal suffrage and have the right to vote on the decisions made by the CASECs.

At the commune level, led by communal councils, each with three members elected through universal suffrage, the Constitution provides for the assistance of municipal assemblies, made up in part of the ASEC representatives and other members elected through universal suffrage from the urban civil society. These assemblies have the responsibility of approving budgets prepared by the councils and deciding by vote on the various programs.

At the department level, the Constitution provides for the election of three-member departmental councils on the part of the departmental assemblies, which are composed of representatives of the municipal assemblies. The departmental assemblies are responsible for electing the interdepartmental council, which, in collaboration with the council of ministers, develops national policies and laws related to local governance.

Thus, as representatives of the people, the assemblies, at various levels of government, are informed by the councils about the latter's management of affairs. And the interdepartmental council checks government access to those areas that affect local governance.

The Real State: Limits in the Application of the 1987 Constitution
In terms of issues related to democratic self-governance, the provisions of the 1987 Constitution are far from being applied. The departmental assemblies

that were to create the interdepartmental council never saw the light of day. Thus, it is impossible to create framework laws to regulate the self-governance of the communes. The majority of government decisions related to this issue are of a de facto nature, whether they are in accord with the intent of the Constitution or not. For example, the order of 13 March 1987, regarding the organization and operation of the Ministry of the Economy and Finance, states in Article 3 that the ministry must assert financial control over the units of government. As such, this order contradicts Article 217, which, as per the 1987 Constitution, advocates decentralizing the finances of these units. The order of 17 May 1990, in Article 3, states that the delegate, the executive representative, is hierarchically superior to the civil and military authorities of the department, while the Constitution provides for the autonomy of the municipalities (Development Alternatives Inc. 2000).

The first problem with the quiet transition from the previous authoritarian regime to a democratic regime came on 29 November 1987, when the army and the Duvalierists sabotaged the first free, general elections in thirty years. At the same time, the semblance of consensus among the different groups that made up the social democratic movement split along radical and moderate lines on the issue of whether or not it was necessary to hold elections. While the radicals saw elections as "booby traps" (*pièges à cons*, in the words of French philosopher Jean-Paul Sartre), the moderates mobilized for the "first elections" of the new political regime (in the sense expressed by Guillermo O'Donnell).

The first elections took place in December 1990, and the political transition formally ended on 7 February 1991, with the installation of the first elected government of the post-Duvalier era and the beginning of the construction of the new democratic order, as intended by the Constitution.

The second problem with the transition came with the overthrow of the new president in a military coup, only eight months after the election, on 30 September 1991. This action signalled the end of the transition as such and the beginning of the political crisis and the involvement of the international community. The Organization of American States (OAS) and then the United Nations imposed economic and diplomatic sanctions on the military regime, and this has had an adverse impact on the socioeconomic structures of the entire country.

The economic sanctions imposed by the Bush administration, the OAS, and the UN at the end of 1991, following the September 1991 coup against the Aristide government, contributed to the accelerated stagnation of local economies in Haiti. According to the Haitian census bureau, the GDP growth rate was −5.3 percent in 1992, -5.4 percent in 1993, and −11.9 percent in 1994. Overall, this embargo (which lasted from 1992 to 1994) threw the country into a period of stagnation such as the one it had experienced under the government of François Duvalier before the short period of prosperity (from 1973 to 1980) under the government of his son, Jean-Claude Duvalier.

The 1994 Peace Operation and Its Aftermath

When diplomatic pressure and economic sanctions failed to unseat the military government, US president Bill Clinton decided on the use of force. The American decision regarding military intervention was based primarily on two factors: (1) the continuous influx of Haitian refugees to the state of Florida and (2) intense media pressure from members of the Black Caucus of the US Congress and African-American civil society organizations.

The negotiated retreat of the military, and the actual return of President Jean-Bertrand Aristide (and, with it, the formal return to constitutional order), raised immense hopes. Despite the considerable resources that the Clinton administration and the international community invested in the intervention, it was very quickly recognized as a failure with regard to the institutionalization of democracy and economic development.

Democratic consolidation did not pass the test of local and legislative elections in June 1995. A pro-Aristide and multiparty coalition led by the Organisation politique Lavalas (OPL) snatched up votes at all levels. Consequently, the electoral process was questioned, and doubt was cast on the regime's capacity to institutionalize democracy, especially since, as defined by the Constitution, elections remain the necessary point of departure for establishing the new state.

With an estimated participation rate of between 20 percent and 25 percent in the first round and between 10 percent and 15 percent in the second round, the elections of June 1995 were indicative of the general dysfunction of the political system. Further, the presidential elections in December of the same year (which were to symbolize the first peaceful transition of power) recorded a participation rate of about 15 percent of the voting population. It was the same for the legislative and local elections of January 1997, which were supposed to continue the cycle as defined in the Constitution by establishing a base of decentralized local power. It was from this new, decentralized local power that the permanent electoral council was to be formed. Despite a high degree of international participation, analysts refer to an electoral collapse, with a participation rate of about 5 percent, and, in the Haitian political tradition of winner takes all, a sweeping success for the new party of former president Jean-Bertrand Aristide.

The contested results of these elections and those that followed permitted neither the formalization of a permanent electoral council (as the independent body provided for in the Constitution) nor the implementation of deconcentration and decentralization measures (also set out in the Constitution). A report recently published by the United Nations Development Program (UNDP) and the Government of Haiti states that, on a recurring basis, the organization of elections places the executive opposite the electoral council. In this way, the elections are exploited as a means of political struggle rather than perceived as a deciding feature of the democratic formalization process (UNDP 2000a).

The economic reconstruction strategy is ambitious and orthodox. It consists of four components: (1) the privatization of public enterprises, (2) the reduction of state administrative personnel, (3) the lowering of import taxes to between 0 percent and 3 percent, and (4) the liberalization of financial markets. These four components were the subject of an accord struck between the Government of Haiti and international financial institutions in August 1994 in Paris, two months before the return of President Aristide. The privatization of two out of nine public enterprises, the recovery of private transfers made by Haitians living abroad, and the government's adoption of the emergency assistance and economic reconstruction program (Programme d'urgence et de reconstruction economique) all contributed to a modest economic recovery: 4.4 percent GDP growth in 1995 and 2.8 percent in 1996 (Comisión económica para América Latina y el Caribe 1997, 24), and there was improvement in some social indicators (such as net enrolment ratio, child malnutrition, and access to safe water) (République d'Haïti 2004). However, the economic recovery did not withstand the political crisis that followed the elections of 1995 and later. The political impasse served to slow down the pace of reforms and to block international assistance.

The Crisis of 2004

Two series of elections were scheduled for 2000: legislative elections in May and presidential elections in November. The opposition parties participated in the first round, and the voter participation rate was around 60 percent. However, a number of irregularities were soon discovered, notably vote rigging by Aristide supporters in several regions of the country as well as an erroneous method of calculating percentages in the senatorial race, which led to the primary candidates of the Lavalas Party being wrongly proclaimed the winners in the first round in almost half of the electoral consultations (ICG [International Crisis Group] 2004c, 8). With the refusal of the Conseil electorale provisoire (CEP) to correct its methods of calculation, the OAS electoral observation mission refused to observe the second round, and the majority of political parties boycotted not only the legislative elections but also the presidential elections slated for November 2000. This was the context within which Aristide won the elections and was elected president, with an estimated voter participation rate of between 5 percent and 10 percent.

Questions raised about the Parliament's legitimacy and the lack of progress in the establishment of effective public institutions led Haiti's principal donors to suspend their assistance to national reform – about $500 million in direct aid. Then, in February 2001, the UN considerably reduced its commitment and withdrew its mission, the International Civilian Support Mission in Haiti (MICAH),[4] primarily because of a lack of cooperation on the part of the government.

In April 2001, the OAS attempted to mediate between the government and an ad hoc coalition of opposition parties in order to reach a negotiated solution to the political and electoral crisis. It focused on three main points: the creation of a new independent and pluralist electoral council, the development of a schedule for new elections, and the establishment of a secure environment. The abuse of authority on the part of the government, as well as blatant violations of human rights, increased tensions and prevented any progress on the part of the OAS. On 17 December 2001, armed gunmen attacked the Palais National. The government called the attack a failed coup attempt, even though its perpetrators had not been identified. However, pro-government groups retaliated by attacking the offices and private residences of several opposition leaders, killing one of them. As a result, negotiations were suspended indefinitely.

Two new developments came about after 2002. First, rising from a small organization known as the Civil Society Initiative (Initiative de la société civile), a coalition emerged, which included 184 civic and popular organizations and some four hundred members. For the first time in Haiti's political history, a very broad coalition of civil society associations and organizations had put itself in a position to demand a role, basing its activities on the promotion of a new "social contract" for a more inclusive government. Primarily because of the weakness of the political parties, in addition to the government's abuse of power, the Group of 184 transformed itself into a coalition with a political mandate and, until his departure, became the most important actor in the campaign against Aristide.

The second development was the rise in physical violence. Pro-government gangs attacked the opposition and an armed group of former military members emerged in the central department and in the nearby border region. In the capital, armed pro-government groups violently assaulted a student demonstration on 5 December 2003 and entered several faculties of the State University of Haiti. After this date, an alliance was formed between the group of opposition political parties, Convergence démocratique, and the Group of 184. This alliance demanded the resignation and departure of Aristide. Despite international efforts to reach a political solution, the trend towards the use of violence took a decisive turn when an armed movement called the Front de résistance de l'Artibonite (Artibonite Resistance Front) for the overthrow of Aristide took control of the city of Gonaïves. On 22 February 2004, another Haitian city fell into the hands of insurgents. The governments of the United States and France pressured Aristide to resign in order to avoid a bloodbath. On 29 February 2004, the president signed a letter of resignation and left the country.

The exceptional duration of the political and institutional crisis in Haiti gave rise to perceptions of a lack of governability. The country was seen as being somewhere between a weakened, totalitarian, centralized state and a democratic, decentralized state that had not yet managed to become operational. Political instability, even within the transition period, had cropped up as though it were a natural occurrence. The Bilan Commun de Pays very aptly commented that, since the overthrow of the dictatorship, Haiti had had twelve heads of state (three of whom led de facto regimes from 1992 to 1994) and that persons in ministerial positions had followed one after the other at such a rapid rate that they had been unable to embark on any reform programs (UNDP 2000a, 16).

In voting on 30 July 1994 for Resolution 940, authorizing the deployment of a multinational force, the UN Security Council chose to address the short-term aspects of the Haitian crisis. In his recent evaluation of this first peacekeeping operation, Minxin Pei (2002, 22) maintains that, "On balance, the international community's intervention in Haiti achieved only its short-term objective: ousting a brutal illegitimate military junta, restoring a democratically elected leader to power, and averting a horrific refugee crisis. Its long-term goal – building viable democratic institutions – remains unfulfilled."

The impact of this situation on the everyday lives of the Haitian people is close to catastrophic. In terms of poverty, according to one World Bank estimate, 80 percent of the two-thirds of the population who live in rural areas are poor, and two-thirds of these people live in extreme poverty. Further, 4 percent of the population possess 66 percent of the country's resources, while 70 percent of the population live on 20 percent of the country's total income.

At the level of government and public services, in the previous regime, the government appeared to be strong but only in the sense of having coercive power. Without democratic legitimacy, it was weak, and its only strength came from the army. At the end of the authoritarian period, economic liberalization occurred in tandem with the withdrawal of the state. This notion of the compatibility between the market and democracy (decentralization) prevailed during the opening of the Haitian economy and the liberalization of its markets. However, it is at odds with the actual changes that took place throughout the world between the crisis of the 1930s and the beginning of the 1980s. During this period, the opening of economies was accompanied by a marked increase in state involvement in the economy, by the considerable development of social protection systems, and by the steadfast practice of stabilization policies (Fitoussi 2004, 92).

The building of sustainable peace can only be accomplished on the foundation of an inclusive democracy that is facilitated by a modicum of economic development. From this perspective, after three lost decades, Haiti is a long way from sustainable development. During the 1970s, per capita GDP increased in real terms by 2.3 percent per year. In contrast, the first half of the 1980s was characterized by stagnation, which occurred against a backdrop of social and political crisis. The 1990s accentuated and entrenched extreme poverty, especially with the shock of the embargo and the economic sanctions imposed between 1991 and 1994. According to the Haitian census bureau and the UN Economic Commission for Latin America and the Caribbean, per capita GDP decreased from 1.9 percent in 1991 to –5.3 percent in 1992, to –5.4 percent in 1993, and to –11.9 percent in 1994. From 1994 onwards, with the infusion of capital from the international community, per capita GDP experienced quick upsurges (9.9 percent in 1995), declining to 0.9 percent in 2000. Per capita GDP further declined to –1.0 percent in 2001 and to a low of –3.8 percent in 2004.

Local Governance and Sustainable Peace

In this section, we examine three community development projects, one each in Gonaïves, Gros Morne, and Marmelade. The guiding question is: How do these local projects fit into broader processes of democratic consolidation, economic reconstruction, and peacebuilding? Specifically, we examine:

1 the contribution the projects made to democratic governance at the local level
2 the contribution projects made to the economic development of the communities in which they are being implemented;
3 the presence or absence in these projects of structures for conflict mediation
4 the implementation of sustainable or non-sustainable structures capable of underpinning local peace.

We discuss the links between these local projects and national processes after we present the case studies.

The three projects that we visited for our case studies should be seen as strategic research sites in that they do not have formally established units devoted to conflict management (which are still rare in Haiti). These projects are: the CARE project in Gonaïves, which is a short-term labour-intensive project; the ADERAM (Asosyasyon pou Devlopman Ekonomik Rivyè Blanch) project in Gros Morne, which is a long-term community-based initiative; and the Marmelade project, which is an experiment in local governance that combines the structures of locally elected or appointed powers, local grassroots associations, and the expertise of national and international personnel.

The case studies presented here are not intended to be representative; rather, they are intended to convey to the reader a sense of the strategies used by various actors to promote local and economic development, democratic governance, and peace in Haiti.

CARE Project in Gonaïves

Located in Artibonite Department, the city of Gonaïves has a population of approximately 66,453 persons (Institut Haïtien de statistiques et d'informatique 1999-2007) and is located about two hundred kilometres from Port-au-Prince. In September 2004, this city's extreme poverty was aggravated by tropical storm Jeanne. Gonaïves has been the recipient of a number of projects aimed at improving the lives of inhabitants and helping to ease their situation (Snow 2001). The city's most populous and conflict-ridden neighbourhoods (Trou Sable, Raboteau, Lòt Bò Kanal, and Ka Solèy) have benefited from special interventions on the part of CARE, the Pan American Development Foundation, and the Cooperative Housing Foundation (with funding from USAID [United States Agency for International Development]).

Since the fall of the Duvaliers in 1986, these disadvantaged areas have gained the reputation of being at the forefront of Haiti's socio-political changes. Many leaders who contributed to the democracy movement gained increased social and political status. Some took advantage of the situation to become involved in all sorts of illicit transactions and were subsequently imprisoned or simply eliminated. At the end of the Aristide period, the same political scheme occurred as had occurred at the end of the Duvalier period: certain political leaders who were former supporters of the dominant regime found themselves persecuted and imprisoned. Once freed from the government prisons, and with access to weapons and ammunition, they joined others who had been victims of the Aristide government to form the Armée cannibale. That group played a key role in ousting the Aristide government in February 2004, with support from the United States and the discontented population (Constant 2003).

Because it has always been a hot spot, between 1996 and 2002 Gonaïves was the site for an infrastructure rehabilitation project funded by USAID (Enhancing Food Security Program, Phase II, EFS II). After tropical storm Jeanne in 2004, the Tropical Storm Rehabilitation Project was implemented with funding from USAID. The CARE project was part of that initiative, and its goal was to help Haitians to re-establish their lives after the devastation caused by Jeanne. This objective had two components: (1) to reconstruct some of the infrastructure used by the general public and (2) to support disadvantaged households that had fallen victim to the storm.

To undertake the infrastructure work (construction and repair of drainage canals) after Jeanne, CARE mobilized the local population through the local management committees. The method used to organize these committees dates back to a food-for-work program implemented from 1996 to 2002. Each committee was composed of a small core group of no more than nine members, with a leader who was elected by these members. The members knew one another and had similar values and attributes (e.g., a certain level of education combined with practical skills and apparent honesty. The committees were re-elected at intervals determined by the members.

The committees formed teams of local workers whose names figured in work contracts granted by CARE. Committee leaders were responsible for managing the team members and for the storage and management of the tools used to undertake the infrastructure work. The municipality provided training in waste management along with CARE technical support workers. CARE provided fuel and covered the costs of repairs, while the Ministry of Public Works provided the trucks to transport garbage.

The economic impact of the project lay primarily in the jobs it created, which were paid a minimum salary that was determined by the government.[5] To illustrate, between April 2005 and January 2006, CARE mobilized 942 teams of twenty-one members each for cleanup work. A total of 19,782 individuals were involved in this piecework. For drainage, during the same time period, CARE mobilized 1,095 teams from a total of 14,926 participants.

With the endemic unemployment that characterizes poor neighbourhoods in most Haitian cities, any job creation, even at a low rate of pay, is generally considered by the population and by the workers themselves to be a great benefit. According to residents of Gonaïves, CARE activities helped diminish popular discontent with the local authorities, who, due to a lack of resources, were unable to meet peoples' needs.

In addition to the creation of jobs, the repair of the canals and the collection of waste contributed to improved accessibility to the slum areas for consumers of products that are sold there. A number of residents of these neighbourhoods benefited because they worked in small trades or as merchants. The construction of a reservoir for safe drinking water in Trou Sable also generated employment.[6] Some fifty thousand people now benefit from a free supply of safe water instead of having to buy it.

The knowledge acquired by committee members contributed to increasing their status among their peers. Given the complex network of relationships that link the committees with the rest of the community, the social status of its members has rapidly become a political asset – to the extent that, according to some CARE employees, some of them have become elected representatives. Women also participated in the working teams. Out of a total of about twenty thousand workers engaged in the cleanup work, about 31 percent were women. With regard to the drainage work, about 33 percent (out of fifteen thousand people) were women. Overall, about one-third of the workforce during this period was made up of women.

Municipal authorities worked with CARE to develop a plan for waste management training that was provided to the committees. CARE provided tools, which remained with the Ministry of Public Works when the project ended, thus contributing to the continued operation of the plan. The neighbourhood committees are seeking to self-manage the waste produced by the residents by creating volunteer brigades that encourage everyone to keep the irrigation canals clean. These committees collect the garbage in the streets and gather it at specific points in the neighbourhood, where the municipality picks it up and takes it away. CARE pays for the fuel. Since CARE's departure in June 2006, the municipality has been working to find another source of funding.

From a local governance perspective, the CARE project had no institutional impact. At best, it could be said that it provided a certain logistical support to the local government – namely, the mayor's office and Public Works Department. The people living in the three areas under study see CARE as an effective structure of local governance working in collaboration with government institutions. Although CARE does not have a unit to manage conflicts among participants, its staff organized a two-day seminar on this theme (based on information found on the Internet) for officials involved in the project. Conflicts that were reported occurred between the local committees and unemployed persons as well as among workers (with regard to "jurisdiction"). Apparently, the committees were able to manage these conflicts, which were in no way a threat to peace in Gonaïves; rather, they were limited events that were resolved to the satisfaction of key parties.[7]

The project ended in June 2006, and the workers who participated in it created a cooperative to maintain its work (the Union des Brigades d'Entretien de Ka Solèy). This cooperative was formed through dues paid to the local committees. As of late 2006, it was involved in the storage and sale of construction materials and has a bank account balance of 120,000 gourdes. Future allocation of part of the profits accrued from this money to the local community would be a definite indicator of this project's sustainability.

Gros Morne Project: ADERAM
With a population of 84,432 inhabitants, the City of Gros Morne (local residents call it a village) is situated in the Artibonite Department, about thirty kilometres northwest of Gonaïves. In the 1980s, a community development project driven by a development centre located in the nearby community of Grépin was implemented through local farmers' associations. Those associations, called "gwoupman" in Creole, chose their members spontaneously. At the time, the project was funded by a German international development association and USAID, and it was executed by Catholic Relief

Services. The project was completed in 1986; however, the gwoupman decided to create a community development association known as ADERAM (in Creole, Asosyasyon pou Devlòpman Economik Rivyè Blanch, Lakil, Moulin).

ADERAM has a "developmentist" ideology, and its interventions fall into several domains, such as storage and marketing of agricultural products, livestock raising, and credit. In 1997, the gwoupman included a total of 1,800 men and women members. Each year, the committee responsible for the association presents the project funds to all gwoupman members who are delegates to the general meeting.

ADERAM has a strong social capital in the sense that the gwoupman is based on trust between members[8] – a trust that has evolved over years of working together in common struggles. In the late 1980s, the leadership was threatened with the label "communist." Though the gwoupman were prohibited from meeting, their agricultural work exchanges provided members with the opportunity to meet and to continue the development movement (spearheaded by the learning centre in Grépin). Thus, although not affiliated with a political movement, the members of ADERAM knew that it was necessary to control their political environment in order to achieve economic success. During local elections in 1996, they managed to win power at local levels.

Established in 1997, ADERAM aims to achieve economic development in the communal sections of Gros Morne. The association's interventions are conducted through the gwoupman, whose members work together to cultivate land leased from other local residents; they are also involved in raising livestock and the storage of agricultural produce. The financial yields coming from gwoupman activities are partially deposited in a local credit union (to support solidarity) and partially reinvested (usually in the same activities). In 1998, ADERAM received a contribution from the European Union and the French Groupe de recherches et d'echanges technologiques for a cane mill project. ADERAM contributed more than one-quarter of the amount invested towards the purchase of the mill.

Thus, by creating its own income-generating activities, ADERAM has dislodged local usurers, whose lending rate could be as high as 30 percent per month. In addition, members of the association pay a preferential rate for the processing of sugar cane into syrup, which they resell on the local markets. About thirty gwoupman composed exclusively of women benefit from ADERAM's investments. Credit provided to women is of great importance since most sales are conducted by women. The need to supply local and regional markets with consumer products creates work for a whole range of persons – gatherers of produce, transporters, tinsmiths who make pots and kettles sold in the market, and so on. From a social perspective, a successful "big business" increases the status of local merchants and helps to increase their access to credit.

At the communal section level, there is no formal governance; there are only attempts at informal governance, which subject local leaders to the demands of the residents. In the case of Gros Morne, these leaders are members of the gwoupman and, as such, benefit from its financial and labour support.

ADERAM has no established structure with which to address conflicts. Thus, a potential conflict around the funding of the mill was resolved after discussions among members. From 1986 to the present, the gwoupman has been able to carry on in spite of the country's socio-political problems. Given the fact that the association's activities are continuing to grow and that there are no major conflicts among its members, it is reasonable to expect that these interventions will last. The gwoupman themselves are involved in maintenance of the mill and other possessions.

Marmelade Projects[9]
Marmelade has a population of 20,054 inhabitants (Institut Haïtien de statistiques et d'informatique 1999-2007). It is a community situated in the mountains, about thirty kilometres northeast of Gonaïves in Artibonite (Institut Haïtien de statistiques et d'informatique 1999-2007). The community is far from being a hot spot; on the contrary, it has built a reputation for being politically calm. The political events that created upheaval in Haiti, from the fall of the Duvaliers in February 1986 to the fall of Aristide in February 2004, left no significant mark on Marmelade. Residents are very proud of this area.

It is no accident that President René Préval, who was re-elected in February 2006, is from Marmelade. Marmelade has benefited from two projects between Préval's first mandate (1996–2001) and his current mandate. One was intended to increase residents' incomes and was implemented by the Fédération des Associations des Caféières Natives; the other was intended to foment sustainable development and was implemented by the UNFAO (United Nations Food and Agriculture Organization) and the Haitian Ministry of Agriculture. Managed by the UNFAO, the second project (usually called the Marmelade Project) was initiated in 1999 with funding from the Netherlands and, later, from Canada. The project focuses on three issues: local development, sustainable agriculture, and environmental management.

To achieve its objective, the project relies on a participatory approach, which includes consultations with, and the empowerment of, residents of Marmelade Commune.[10] The various stages of the project were put into place after this approach had been tried in an experimental phase. During Phase II (2003–05), the project established its basic operating structure:

1   a Marmelade communal committee for joint action and planning[11]
2   three local development committees, one per commune[12]
3   a communal development plan
4   three local development programs, one per communal section.

Thus, the project revolves around a communal committee and three local committees. These two levels of planning integrate local elected representatives from the territorial communities. The project seeks to respect as well as put into practice the law of 4 April 1996, which requires that elected representatives be involved in development activities that take place within their jurisdiction.

Delegates to the general assembly include members of the rural and urban committees as well as other civil society participants. The local development programs, prepared by the local committees in collaboration with the population of the communal sections, are used by the general assembly to prepare a communal development plan. The project is managed by a national director, who is also the director of the communal agricultural office and receives technical support from the UNFAO through its chief technical adviser.

The project's social and economic impacts can be observed on two levels: an immediate level, in the form of access to credit, and a long-term level, in the form of environmental protection. The two levels are linked to each other. Indeed, one of the UNFAO's conditions for the peasant farmers' access to the Marmelade credit union (a savings and credit union whose purpose is the advancement of Marmelade) is their capacity and willingness to manage a tract of land so as to prevent erosion. The planter's file is sent to the main office in Marmelade and is only approved if he or she agrees to establish a plan to manage the land sustainably, in collaboration with the local committee. According to one project manager, between fifteen hundred and two thousand planters have sold their products to processing plants in Marmelade.

Credit is provided in three areas: livestock, storage, and marketing of products and farm inputs. Storage ensures increased income for the planter and his/her family because the products will be resold, either abroad or on the local market during periods of shortage. In this way, sellers of agricultural products make a profit from the difference in price between the markets in which they sell their goods and the price paid to suppliers. Now, through UNFAO funding, each local committee has a mill to process sugar cane. Once they receive training, committee members manage the mills.

Apart from the farm credit provided to women, the project organized a gender equity seminar in March 2005 with the assistance of a national research department. Men, women, youth, and representatives from the territorial communities participated in this seminar. According to one of the project managers, this was one of the Canadian Development Agency's funding requirements, as was capacity building for both men and women with regard to the equitable management of business relations.

Women participate in decision making at the level of the local committees. For example, of the twelve persons who participated in the planters' meeting in one communal section on 25 April 2006, two of the committee leaders were women. At the meeting, with the support of an internationally recognized Haitian NGO that specializes in the promotion of micro-enterprises involved in dairy processing, they announced their decision regarding the conditions for the establishment of a dairy plant.

The project is a major first in the area of local governance. Its participatory approach is all-encompassing, and residents have learned to undertake and implement projects in collaboration with the local authorities, both elected and nominated. There are even examples at the level of the local committees. First, residents carry out their own development program in collaboration with the local authorities and with other participants from the communal sections. Then, independent of the local committee, they undertake to finance their activities. For example, the elected local leaders and the members of one communal section, Crête-à-Pins, developed a plan to supply safe water to a local area. They have obtained funding from the Japanese mission in Haiti, initiated project implementation, developed water sources, and built water tanks.

In addition, the commission responsible for education obtained funding from the Haitian Fonds d'aide économique et sociale to finance the rehabilitation of the community's school. This commission has also submitted a proposal to the Canadian education and health fund to finance a project to rehabilitate the school in another community. However, the Marmelade project still faces a challenge: the need to secure operational funding from local sources in the absence of international funding.

The Marmelade project does not have a formal conflict management unit, but its field officers think they can manage conflicts that occur in an ad hoc manner. According to the local committee coordinator (i.e., the local mayor), project managers can form a support committee to manage conflicts. This committee would be composed of the mayor and deputy mayor, other locally elected leaders, members of the population, and representatives of the decentralized state agencies. During the aforementioned seminars, there was also a module on conflict management. Given that the project managers consider Marmelade to be a tranquil area, there does not seem to be a pressing need for major investments in conflict management at this juncture.

In terms of sustainability, the project adopted an entirely original approach. The two committee coordinators must remain with their replacements for one year in order to convey their knowledge about project management and coordination, which must be in accordance with the wishes

of the local population. In other words, they must hand over the coordination activities before relinquishing their position as coordinators. None of
the members of the coordination committees receives a salary for their participation in the project. However, they benefit from the training programs
and study trips, which help them become more efficient in carrying out
their tasks.

On an experimental basis, the Marmelade project will be extended to
other communes in Artibonite Department and northern departments.

Conclusion

At the Local Level
The implementation of labour-intensive projects or local economic development projects relied on local groups that, although encouraged by project
managers, were created due to local initiative. These groups are made up of
local participants who have a close and trusting relationship with the
populations who benefit from the projects. Thus, they serve as contact points
for the projects (as in the case in Gonaïves), integrate them (as in the case in
Marmelade), or replace them (as in the case in Gros Morne). In all cases, the
groups seemed to establish a democratic structure, with provisions for elections and without exclusions based on gender or economic status. Participation in decision making was open to all members, with the right to oppose
established by internal voting mechanisms. The local groups, however, operate in a political vacuum – that is, without fitting into any overarching
plan or strategy to promote the extension of democracy (e.g., the National
Solidarity Program in Afghanistan).

The three projects address different levels of local governance. In Gonaïves,
CARE provided technical, financial, and logistical support to state agencies
that were supposed to train the neighbourhood committees. These committees sought, with support from the municipality, to self-manage the
cleanup of the neighbourhoods in which they reside. The project has no
institutional outcomes from a local governance point of view. In Gros Morne,
there are attempts at informal governance in which the elected local leaders
are subject to the requests of the residents. As members of the local cooperative, they sometimes receive financial and human resource support
for their activities. Marmelade has experienced a first in terms of institutional governance as the residents conceive of projects and implement them
in collaboration with the local (elected and appointed) authorities.

The social and economic impact of these projects also varies. In Gonaïves,
the economic impact is felt directly in the form of the jobs that the project
creates and indirectly through the cleanup activities (including the repair
of the canals) that make the slum neighbourhoods more accessible for the
consumers of products. In Gros Morne, the gwoupman have implemented

their own income-generating activities: a savings and credit cooperative and a sugar cane mill. These two enterprises, which gwoupman members are managing themselves, have a significant impact on the local communities. The savings cooperative provides credit to its members at a preferential rate, and the mill provides services (processing sugar cane into syrup) to gwoupman members at a preferential price. In Marmelade, the project has both an immediate and a long-term impact, in the sense that the credit provided at a favourable rate to the planter for the raising of livestock, storage of products, and marketing of products and farm inputs is tied to her or his willingness to manage the land so as to fight erosion. This is in accordance with a plan established with the local development committee to protect the soil by using plants that help to counteract erosion.

These three projects all manifested a certain extent of gender equity. In all three sites, women were forming groups, participating in decision making, taking part in the work, and enjoying equal access to all the services (training, farm credit, processing activities).

All the groups seemed to adopt the idea of sustainability. In Gonaïves and Gros Morne, the creation of local cooperatives based on the collection of membership fees is an indication of this. In Gros Morne, the gwoupman also created a savings and credit cooperative. In Marmelade, the sustainability of project outcomes will depend on the ability of participants to manage the funds necessary to follow up on them.

Nonetheless, these case studies highlight constraints to local governance, economic development, and peacebuilding. First, they show that there is little coordination between local projects. If economic development and democratic governance is to spread, then local initiatives need to be embedded in a national plan and in relevant national programs. If this does not occur, then the experiences of these various communes will not reach the point at which they would have a significant impact at the departmental level and, eventually, at the national level.

Second, the direct and continued participation of the project members in the creation of public goods helps to foster the motivation needed for the collective ownership of project outcomes and even of the projects themselves. This participation also ensures the strengthening of local democratic governance. However, the participation of the local population must be institutionalized through the assemblies that, at various levels, share sociopolitical jurisdiction. This is to ensure that those who have previously been excluded will now have an influence on public policies, as provided in the Constitution of 1987. The legitimacy of the new government will depend on its ability to move towards a policy of decentralization that favours the institutionalization of local governance. Without this policy, the successes of the local actors will remain short-lived.

Third, many socio-political risks persist. The populations of these areas are similar to those of other areas in Haiti. They are generally poor, lack training, and are unemployed. Individuals with ill intents can rally them around all sorts of demands, particularly while a climate of impunity flourishes. The calmness seen in Artibonite and elsewhere in Haiti is in no way an indication that the climate is right for a sustainable peace. The defusing of the forces that counter the maintenance of socio-political peace will depend on the new government's ability to hold them in check by involving the local population in income-generating employment that is also socially valued. This ability is hampered by the economic stagnation in which the country is mired. The influx of foreign capital from the international community, in addition to the proper management of this capital, is an urgent necessity. The extension of the governance model undertaken in Marmelade to other parts of the country remains conditional on the government's ability to provide the necessary financial resources and institutional environment.

Fourth, there are no formal local structures in place for conflict management. Problems are resolved as they arise, through the intervention of the local population. The success of people's local enterprises depends on the institutional framework that the government is able to offer. Most areas of governance fall under the control of monopolistic elites, and this makes it almost impossible to establish rules aimed at achieving equity in the production of goods and services. Gros Morne's production and overseas sale of mangoes provides one illustration of this point. At the national level, as well, the decline of products such as sugar, coffee, and rice is linked to the fact that their import and resale on the local market brings large profits to certain monopolistic sectors. In other words, the material interests of monopolistic elites have adversely affected the ability of the state to fulfill one of its main functions – to mediate between divergent vested interests in the search for peace. Continuing and sustaining the positive outcomes of local governance will depend on the state's ability to settle conflicts of interest between those who, in the past, have been excluded and those who have been influential.

These observations underscore a disturbing pattern in Haiti – a pattern that may be common in other peacebuilding contexts: although local development projects can help key actors develop democratic values and practices, the state remains too fragile to create the institutional framework to bolster that change and to link it to sustainable peacebuilding. Thus, the experience of those projects in local governance seems to be limited to the settings in which they occur: there are no links with broader processes of democratic governance and peacebuilding. Indeed, in Haiti, local projects tend to remain isolated despite the dream of using Marmelade as a model for broader initiatives.

At the National Level

Interestingly, the international community and the transitional government that held office from 2004 to 2006 did apply those lessons learned from the failure of peacebuilding in the 1990s. Though the military intervention that began in February 2004 led to the installation of a transitional government of dubious legitimacy, the international community and that government cooperated to lay foundations for democratic change. Former army personnel, who led the uprising against President Aristide, were not brought into the transitional government. Yet, despite numerous attempts to restore public security, violence escalated, with the involvement of national police and UN forces, especially in the poorest areas of Port-au-Prince.

These mixed beginnings notwithstanding, the presidential and legislative elections held in early 2006 were largely free and fair. The international community and most other political parties recognized the victory of Lespwa candidate René Préval in the first round of the presidential elections, despite initial confusion over the count and despite Lespwa's links to Parti Lavalas. When Lespwa did not win a majority in either chamber of the National Assembly, it and other political parties committed themselves to work together to ensure legislative progress and to consolidate democracy.

An innovative approach to "adjustment for peace" was also applied in the domain of economic and social policy. The Cadre de coopération intérimaire (CCI), which provided the framework for economic recovery during the transitional period, clearly moved beyond earlier orthodoxies. Indeed, it combined measures to stabilize prices and to restore a balance in public finances with measures to address urgent needs in urban and rural areas as well as with steps to rebuild infrastructure and public sector capacities in areas like health, education, and public security. The international community put huge resources behind the implementation of the CCI.

Although the CCI could not meet pent-up demands for an immediate improvement in the living conditions of average Haitians, its utility was confirmed by President Préval's request that it be extended to late 2007 to allow his government, on the basis of wide consultations, to prepare a poverty reduction strategy paper (PRSP). Haiti still faces huge challenges in the areas of economic and democratic development, especially at the local level. The difficulties experienced in 2006-7 in the attempt to forge a broadly consultative PRSP process are not encouraging.

It is still too early to pass definitive judgment on the results of the 2004 intervention or the 2006 elections. Yet, in contrast to the outcome after 1994, developments since March 2004 suggest that it is possible for committed national leaders and the international community to open the door to sustainable peacebuilding, even on the heels of a controversial stabilization operation. Taking the time needed to organize free and fair elections, respecting the outcomes of those elections, fostering cooperation among political parties, and jointly formulating policies that revive markets while renewing public sector capacity and focusing on poverty reduction all seem crucial to the *relatively* positive outcomes of the 2004 intervention (at least to date).

Finally, the case of Haiti strongly suggests that peace cannot be built on the foundations of a weak state: it requires legitimate and effective public institutions. This applies as much to the realm of public security as it does to the realms of political democracy and economic recovery. Without a capable, professional, and politically neutral public service, it is not possible to implement decentralization, to reform the police, or to institute other changes required to sustain a future peace (Hector 2007, 15-16).

Recommendations

1   The political and institutional backdrop in present-day Haiti offers many opportunities. Over the coming years, the current coalition government should build on the December 2006 local elections and on the current PRSP process to adopt a bold approach to democratic decentralization.

2   The legitimacy of local leaders is an essential condition of good local governance. That legitimacy is related to the ability of the Conseil électoral provisoire to ensure free and fair elections. Strengthening that institution at the local level is therefore of the utmost importance. Since the permanence of the CEP depends upon the existence of the departmental assemblies and other authorities based in the territorial communities, following the December 2006 local elections, the new government should make the establishment of those bodies a top priority.

3   The dissemination of information through community radio will contribute to strengthening the public's knowledge of conflict management. At the local level, it will be necessary to create civic committees to defend citizenship rights. Such committees should permit regular dialogue among the various sectors of the population, police authorities, and judicial powers, with the aim of rebuilding justice and security. These committees should also create spaces in which citizens will be able to express their grievances in a peaceful and lawful manner (ARD 1996).

4   Local governance is still in its experimental stages and, therefore, requires the development of the local economy to ensure its survival; it also needs the future interdepartmental council and the future council of ministers to develop framework laws. The existence of certain legal provisions should enable local municipalities to expand their tax base to obtain the funds necessary for development activities in their communities. Newly elected mayors should seek the national and international collaboration necessary to implement these fiscal measures.

5   One of the priorities of the new government should be the creation and strengthening of the lines of communication between the various levels of local and national authorities and international donors, with the aim of linking isolated local development projects to the national decentralization strategy.

5

Palestine, 1993-2006: Failed Peacebuilding, Insecurity, and Poor Governance

Khalil Shikaki

Thirteen years after the start of the Palestinian-Israeli peace process, military occupation remains the most fundamental problem for the Palestinians, just as violence remains the most fundamental problem for the Israelis. While successful in building a national authority, Palestinians have not succeeded in building effective and democratic governance at either the national level or the local level. During six years of the second intifada, peacebuilding among the Palestinians has confronted new threats: internal chaos and power struggle; the election of a new Parliament dominated by forces committed to armed struggle and opposed to the Oslo peace process with Israel; fragmentation within the mainstream national movement that lost the 2006 parliamentary elections; disintegration and potential collapse of the central government; and the inability of local government to provide an alternative source of support. Although the initial consequences of President Arafat's death in November 2004 were positive, opening the door to democratization, a temporary halt in the violence, and better governance, the future of the Palestinians and Palestinian-Israeli peacebuilding remained uncertain, particularly in light of the Hamas electoral victory. The formation of a Hamas government in early 2006 brought further domestic upheaval, international financial sanctions, and diplomatic boycott. The formation of a national unity government in March 2007 helped reduce domestic tensions but did not bring an end to international sanctions.

This chapter examines the failure of peacebuilding in Palestine, focusing on the unfulfilled short-term expectations of ending violence and curtailing occupation as well as on the long-term objectives of state building and good governance. Since Palestine is a case of two-level conflict – state-to-state and intrastate – the study highlights the interplay between these two levels. In doing so, it addresses a question posed in the introductory chapter concerning the best way in which to meaningfully assess peacebuilding. Palestinian-Israeli peacebuilding has involved a state-to-state peace process that has entailed political agreements, security components, and a "normalization" of extensive economic and administrative relationships between the two entities. However, it has also involved a much more complicated state building process, with elements of domestic governance, economic reconstruction and growth, and social development. These two levels influenced each other in significant ways, and the record of the past decade has demonstrated that they are highly interdependent. Indeed, in the short run, the sustainability of peacebuilding has proved highly dependent on the success of the long-term objective of state building. Similarly, the success of state building has been conditional on meeting short-term expectations of ending violence and occupation.

The viability of Palestinian state building has proven to be greatly dependent on the terms of the negotiated settlement with Israel. In the eyes of its constituency, the failure of the Palestinian Authority (PA) to translate the 1993 Oslo Agreement into actual measures to end the occupation greatly reduced both its legitimacy and the legitimacy of the agreement it had signed. Having lost the legitimacy it acquired by signing the peace agreement, the old guard leaders of the Palestinian Liberation Organization (PLO) relied more and more on force to maintain control, and this led to the creation of an authoritarian regime. An exclusive political system marginalized young guard nationalists and Islamist forces. It also marginalized local government by ensuring that the central government had control over local councils, their finances, and decision making. Opposition to the old guard within the nationalist movement, expressed by young guard violence against Israelis and the formation of armed militias, undermined the short-term stability of the peace process. A weak local government was unable either to provide legitimacy at the grassroots level or to deliver services when the central government became dysfunctional. The nationalists' twin failures of not delivering peace, on the one hand, or good governance, on the other, led to a strong showing for the Islamists in local elections in 2005 and culminated in January 2006 with the parliamentary elections, in which Hamas, a faction opposed to the Oslo peace process and committed to continued armed struggle against Israeli occupation, won a clear majority of seats.

The centrality of the relationship between state building viability and the legitimacy of the interim and, later, the permanent Palestinian-Israeli agreements should not be underestimated. Only an agreement acceptable to the majority of Palestinians would be approved by the major political forces – namely, Islamists and nationalists. Without the support, or at least the acquiescence, of these groups at both local and national levels, it is questionable whether sustained peacebuilding can be achieved. An agreement that lacks legitimacy in the eyes of the majority of Palestinians will render the state and the process of state building illegitimate; the greater the legitimacy of the peace agreement, the more likely that it will be able to create a legitimate and viable state. Therefore, anyone attempting to understand the failures and successes of peacebuilding in Palestine must be fully aware of the interplay between intra- and inter-state processes (on two-level game theory, see Putnam 1988).

Moreover, the state-to-state peacebuilding process has been greatly influenced by international politics. The end of the Cold War made Israeli-Palestinian peacemaking possible, allowing a small country like Norway to play a significant role in that effort – a role unimaginable a few years earlier, when the PLO was highly dependent on the Soviet Union for support. However, the emerging structure of the international system in the post-Cold War era shaped not only the incidence of peacemaking but also the nature of peacebuilding outcomes. The post-Cold War dominance of the United States created conditions that constrained the substance of the Norwegian peace efforts. The Oslo Agreement could not force Israel to fully end its occupation of Palestinian territories as Israel could easily count on full American backing. The international community's tendency to focus on short-term needs (i.e., security for Israelis) rather than on long-term needs (i.e., Palestinian needs for the full end of occupation and for good governance) was determined by a disparity in power relationships favoured and sustained by the United States.

The presence and intervention of the international community, particularly the donor countries, has also had an impact on peacebuilding. The interplay between peacemaking and state building lies at the heart of the international involvement in Palestinian peacebuilding. The Quartet's "Road Map for Peace" illustrates this link.[1] If one examines the international interest, one can quickly conclude that the peacebuilding goal of a "viable Palestinian state" is predicated on the assumption that the same state would be compatible with the vital interests of the other major parties to the conflict, particularly Israeli peace and security, and that it would not threaten regional stability. While Palestinians in the post-Oslo period were confronted with the challenges of an unfinished peace and national reconstruction, the international donor community was faced with meeting the requirements of promoting good governance and, at the same time, supporting peacemaking. When a contradiction emerged, as in the aftermath of the Palestinian parliamentary election of January 2006, which brought to power a Hamas majority opposed to the Road Map, the international community was quick to abandon the interest in good governance altogether in favour of imposing Israeli-inspired peace and security-related conditions. The international community has clearly demonstrated that it is willing to risk pre-empting a nascent Palestinian transition to democracy in favour of promoting a security and peace agenda determined by non-Palestinians.

This peacebuilding outcome did not come as a surprise. To many donors and Palestinians, the objectives of peace and good governance were linked:

support for peace was based on certain expectations regarding governance and national reconstruction. While donors wanted to promote Palestinian ownership of good governance, reconstruction, and socioeconomic development, they were grappling with the question of how international assistance could promote a commitment to peacemaking and, at the same time, hinder the strengthening of an elite that was authoritarian but also essential to the success of the first objective. International efforts to deal with this dilemma yielded mixed results. While early 2006 witnessed the holding of parliamentary elections and significant progress towards Palestinian good governance, the international community, alarmed by the victory of Hamas, terminated all its direct assistance and most of its developmental assistance to the Palestinians. Instead of encouraging the emergence of a national unity government of Islamists and nationalists that would help moderate the attitudes and policies of Islamists and provide a strong impetus to peacebuilding, the international community chose a policy of containment.

The rise of Hamas in local and parliamentary elections and the continued violence during the years of the peace process demonstrate the failure of peacebuilding to pay attention to long-term considerations (e.g., the terms of the Oslo Agreement, the need to integrate the Islamists and nationalist young guards into the domestic political system, and the need for empowered local government). This could also have serious implications for short-term expectations. One would expect that, in future Palestinian peacebuilding, the tension that emerged during the last decade between the requirements of short-term expectations and the imperatives of long-term objectives would not be resolved at the expense of the long-term future of the Palestinians.

In preparing this chapter, we reviewed the existing literature on the status of the peace process and the Palestinian domestic political scene. We also combined findings from surveys of public opinion and exit polls with insights gained from interviews with policy makers and elected officials at both national and local levels.

This section situates the examination of peacebuilding in the context of Israeli-Palestinian peacemaking – with its two main goals of war termination/end of occupation and state building. It traces the development of the three main phases of the peace process: the Oslo bilateral agreements (1993-2000), the return to violence during the second Palestinian intifada (2000-5), and the turn to Israeli unilateralism (2004-6). During these phases, we saw, in 2000, the collapse of the objective of war termination and, in early 2005, its partial restoration. Parallel to this, we saw the transformation of the PA into an authoritarian regime under Yasir Arafat as well as Palestinian efforts, in the post-Arafat era, to reopen their political system and to allow a transition towards a more accountable governance.

From the Oslo Agreement to Israeli Unilateralism

To many Palestinians and Israelis, the Oslo peace process represented a grand bargain. The Israelis expected it to deliver an end to Palestinian violence, and the Palestinians expected it to deliver an end to Israeli military occupation of their land. While violence was indeed reduced and the Israeli army did redeploy its forces out of Palestinian populated areas, the expectations of most Palestinians and Israelis were never fulfilled. Violence against Israelis continued, while the number of Israeli settlers in the occupied Palestinian areas doubled during the first six years of the peace process. Internal forces that had been marginalized and somewhat delegitimized by the peace process (e.g., Hamas on the Palestinian side and Jewish settlers on the Israeli side) sought to sabotage the process. Mutual violence and expansion of settlements were the tools that were effectively used to cause delays and distrust and that eventually doomed the whole process.

That process brought the PLO and Israel to the negotiating table and led to the signing of the Declaration of Principles, or Oslo I, in Washington, DC, in September 1993 and the Interim Agreement, or Oslo II, in October 1995. The agreement called for an immediate Israeli withdrawal from a small part of the occupied Palestinian territories and a phased withdrawal or redeployment from other parts, pending a final agreement on borders and other core issues, such as the return of Palestinian refugees to their homes and property inside Israel and the future of Arab East Jerusalem and its holy places. The PA was formed in May 1994 in the Gaza Strip and the Jericho area as a first step in a long process of national reconstruction and as part of a five-year interim arrangement whose goal was a permanent peace settlement. A permanent status peace agreement was supposed to be reached in 1999, but negotiations did not take place until mid-2000.

A Camp David Summit called by the US president in July 2000 failed to produce a final status agreement. In September, a visit by Israeli prime minister Ariel Sharon to al Haram al Sharif (known to the Israelis as the Temple Mount) triggered a Palestinian intifada that has led to the death of more than four thousand Palestinians and 1,100 Israelis. Efforts by the international community to put an end to the violence and to bring the two sides back to the negotiating table failed between 2000 and 2005. The most comprehensive effort has been the Quartet's development of a "Road Map for Peace." While the Road Map was presented to the parties in early 2003, between 2003 and 2005 little was done to implement it. In mid-2004, Israel abandoned bilateral negotiations in favour of unilateralism when its government approved a disengagement plan. The plan called for an Israeli evacuation of all Jewish settlements in the Gaza Strip and of four settlements in the northern West Bank. In September 2005, the disengagement plan was successfully implemented, without Palestinian-Israeli violence or much resistance from the settlers.

The Oslo peace agreements (which created the PA and its institutions) imposed severe constraints on Palestinian jurisdiction and control in both internal and external spheres. The very limited territorial jurisdiction of the PA has gradually expanded to include additional areas in the West Bank. By 2000, the PA had territorial and functional control over most of the Gaza Strip and about 40 percent of the West Bank. Functional control in the West Bank, however, is far from complete, even in theory, as Israelis retain overriding security responsibilities in more than half of the areas supposedly under Palestinian control. Since the start of the second intifada in September 2000, the Israeli army has, from time to time, reoccupied towns and cities under PA control. Indeed, since March 2002, the Israeli army has reoccupied almost all PA territories in the West Bank.

Despite the optimism and economic achievements of the early years of the peace process, as Table 1 shows, the underlying promises of peace remained largely unfulfilled, with the viability of the Palestinian economy proving difficult to attain. Four decades of Israeli occupation have made the Palestinian economy very dependent on Israel and have isolated it from the rest of the world. Israel is the PA's sole trading partner, and a large segment of Palestinian labourers rely on jobs inside Israel. The Palestinian economy remains a captive economy and, in the Palestinian territories, Israel has maintained a captive market. As such, the PA's trade deficit with Israel has always been lopsided, and increases in foreign aid go mainly to finance this deficit. The PA budget is dependent on external financial support, and even the part that comes from Palestinian customs and taxes has to come mostly through Israel, which collects those revenues on behalf of the PA. Movement of people and goods, particularly between the West Bank and the Gaza Strip, is restricted by Israeli decisions. Israel continues to control Palestinian borders and international crossing points. The last six years have witnessed a continued steep and unprecedented decline in all Palestinian economic indicators, with the Gross National Income in 2003 amounting to less than 50 percent of that of 2000. Real per capita incomes are now less than half of their 2000 levels. In a March 2006 report, the World Bank (2006, 1) concluded that, "despite positive growth rates during 2003-5, Palestinian incomes remain considerably lower than their pre-*Intifada* levels, with real GDP per capita in 2005 about 31 percent lower than in 1999."

Israel initially responded to the second intifada with a massive use of force, seeking to convince the Palestinians of the futility of violence and to compel the Palestinian leadership to crack down on groups involved in violence against Israelis. However, it was Israel that was quick to learn a lesson in the limits of force and to opt in early 2004 for a "unilateral separation." The Israeli right-wing government of Ariel Sharon reached the conclusion that there was no Palestinian partner for the kind of peace negotiations in which it was willing to engage. Sharon preferred a long-term interim deal in which Israel would avoid making hard choices about Jerusalem, settlement blocs in the West Bank, and refugees. The Palestinians wanted to continue the January 2001 Taba permanent status negotiations, which were frozen when Sharon became Israel's prime minister in February of that year. Fearing the loss of its Jewish majority should the status quo remain unchanged, Israel sought to change its strategic environment by unilaterally withdrawing from the Gaza Strip (with its 1.3 million Palestinians). In April 2004, Sharon presented his plan for unilateral disengagement to an Israeli public that was eager to embrace it.

Through this disengagement plan, Sharon and his successor, Ehud Olmert, now leading a new parliamentary faction called Kadima, signalled a willingness to take short-term risks for the sake of long-term Israeli benefits. The Israeli elections in March 2006 strengthened Kadima's ability to advance its unilateral vision in Gaza. However, the Palestinian public and Islamist militants saw the Israeli disengagement plan as a victory for the intifada. Riding on its added popularity, Hamas won the Palestinian parliamentary elections in January 2006. The Israeli-Hezbollah war in the summer of 2006 greatly reduced Israeli public support for further unilateral withdrawal from the West Bank, leaving Kadima without a clear vision for the future of the Israeli occupation.

Yet, even if Israel returns to unilateralism, the consequences for the Palestinians could be bleak. Most Palestinians recognize that a unilateral disengagement plan could hurt them in the short term by threatening the political unity and the territorial integrity of the two geographically disconnected areas of the West Bank and the Gaza Strip. If this occurs, political and territorial breakup could speed up the fragmentation and eventual demise of the PA, paving the way for the emergence of more radical entities. The result would be that, for a long time to come, there would be no one able to speak for the Palestinians. A World Bank report concluded that the Israeli disengagement from the Gaza Strip would not make an appreciable difference to the devastated Palestinian economy. It called for fundamental changes in the political-security environment – changes that would do away with restrictions on the movement of Palestinian goods and persons that had been imposed during the intifada (World Bank 2004b). Moreover, the Israeli response to the election of Hamas – withholding the monthly transfer of about US$55 million of Palestinian revenues collected by Israel on behalf of the PA – coupled with the donor community's suspension of financial support, threatens to bring the PA to the point of total financial collapse. According to the World Bank (2006), in 2006, real GDP per capita declined by 27 percent, personal incomes dropped by 30 percent, unemployment reached 40 percent, and poverty reached 67 percent.

Achievements of the Peace Process

The three phases of the peace process – the Oslo bilateral agreements, the return to violence, and the turn to Israeli unilateralism – point not only to the collapse of the goal of war termination but also to the utility of diplomacy and negotiations. Despite the changes in the Palestinian environment since the death of Arafat, the two sides have failed to return to negotiations. By early 2006, Palestinians had elected a government that believes in the Palestinian right to resort to arms, and the Israelis had elected a government that seeks to determine Israel's borders with Palestine unilaterally. In the aftermath of the Israeli war with Hezbollah and the Israeli questioning of unilateral withdrawal, the lack of direction is more glaring than ever. Despite the progress made in the formation of a Palestinian national unity government, the ability of the PA to embark on serious state building remains in doubt. Yet, it would be a mistake to end this section on a purely negative note. It is worth recalling the following early achievements of the peace process:

1   The initial period witnessed a partial end of Israeli military occupation of Palestinian areas, including an Israeli withdrawal from all Palestinian populated areas (with the exception of Arab East Jerusalem) and a major reduction in the frequency of Palestinian violence against Israeli targets.

2   Mutual Israeli-Palestinian recognition, with Israel recognizing the PLO as the representative of the Palestinian people and the PLO recognizing the State of Israel, took place in 1993 and represented a significant breakthrough in Palestinian-Israeli relations. It was a clear move away from mutual denial, which is what had characterized their relationship until that moment.

3   The establishment of the PA took place in 1994, and the process of state building gained momentum after the 1996 elections leading to the creation of state-like institutions and security services. In the first few years of its formation, the PA succeeded in establishing a functioning cabinet; conducting general elections for the presidency and the Legislative Council; delivering education, health care, and other basic services; revitalizing tax collection; drafting enabling legislation and regulatory frameworks for the conduct of public administration and of private economic and commercial activity; and maintaining security and public law and order. By 1999, Palestinian civil and territorial control was extended to over 42 percent of the occupied territories, of which less than half also came under Palestinian security control. The PLO moved its offices, bureaucracy, and armed forces into Palestinian areas under PA control. As a result, almost 100,000 Palestinians linked to the PLO returned from the diaspora to live in PA areas.

4   The first national elections took place in January 1996, leading to the creation of the first Palestinian parliament – the Palestinian Legislative Council (PLC), with eighty-eight members. The total number of candidates reached 672, of whom twenty-five were women (five of whom won seats). Three-quarters of Palestinians living in the West Bank and the Gaza Strip, of whom 43 percent were women, participated in the elections. In 2005, four rounds of local elections and a presidential election were held, and in January 2006 the second Palestinian parliamentary elections took place.

5   International financial support, averaging about half a billion US dollars between 1995 and 2000, helped the Palestinians start a process of independent economic development and to rebuild Palestinian infrastructure (see Table 1). In October 1993, two weeks after the signing of the Declaration of Principles, donors pledged US$2.4 billion to support Palestinian socioeconomic development over a period of five years. Donor funds were crucial to the establishment phase of the PA, covering a significant portion of start-up and running costs for both the civil service and the Palestinian police force. The financial sector was strengthened, and major investors, mostly Palestinians living in the diaspora, returned to Palestine. The PA was able to build trade links to several external markets. During the first six years, some progress was made towards economic growth and poverty reduction. Between 2001 and 2005, donor support averaged US$1 billion. In both absolute and per capita terms, the donor effort for the Palestinians has been one of the largest ever undertaken by the international community.

Table 1

Major socioeconomic indicators, 1994-2005

Year	Population (in millions)	GDP ($US millions)	Growth rate (%)	Poverty (%)	Unemployment (%)
1994	2.3	3,283			
1995	2.5	3,587	6		
1996	2.6	3,791	2	27	23
1997	2.8	4,290	12	25	20
1998	2.9	4,821	12	23	15
1999	3.0	5,095	9	21	12
2000	3.2	4,939	–5	32	15
2001	3.3	4,326	–15	44	26
2002	3.4	4,169	–10	60	31
2003	3.5	4,011	6	72	26
2004	3.6	4,131	6	61	27
2005	3.8	4,044	8	44	23

Source: Various reports issued by the Palestinian Central Bureau of Statistics, the Palestinian Economic Policy Research Institute, the IMF, and the World Bank.

PA Governance

During the last decade, questions have been raised about the authoritarian political culture and corruption of Palestinian elites, and about the weakness of Palestinian public institutions. Since the formation of a Hamas government, questions have been raised about the ability of the Palestinians to forge a national coalition of Islamists and nationalists and, in the absence of such a coalition, the ability of the PA to survive international sanctions and in-fighting. The inability of the ruling mainstream national movement to integrate young nationalists into the political system, along with the exclusion of the Islamists from the political process during the last decade, led to the creation of an authoritarian regime that gradually lost much of its legitimacy. Palestinians have also complained of weak local government, especially during the last six years as more and more people turned to local councils for help. As the PA's capacity to deliver basic services diminished, the role of local councils became paramount. Yet local councils, all appointed by the PA, were unable to meet these demands as they not only lacked the capacity to provide the needed services but also continued to suffer from a centralized system of local government and a lack of public legitimacy.

We now turn to PA governance and, in so doing, address three issues: (1) the authoritarian nature of the PA, the centralization of its authority under nationalist rule, and its potential collapse under the rule of Islamists; (2) the reasons for PA authoritarianism and potential collapse; and (3) the way towards good governance and more decentralized local government. However, first we briefly describe the institutional structure of the PA.

Overview of PA Institutions

The Palestinians have made significant progress towards the creation of public institutions. In 1993, immediately after the Oslo Agreement, the PLO Legal Committee began to draft a Palestinian provisional constitution. In 1996-97, the PLC approved a basic law in its third and final reading. The new constitutional document was debated in full view and with the participation of the Palestinian public. But, for five years, former PA president Arafat refused to sign the Basic Law. He was finally forced to do so in May 2002, after tremendous internal and external pressure. The Basic Law calls for a democracy based on the rule of law and a limited form of separation of power; it affirms a commitment to basic civil rights and freedoms; and it calls for a strong legislature. The legislature is to be directly elected by the people, to be entrusted with the tasks of legislation and oversight, to have immunity for its members, and to have the right to grant and withdraw confidence in the executive and to approve its proposed budget. However, the Basic Law lacks the means of bringing the PA president to accountability, a fault that, until March 2003, made the task of parliamentary oversight almost impossible. At that time the Parliament amended the Basic Law by shifting most of the powers and responsibilities of the executive away from the president to the cabinet and to a newly created position of prime minister. This 2003 constitutional change left many issues unanswered, and this led to a great deal of confusion over the limits of presidential powers versus cabinet powers. In any case, the president remains unaccountable, even if, on paper, he has much less power to use or abuse.

With the 2003 constitutional changes, the Palestinian political system became a mixed government, with parliamentarian and presidential elements existing side by side. The parliamentarian element is manifested in the presence of an elected council (Parliament) that has the power to grant and to withdraw confidence in a cabinet and a prime minister. The president is directly elected by the people, is responsible for appointing and dismissing prime ministers, and has the ability to veto legislation and to issue decrees regarding critical public issues.

The Palestinian executive is comprised of a president, a prime minister, a cabinet or council of ministers, ministries, government authorities, agencies and services, and the support offices of the president's general secretariat and the cabinet secretariat. Theoretically, the executive power is placed mainly in the cabinet; in practice, the president enjoys greater powers, particularly in the areas of security and legislation. The executive carries out the following tasks: it lays down and implements the general policy of the government; it supervises the administrative and security organs; it prepares and approves the annual budget; and it participates in setting up courts and appointing judges.

In January 1996, Palestinian residents of Gaza and the West Bank, including East Jerusalem, elected an eighty-eight-member legislature – the PLC. The Palestinian elections represented a significant step in the process of institutionalizing a parliamentary life in the West Bank and Gaza. The promulgation of an election law, the establishment of a permanent election committee, the division of the country into electoral districts, and the successful holding of elections have all contributed to this process. The second PLC was elected in 2006 and is larger than the first (with 132 members), and the electoral system has changed from an entirely district-based majority system to a mixed system of proportional representation and district-based majority.

In theory, the PLC has several means of holding the executive accountable: it has oversight power and can supervise the performance of the prime minister and the cabinet; its committees can hold hearings for officials suspected of violations and breaches of conduct; it can withhold support from the cabinet by withdrawing confidence. But its legislative power is constrained by a presidential veto, which it can override by a two-thirds majority. Moreover, a combination of reasons has hindered the PLC efforts to exercise accountability. These reasons include constitutional ambiguity regarding the powers of the president, the prime minister, and the cabinet. The political composition of the first PLC (70 percent of its members are from Fateh) has facilitated the executive's attempts to ignore the legislature, while the composition of the second PLC (about 56 percent of its members come from the Islamist Hamas) may similarly reduce its effectiveness.

For a long time, there have been two judicial systems, one in the West Bank and one in Gaza. Each was organized according to its own legal framework. Serious differences existed between the two, and the PA made few unification efforts during the first eight years of its existence. The Law of the Judiciary was signed by the president in 2002, but significant impediments continue to prevent the coordination of functions between the ministry of justice, the Attorney General's Office, and the Supreme Judicial Council. The performance of the court system is very weak. There are serious shortages of courts, judges, bailiffs, clerks, and equipment. The congestion and overload of casework have led to the deterioration of the whole system and have made administrative intervention in court work possible. Decisions of the regular courts have not always been implemented. Indeed, in most security and political cases, decisions have been ignored and the judges who issued them sometimes dismissed. Security services resorted to intimidating judges in order to prevent them from examining security cases. Many judges have been demoralized. There is a pattern of clear lack of cooperation between courts and enforcement agencies, particularly when it comes to political and security related cases.

At the local level, the PA allowed the establishment of councils with limited powers and responsibilities. A ministry of local government was established to oversee the functioning of local councils. The Law of Local Authorities mandated the election of these councils, but the PA executive prevented elections for local councils and ensured that laws adopted by the PLC deprived them of the ability to determine local policy or to secure the needed resources to be able to effectively deliver services. It was not until December 2004/January 2005 that the PA finally allowed a first round of local elections to take place in thirty-six out of about four hundred local councils. A second round of local elections took place for eighty-four councils in May 2005, a third round for about one hundred councils in September, and a fourth round for about forty councils in December. No final date has been set for the final and most important round, which involves elections for the remaining councils (including those for most of the big cities and towns).

The Road to PA Authoritarian Governance

The PA gained electoral legitimacy once a Palestinian parliament was elected in January 1996. Seventy-five percent of eligible voters participated in the election, despite a call by opposition groups for a boycott. However, the PA soon turned into an authoritarian regime and began to lose public confidence. The second intifada changed the domestic balance of power, weakening the ruling party, Fateh, and strengthening Hamas and other Islamists. It also increased the level of public disappointment with the PA's performance in areas of efficiency, democratization, and clean government. Finally, it crystallized a split within the Palestinian nationalist movement, leading to the emergence of a rebellious young guard at the expense of the PLO old guard. The net effect of all three developments, as well as the perceived failure of the peace process, was the decline of the PA's legitimacy in the eyes of the public and increased support for alternative sources of legitimacy. Groups and activities relying on "revolutionary," or Islamist, legitimacy gained public support. Moreover, the return to violence in Palestinian-Israeli relations during the second intifada exacted a social cost from the Palestinians. The rise of Hamas, a conservative faction with a socio-political agenda, has been one of the consequences of the militarization of the intifada. In addition to a collapsing peace process and deteriorating economic and living conditions, other factors have also caused the diminishing support for Arafat and Fateh. The Palestinian public has been highly disappointed and disillusioned by the perceived failure of the process of national reconstruction and good governance. Over the years, the evaluation on the street of the status of democracy, PA performance, and levels of corruption has moved from bad to worse.

Three factors led to the state of affairs described above: (1) the nature of the Oslo peace process; (2) the divisions in the nationalist movement between young guard and old guard, along with the exclusion of Islamists from the political process; and (3) the role of the donor countries in turning the PA into what can be called a rentier state.

Governance in the Shadow of the Oslo Framework

The Oslo peace process reflected the dramatic disparity in the power relationship between Palestinians and Israelis. It front-loaded benefits for the Israelis (e.g., a permanent end to Palestinian violence) while back-loading benefits to Palestinians, postponing the resolutions of all the major issues of the conflict, including the issue of Palestinian independence and statehood. Meanwhile, Israel continued to build Jewish settlements in the occupied Palestinian territories. As the weak party, the PLO was forced to accept these conditions even if they were unpopular. To confront dissent at home, the PLO elite, if it wanted to protect the peace process and remain in power, needed to crack down on those opposed to them. Thus, the Oslo context for Palestinian governance was not conducive to the successful promotion of good governance.

The transitional nature of that process, with its limits on Palestinian independence and its emphasis on security for Israelis, imposes many constraints on the ability of the PA to perform the normal functions expected of any sovereign authority. These constraints include lack of control over land and resources, the movement of people and goods, international crossing points, economic policies, foreign relations, and security matters. They also include lack of full jurisdiction over legislation and over Israelis residing in or passing through PA-controlled areas. All of this undermines the judicial system and consequently hurts its ability to secure its independence.

In the early stages of PA development, Israel secured for itself the ability to oppose legislation that it saw as exceeding the powers and responsibilities transferred to the PA or inconsistent with the provisions of the peace agreements. Similarly, according to the transitional agreement, Israel maintains the right to oppose any legislation that it deems to be "inconsistent with the provisions of the Declaration of Principles, this Agreement, or of any other agreement that may be reached between the two sides during the interim period." Such legislation "shall have no effect and shall be void."[2]

The unfinished nature of the peace process produced three additional outcomes that had a significant negative impact on the process of governance:

1   The PLO signed the agreement with Israel, authorizing the creation of the PA. The fact that it was the PLO that signed the peace agreement had far reaching consequences for state building. It was the PLO, not just the peace agreements, that shaped the PA and that conferred legitimacy upon it. That legitimacy implied that the PA would be required to govern not only along the lines delineated in the peace agreements and existing constitutional and legal bases but also in ways that would not represent a fundamental departure from PLO norms and practices. The potential tension between the imperatives of the two sources of legitimacy always remained a source of irritation and discord among Palestinians as they embarked on the process of national reconstruction with the aim of achieving a successful transition to good governance and a system of law and justice.

    The continued PLO role has been essential for the peace process, but it has led to a PLO-PA duality, with negative effects on the process of creating effective and viable public institutions and the promotion of good governance. One of the most consequential steps has been the decision to maintain the existence of the PLO semi-state institutions and functions even as Palestinians have been engaged in a process of building similar PA institutions. The continued existence of the PLO provides Palestinians with a mechanism to maintain their institutional national existence even if the peace process collapses or fails to reach its goal – the establishment of a Palestinian state. The most serious outcome of this decision has been the development of what one may call a PLO-PA duality.

For decades, Palestinians, under the PLO umbrella, have built an extensive network of political, military, and socioeconomic institutions. Though not elected, the Palestine National Council – at times, the Palestine Central Council – has served as a parliament in exile, while the PLO Executive Committee has served as the executive. For over thirty years, Arafat served as the chairman of the PLO executive. Many other PLO institutions provided services to Palestinians under occupation before they came under the jurisdiction of the PA. Today both PA and PLO institutions operate within the same territories. At times, especially when constitutional and legal ambiguity prevailed in the West Bank and Gaza, it has not been easy to clearly define the boundaries and mandates of the two Palestinian governing bodies. This has given rise to problems in major areas of governance (including accountability, the rule of law, and constitutionalism) as PLO or non-PA institutions began to make decisions that had a fundamental impact on Palestinians without subjecting themselves to political accountability or due process of law. Sometimes this has hampered the process of institution building by fostering rivalries between PA and PLO institutions with similar mandates. Given the outcome of the 2006 parliamentary elections, the Fateh-controlled PLO seems to be on a collision course with the Hamas-led government. With Hamas refusing to recognize the authority or supremacy of the PLO or the agreements signed by it, the entire process of peacemaking, let alone state building, may come into question.

PLO-PA duality may have fuelled other problems as well, including a lack of transparency in some PA institutions, as the PLO needed to continue to fund its institutions using undisclosed PA resources. The diminished accountability in PA and PLO institutions not only weakened the process of institution building but also led to widespread corruption.

2   The open-ended nature of the Oslo framework affected the Palestinian hierarchy of priorities by justifying a continued emphasis on a national political agenda and economic progress rather than on issues of democratic governance. The need for a stronger and more consolidated process of institution building loses its urgency while Israeli military occupation is still dominating Palestinian life. Continued occupation affects the ordering of the hierarchy of priorities for most Palestinians, thus promoting issues like the completion of the peace process and securing economic development, even if they come at the expense of good governance. For a long time, grassroots demands for stronger institution building and a transition to democracy has remained weak and hesitant.

The primacy of security in this initial phase of the peace process further marginalized the judiciary as security considerations took precedence over the requirements of institution building or the need to respect human rights and the rule of law. The PA executive, without any basis in law, significantly curtailed the jurisdiction of the Attorney General's Office in order to keep security prisoners in PA jails. The executive has routinely ignored the High Court's decisions dealing with security detainees. Furthermore, in the early stages of the peace process, requirements of national reconstruction led to a focus on strengthening the capacity of the central government and its security forces. Little attention was given to the impact of such policies on the rational allocation of resources and the transition to democracy. In particular, some abuse of human rights was tolerated when it was seen as contributing to the success of the peace process.

3   Political and security-motivated Israeli policies greatly constrain the process of institution building. Freezing monthly revenue transfers to the PA in 2001-2 and again in early 2006, the reoccupation of Palestinian cities in the West Bank since March 2003, the partial severance of links between the West Bank and Gaza during most of the period of the peace process, continued closures and sieges of cities and towns during the second intifada, the restriction of the movement of Palestinians, and denial of access to certain areas – all of these phenomena have a negative impact on the performance of PA institutions. The partial severance of geographic links between the West Bank and Gaza led to a waste of resources and a lack of coordination, forcing PA institutions to create redundant offices and to hire more staff than needed. Ministries opened main offices in the two areas and face the daunting task of coordinating them. Palestinian private investment also dropped significantly after Israel began to impose closures in the aftermath of violent attacks against Israelis, particularly during the last four years. Likewise, the Israeli policy of denying PA access to areas still under occupation, those known as "C areas," prevents the effective implementation of infrastructure and other development projects.

Palestinian Divisions

The peace process created a political system that rewarded Palestinian nationalists while marginalizing the Islamists who, at that time, had the support of almost one-third of Palestinians. The Islamists, who had a widespread network of social, economic, and political organizations and activities, were excluded from political participation. For them, the process was illegitimate to begin with because, in their view, it made uncalled for concessions to the Israelis. The Islamists therefore never agreed to the cessation of violence against the Israelis and, indeed, continued to engage in it on a sporadic basis throughout the period between 1993 and 2000.

Moreover, linking the 1996 Palestinian national elections to the peace process and the selection of a majoritarian electoral system, rather than to the more popular proportional representation system, was part of the nationalists' strategy to exclude the Islamists from the political process. However, by excluding the Islamist groups, the new political system succeeded in ensuring that Islamists perceived it as illegitimate. When large-scale violence finally erupted around the end of 2000, Islamist militias created a state within a state. This led to serious deterioration and, eventually, to the almost total collapse of law and order. By January 2006, the Islamists managed to emerge as the most popular political factions among Palestinians in the Gaza Strip, winning 44 percent of the popular vote in the parliamentary elections and 59 percent of the seats. By contrast, Fateh won 41 percent of the popular vote and only 34 percent of the seats. Four other nationalist-secularist groups won 15 percent of the popular vote. The Islamists did very well in the local elections that took place throughout 2005, winning 34 percent of the popular vote to Fateh's 37 percent. Other groups and candidates won 28 percent.

To make things worse, the new political system created by the peace process relied almost exclusively on old guard nationalists, the founding fathers of the nationalist movement, who lived most of their lives in the diaspora and who signed the peace agreement with Israel. The old guard derived its legitimacy from the legacy of the PLO as well as from the Oslo Agreement and its outcome. Its also derived power from its control over the financial resources of the PLO and the PA, the diplomatic recognition accorded it by the international community, and the control it exercised over the main bodies and institutions of the PLO and the PA, including the bureaucracy and the security services (Shikaki 2002).

While the old and the young guards shared common views regarding the basic components of the peace process, agreeing on the two-state solution, they have fundamental disagreements over issues of governance. Leaders of the old guard quickly proved that they were not democrats, having become accustomed in the diaspora to an Arab political culture that encouraged authoritarianism. The secretive nature of the Palestinian resistance movement before the start of the peace process did not encourage openness, transparency, or respect for the rule of law. Public perceptions of PA corruption and lack of democracy worsened during the years of the peace process. Young guard nationalists who led the first intifada felt deprived of the fruits of their victory as they were quietly marginalized by the new authoritarian political system.

The old guard sought to exclude members of the young guard from senior PA positions and went further by deliberately aiming to weaken civil society organizations and marginalize local government, the two primary homes of the young guard. While the first Palestinian intifada in the second half of 1980 intensified Palestinian grassroots and civil society efforts to deal with societal needs in the face of a harsher and more brutal Israeli military occupation, the old guard, empowered by the peace process, sought to undermine organized civil society. A large number of NGOs established in the 1980s gave the young guard the means to rely on decentralized and pluralistic networks that sought to encourage self-help and to deliver services while encouraging Palestinians to disengage from Israeli military institutions. Tensions at times emerged between local young nationalists and old guard leaders in the diaspora over decision making, with the younger activists seeking a more decentralized system of government and the PLO seeking to maintain tight centralized control. After the establishment of the PA, these NGOs fought, with limited success, to defend freedom of expression, freedom of association, political pluralism, and decentralization of authority. Soon, however, many of the NGOs were incorporated into or lost their best staff to the PA. At the urging of the old guard, international donors that, in the past, had supported the NGOs diverted their resources to the PA, forcing many NGOs to scale down their activities or close down. Moreover, the old guard's disregard for local government and its concerns and needs became endemic as the central government eventually appointed all local councils and their heads and made them subordinate to the minister of local government. In sum, the old guard sought to centralize authority, while the young guard sought to attain a more diffused and decentralized power structure – one that would empower grassroots organizations (a legacy of the first Palestinian intifada, which had been led by the young guard).

The second intifada provided the angry young Palestinians with the opportunity to gain primacy in Palestinian politics, weakening the control of the old guard over the domestic political system and significantly reducing the room it had to manoeuvre with regard to its peace-related contacts with Israel and the international community. The old guard's failure to build strong public institutions, to deliver clean and good governance, or to end the Israeli occupation through negotiations provided fertile ground for the emergence of the young guard. The young militants wanted to emulate Lebanese Hezbollah methods by forcing the Israelis to unilaterally withdraw from the occupied Palestinian territories just as they had been forced to withdraw from South Lebanon. Resorting to violence against the Israelis gave the young nationalists popular legitimacy to carry arms and to form militias and, thereby, to intensify their fight against the old guard. To improve their position vis-à-vis old guard, young guard militants sought an alliance with the Islamists. However, they also sided with refugees and the poor in the inner cities rather than with the wealthy and more established urban commercial class. The resulting empowerment of the Islamists and the neglected and deprived groups helped sustain the armed intifada despite the tremendous costs it exacted from the Palestinian middle class. Tensions between the young and old guards exploded in open clashes during the July 2004 turmoil.

The death of Arafat deepened the divisions among the nationalists and emboldened the Islamists. The young guard saw it as an opportunity to take power away from the old guard. Marwan Barghouti, their most recognized leader, almost ran against Mahmud Abbas, the official candidate of Fateh, for the office of the presidency. The election of Abbas as president of the PA in January 2005 took place only after he and other members of the old guard agreed to hold the Fateh Sixth Convention, a meeting that the old guard had delayed for sixteen years. The young guard hoped to use the occasion to gain control of Fateh's institutions and decision-making authority. Without Arafat, the Palestinian political system became more open, and Hamas now actively sought to be integrated into it. However, when Hamas won the elections in January 2006, the divided Fateh, at the strong urging of the international community, refused to join a national unity government – one that would have given a strong impetus to peacebuilding.

Donors

The role of the international community in Palestinian peacebuilding has been enormous. It contributed to peacemaking, funded significant components of PA activities, and sought to influence Palestinian governance and peace policies. The outcome has been mixed. In the critical period of PA formation in the mid-1990s, donor support helped the Palestinians conduct their first elections, start the process of economic development and reconstruction of basic infrastructure, build public institutions, and improve service delivery. However, the international role did not always meet the expectations of the Palestinians, either in protecting them against Israeli occupation policies or in providing assistance in the transition to democratic governance and sound economic development. In that early period, the donor-driven development agenda was set, giving primacy to war termination even if it came at the expense of long-term good governance. Indeed, donors' policies aimed at promoting peace led to entrenchment of authoritarianism, tolerance of corruption, and absence of good governance. Even when the international community compromised its position on good governance and gave priority to war termination, with its emphasis on security considerations, the goal of ending violence was not fully achieved. Palestinians were also frustrated with international ineffectiveness in forcing Israel to end its occupation of Palestinian territories or even freeze the building of Jewish settlements in occupied Palestinian land. When Palestinians finally managed to hold democratic elections in January 2006, the international community, seeking to isolate Hamas, "rewarded" them by cutting off most donor aid, making its resumption contingent upon the Hamas government's compliance with peace-related conditions. To most Palestinians, the behaviour of the donor countries is proof that the commitment of the international community to Palestinian democracy is hypocritical.

International assistance has had a major impact on the development of all branches of the Palestinian government. The PA initially lacked the ability to determine long-term needs and to prioritize short- and medium-term objectives. In such a situation, programs were partly or largely donor-driven. By providing funds to the PA, donors sought to support the peace process. These funds helped improve Palestinian living conditions, providing peace dividends and, thus, increasing Palestinian support for the peace process. Donors were interested in supporting a *successful* peace process, and this required strengthening the PA so that it could meet its commitments to the donors and to Israel. Donors were not interested in wasting money on an unsuccessful peace process. Thus, while Palestinians prioritized such issues as combating settlement expansion, protecting their interests in Jerusalem, and developing areas still occupied by Israel, donors refrained from supporting such issues because they did not want a clash with Israel. Donors also steered away from problematic areas or areas that lacked the capacity to shop for funding (e.g., the agricultural sector), thus compounding their weakness. As a result, some institutions became stronger than others, even when this was incompatible with or even contradictory to Palestinian needs. In some cases, different donors supported competing institutions, thus reinforcing institutional fragmentation. When, in January 2006, the Palestinians elected a government that refused to recognize Israel or the Oslo peace process, donors were quick to terminate aid.

During the years of the second intifada, the international community went beyond its previous commitment by directly supporting the Palestinian budget, an action it doggedly refused to take previously (with the exception of the establishment phase of the PA in the first two years of the peace process) due to domestic pressure at home, mostly related to concerns about PA corruption. This direct financial support went to pay a large portion of public sector salaries. In doing this, the international community sought to prevent the collapse of the public sector and a probable serious escalation in violence, which may have led to a much more expensive international military intervention. Moreover, the intifada added to the PA's loss of control over law and order, threatening to turn it into a dysfunctional authority and, indeed, a "failed state." Fearing being blamed for this outcome, the international community sought to continue to provide support in order to prevent the total collapse of the PA, even if this meant what some Palestinians saw as subsidizing continued Israeli occupation.

During the years of the peace process, efforts on the part of the international community to save the PA through direct aid did little to help the Palestinian economy. The outcome of international aid efforts a decade later, after more than US$6 billion had been spent in development aid, is at best disappointing. Take, for example, the period of the intifada, which witnessed the doubling of donors' annual disbursements to almost US$1 billion per year. This amounted to over US$300 per person per year, itself a record in the history of foreign aid. Yet, at the same time, as the World Bank records show, in real terms Palestinian personal incomes contracted by almost 40 percent. Indeed, the skewed Palestinian trade structure with Israel meant that a large chunk of international aid has benefited the Israeli economy. A July 2003 study by the United Nations Conference on Trade and Development (UNCTAD) shows that the large Palestinian trade deficit with Israel in 2002, both as a percentage of the total trade deficit and as a percentage of GDP, caused "some 70 percent of donor funds to pay for Israeli imports" and "some 45 cents of every dollar produced domestically to be channelled to the Israeli economy." Under these circumstances, it is difficult to see how donor funds injected into the Palestinian economy would have a noticeable domestic multiplier effect. "On the contrary," the UNCTAD study concludes, "a positive income multiplier effect of these funds would be felt in the Israeli economy" (UNCTAD 2003; see also UNCTAD 2002, 2005).

The reason for this international failure is political. The political-security environment of peacebuilding was highly destructive. The international community understood this but was unable or unwilling to do much to change it. As the representative of the World Bank in the West Bank and the Gaza Strip, Nigel Roberts, stated in April 2005, "donor developmental assistance can only bring sustainable growth if the policy environment changes first" (Roberts and Mocci 2005). The World Bank highlighted Israeli closure policy as a fundamental impediment to Palestinian growth. In light of the Israeli disengagement plan, the World Bank (2004b) concluded that, if the closure regime remained in place, no amount of aid would have an impact. Palestinians, however, believe that, without serious international pressure and, indeed, direct intervention, Israel is not likely to make any changes to its closure policy. Palestinians believe that Israel prefers to see them receiving just enough international handouts to keep the lid on the pressure cooker and to keep the PA functioning.

Palestinians would view positively an international intervention that would address the disparity in the power relationship between them and the State of Israel. The divisions among the main actors in the international community, which led to their inability to force Israel to end its occupation of Palestinian areas and to cease those activities that violate international law (such as the annexation of Arab East Jerusalem and the building of settlements in occupied territories), has been a major source of

Palestinian frustration. At times, particularly during the years of intifada, Palestinians presented the role of the international community as one of defending the Palestinian territories against Israeli occupation policies, considering this to be part of the international responsibility to protect people under occupation.

Palestinians have seen international intervention to end the Iraqi occupation of Kuwait and in places like Rwanda, Bosnia, Kosovo, and East Timor. And they believe that the international community, due to US dominance of the international political system, has sided with the occupying power in its violations of international norms and laws. With regard to their conflict with Israel, Palestinians want the international community to help them consolidate their international legitimacy and to implement international law. While showing interest in playing a larger role, the international community has been reluctant to take on a security role because it does not want to get entangled in a violent conflict, particularly when the United States is seeking to dampen international enthusiasm for this. Israel sees such a role as constraining its room to manoeuvre, particularly in the security realm.

In its 2001 report on the "Responsibility to Protect," the International Commission on Intervention and State Sovereignty made it difficult for Palestinians to achieve this kind of intervention since it required evidence of massive human rights violations, such as genocide or ethnic cleansing, not to mention the explicit authorization by the UN Security Council. This makes it extremely difficult for Palestinians to advance their case. Instead, the international community prefers, as in the case of the Road Map, to follow the examples of the early post-Cold War period, in which it sought to navigate an internationally negotiated solution to the Palestinian-Israeli conflict. While the Road Map provides for a larger international role than has so far been possible in Palestinian-Israeli peacemaking, it pays little attention to the root causes of the conflict and ignores lessons learned in other cases. For example, it ignores the need to integrate armed groups into the political process by making their disarmament a precondition for any further progress towards domestic reform (e.g., elections) or peacemaking (such as Israel's return to pre-intifada lines or a freeze on settlement construction). Yet, it is now clear that even this "soft" international approach was unacceptable to Israel and, thus, to the United States. The international community failed to apply pressure on Israel to implement its commitments under the Road Map, even after the death of Arafat and the election of a new Palestinian president who was committed to ending the violent conflict.

Similarly, the international community failed to pressure the PA to build an open and democratic political system. While on paper donors sought to encourage good governance, in reality this came second to the goal of advancing the peace process. Donor support for the process of democratization involved support for the first Palestinian general elections, support for local elections, support for the PLC, support for NGOs, support for public administration reform, support for the rule of law and the judiciary, the training of judges, financial reform, and so on. These efforts, however, were not sufficient to hinder the consolidation of authoritarianism. One of the reasons for this failure is the dilemma facing the international community, which had to choose between the requirements of the peace process and the needs of good governance.

The 2001 Responsibility to Protect report, with its emphasis on the need to take into account long-term conflict prevention needs, came too late for the Palestinians. During the early years of the peace process in the early and mid-1990s, the international community was entertaining different political concepts regarding governance and the peace process. Perhaps the most important of these involved the belief that security is the cornerstone of Israeli-Palestinian peace. This belief led to the widespread assumption that all can be sacrificed for the sake of promoting security, including justice and democracy for the Palestinians. With international acquiescence, primacy was given to Israeli security interests. Israeli security imperatives, which clashed with the needs of good governance and economic development, required the creation of a state not much different from a police state.

A second prevailing concept is the view that strong government is an essential component of stability in a post-conflict society. This concept affected the behaviour of donors. As indicated earlier, by providing funds to the PA, donors sought to support the peace process. By strengthening the PA, donors aimed at providing it with the capacity to implement its commitments under the peace agreements. At one point, this policy meant shifting resources away from civil society organizations to the PA.

A third concept is the belief that democracy cannot survive the challenge of political Islam. Donors were happy to see Islamists, such as Hamas and Islamic Jihad, excluded from the political process. Many in the international community feared that democracy and the rule of law for Palestinians might bring about a victory for Hamas. Election results for student and professional associations, which showed impressive victories for the Islamists, heightened this fear, despite the fact that the Islamists had lost half of their support: as documented by numerous Palestinian public opinion polls, it was down to less than 20 percent during the more successful period of the peace process (between 1995 and 2000). Essentially, the success of Hamas in the January 2006 elections was due to the failure of the processes of peacemaking and state building, and this included the old guard's early exclusion of the Islamists.

Moreover, international financial support distorted the Palestinian political economy, leading the PA to pay more attention to outside pressure and less to the concerns and needs of its constituency. A disproportionate percentage of PA budget revenues came from international donors. Moreover, an important part of the PA budget came from revenue transfers that came from taxes and customs duties that Israel collected on Palestinian-imported goods passing through Israeli ports. Israel has occasionally suspended such transfers in its efforts to restructure PA motivation and to change its policies. Instead of relying on Palestinian society for budgetary revenues, the PA grew accustomed to receiving, from outside sources, an average of $500 million annually between 1995 and 2000 and more than that since the eruption of the intifada. During the last ten years, the percentage of donor- and Israeli-transferred money averaged 70 percent to 80 percent of the PA annual budget.

The reliance on outside sources and the mostly one-way flow of resources from the PA to Palestinian society weakens the ability of Palestinians to make demands on the PA. This condition has also probably contributed to the weakening of PA institutions because it leads to a lack of accountability and encourages authoritarianism. It may have also encouraged the depoliticization of a large segment of the Palestinian public. The Palestinian Center for Policy and Survey Research (PSR) public opinion polls indicate that the percentage of those who consider themselves non-affiliated with any Palestinian political faction has multiplied several times, from 9 percent in 1993 to more than 40 percent in 2000. This structure of the Palestinian political economy may have also contributed to the PA's tendency to avoid a decentralized local government.

Towards Good Governance

In order for Palestinian peacebuilding to succeed, the system of government must be reformed. Reform should involve: (1) strengthening public institutions, (2) respecting the outcome of the January 2006 parliamentary elections and establishing a national unity government, and (3) empowering local government. The January 2006 elections represented the most successful Palestinian effort towards good governance since the first elections in January 1996. It goes without saying, however, that the election of a Hamas government will not make the task of governance easy. More seriously, the response to the Hamas victory on the part of Fateh, Israel, and the international community – all of whom are seeking to isolate the new government and are rejecting calls for a nationalist-Islamist coalition – could deliver a pre-emptive blow to the whole process of peacebuilding.

Reforming the PA

Demands for the reform of the PA, which started almost immediately after its establishment but, by 2006, had still met with little success, led to the electoral victory of Hamas. Failure to carry out serious reform altered the domestic Palestinian political landscape in ways that ultimately gave increased weight, and indeed a parliamentary majority, to Islamists, who adopted substantially different attitudes and policies towards peacemaking and state building than did the PA.

The first warning signs came during the Israeli March 2002 reoccupation of Palestinian cities, when the PA failed to deliver any services whatsoever, thus provoking internal Palestinian debate on the immediate need for fundamental political reform. Overwhelming public demand was coupled with urgent requests from the PLC and the Fateh Revolutionary Council. A fully detailed reform program emerged, receiving an almost unanimous Palestinian consensus. The international community jumped on the bandwagon with its own list of reform demands. After some hesitation, President Arafat grudgingly conceded. Some constitutional and institutional reforms were approved, and a date for national elections was set.

The framing of reform in terms of regime change, as adopted by the Bush administration in 2002, and the prevailing perception that the United States was seeking to impose reform as a precondition for peace, constituted a slap in the face to the reformers, who took risks by advocating good governance. The internally driven but externally supported reform campaign began to lose steam. Before it was temporarily halted, the May-June 2002 reform campaign did manage to bring about important changes. The temporary constitution, the Basic Law, and the Law of the Judiciary were finally signed by the president, after having been frozen by him for several years. A reformist finance minister, Salam Fayyad, was appointed, and this quickly led to substantial progress with regard to placing PA expenditures and revenues under the control of the Ministry of Finance. But reforms in the public security and the judiciary sectors were short-lived and remained cosmetic. Efforts to push for national elections were abandoned as Israel adamantly refused to consider withdrawing its forces from Palestinian cities, thus providing the old guard with a good reason to shelve the issue.

However, by early 2003, the Palestinian reform movement gained significant impetus from international support for constitutional reform, and this led to the creation of the office of prime minister. With an overwhelming majority, in March 2003 the Legislative Council introduced amendments to the Basic Law (creating the office of prime minister) and, in a historic move, relieved the PA presidency of most of its powers and responsibilities – including those related to public finance, civil service, law and order, and internal security – and gave them to the cabinet, which was under the leadership of the prime minister. Soon after, Mahmud Abbas (Abu Mazin), the most senior old guard Arafat associate, received a parliamentary vote of confidence – a vote that was supported by both old and young guard members.

This constitutional change in the Palestinian political system was followed by serious efforts on the part of the Abbas government to institutionalize the reform process. Reforms in the judicial system and public administration were encouraged. For example, security courts were abolished, and the Supreme Judicial Council was appointed in accordance with the Judiciary Law. Several PA authorities and agencies that nominally reported to Arafat were integrated into the government and, hence, brought under its jurisdiction. Public finance witnessed major improvements, including better control over public investments and the salaries of some security services.

Yet this, too, did not work. The Quartet Road Map envisaged an empowered prime minister as being the shortest way to restore the lost credibility of the Palestinian leadership. The hope was that this would lead to more political reforms, to a reduction in the level of mutual violence, and to the resumption of peace negotiations whose purpose was to put an end to the Israeli occupation. In this sense, this step was the most critical the Road Map had to offer. However, Abbas was forced to resign a few months after assuming office as Arafat managed to find ways to undermine his authority and to effectively deprive him of his constitutional powers.

Before his death, Arafat had failed to reform the political system, which remained corrupt and authoritarian. With his death in November 2004, a window of opportunity was opened. The changed political-security context in the post-Arafat era changed the calculations of the main actors with regard to Palestinian reform. Local elections became possible and were followed by presidential elections. Parliamentary elections, first scheduled for July 2005, took place in January 2006. The emergence of Abbas – a man who, in the past, had expressed support for far-reaching political reform – as the chairman of the PLO and his election as president of the PA was another result of this new environment. Basically, the death of Arafat weakened the influence of the old guard in the political system.

While these internal dynamics provided a more hospitable environment for reform, serious difficulties remained and prevented other reforms before the January 2006 elections. The need to contain public sector employment (if not reduce it) and to significantly reduce the salary bill for the PA may have contradicted President Abbas' political need to ensure Fateh loyalty, to co-opt the public sector, and, in general, to encourage people to vote for Fateh rather than for Hamas. The need for security sector, electoral, and ministerial reform was already being resisted by those within the security and political establishments who had a vested interest in the status quo and whose support was necessary if the new president was to achieve his immediate political and security objectives. Moreover, forces opposed to reform were quick to frame some of its aspects (e.g., its anti-corruption elements) as conflicting with security needs because they were likely to target senior security officials. Posing such a false "security dilemma" might have deterred the new leadership from embarking on far-reaching reforms in the security services. Moreover, reforms, particularly those that were likely to empower the young guards (e.g., internal Fateh primaries), angered the old guard, which opposed them. Senior bureaucratic and security officials, wishing to protect their own personal privileges, resisted any significant changes in their institutions. But without all these reforms, conditions on the ground continued to deteriorate, with Fateh's fragmentation leading to the public becoming even more convinced of its responsibility for PA corruption and the lawlessness that prevailed throughout 2005.

Externally, it was not self-evident that the international community sought genuine and deep-seated reform in the PA, not even in the security sector. This was especially true with regard to the United States and Israel. While, in June 2002, US president Bush made the issue of Palestinian reform and democratization a sine qua non for the peace process, it seemed that reform of the security sector was not intended to go much deeper than the cessation of violence and decisive action against terrorism. The Quartet's work plan did not deal with security sector reform as an integral part of overall PA reform and, indeed, allocated it the least attention and resources. Not surprisingly, then, security is the area in which the least reform has taken place.

One year of Hamas rule made conditions worse. Efforts by the Islamist group to control the security services and civil bureaucracy were met with resistance from Fateh and a major public sector strike. Yet, the formation of the national unity government in March 2007 provides a better environment for political reform than had existed before. Given the internal and external dangers confronting the PA, the following reform areas should top its priorities:

1 *Security sector reform.* Security conditions remain fragile as the Palestinian security services lack the capacity to enforce law and order or to maintain the current limited ceasefire. Reforms in the security sector will allow for a more optimal means of rebuilding the security services. Rebuilding these services before instituting fundamental reforms may be a waste of time, effort, and resources. The main goal of the security reforms should be the unification of the security forces into three services under the control of the interior ministry and the cabinet. As the Basic Law states, the cabinet should be the sole body in charge of setting the PA's security policy. In the past, the so-called National Security Council proved highly ineffective and redundant. This reform measure would allow for civilian control over security and for legislative oversight. A clear chain of command, with explicit mission statements for the three

services, would allow for more effective functioning. Currently, the PLC is considering several proposed laws dealing with PA security services that contain several major contradictions. The cabinet should immediately present the PLC with proposed legislation that would unify all proposals and incorporate the elements mentioned above.

2 *Corruption and the rule of law.* The outcome of local and national elections demonstrates the top priority that the public has given to corruption and the extent to which it has lost confidence in the ability of the nationalists in the PA to fight it. Now under the control of Islamists, the PA needs to embark on an immediate anti-corruption campaign. Efforts in this area must integrate legal reforms along with reforms in the judiciary, law enforcement agencies, and the Office of the Controller General. Restoring confidence in the PA through the enforcement of the rule of law should be the main goal of reform in this area. To achieve this, the following steps should be implemented as soon as possible: (a) The Office of the Attorney General should be strengthened by providing it with sufficient budget and professional staff. The office must function independently of politicians and security services and must have a clear and sufficient mandate to examine, in a timely manner, all cases of corruption and other serious violations of the law. (b) The PA must also reorganize the police and ensure that its head works closely with the attorney general and the courts to implement all decisions made by those institutions. (c) Similarly, the controller general should be empowered, and his office should be made accountable to the PLC, not just to the president. The office should make public and submit to the PLC all annual audit reports that have previously been presented to the office of the president. (d) The PLC should allocate sufficient funds to allow for the smooth and effective functioning of the three institutions mentioned above. (e) Finally, the Law of the Judiciary should be amended to ensure the independence of the judiciary, while assuring a smooth functioning relationship with the Ministry of Justice.

3 *Changing the electoral system.* After several false starts, in late 2005 the PLC managed to amend the electoral system, thus allowing parliamentary elections the following January. The Parliament adopted a mixed proportional representation-majority system as opposed to the previous purely district-based majority system. This system is sometime called a "plurality multi-member district system," or a "block vote." In this system, voters have as many votes as there are seats to be filled in their districts and the highest-polling candidates fill the positions, regardless of the percentage of the vote they achieve; a majority is not required. The advantage of this system is that it allows voters to vote for those

individual candidates whom they trust. It also allows for a fair representation of the different districts in the country. Political parties play a
significant role in this system, allowing for the gradual emergence of a
credible party system. Parties that are disciplined can do better than can
those that are fragmented and incoherent.

However, this tends to exaggerate the smallest advantage one party
might have over others by giving it disproportionately more seats than
it deserves based on the popular vote. Given the tendency of voters to
select all or most district candidates who belong to the same list they
have voted for in the national vote, the system generously rewards any
faction that has the slightest edge over the other factions in any given
district. While Hamas won only 44 percent of the popular vote, it was
able to win 59 percent of the seats. A fully proportional representation
system would provide the best opportunity for all factions to gain fair
representation in the legislature. This amendment is likely to provide
Palestinians an opportunity to open the political system further, to encourage a genuinely inclusive process, and, thereby, to allow the integration of all forces and to give the political system a significant increase
in legitimacy and credibility.

Respect the Outcome of Elections and Support a Nationalist-Islamist Coalition

The holding of parliamentary elections in January 2006 started a genuine
process of democratization. While Hamas sought to establish a national
unity government based on a nationalist-Islamist coalition, Fateh hesitated
for a year before agreeing to join the coalition, partly as a result of international pressures. The international community responded to the Hamas victory with grave concerns about the domestic and peace-related implications.
To keep its economic and financial support and to remain politically engaged with the Hamas-led PA, the Quartet was quick to articulate its conditions. It demanded that Hamas must recognize Israel, renounce violence
and dismantle its militia, and observe existing peace commitments and
obligations undertaken by the PA and the PLO during the years of the peace
process since 1993. Even after the formation of the national unity government in March 2007, the donor community refused to end its financial
sanctions, although it did ease the diplomatic boycott.

The holding of elections in the Palestinian territories has helped to achieve
four objectives. First, elections have renewed the PA's legitimacy and provided it with the opportunity to project leadership at a time when its unity
of representation, and indeed its mere existence, was at stake. Second, elections have provided Hamas and the nationalist warlords with the opportunity to capitalize on their popularity, gained during the intifada, and translate

it into parliamentary seats. Third, if the election outcome is respected, elections could provide Palestinians the means of finding their way back to democratic governance. No single person, no matter how authoritarian, would again be able to concentrate so much power in his or her hands. Finally, an Islamist-nationalist coalition could help Palestinians deal effectively with the challenges of the processes of peace and state building by helping to moderate Hamas peace policies and to consolidate the democratic transition.

However, current efforts by Fateh to transfer powers and jurisdiction from the cabinet and Parliament to the Office of the President, which it controls, undermine the credibility of the elections. Such efforts cover areas such as public finance, security, international crossings, the judiciary, and legislation. Similarly, the international boycott of Hamas (and, later, the national unity government) and the termination of financial support show a total disregard for the will of the people who exercised their democratic right to vote in fair elections funded and supervised by the international community.

Reforming Local Government
During the last six years, due to internal weaknesses and Israeli coercion, the capacity of PA institutions to deliver basic services to Palestinian society gradually diminished. Many people turned to local councils for help. But the councils, appointed and controlled by the PA Ministry of Local Government, lacked the capacity and the legitimacy needed to be able to respond to local constituencies (see Bush 2004 for details of a Rafah case study).

Three problems in particular hindered the attempts of Palestinian local councils to play a more active support role during this period of extreme need. First, the PA tendency during these years was to centralize authority, exercising higher levels of control over local revenue generation, administrative affairs, and budgeting. Second, local councils suffer from a long history of weak fiscal, organizational, and management capacity. This weakness has been exacerbated by a lack of accountability and oversight. Third, local councils lacked legitimacy in the eyes of the public, which hindered their ability to take measures and to make decisions that might affect people's lives. Until 2005, the last time elections were held for almost all cities and towns was in 1976. As a result, public participation in local government activities has been very limited.

Strengthening local government is an essential step towards reforming Palestinian governance. PSR fieldwork and meetings with elected and appointed heads of local councils have indicated several bleak areas that must be addressed: a dismal relationship between local councils and the PA as well as serious financial and administrative difficulties within local councils. Empowering local councils serves several peacebuilding purposes, and it is essential to the political system's becoming more legitimate, inclusive, and responsive to the needs of its constituencies. It would also help to promote the empowerment of women as well as to enable local councils to play a role in local conflict management.

PSR fieldwork research found three major difficulties with regard to the work of local councils:

1   *Relationship with the PA.* Council members complain that the existing law limits their authority at a time when public expectations are high, given the weakness of the central government. Moreover, they complain that officials from the Ministry of Local Government are interfering in their affairs. These officials are perceived to be violating existing laws, thus further restricting the little authority local councils have. Municipal courts are unable to operate effectively due to a lack of judges. Local councils lack an enforcement mechanism to use against those who refuse to pay local fines or taxes, and they complain that the law enforcement agencies show little interest in enforcing court or council decisions regarding building codes and violations of other regulations.

2   *Revenues.* Almost all local councils suffer from financial difficulties. Deficits are chronic, threatening to eliminate the ability of the councils to engage in any serious developmental plans. Most are in debt as they are unable to pay for their electric and water bills, which are owed mostly to Israeli suppliers. Residents also avoid paying their utility bills because of increased poverty or because they know that local councils lack either the capacity or will to disconnect such basic services or force residents to pay them. The PA itself contributes to this problem as it often delays payment of taxes and fees it collects from citizens on behalf of local councils. Over the years, the PA-appointed local councils made their financial situation even worse by increasing their salary payments, which, in many local councils, have now reached about 70 percent of the budget. But perhaps most important, the ability of the councils to find new revenue sources is highly constrained by law and by the devastating economic conditions over the last five years.

3   *Administrative difficulties.* Three major administrative problems plague most Palestinian local councils. Most councils employ twice as many persons as they need. Skyrocketing unemployment during the years of the second intifada forced local councils to provide jobs in an attempt to help reduce the gravity of the unemployment problem. Moreover, it is not uncommon for hiring to be motivated by political or family loyalties. But this also means that most staff and technical teams lack the

necessary academic qualifications and/or practical experience, which, in turn, affects the ability of the councils to deliver efficient services. Finally, local councils tend to lack administrative structures with clear job descriptions and chains of responsibility.

If the system is to become more legitimate and to be more responsive to the needs of its constituency, then it is essential to reform local governance. Yet no serious efforts have so far been made to do that. It is clear that any such reform would have to focus on making local governance more accountable, decentralized, and efficient in the following ways:

1   *Empowerment through legitimacy and accountability.* Elections provide the most effective means of increasing the legitimacy and accountability of local councils. The PA has delayed these elections since 1996. In December 2004, the PA started to conduct local elections. By December 2005, four rounds of elections had taken place, covering a little over half of the local councils. Palestinians have shown greater interest in local elections than in presidential elections, with the turnout in the latter (which were boycotted by Hamas and other Islamists) reaching 45 percent and in the former reaching 68 percent. Female participation in local elections was encouraged when the PLC amended the law, assigning a female quota, whereby at least two women must be elected to each local council. In at least four localities, including Ramallah, a majority of men elected women as mayors. But the victory of Hamas in many of these contests and in the parliamentary elections has created concern that the PA might not be able to hold the final round of local elections. Only by continuing the election process will the local councils be empowered to act in the interest of local constituencies. These elections encourage political participation, empower women, and create greater public confidence in the political system.

The election of about five thousand local government officials (once all rounds are completed) will have an enormous impact on political participation. The experience gained in the election process and in office makes these individuals stronger candidates for public office at the national level and, thereby, increases public participation and competition. More important, in the short run, this development would provide marginalized groups – mostly young guard nationalists, the Islamist opposition, women, and leftist political factions – an opportunity to influence public life and to be integrated into the political system. Due to the traditional nature of Palestinian society, it has been much easier for women to participate in local government activities (including local elections) than in national government activities. It has also been easier for the legislature to mandate a female quota in the local elections than in parliamentary elections. Success of women at the local level will play a role in educating society on the benefits of female participation and make it easier for women to move forcefully into the national arena.

2 *Empowerment through decentralization.* Weak local government does not provide enough attractions, opportunities, and challenges for politically marginalized groups. Strong local government makes it easier to enhance the chances for political development in Palestine as it makes the transition from local to national politics, from local councils to Parliament and ministries, easier and more worthwhile. In other words, the greater the empowerment at the local level, the greater the chances for making the political system more inclusive. And this, in turn, may engender further political development.

Given the legacy of the occupation and the strong political role played by local councils in the absence of representative government, the majority of Palestinians would appreciate the strengthening of local government. Indeed, PSR surveys and fieldwork clearly indicate overwhelming support for greater mandates for local councils.

Decentralization is one of the means of strengthening local councils. To achieve decentralization, it is essential to introduce changes in the legal framework and the functioning of local councils. Significant changes need to be made in three legal documents – the Basic Law, the Law of Local Councils, and the Law of Elections for Local Councils. At the legal-constitutional level, it is proposed that the legislature examine amending the Law of Local Councils to change its underlying philosophy so that it supports creating local government rather than local administration. Such a change would require introducing changes to the Basic Law. Currently, the Basic Law mandates the creation of units for local administration. For its part, the Law of Local Councils envisages a limited role for local councils with regard to managing local life, while giving the central government (in the form of the Ministry for Local Government) greater control over the activities of these councils. The authority of the central government should be reduced, while the authority of local councils should be extended to include wider areas of revenue collection, municipal policing, and socio-political development.

Decentralization must focus on fiscal and administrative issues, both of which are regulated by the existing laws, which are too restrictive. Improved legal, regulatory, and financial frameworks that ensure clear division of responsibilities and accountability must be incorporated into the amended laws. It is also necessary to increase the ability of local councils to generate revenues from internal and external sources in order to attain sustainability. Local councils should aim to carry out functions already assigned to them by the law. So far, due to lack of funding, they have not been able to do this. Finally, the Ministry of Local Government should be encouraged to relax restrictive administrative controls over local councils. These controls currently restrict the ability of the councils to address essential needs, such as budgeting, planning, and hiring.

3   *Improved capacity.* The fiscal, organizational, and management capacity of local councils should be strengthened. In order for the councils to carry out their decentralized responsibilities, their capacities must be improved. This should involve better interaction between local and central government and inter-municipal coordination and cooperation. Improved administrative capacity allows for better service delivery and overall performance. Palestinian town plans have traditionally been based on the needs of the central government rather than on those of the local communities. Improving the technical and financial capacity of local councils would allow them to assume the responsibilities for town planning. While the Ministry of Local Government has prepared more than one hundred town plans in the last several years, many more are needed. Local councils are in a better position to assess that need.

Local councils could help themselves by seeking innovative ways to increase revenues and by encouraging residents to pay their bills. They should resist the temptation to hire more persons than they need, even if this helps their community address short-term problems. In addition to promoting legitimacy by making the system more inclusive and promoting the participation of women, empowered local councils are able to play a role in local conflict management. Councils with representation from all factions have greater ability to mediate differences and to enforce laws within their jurisdictions.

Conclusion

Five main conclusions emerge from this study:

1   Interim agreements that delay the resolution, or at least the development, of clear guidelines for how to resolve core issues of the conflict provide a shaky basis for sustained peacebuilding. While it is unclear whether a comprehensive peace agreement is possible under the current great power disparity, only such an agreement will pave the way for successful peacebuilding – peacebuilding that can terminate war, provide good governance, and lead to a successful Palestinian national reconstruction. A permanent agreement would provide assurances to Palestinians and Israelis regarding their vital long-term rights, needs, and interests (such as

final borders, political sovereignty, demography, and economic resources) and thus pave the way for cooperation in areas pertaining to short-term needs (such as security and war termination). Herein lies a first peace-building predicament. To encourage Palestinian democratization and to deliver greater security, a permanent status deal is essential. Yet, given the existing power disparity and the US tilt in favour of Israel, the international community has now made a permanent agreement (indeed, the mere return of Israel and the Palestinians to bilateral negotiations) contingent upon Palestinians' achieving a significant degree of democratization and security.

2   Focus on short-term security needs contributed to the emergence of authoritarianism in the PA while failing to deliver security. Indeed, the failure of the PA to build strong pubic institutions and to develop an inclusive political system has generated greater internal and external insecurity. Poor governance and increased insecurity contributed to the collapse of law and order in areas controlled by the PA, with de facto power transferred from PA hands to the hands of armed groups and militias. As the Palestinian political system became dysfunctional, the PA looked more and more like a "failed state." Only by making the system open and inclusive (by respecting the outcome of the parliamentary election and supporting a national unity government, continuing with the local elections, and strengthening local government) and by reforming and strengthening Palestinian political and security institutions can the Palestinians succeed in state building and peacemaking. Herein lies a second peacebuilding predicament. The security-first approach leads to greater authoritarianism, which, in turn, leads to less security, while the end of authoritarianism promises less violence. But the ability of the Palestinians to reform their political system is highly dependent on progress in the peace process – a goal that can only be achieved by ensuring security.

3   Efforts by nationalist old guards to exclude young guards and Islamists from the political system have had devastating consequences for peacebuilding. Today, the international community's rejection of the unity government – because Hamas refuses to explicitly accept international conditions – could lead to its collapse. Herein lies a third peacebuilding predicament: given the outcome of Palestinian elections, only an Islamist-nationalist coalition – by providing Islamists with an environment conducive to moderation – can provide the means to sustained peacebuilding. Yet, given the international response to the unity government, it is highly unlikely that such a coalition would be able to survive long enough to allow Hamas to moderate its views.

4   Weak local government deprives Palestinian peacebuilding of a major source of legitimation. Strengthening local government would contribute to reforming national governance. Yet, the current weak political system is unlikely to take the necessary steps to ensure such an undertaking. Herein lies a fourth peacebuilding predicament. While it may seem easier to reform (and hence empower) local government than it is to address the larger issue of sustained national unity and democratic reforms, it is only through the latter that the former can occur.

5   The international community has a critical role to play in helping Palestinians (and Israelis) return to a more meaningful peace process and in building a viable democratic and prosperous Palestinian state – one that is able to deal with the many challenges it is likely to confront, including governance. Yet, so far, the only conceivable international role (given the Israeli-Palestinian power disparity, US dominance of the international system, and the post-9/11 environment) is unlikely to produce such outcomes. To the contrary, at times donors have contributed to Palestinian authoritarianism, refrained from taking effective measures to enforce international norms, and lacked the political will to articulate and promote a permanent status vision – one that does not disregard those international norms. While Palestinians are satisfied with international humanitarian and economic assistance, they are critical of the unwillingness of the international community to protect them against Israeli violence and colonization of the occupied territories. Moreover, one of the unintended outcomes of international economic aid has been the facilitation of continued Israeli occupation while making it more difficult to promote governance that is accountable to Palestinians. And herein lies the fifth and final predicament of peacebuilding. Little progress is possible without solid international intervention. Yet, in the post-Cold War and post-9/11 era, successful Palestinian peacebuilding is likely a mission impossible for the international community.

For peacebuilding in Palestine-Israel to succeed, peace- and state-building efforts should be focused on three objectives:

1   Building a clear political framework, preferably a final status agreement, that clearly meets the parties' vital needs and resolves all the issues of the conflict.
2   Opening the Palestinian political system and making it more inclusive by implementing security and political reforms, respecting the outcome of the January 2006 parliamentary elections, supporting the national unity government, and holding the fifth and most important round of local elections.

3   Empowering local government by allowing elected councils greater autonomy from the central government, holding elections for all local councils, and improving the capacity of these councils to deliver services and to independently generate revenues.

6

Afghanistan: What Kind of Peace? The Role of Rural Development in Peacebuilding

Omar Zakhilwal and Jane Murphy Thomas

Afghanistan is often depicted as being in a postwar situation, but questions remain as to whether this is an accurate description. While peace could be on the horizon, the distance to that horizon is unclear; and, as time goes by, uncertainty grows. What kind of peace is actually possible in Afghanistan? One source refers to the present situation as "conflictual peace" (Suhrke, Harpviken, and Strand 2004). Upon what is sustainable peace conditional?

Peace in Afghanistan is determined and threatened by numerous factors. As this chapter's title suggests, development in rural areas, where most of Afghanistan's citizens live, could perhaps be the most critical issue in determining the future. In many ways, the war in Afghanistan can be attributed to past rural development policies (or lack thereof).

In seeking to best understand the role of rural development in sustainable peacebuilding, we address several key questions: What is the background that led to the present situation, and what implications does this have for today's policy makers? What factors or conditions will determine or threaten peace? What efforts have been made to rebuild the state structures and to create conditions that at least make peace feasible? How does the foreign military presence relate to rural development and peacebuilding? What lessons have been learned elsewhere in rural development and can now be applied in Afghanistan? What lessons can be drawn from Afghanistan's history and its one major rural development program – the National Solidarity Program (NSP) – and applied to the country's broader rural development and peacebuilding efforts?

The situation in Afghanistan illustrates and reinforces a number of the propositions of the WKOP project: notably, that, in order for peace to take hold, it is essential to engage a broader range of stakeholders, especially those historically excluded. The international community must address these groups' legitimate political, socioeconomic, and cultural demands, and it must help to strengthen the Afghan government's capacity for participatory policy making.

We have been involved, as participant observers, in relief and development programs in Afghanistan for twenty years, and we begin this chapter by discussing how past rural development policies, or lack thereof, have fuelled war in that country. We review state building since the fall of the Taliban, consider what kind of peace is possible, and then examine its main determinants. A section that emphasizes participatory rural development and its importance to peacebuilding is followed by an analysis of the country's main effort to bring about this rural participation – the NSP. We then offer some conclusions, recommendations, and a brief look at the future. Information for this chapter was collected through an extensive review of the published and grey literature, participant observation, and field research.

Historical Background

Afghanistan presents a striking example of the connections between rural development, war, and peace. One constant has been relations between Kabul and the rest of the country – relations that, at best, have hardly existed and, at worst, have caused unrest and war. While roughly 80 percent of the population remains rural, development infrastructure and services have historically been concentrated in the cities, especially Kabul (Afghanistan National Human Development Report 2004). The self-serving reputation of Kabul began in the 1950s, and it increased with the politicization of aid from Western countries and the USSR and with decades of war.

A major turning point in Kabul-rural relations came in 1978, with a coup d'état that placed Nur Mohammad Taraki in power. He and his Communist government immediately began introducing and rapidly enforcing eight major reforms that were directed at rural populations. While all the reforms were unpopular to varying degrees, the land reform and literacy programs are remembered by many as being the most severe and unacceptable. In its attempt at land reform, Taraki's government sent representatives, backed by government troops, to the villages to confiscate land and redistribute it. A nationwide literacy program was also imposed. It was compulsory for everyone who could not read or write, and it treated villagers and the rural way of life with contempt. Even old people, who are held in esteem by Afghans, where forced to attend. Literacy textbooks illustrated that being a farmer was a "backward" way of life, while working in a factory or office was not.

All these reforms were enforced by the military. This led to uprisings around the country and to the 1979 invasion by the USSR, which wanted to prop up the Afghan regime it had created. A decade later, after millions had been killed or became refugees, and the country's education/health system and infrastructure had been destroyed, the USSR withdrew its troops. Over the next decade, the mujahideen and Taliban added their own chapters of conflict and destruction.

While journalists and the media covered the more than twenty years of war, according to Atmar and Goodhand (2001), "compared to many other conflict zones, Afghanistan has received limited attention from researchers and analysts." This is especially true with regard to aid, how past aid and development policies contributed to the conflict, and how effective or ineffective relief or development assistance has been in the meantime. Even five years after the overthrow of the Taliban regime, there is little critical analysis of these aid policies and programs and how they relate to the overall context of Afghanistan. This chapter is one small attempt at such an analysis.

In the next section, we examine what has happened since the 2001 Bonn Agreement and offer a general analysis linking the challenges of state building, peacebuilding, and rural development. We emphasize how, in a country where rural development policies have meant either almost no government services or the opposite (i.e., unwanted reforms forced on the people leading to uprisings and war), drastically different rural policies are needed – ones that are sensitive, sustainable, and participatory. Unlike before, the Kabul government must make a visible difference to the rural areas.

Early State Rebuilding

In Afghanistan, a new crossroad was reached in 2001. In response to the terrorist attacks on the United States on 11 September 2001, the United States invaded Afghanistan and toppled the ruling Taliban regime. This military intervention was coupled with a UN-mediated political framework, the Bonn Agreement, signed on 5 December 2001. The Bonn Agreement set into action a number of steps pertaining to state building. Most significantly, it established an interim authority and transitional government; in January 2004, a new constitution was adopted. In October 2004, national presidential elections were held, in which Hamid Karzai became the first elected president of Afghanistan. Parliamentary elections were held in September 2005. Other hopeful results included the voluntary return of over 4 million Afghan refugees from Pakistan, Iran, and elsewhere; the return of some 5 million children to school, one-third of them girls; and the successful launch of several major development and reconstruction initiatives.

In line with the Bonn Agreement, specific commissions were established to directly facilitate political processes and to lay the foundations for specific tasks: legal reform and rule of law, the observance and protection of human rights, and the establishment of a future public administration and its needed reforms. The Bonn Agreement also addressed the need to fill the security vacuum by requesting the deployment of an international security assistance force (ISAF), and it specified the role of the United Nations in supporting state-building processes.

As outlined below, other elements of particular concern in Afghanistan's state building and peacebuilding include the participation of civil society and the state's capacity to govern and provide services (and to acquire the financial resources to do so).

In these five years, Afghan civil society has, in varying forms and degrees, become more engaged. The country already has various institutions and groups that have long histories of self-help in their own communities (e.g., *shuras*, or village councils), traditional mechanisms (e.g., *Jirgas*, dispute resolution bodies), and religious networks. There are also a number of indigenous non-governmental organizations, which emerged following the 1989 withdrawal of Soviet troops, as well as professional associations, which emerged more recently. All these groups have a strong potential for playing new or additional roles in their own communities. Other indicators of some level of grassroots confidence include increasing numbers of civil society groups, the scale and rate of reconstruction, and, in many areas, a relatively booming economy.

Despite these positive developments, great challenges continue. Kabul's relations with the rest of the country remain unsettled; while a careful balance was articulated in the new Constitution, translating this balance into reality is a formidable challenge. The central government has established a basic presence in the provinces and districts, but even five years later, its capacities are weak. In those locations, under the present conditions, the loyalty of government personnel to their employer has taken precedence over competence. As a result, the central government's attempts to bring about needed changes have thus far had limited success. While the rebuilding of the Afghan state has begun, security conditions remain unsettled. In fact, in some parts of the country, security has deteriorated and the Taliban has returned in force.

In some areas, powerful strongmen, or "warlords," still dominate and are largely blamed for the country's divisiveness and insecurity. The central government attempted to rein in the warlords by including some of them in the interim government, but several of these people have since been elected to the Parliament, drawing sharp criticism from human rights groups and Afghan citizens alike. Pessimistic predictions that the vote would entrench and legitimize these warlords and, thus, increasingly weaken Parliament are coming true far too often. As elected officials of all backgrounds are increasingly being associated with self-serving activities, corruption, and mismanagement, earlier optimism that an elected Kabul government could make a difference has faded significantly.

The strength of the Kabul government is hampered by two additional factors: its finances and its capacity to carry out administrative roles. By 2007, it still had limited financial resources of its own, and less than 30 percent of international aid was being channelled through the government.

President Karzai (2007), in his recent speech to the donor community, stated that this was undermining the government and its potential. Accusations and counter-accusations by government, donor government representatives, and NGOs regarding waste or poor use of existing funds on the part of the Afghan government and NGOs have been rampant (Salahuddin 2005). Nevertheless, early in 2006, as a result of the London Conference, the Afghanistan Compact committed donors to make more effort to increase the share of the total external assistance that goes to the core government budget (Government of Afghanistan, United Nations, and International Community 2006) and to help put into effect the interim Afghanistan National Development Strategy.

One of the main problems, and one likely to last for some time to come, is the government's weak administrative capacity. Since 1978, many senior managers have been killed or compelled to flee successive regimes. The country now, as in the past, has very few people with a higher education; probably less than 1 percent of the population has a university education. Complicating this scenario is job competition. Most educated Afghans are highly sought after and are currently employed by international agencies, which pay them much more than does the Afghan government. To illustrate, government civil servants are paid an average of US$60 per month, while Afghans working in UN or donor agencies and NGOs earn an average of $1,000 per month (Government of Afghanistan, United Nations, and International Community 2006).

The extreme shortage of highly skilled Afghans in the civil service has resulted in the engagement of an increasing number of foreign advisors. These people work in the ministries, primarily in order to increase the Afghan government's aid absorbency. However, the result is that the Afghan government's capacities are being enhanced rather than being built (Afghanistan National Human Development Report 2004).

What Kind of Peace? Underlying Determinants and Threats

What is the status of peace in Afghanistan? One report says that, because of the "built-in elements of conflict that were either ignored or deliberately set aside" during the Bonn process, Afghanistan has what may be termed a "conflictual peace" (Suhrke, Harpviken, and Strand 2004, 3). Among the most obvious problems is the fact that "the UN did not bring together warring parties to make peace" (Rubin n.d.). Solutions have been initiated by the Government of Afghanistan since the Bonn Agreement, with the introduction of an amnesty for former Taliban. However, this is meeting with limited success, perhaps because of a lack of suitable incentives (ibid.).

Another study considers the extreme complexities of the conflict and its root causes and how this calls for going "beyond simplistic formulations such as 'peace' or 'ending war' to 'conflict transformation': an emphasis on transforming institutions, regionally, nationally and locally" (IRIN 2005). This transformation means addressing the links between scarcity, inequality, and institutional weaknesses.

Despite some early successes in state building, Afghanistan's transition to peace and stability is not yet assured (Afghanistan National Human Development Report 2004, 201-20). It is difficult to speculate on what kind of peace is possible; however, we may certainly speculate on what might make peace possible. In order to do this, we must take into account a complex mixture of dynamic and interdependent factors. These include basic living conditions, inclusive balanced development, local values as well as social and cultural issues, the regional and international community, drugs, and security arrangements (which, of course, include a foreign military presence). All of these factors are discussed below in more detail, and it is their tense interdependence that provides the main context for rural development.

Basic Living Conditions

Hope for the future might be most accurately assessed by the basic, day-to-day living conditions of most Afghans. After so many years of living in extreme poverty, and hearing the international community's promises of assistance, Afghans have high expectations that the central government will finally alleviate at least some of their living conditions. Over the past decades, already poor living conditions deteriorated further. As stated in Afghanistan's first National Human Development Report (Government of Afghanistan, United Nations, and International Community 2006), child and mother mortality rates, low literacy rates, and a lack of access to health care and safe drinking water have resulted in Afghanistan placing 169th out of 174 countries. War damage to infrastructure, the subsequent plunge in food production and the country's main exports – all agriculturally based – led to further poverty. Five years on, although some positive steps have been taken, around the country there is an apparent and growing dissatisfaction with the central government, which has made little improvement in the basic living conditions of most people.

Public dissatisfaction has been most strongly expressed in the results of a national survey report entitled *Breaking Point: Measuring Progress in Afghanistan*. "If the progress made since 2001 is to be restored in Afghanistan, dramatic changes are needed. If a critical mass of Afghans experiences positive change, negative trends are reversible. The year 2007 is the breaking point" (Patel and Ross 2007, 9).

Inclusive, Balanced Development

The rural areas of Afghanistan represent a diversity of cultures, topography, and histories. Their accessibility to the capital city also varies. Rural development strategies, therefore, must address these diversities, must be balanced and inclusive, and must address inequalities of gender, regions, religions, ethnicities, and locations. Historically, Afghan women have been victims of imbalanced development; they are often excluded from decision making that affects them and underrepresented in education, health, and many other services. The successful introduction of change will depend on many factors, not the least of which will be how the international community chooses to support the changes Afghans wish to make. In rebuilding the country's institutions at all levels, it is especially important to ensure that women as well as men (from all cultural groups) are included in the assistance programs, capacity building, and hiring.

The fall of the Taliban finally brought the situation of Afghan women to the world's attention, but the problems are long-standing and have become more complex since the Soviet invasion twenty-five years ago. Yet, even by 2006 – five years after the Taliban – the basic conditions of some women have still not improved. For example, one of the earliest reports on the mortality rates of Afghan mothers, published by the US Centers for Disease Control and Prevention in 1986, indicated that Afghanistan had the highest birthing-related mortality rate in the world (Thomas 1990). By 2004, the United Nations Development Program's (UNDP's) Afghanistan National Human Development Report showed that Afghanistan still had the world's highest mortality rate for mothers – 1,600 per 100,000. Other conditions indicate interconnected challenges: the life expectancy of both men and women is estimated at only 44.5 years, while the literacy rate of men is 16 percent and that of women is 12.7 percent. Such poor conditions for both men and women suggest that inclusive, balanced development must include both genders.

Inclusion requires that Afghan women assume leadership positions – that they become doctors, entrepreneurs, policy makers, planners, social mobilizers, and legislators. However, even with constitutional guarantees for women, and with seats reserved for them in the 2005 parliamentary elections, so many of their obvious needs have yet to be addressed. The situation raises many questions about the international community's commitment to action. As one report states:

> Twenty-three years of conflict – Soviet occupation, civil war, the Taliban, and finally the US-led bombing campaign – have taken a toll on women in Afghanistan. Since the fall of the Taliban regime in 2001, Afghan women have been the focus of much international attention and the cornerstone of the largest gender-focused aid intervention. Yet today, many people in Afghanistan believe that there is less funding for women and for gender programs than there was three years ago "because we think we have solved the problems." (Abirafeh 2005, 3)

The above report, entitled, *Lessons from Gender-Focused International Aid in Post-Conflict Afghanistan ... Learned?* is the most comprehensive analysis of this subject available. It argues that many of the problems of Afghan women lie in the aid community's lack of understanding of Afghan culture; its inability to recognize indigenous capacities and how, in Afghanistan, "gender" has been seen as being only about women (which further divides Afghan men and women); its failure to match rhetoric with political will and funding; and several other shortcomings. As the report suggests, peace is crucial to women and men, but this requires supporting both women and men in ways that do not fuel further distrust and backlash.

Local Values and Social and Cultural Issues
In 1978 there was an attempt to force reforms on the rural people – reforms that rejected Afghan social and cultural values. The situation was then made far worse with the 1979 Soviet invasion and occupation and a decade of killing, destruction, and culturally insensitive behaviour on the part of the Soviet military. For centuries Afghans have resisted invaders, often violently, for trying to impose outsider priorities. Military occupation and behaviour – indeed, even the imposition of well-intended ideas or aid – now as in the past, is almost sure to fuel conflict.

It by focusing on some of the local Afghan values that development and peacebuilding could be strengthened. In particular, international assistance has suffered from a failure to understand Afghan culture and religion (Maley 1998). Yet to be developed are strategies for translating Afghan cultural and religious values into governance and assistance issues so as to avoid polarizing domestic and international actors (Karim and Hess 2001). For example, during the time of the Taliban, opium growing was dramatically less prolific than it is now, partly because it was strongly condemned as anti-Islamic. Aid effectiveness and conflict prevention can both be improved if the international community learns about and respects the potential of local beliefs and values.

Supportive International Community, Regional Cooperation
Long-term development support will be needed to make peace feasible. For many Afghans, international commitments pledged now are a déjà vu from the 1989 era, when the Soviets withdrew their troops and the international community made large pledges of assistance, most of which were not realized. Despite what has been learned internationally since then about the risks of abandoning "failed states," Afghans remain anxious about what is happening with the present international assistance promises, worrying that, like before, they will disappear when the international community grows tired of the unsettled situation.

The regional political environment is also critical for progress in peace-building. Although alignments have been considerably altered since 11 September 2001, most nations in the region maintain and cultivate their networks in Afghanistan. Although there has been partial progress towards converting harmful interference into constructive engagement for the rebuilding of the country, at present the involvement of Afghanistan's neighbours seems to be aimed as much at maintaining options in case of renewed conflict as at contributing to peacebuilding and reconstruction.

Security Arrangements and Taliban Resurgence

With the central government unable to extend its full authority to the whole country, in some Afghan provinces control remains in the hands of powerful regional figures. With a resurgence of the Taliban in some provinces, along with other problems, the hope that the central government might be able to take control has diminished further.

Since late 2001, two sets of international military forces have been present in Afghanistan to shore up security and the central government, with each having different roles. By the end of 2006, the foreign military presence had grown to about thirty thousand personnel. These include roughly twenty thousand personnel under the US-led coalition Operation Enduring Freedom (OEF), whose main goal remains to rout out al Qaeda and its Taliban base, which is located mainly in the south and east. The second force is the UN-mandated, NATO-led International Security Assistance Force, which numbers about 8,500 personnel from twenty-nine countries. These people are stationed mainly in Kabul, and their role is to secure the capital and main airports, to train the Afghan National Army and National Police Force, and to provide provincial reconstruction teams (PRTs).

From 2001, the foreign military – mainly Americans but more lately Canadians as well – has taken an offensive role, actively pursuing the Taliban, insurgency, or resistance in any form. Their strategies (especially aerial bombardments and other attacks), which they believe necessary to meet their objectives, are similar to those used by the USSR during its decade of war in Afghanistan. The resulting growing number of destroyed villages and civilian deaths fans retaliation and creates an atmosphere conducive to further empowering the Taliban.

The deaths of civilians during military offensives undermines peace operations in stable areas. Human Rights Watch (2007) has estimated that, in 2006, some one thousand civilians were killed, making it the deadliest year for Afghan civilians since 2001. Poor coordination between combat and non-combat forces foster such tragedies. As reported in the Canadian media, one day in May 2006, the Canadian PRT was in Azizi, a village in north Khandahar, launching a Canadian International Development Agency (CIDA)-created

project called "Confidence in Government," which was aimed at "rebuilding the shattered authority of Afghanistan's local government" (York 2006).
A few hours later, American forces bombed the village, killing several dozen
villagers, including at least twenty civilians. While an "aid" visit by one set
of military personnel may have no connection with an attack by another,
in local eyes these differences hardly matter.

The PRTs have become very controversial in the attempts of international
security forces to win the "hearts and minds" of Afghans. Some foreign
forces have "embedded" PRTs within their operations in order to carry out
reconstruction and to provide humanitarian aid. While the military apparently believes this helps their efforts, NGOs suggest that this militarization
of aid and the dual roles played by the PRTs cause many problems. Because
the military has no training in or experience with aid and development, it
is making classic mistakes. An example is "quick impact projects," which
involve free handouts of goods such as tractors, cash, fertilizer, small-scale
construction projects, and the like. Rather than seriously aiding development, these are seen as little more than an attempt to buy favour. And, as
the military has little understanding of local power structures, such "projects" simply reinforce local problems. They also lead to confusion within
the Afghan public: Which aid personnel are neutral humanitarian helpers
and which have intelligence-gathering or other military objectives?

In response to the above complications, through the Agency Coordinating Body for Afghan Relief (2003), NGOs maintain a unified stance against
the dual roles of PRTs. This agency points out how the idea of presenting
soldiers in sheep's clothing is both contradictory and counterproductive.
This stance was repeated at the 2006 NATO conference in Riga, with the
agency appealing to the military to stay out of reconstruction and development and to increase its security roles (e.g., training the Afghan military,
police, and so on).

Training the planned seventy-thousand-member Afghan army to take over
the security role is under way and has been seen by many as essential. Yet
analysts have pointed out many problems with building the army, including the slow pace of training, failure to get the multiethnic mix needed, and
a high rate of desertion. In particular, there is concern that, in any case, the
Afghan National Army could well be outnumbered by the illegal militias.
As Arne Strand points out in Chapter 9 of this volume, even five years after
the toppling of the Taliban regime, and the completion of the UN-backed
disarmament, demobilization, and reintegration of ex-combatants program,
there are still an estimated 1,800 illegal armed bands of men consisting of
up to 100,000 individuals who pose a security concern in many parts of the
country (IRIN 2005). If the ISAF and OEF forces withdraw before needed
resolutions and transformations, many fear that Afghanistan will revert to
the post-Soviet, pre-Taliban internal conflicts of the 1990s (Maloney 2004).

Opium Growing/Drugs

Despite unprecedented eradication and "alternative livelihoods" programs, by 2006, some of the highest levels of production of opium ever to grow in Afghanistan were reached. In Afghanistan, opium growing, driven by demand from the West, is a major power issue – one that, in some rural areas, perpetuates the cycle of poverty. The growers, most of whom are the smallest farmers, become indebted to the powerful traders and opium "mafia," whose quest to maintain control fuels the conflict. They lend money to the small farmers to grow their crops in the coming year. Due to many other demands on the farmers' limited financial resources, such futures buying, or advances, keep them borrowing from the same source, binding them to the powerful figures who protect their territories with their own militias. Perhaps the only way out of the vicious cycles created by the drug trade is to create alternatives that would allow those trapped to escape. We need programs in the West that lessen demand and programs in Afghanistan that give options to the poor farmer-grower.

Participatory Rural Development in Peacebuilding

While challenges to peacebuilding in Afghanistan may appear overwhelming, one of the main determinants of peace goes back to a proposition that emerged out of the WKOP project, which had to do with the need to draw stakeholders into participatory policy making and other development processes. It is not only rural development that is essential to peacebuilding in Afghanistan, *participatory* rural development also needs to be seen as a main vehicle for peacebuilding, both among the people and between the people and the government.

What do we mean by rural development? Although there is an enormous body of literature on rural development and different concepts and trends have evolved, for the purposes of this chapter we refer to it in two ways. First, rural development may be generally defined as providing efficient quantities of assistance to rural areas (in Afghanistan, this alone is a major change from the past). Second, "rural development can be defined as the process whereby rural communities progress from given situations to more desirable situations in terms of quality of life. It depends on the utilization of local, physical and human resources, supplemented by investment, technology and services with full participation of the local people in decision making" (International Network for the Availability of Scientific Publications 2004).

What do we mean by participation? Narayan and Rietbergen-McCracken (1998, 4) define participation as a "process through which stakeholders influence and share control over development initiatives, decisions and resources which affect them." During the years that Afghanistan has been at war, the participation paradigm has come into existence internationally (having evolved out of NGO work in Latin America, Africa, and Asia) largely because of dissatisfaction with top-down aid programs that simply were not getting the desired results. The theories and practices such as those of Paulo Friere (the Brazilian educationist), the liberation theology movement in Latin America, and the cooperative movement in India and Bangladesh provided poignant examples of how to effectively address poverty by working directly with people at the grassroots level in order to design and to implement policy and programs. By the 1980s, specific attitudes and methodologies – such as rapid rural appraisal, participatory rural appraisal, and so on (introduced by Robert Chambers and others) – had emerged. Their focus was on working with the poor so as to put them in charge of analysis and decision making, with their empowerment being the intended goal. Since then, donor agencies, including the World Bank, the Asian Development Bank, the United Nations, and various donor governments, have, at least in theory, required "beneficiary participation" in virtually every project.

The trouble is that while "participation" has, in theory, become accepted in the broad development field, in practice it has not. Internationally, lessons learned and some of the best practices include the following: the need for clear concepts, methodologies, and tools for participation, motivation, and empowerment; realistic time and resources; political will and the buy-in of all stakeholder groups with regard to sharing power; instilling local ownership; the need to recognize local social contexts; the need for high levels of training, supervision, and support of social mobilizers; capacity building and long-term follow-up in communities to help avoid the breakdown of groups formed (which often happens when such groups are introduced by any source outside the community); tools for targeting the poor and empowering them while still dealing with the elites; identifying and addressing root causes; avoiding dependence; setting up sustainability; managing expectations; creating and maintaining links among villages, government, and other stakeholders. These best practices are more likely to be achieved when specifically targeted beneficiaries and the whole community are involved, rather than just the usual leaders and powerful people.

Such lessons and best practices are long overdue in Afghanistan: attempts at participation and empowerment should not be only "community-led" or only "government-led" but, rather, a two-way dialogue. This approach would represent drastic change in Afghanistan, a country historically run along highly centralized, top-down lines. This would also require major changes in the international aid programs that, over the years, have operated by employing different degrees of outside, top-down imposition. By default, there having been no recognized central Afghan authority for many years, aid programs have been "parachuted in" with little to no local consultation. The UN, donor governments, and NGOs have decided what is needed and, to the extent possible, tried to provide it, usually to targeted parts of the population (especially the most vulnerable). Thus community development, involving the whole community participating in the decisions that affect them, is very new. With few exceptions, such attempts have been made only since 2001 and, as elsewhere, will need many years of learning and applying the above lessons to achieve the desired results.

How conducive is the present situation to people's participation? In the constitutional sense, the timing couldn't be better – at least in theory. The new Afghan Constitution took a bold step in officially recognizing and requiring local-level participation. Article 140 states: "In order to organize activities and provide people the opportunity to actively participate in the local administration, a council shall be set up in districts and villages in accordance with the law. Members of these councils shall be elected by the local people through free, general, universal, secret and direct elections for a period of three years."

While participatory development is important everywhere, it is crucial in Afghanistan, even in its conflictual state. It is a main way to counter the tensions between perceptions of a modern state with its modern, urban elite and a conservative, rural tribal people. Such dialogues and processes are especially important in rural Afghanistan as fast paced change is often understood by conservative rural Afghans as influence from the West – change they perceive as anti-Islamic and are quick to reject (Afghanistan National Human Development Report 2004).

Despite the challenges, the Kabul government began practical work in many rural areas, instituting projects financed by donor governments, UN agencies, the World Bank, the Asian Development Bank, and others. One of these national priority programs is the National Solidarity Program (NSP). It is particularly relevant to analyze this program since it constitutes the first major attempt at country-wide, community-based development. We examine this program to see whether or not it is applying the lessons learned elsewhere. Is it going to make even the slightest difference in daily living conditions? Is it going to better equip rural Afghans to be able to bring about needed changes themselves? Is it going to give Afghans any real hope that things will get better? What is still needed? What might the NSP suggest for the country's rural development as a whole, including such instruments as the Afghanistan Compact, the interim National Development Strategy, and other donor and ministerial programs?

National Solidarity Program

"At present, the most complicated and high stakes IFI-financed program in Afghanistan is the World Bank-financed ... NSP" (Carlin 2003, 8), which was introduced in 2003 by the Afghan government's Ministry for Rural Rehabilitation and Development (MRRD) with a budget of US$800 million (GOA/MRRD/NSP 2003a). Towards this budget, by the end of March 2007, the NSP had received approximately US$450 million from the World Bank and donor countries, including Denmark, Japan, the United States, Canada, and the European Union (GOA/MRRD/NSP 2006b), as part of the funds administered by the Afghanistan Reconstruction Trust Fund. In three years, this amount was to cover the country's qualifying villages (GOA/MRRD/NSP 2005a). As the first program of its kind, the NSP's main goal is to get the government to introduce community-based local governance and development – a crucial step for the country's stability.

The NSP is implemented for the government's MRRD by the UN Habitat and about twenty-five international and Afghan NGOs, all of which are referred to as the facilitating partners (FPs). The FPs were selected based on their existing expertise in Afghanistan and their capacities to expand operations. They include such international NGOs as CARE, the Swedish Committee for Afghanistan, the Aga Khan Foundation, Oxfam, and ActionAid. The FPs are responsible for approaching communities and letting them know about the NSP, its eligibility requirements, and what it has to offer. They help the village through the whole NSP process. German Technical Cooperation, a German government agency, was appointed as oversight consultant, along with Development Alternatives Inc., an American consulting firm. Starting 1 March 2007, the latter two agencies were replaced by Maxwell Stamp, a British consulting firm.

NSP documents describe the program as consisting of four core elements: (1) a facilitated participatory planning process at the community level to assist with the establishment and strengthening of community institutions; (2) a system of direct block grant transfers to support the rehabilitation or development activities for such institutions; (3) capacity development to enhance the competence of communities for financial management, procurement, useful technical skills, and transparency; and (4) activities that facilitate links to other institutions and programs with available services and resources (GOA/MRRD/NSP 2003a).

The block grants are allocated to villages comprised of over fifty families at US$200 per family up to a maximum of US$60,000 per village (GOA/MRRD/NSP 2003b). These block grants are to provide resources for public infrastructure, community assets, revolving funds, social services, and training identified as priority needs through an inclusive, participatory village planning process. The village is to manage the block grants, including preparation of project proposals, with technical assistance from the MRRD.

To be eligible for a development grant from the NSP, communities are required to elect a community development council (CDC), which should be a representative, decision-making body made up of both women and men; or, out of cultural sensitivity, men and women could organize separate councils. The CDC is to hold a series of community meetings to make decisions on development priorities, final choice of projects, size and composition of community contributions, use of project funds, project implementation and management, transparency arrangements, and plans for the operation and maintenance of completed projects.

Government documents refer to the NSP as its "flagship" program. It is by far the largest government program in the country in terms of financing and geographic reach. At its inception, the NSP was to be implemented in nearly every Afghan village within three years. The scale and speed of this project as, perhaps, unprecedented. As the NSP is the first contact that many rural Afghans have with the new government, the potential importance of results of this program cannot be overstated.

What has happened? Under the NSP, Afghanistan's first CDCs were elected from August 2003 onwards, and the first block grant disbursements began in December 2003. By the end of March 2007, about 16,500 villages had elected CDCs, and nearly 22,500 village projects had been funded. The projects are divided into those for drinking water, irrigation, reconstruction of schools, clinics, community centres, transport, and energy, with a smaller number pertaining to livelihoods and income generation (GOA/MRRD/NSP 2005b). Villages that are able to successfully implement projects during the first year are to receive additional small block grants during their second and third years (GOA/MRRD/NSP 2005a). After this time, the CDCs and the villages are to sustain the projects themselves.

For this chapter, we conducted research in twenty-nine villages in five provinces – Nangarhar, Logar, Wardak, Parwan, and Herat – in which the NSP is under way (see appendix at end of chapter). In each of these provinces, villages were randomly selected. On the first visit to each of the villages, surveyors conducted a survey using a questionnaire. One of the authors (Omar Zakhilwal) and his research assistants then revisited the same villages, collecting qualitative data through participant observation, attending meetings, and conducting interviews with key informants. They also facilitated partners, leaders, members, and non-members of CDCs in the villages and on CDC project sites. We also analyzed formal and informal interviews with other actors involved in the NSP. Finally, our early participation in the program and our ongoing observation of its performance provided other insights.

From these twenty-nine villages, we present five illustrations. These were selected to present qualitative data on the NSP and to be at least roughly representative of the villages visited. Of course, we make no claim that these five are representative of all the villages participating in the NSP. Nevertheless, we observed that, even in these few villages, both positive and negative results were occurring. Of concern is the fact that some of the risks are already apparent, providing cautions that should be addressed as the NSP moves forward and suggesting the kinds of problems that need to be prevented with regard to rural development as a whole.

Case Illustrations

Illustration 1: Upper Nawach Village, Parwan Province

The Nawach villages are located about 150 kilometres north of the capital city of Kabul in the District of Salang in Parwan Province. Lower Nawach is across the main road that crosses the Hindukush Mountains at the Salang Pass, connecting the north of the country with the south. Between the village and the road flows the Salang River. Upper Nawach is about five kilometres, or two hours uphill walking distance, from Lower Nawach. Each village is made up of about one hundred families. The villagers come from a single ethnic and tribal group, and most are related by intermarriage.

When the NSP came to the two villages in the fall of 2003, the choice of what could be done with the money was obvious for Upper Nawach but not so obvious for Lower Nawach. "When community mobilizers of the MRRD came to our village and told us about the NSP, we first didn't believe anything they were saying," says Abdul Habib, the chair of the Upper Nawach Community Development Council. "Never in the history of Afghanistan had the central government taken people into confidence and put them in charge of a development project, so how could we believe it now?" he reasoned. However, when they realized that the program was real, they elected a CDC. The project they selected for their allotted NSP fund, after a village-wide consultation, was the building of a tertiary road to connect them to the main road.

The villagers of Upper Nawach did not wait for the NSP money to arrive before they started work on the road. Indeed, the road was 80 percent complete before they got their first 20 percent of the US$25,000 block grant. "The NSP was sort of a trigger. For years we knew the road to be of need but we just couldn't get ourselves organized to go about building it – the NSP pushed us in that direction," Habib explained. "And we don't see this as just a road," he said, "It is way more. It is access to health, to school, to the market and to information."

An engineer from UN Habitat, the FP in Parwan, said that the estimated cost of the road was over US$50,000 if the work were to be carried out by an NGO, but the village people completed it for half that amount. The CDC believed that the road would make higher education more accessible and would help with other village problems as well. To continue studying beyond Grade 4 (which is as high as they could go in the village), the children had to walk to and from the upper school each day – a total of four hours of walking per day. A road and vehicle transport would make it more realistic for the children to make that journey, and there was hope that both girls and boys would be encouraged to go to school and stay in school. Others also looked forward to being able to reach a hospital for treatment for critical illnesses.

Prior to the CDC, Upper Nawach had never had a village development *shura* (council). As the villagers explained, all of them knew what the village's needs were, but they never sat down to discuss them. The NSP provided them with that opportunity. The CDC is now a development council and an authoritative dispute-resolving body. One elder who is a member of the village's CDC said, "The power of decision making was transferred to people. Therefore, whoever designed the NSP made the right decision. This is bringing unity to people."

There was, however, a major problem with the road. It took many months of hard work to build it over difficult terrain. The road was finished from Upper Nawach to the upper edge of Lower Nawach. It then had to go through Lower Nawach to get to the river, at which point a bridge would need to be built in order to connect it to the main road. The problem is that the villagers of Lower Nawach would not allow the road to go through their land because, if they did so, they would lose scarce agricultural land. Besides, the bridge would require much more money. Who will pay for it? "Why didn't they ask us first, before they built the road, if we would allow them to go through our village?" an elder from Lower Nawach stated. "And without the bridge this whole road is useless. Why didn't they think of that first either?"

Illustration 2: Lower Nawach Village, Parwan Province
Lower Nawach is an internally divided village. Unlike Upper Nawach, which is made up of closely knit families, Lower Nawach was divided long before the presence of the NSP. This village chose to spend its block grant on a micro-hydro plant. "The first day, when NSP facilitators came to explain to us the program, I said we wanted to do electricity for our village," the CDC chair said. "The reason we picked this is because every other village along the river is doing the same. We don't want to be different from the other villages." The researcher asked, "But did you discuss this in comparison to other things you could do with the money?" "There was no need to do that – this was it," the chair responded.

Other villagers, in private conversations with the researcher, said that they had requested a drinking water facility, but the chair did not listen because he had personal interests in the project. "What interests?" the researcher asked. "The chair contracted out the project to himself," a villager responded. "He claims that nobody else stepped forward. So what else could I do?" When asked about this, the chair replied, "I am actually losing money on this project – but I am doing it because I, as the chair, am responsible for the successful conclusion of this project."

When the researcher went to see the project, he heard about a disturbance. Two farmers, a father and a son, knowing that someone from Kabul was visiting the project, protested that it had damaged their land. Two more farmers joined in, claiming the same. The researcher saw that their land was, indeed, vulnerable to the water intake needed for the project. "But this is your project, you as a village picked it, so why complain about it?" the researcher asked. "No, this is the chairman's project. We were not consulted. We don't want this," the farmers replied, raising their voices. "But you need to resolve this through your CDC," the researcher advised. "The CDC is not a council [*shura*] that can resolve things. I want you to resolve this!" one of the farmers demanded of the researcher.

Illustration 3: Char Kabutarkhan Village, Herat Province

Char Kabutarkhan is located in the District of Guzara in Herat Province. It is located fifteen kilometres to the south of Herat City and about four kilometres off the main road. According to the NSP village file, there are 735 families inhabiting the village, which had been located at the front line during the Soviet presence and had been heavily damaged during the war. After the defeat of the Communist regime in 1992, many of the village's exiled residents returned and rebuilt their homes. Many of the villagers are farmers. The village lies by a river; its land is fertile and is, therefore, very green. According to Abdul Wahab, the chair of Char Kabutarkhan CDC, when the NSP came to the village in the fall of 2003, "We already were a united village, but we did not have a structure and therefore could not take advantage of our unity for development. What the NSP did was to give us that needed structure through the formation of CDC." Abdul Qudus, a member of the village CDC, and Said Shiragha, a villager, agreed. "We did form *shuras* off and on but only for dispute resolutions. We never attempted, or probably never thought of, putting one together for development," Qudus explained. "Our CDC now does both, the traditional dispute resolution and also its tasks under the NSP."

Sher Agha pointed out that, after the NSP arrived, the incidence of disputes had fallen. He believes that the NSP probably strengthened unity among the villagers, and hence the decline in disputes. For their NSP entitlement (about US$60,000), the village built a school, repaired the village's public bath, and also built a number of culverts. "All these were the village's priorities and we would not change them if they were to start all over again," Wahab said. "For example, our school did not have a building and therefore it was not conducive for studying. The closest school with a building is seven kilometres from here. That was too far for our children. So the school was our top priority."

Now that the NSP projects are concluding in the village, what will happen to the CDC? The villagers were of the view that it would continue functioning, and they had already taken steps to sustain it. For example, they have agreed to use the NSP account as the village's trust fund and have encouraged their fellow villagers to donate to it. In addition, the CDC would act, as it already had on numerous occasions, as the village's representative body. As such, it would inform the government, NGOs, and international organizations of its problems and to ask them for development assistance.

The women of Char Kabutarkhan have their own CDC and are very active, a situation that may be aided by the high female literacy rate in this village. The school that the village built with the NSP block grant was, in fact, pushed by the women. The women's CDC also serves as the focal group for other organizations that are interested in women-related issues. For example, it meets regularly with the regional office of the Afghanistan Independent Human Rights Commission to discuss women's rights and to receive training.

The villagers claimed that, so far, the NSP has been the best government project they have seen. "It delivered on what it promised. It created jobs for the poor. Its money was also spent within the village. It produced projects that shape up the future of our village," Wahab explained. However, he added that it could be further improved. For example, the NSP could pay the instalments in a timelier manner. "Right now there are delays that affect the continuity of our work," Qudus complained. Another male villager felt that there could be more emphasis on women's training that goes beyond the NSP: "They need to know about their role, their options and also their rights."

Illustration 4: Zakhil Village, Nangarhar Province

Zakhil (the home village of co-author Omar Zakhilwal) is located about twenty kilometres to the southeast of Jalalabad City, the capital of Nangarhar Province. It is inhabited by about 350 households, comprised of five or six extended families. The village has never had a shortage of family quarrels and disputes, which, in turn, has resulted in two or three rival blocks – each one with its own *malik* (leader) and its own program and function with regard to social occasions and gatherings.

Such divisions often have a greater impact on male-to-male relationships in a village than on female-to-female relationships. There are two reasons for this; first, unless the disputes are serious, the men usually do not put pressure on the women to adhere to these divisions; second, women often socialize among themselves more then men do, assisting each other with numerous domestic tasks and thus establishing bonds. In Zakhil, as throughout the eastern provinces, what brings women together (and where they often socialize) is the *gudar*, which is a water-point (a *karez*, a water spring or stream). It is here that women come to get drinking water or do their laundry. In the morning, when men are away working in the fields, women and girls put their pitchers or laundry on their heads and walk to the *gudar*. There they spend time working and sitting with other women, talking, doing the laundry together, helping others with theirs, asking for advice, or simply sharing their latest stories and news. The *gudar* is also known as a place for young people to watch for and to attract the attention of suitors. Interested young men make sure they cross by somewhere between home and the *gudar*. Although chores at the *gudar* are hard, in many villages it is a popular place with women. In a conservative culture in which they spend their time inside the family compound, rarely venturing into town, the *gudar* is an important space for women to frequently get outside and socialize.

Like many such villages, Zakhil had a *gudar* for as long as the villagers with whom the researchers spoke could remember. While over the years there were many village disputes, these did not affect the *gudar*. At least not until the NSP arrived.

Given the divided state of the village, it is not surprising that village involvement in the NSP reflected those divisions. While the CDC held many village meetings, members could not come to an agreement on what they could do with the NSP money. For every project idea discussed there were some who would benefit more than others, and that was unacceptable to the council as a whole. After many months of quarrels, two members of the CDC pushed for a well in front of their home compounds. The rest of the villagers and their representatives would accept it only if there was a well in front of *every* compound. They finally agreed on eighteen wells, one for every compound in the village. These eighteen wells were in addition to the only functioning well already in the village (and three that were not functioning due to lack of maintenance). Such an increase in the number of wells in a location known to have seasonal water shortages, and where wells already had a history of not being maintained, should have raised questions about this village's project choice. Not only were the wells a questionable choice but they also put an end to the *gudar* – an important part of village culture and social life. "We incorporated women's needs in our decisions – in fact we did the wells for women because they don't have to leave their house for drinking water and laundry," responded Maeen Khan, chairman of the CDC. But when the researchers interviewed some of the village women, they said they had not really been involved in the decision making and that they missed the *gudar*, as did some male bachelors.

Illustration 5: Mahalai Pusht Village, Herat Province

Mahalai Pusht is a village located about thirteen kilometres from Herat City and two kilometres to the north of Char Kabutarkhan. It is inhabited by nine hundred families. Mahalai Pusht, like other villages we visited, was also affected by the war during the Soviet invasion. The literacy rate of both men and women is relatively high, and the village, which is agricultural, has plenty of land and water. Many of its houses were rebuilt after the collapse of the Communist regime and the return of the exiled population in

1992. Prior to the arrival of the NSP, the villagers lived in harmony with each other; however, like those in Char Kabutarkhan, the villagers of Mahalai Pusht were not organized so as to be able to use their "strengths" for development. As the villages themselves claim, the NSP gave them the needed organizational skills.

The project the villagers built for their US$60,000 NSP allotment showed not only the CDC's organizational skills but also its potential for sustainability. Their drinking water project involved the digging of only one deep well for the whole village, as opposed to dozens (as was the case in some villages in the east and as discussed above). Above the well they have built a water tank big enough for the whole village. Water pipes run about three kilometres east and west through the village. Each family that receives water at its house from the main pipe must pay for the extension and for a water metre.

Next to the village, two rooms were built. These house an electricity generator, a water pump (both paid for by the NSP block grant), and an office for the project's hired manager and a mechanic. The mechanic is responsible for the maintenance of the machines, while the manager's job is to ensure that there is water in the pipe twenty-four hours a day. He also issues bills for each water metre at the end of the month and collects payments. This money pays for the salaries of the two hired personnel and the operation and maintenance of the system, yet there is often a surplus for the village's trust account.

The villagers claimed that, after the NSP, the solidarity in the village was strengthened. They have already put this solidarity and their organizational skills to other good uses (e.g., dispute resolution and securing more projects for the village, such as the road and school, which were built by other organizations).

NSP Limitations and Possibilities

What patterns can be observed based on this sample? Although the twenty-nine villages visited in these five provinces represent a diversity of situations, topographies, ethnic groups, economics, security, and other conditions, we observed that there are both weaknesses and strengths in the NSP and that these results are relatively similar across the sample. Although the sample visited was fairly small, the observations made in these few villages are important, especially since they are so similar to the later assessments of villagers who represented Afghanistan in a national conference held in Kabul in mid-2005 (see below).

From our field study, we are able to make a number of observations. These need to be considered across the NSP, for rural development as a whole, and for lessons in state building and peacebuilding. Our main observations are as follows:

1   *Lack of genuine participation.* In the villages visited, there were often ques-
    tions about the genuineness of community participation and empower-
    ment. In one of the villages (Lower Nawach), we observed the outright
    "elite capture" of an NSP project. We note the lack of meaningful par-
    ticipation on the part of women throughout our fieldwork, except in
    the Herat villages. In most of the CDCs, it has been reported that women
    are part of the overall CDCs or that they form separate women's coun-
    cils, but in most villages their inclusion is only nominal.

2   *Who got elected.* General observations in the villages raise questions about
    those who were elected to CDC leadership positions. Often they were
    the same powerful, influential, and relatively well-off persons who had
    been in charge all along (e.g., schoolmasters, imams, landowners, elders,
    etc.) and who are also sometimes part of the traditional leadership.
       While it is not surprising in such first-ever elections that influential
    people would be elected, to include the voices of the poor will require
    strong plans, many years, and resources that were not included in the
    NSP. Such realities about CDC leadership raise many questions about
    inclusion and whose interests the projects really serve.
       In the long term, the traditional forms of community leadership may
    still be the most predominant and most enduring. Perhaps an Afghan
    hybrid will emerge, in which the traditional leadership will use some
    new organizational, management, and resource-building skills, presum-
    ing these can still be acquired through the NSP or other sources.

3   *Skills of FPs and their social mobilizers.* In the villages visited, it was appar-
    ent that there is wide variation in the level of skills of FPs and their
    social mobilizers, many of whom were workers diverted from other pro-
    jects or taken on as new staff, often with little or no community de-
    velopment experience. Social mobilizer training has been mainly
    concerned with NSP procedural and logistical matters, but training in
    participation and community development is largely missing. Most so-
    cial mobilizers had been assigned to far too many villages and had been
    provided with too few resources to handle the workload expected. This
    contributed to many of the problems observed.

4   *Limited capacity building in villages and government.* The NSP is building
    capacities almost entirely in the FPs rather than in the government.
    MRRD had about eighty of its Kabul personnel integrated into the oper-
    ations of the NSP Oversight Consultant in Kabul, with roughly the same
    number in the provinces and a few others located with FPs; however,
    the total is far under the number needing training (Asif Rahimi, e-mail
    to Jane Thomas, 15 November 2005). Capacity building at the village

level was also observed to be weak. Villages visited had received little to no training or resources to assist them in future village development when the NSP ends.

5 *Links between CDCs, and between CDCs and others.* In the villages visited, there was a lack of CDC links with other CDCs in the areas, where projects might overlap (as in Upper Nawach and Lower Nawach villages). Although clustering by NSP villages is reported to have begun in some locations in Afghanistan (Asif Rahimi, e-mail to Jane Thomas, 15 November 2005), it was not yet seen in the villages visited. There was also little to no NSP connection with other assistance programs or government ministries and almost no involvement on the part of government personnel. In none of the case study villages had the CDCs been linked with other services, although such links are one of the NSP's stated four core elements. These opportunities are being missed, and many district administrations perceived themselves as having been sidelined.

6 *Sustainability of CDCs and their projects.* Observations in the villages visited raise questions about the sustainability of CDCs, and it is this that could pose the biggest risk to local governance and community-based development. Within the international aid community and MRRD there is high hope for the CDCs, but their future depends on many complex realities. If these CDCs fail, it will take a very long time to build up enough trust to enable such efforts to work again.

As pointed out earlier, over the last decades NGOs in many countries have implemented their work by forming groups. From such group formation experiences many lessons have been learned, the most significant being that it is common for groups to fold once outside assistance or leadership is withdrawn. In order for groups to survive, they require long-term follow-through comprised of social mobilization and advocacy. At the same time, they need input to keep building and renewing their own skills, resources, and other capacities so that they can deal with the local power structures and engage in more development.

However, as planned at the beginning, the maximum time a village will have contact with the NSP is only three years, which, according to lessons learned elsewhere, is far too short a time span within which to make sustainable differences. So far the emphasis is on CDCs holding elections and spending their block grant. Besides the fact that CDCs have received little to no training on how to manage their organizations, there has been little to no planning with regard to helping villages set up their own financial resources (e.g., savings, credit, revolving fund, etc.). These two factors – the short contact time and villages still being without their own financial resources – make it challenging for many CDCs to last. It is also doubtful whether the NGOs can carry the villages forward on their own. Before the NSP, NGOs were operating in only a small percentage of the villages that the NSP was to reach. Post-NSP, due to funding and other limitations, it is unlikely that NGOs can maintain the NSP-planned scale. There is also the large question: If there is to be follow-up, who will do it? NGOs? Government?

The sustainability of the projects undertaken by CDCs will be a large part of the credibility and life expectancy of these organizations. Although NSP guidelines require plans for operation and maintenance, many factors make meeting these requirements difficult. If the project falls apart, what happens to the CDC? In many of the villages visited, the sustainability of the NSP projects was uncertain, and this, in turn, affected the CDC and local relations. For example, in the Herat village, what will villagers think of the CDC if it turns out that the school they built cannot be operated effectively? What problems are likely to occur among people in Upper Nawach when they find they have a road that comes to a dead end? Can the people in Lower Nawach afford the micro-hydro plant, and is it being maintained? Will the disunity in Zakhil worsen if the poorly chosen wells dry up? Failed projects can mean not only the end of the CDC but also tension and yet more mistrust between the villages and others.

7   *Social capital.* The NSP presents examples of both positive and negative effects on social capital. In some places visited, it was observed that, when unity existed before the arrival of the NSP, the money and opportunities the program brought appeared to complement or even increase that unity (as in Upper Nawach and Char Kabutarkhan). On the other hand, where social capital was already in short supply (as in Zakhil and Lower Nawach), or where disunity existed before the arrival of the NSP, the outside money and organizing could exacerbate the strife.

There was some concern that the NSP projects could negatively affect social capital (as in the *gudar* at Zakhil) as well as the customs of *hashar*, in which community members voluntarily contribute labour and resources. Village NSP construction projects pay villagers to perform labour they would normally have performed for free as a community obligation. Community contributions to projects, required by the NSP, were often of a token nature. This problem did not start with the NSP, but it is important to be aware of the long-term negative impacts of any program that undermines customs pertaining to self-help and to the pooling of community resources.

8   *Monitoring and evaluation.* In the villages visited, monitoring and evaluation of the NSP was late or non-existent. Had monitoring and evaluation

been introduced in a timely fashion, problems could have been caught before getting out of hand (e.g., the wells at Zakhil).

9 *Financing.* Financing has remained a main risk. For the planned level of activity at the beginning of the NSP, the budget required was US$800 million, but by roughly more than two-thirds of the way through the project, a little over a half of the needed budget had been secured from the World Bank and donor countries (GOA/MRRD/NSP 2006b). Unlike other large projects in other countries, where funds are fully allocated before the project begins, donors are deciding on funds for the NSP on a year-by-year basis, which leaves the NSP vulnerable. Any major national or international security event, or even simple changes in policy, could render the NSP broke. Moreover, the NSP puts a major obligation on government, and this may be difficult or impossible to sustain. Given that the NSP has been publicized nationally as going to every village with money, it is especially risky that it is being implemented without full guaranteed funding.

10 *NSP background and preparation.* Overall, NSP weaknesses can be directly linked to its hasty preparation and implementation, its rapid growth, and its huge scope. While best practices in development show that the most successful projects go through many months or years of preliminary study and design, often involving pilot projects, the NSP in Afghanistan did not pass through any of these stages. Instead, it was adapted from the design of similar World Bank projects in East Timor and Indonesia, and it was initiated at full scale in Afghanistan on a very short timeline. Introduced in December 2002, NGOs held workshops in February and March 2003 to try to overcome the project design flaws,[1] but the main in-built risks remained: the scale and the speed. Adequate time was not allowed for many crucial activities, especially crucial capacity building. Although the NSP constituted a very new approach in Afghanistan, it was assumed that each FP had the requisite participation and broad community development skills. Within only a few more months, by September 2003, NGOs were already implementing the program on a large scale.

The NSP rush was part of the run-up to the Afghan presidential elections, which were to follow the next year, and this put pressure on donors, the MRRD, and the FPs to operationalize immediately. Careful preparation was given far less priority than was the perceived need to make it appear as though things were happening quickly and on a large scale. Details such as thorough training would have to come later. Possible additional roles, such as peacebuilding and poverty alleviation, were not clearly integrated into the NSP as planned strategies; rather, these major roles may have been assumed only as possible consequences. Given the lack of normal preparation, the rushed start-up, and the scale and scope of the NSP, it is not surprising that problems arose.

Villagers' Assessment of the NSP

The most important overall analysis of the NSP comes from villagers themselves, and their observations are remarkably similar to ours. This emerged especially from the first ever *jirga*, or conference, of village representatives held in Kabul in July 2005, which we attended. The *jirga* brought together 350 select CDC representatives, one-third of whom were women, from every province, where they were addressed by President Karzai and several other officials and given prominence in the national media. During the week's proceedings, delegates were also asked to evaluate the NSP and their villages' roles in it – a discussion that produced results applicable to aid agencies. Like us, delegates concluded that the NSP had several strengths, the most important of which was that it was helping to build relations and trust between the central government and rural people and that it was transferring responsibility and skills to communities.

Significantly, the CDC representatives also identified areas in need of improvement. Divided into twenty discussion groups, delegates identified such weaknesses as the low involvement of women, the lack of a long-term strategy, the undue influence of powerful persons in communities, the lack of planning for sustainability, the lack of formal links with district administrations, the late arrival of block grants, and the occurrence of some weak projects. To overcome these weaknesses, delegates suggested that the central government should legally recognize the CDCs; assistance should be given to developing bylaws for the CDCs; CDCs should be linked to district administrations, where they could play advisory roles; the financial sustainability of the CDCs should be improved by creating financial resources and systems as well as by providing training and continued technical and financial support; where culturally preferable, separate CDCs should be created for men and women so that both can more freely express themselves; training should be provided to both men and women with regard to development and women's rights; and so on (GOA/MRRD/NSP 2006b).

The villagers' own overall analysis of the NSP indicates the value of having them carry it out. The opinions and observations expressed by villagers are most important with regard to building the NSP as well as with regard to national and rural development in general.

Conclusion

Given the history of Afghanistan, and the fact that rural development policies either did little to benefit most of the population or actually caused conflict, it is clear that the Government of Afghanistan and aid agencies now need to adopt different strategies. However, the Kabul government is still limited in its abilities to serve the country and is rapidly losing what trust the public electorate had in it. The presence of foreign military forces whose purpose is to shore up government power also sometimes adds to the confusion and conflict.

What cannot be emphasized enough is the fact that the most basic objective of the NSP – to initiate and strengthen strong community organizations – may still be the greatest hope for rural development and peacebuilding. The hope is that, by developing their own grassroots organizations, skills, resources, and links with each other, members of communities will be able to improve their own livelihoods, health, and educational opportunities. Such improvements may be the country's biggest development – building unity, cooperation, and peace from the bottom up.

While there are weaknesses in the program, all things considered, it is commendable that the NSP has achieved as much as it has. By the end of March 2007, the NSP had reached 16,500 villages in 279 of the country's 360 districts – a major achievement (GOA/MRRD/NSP 2006b). This growth is all the more remarkable as Taliban attacks on aid programs have increased and more aid workers have been killed.

The rapid, wide-scale start-up and lack of preparation were the main causes of problems in the NSP's first years; but what difference does this make now, further down the road, in the program's fourth year of operation? At this point, how the NSP operates may be even more important than it was at the beginning. While its achievements can be admired, unless it adds significant depth and longevity at the level of each community, the NSP will just be skimming the surface. If bottom-up development and stability is really to happen, it will require many years of continued secure funding and capacity building at all levels.

Recommendations

Committing to long-term support for community-based rural development:
- Donors, government, NGOs, and the international community can most effectively help build peace in Afghanistan by providing sustained, long-term follow-up and improved support to villages so that they may achieve their own development and be able to participate in both local and national scenes. For years to come, such support will be essential.
- Increase, sustain, and secure funding. Ways should be found to ensure that donor pledges are made and paid, committing the money upfront on a multi-year basis, placing it in secure trust funds or other mechanisms that make possible not only longer-term planning but also timely, performance-based payments.

- Build on what has been started. Fund the NSP and other programs to increase the capacities of the CDCs. Ensure rural development funding, recognize and respect community leadership, and help build its capacities. As the capacities of CDCs increase, all programming – agriculture, water, health, education, and so on – should be funnelled through these councils.
- Make sure that significant funds go to the rural areas. Until most of the population sees significant improvements in their own rural locations, the self-serving image of Kabul will remain.
- Expanding the NSP further might be important, but deepening it is even more important. Insist on greatly increased and improved training for all involved.
- Improve coordination between donors, government, and NGOs. Implement mechanisms committed through the Afghanistan Compact, the Afghanistan National Development Strategy, and other agreements.
- Develop government-NGO relations. Special initiatives are needed by NGOs and government regarding how to more effectively deal with each other. In the long term, how will work be implemented in the villages? How can NGOs best support government leadership? How can government support the specialized services NGOs provide? Given that both government and NGOs have distinct roles to play, what can be done to ensure mutual benefit?
- Addressing the narcotics industry requires a multidimensional approach: government policies and enforcement; international programs to lessen the demand for narcotics; efforts to create a better understanding of the power structures that trap farmers; and realistic options at the farm level, both short term and long term.

Improving security arrangements:
- The military should limit its activities to what it specializes in – providing security and peacekeeping activities. This would create a more secure environment for the humanitarian agencies, who could then carry out their specialized work. The military should also focus its efforts on capacity building with the Afghan police, army, and related national security so as to most effectively contribute to peace and security. It should stop engaging in its present dual and contradictory roles. Rural development, and all the specialized expertise it takes, should be left to government and civilian humanitarian agencies: the UN, donor programs, NGOs, and the communities themselves.
- Continued and improved funding is needed to continue capacity building for Afghan military and security forces.

Promoting Afghan voices, ownership, and policy making:
- Give villagers a far greater voice in development. National forums of villagers, such as the 2005 Kabul conference, should be held regularly to receive feedback and to help guide rural development policy and planning. Similar forums should be established at the provincial, district, and village levels and play ongoing roles in monitoring and evaluation, annual planning, coordination, and other such functions.
- Support Afghans and help them take and keep the lead at all levels. All forms of foreign assistance must avoid over-stepping Afghan leadership; rather, it must acknowledge and encourage Afghan ownership and initiatives.

Building local and national capacities:
- In the NSP, capacity building has been almost exclusively focused on the FPs, with little capacity being been built into the government. Especially needed is capacity building between ministries with regard to the raising of awareness; the development of common visions and approaches in rural development; and the coordination of plans, policies, and programs to support integrated rural development.
- Stabilize salaries. Salary stabilization between government and other sources is a necessary part of Afghan government capacity building. If NGOs, donors, and the UN continue to out-pay the government, the most skilled Afghans will continue to avoid government in favour of foreign agencies.
- The NSP could benefit from multi-ministry involvement. This joint involvement would encourage a unified approach to the villages.
- Build capacities at the village level. Long-term follow-through is needed with the CDCs in order to build skills in group management (including bylaws) and make links with government and non-government sources for development in agriculture, health, livelihoods, education, and so on. Helping villages build up their own financial resources through savings, credit, revolving funds, or other micro-finance instruments is a necessary part of poverty alleviation.
- Recognize villages' own resources and place more demands on them to mobilize these resources. Encourage attitudes of self-help and partnership with government, donors, NGOs, and so on. Discourage dependence on outside sources. Encourage cooperation between villages.
- Build the capacities of social mobilizers, FPs, other NGOs, the government, and others who need the skills and resources for integrated, community-based rural development. Ensure better support and more realistic workloads for social mobilizers.

- Clarify the legal status of CDCs. There is some confusion about the legal status of CDCs, specifically about their roles in relation to "government versus governance." Some sources refer to CDCs as "local governance," but the lowest level of government in Afghanistan is the district level. As elected bodies, the CDCs are a new category of institution in Afghanistan. It needs to be made clear that the CDC is *only* a voluntary village development organization and not a level of government (where "government" means having power or authority, such as taxation, laws, right to arrest, imprisonment, etc.).

Ensuring inclusive, balanced development:
- Target assistance, while supporting community-based development. Only in this way will genuine participation of the poor, marginalized groups, and women be feasible.
- Turn talk into action to help Afghan women. Create strategies that are proactive and culturally sensitive, including cultural practices that separate men and women. Ensure the recruitment of women; help Afghan women help Afghan women, especially to work in rural areas; provide gender sensitization and more gender know-how at all levels. Women's programs and "gender programs" (which also help Afghan men) are both important.

Sharing lessons through open monitoring and evaluation, and support development studies:
- Support research, dialogue, and training for development in Afghanistan. Explore and analyze aid and development history, trends, issues, theories, practices, development management, and their application across various sectors. Such programming should also serve as a centre for dialogue, critical analysis, communication, and the building of common visions and practices for development. One of many priority subjects is the role of aid in unity and/or conflict.
- Raise awareness, develop skills, policy, and the practice of participation. As "participatory development" is relatively new in Afghanistan, training regarding the rationale and methods to be put into practice in all sectors is needed in the government, NGOs, the private sector, and communities.
- Promote better monitoring and evaluation, and share best practices. A system of repeating opportunities (workshops, conferences, seminars, publications, etc.) should be held to identify best practices, and this information should be used in policy development, training, and other forms of capacity building.

The NSP is an example of WKOP's observations on disjunctions between policy and practice. Ideas and lessons learned internationally *do* form the basic ideas of the NSP, but it is a victim of the "tensions between short-term measures and the longer-term structural changes necessary to prevent the recurrence of armed conflict" (Baranyi 2005c, ii). Community-based rural development and community-government dialogue must move forward if there is to be any hope of real, lasting peace. The building of this cohesion will be a long, slow process.

What does the future hold? Although most factors are dynamic, with many possible directions for change, we can think in terms of two main possible long-term scenarios. First, the NSP's weaknesses could be greatly reduced by implementing the above recommendations. The NSP is only one project; however, because of its scale and intent, it could be seen as a core around which other development could be built. With the implementation of the Afghan Compact and the interim National Development Strategy between 2006 and 2011, several new projects are being introduced, including some megaprojects. This makes it especially timely to consider the NSP in the context of the overall aid scene in Afghanistan. If the kind of recommendations made in this chapter are put into effect, and if the new levels or forms of assistance are well planned and coordinated, then rural development and peacebuilding could benefit significantly.

The second scenario continues, or perhaps even enlarges, the risks. If donor funding or government resources remain uncertain, incomplete, uncoordinated, or short term, so that the capacities that need to be built remain unbuilt, the result, at best, will be maintenance of the present "conflictual peace." Factors such as the confusing and contradictory military roles (e.g., PRTs), the unresolved narcotics trade, the continued lack of cohesion in and benefits to rural areas may simply perpetuate the causes of conflict.

Appendix

Villages in Afghanistan WKOP study

	Province	District	Village
1	Herat	Guzana	Mahalai Pusht
2	Herat	Guzana	Charkabutarkhan
3	Logar	Baraki Barak	Ahmadshah
4	Logar	Moh'd Agha	Babuki
5	Logar	Moh'd Agha	Zaqum Khil
6	Logar	Moh'd Agha	Rahmat Abad
7	Logar	Moh'd Agha	Qazi Village
8	Logar	Moh'd Agha	Kahi
9	Nangarhar	Achin	Chelgazi
10	Nangarhar	Achin	Pekha
11	Nangarhar	Achin	District Bazaar

▶

◄ *Appendix*

	Province	District	Village
12	Nangarhar	Achin	Kandi Bagh
13	Nangarhar	Chaprahan	Charkala
14	Nangarhar	Chaprahan	Hadiyakhil
15	Nangarhar	Chaprahan	Sholana
16	Nangarhar	Chaprahan	Kadi
17	Nangarhar	Rodat	Zakhil
18	Nangarhar	Rodat	Hesar Shahi
19	Nangarhar	Rodat	Chaghari
20	Nangarhar	Rodat	Chenar Kala
21	Nangarhar	Rodat	Hikal
22	Parwan	Bagram	Skandi
23	Parwan	Bagram	Nawach Safla (lower)
24	Parwan	Bagram	Nawach Bala (upper)
25	Parwan	Salang	Jawarsang
26	Parwan	Salang	Chakdara
27	Wardak	Maidan Shahr	Jami Khil
28	Wardak	Maidan Shahr	Shater
29	Wardak	Said Abad	Sadudin

7

Transition from Civil War to Peace: Challenges for Peacebuilding in Sri Lanka

Jayadeva Uyangoda

Against the background of a failed peace process, Sri Lanka provides a useful case study of what kind of peace is possible and necessary in a protracted ethno-political conflict. The central problem I explore in this chapter is this: how could an actually existing, limited, and short-term peace process develop into a long-term and sustainable process of political, economic, and social transformation? I examine this question in relation to the peace process that was inaugurated in February 2002, when the Sri Lankan government and the Liberation Tigers of Tamil Eelam (LTTE) signed a ceasefire agreement.

The peace process that began in 2002 remained incomplete as a process for conflict transformation. It could not move beyond the essential limitations of a "strategic peace" – defined here as the no-war relationship developed by the Sri Lankan state and the LTTE. It was limited peace because the scope of peace was essentially a condition understood as a temporary absence of war. The ceasefire agreement signed in February 2002 was the bedrock upon which this strategic peace was established. Its defining characteristic has been the balance of military power between the two sides (Uyangoda 2003). Strategic peace, as I point out in this chapter, brought the two sides to a ceasefire agreement and negotiations, but it did not have the capacity to produce a significant political outcome, even an interim settlement agreement, because the parties tended to evaluate such political outcomes from partisan, zero-sum perspectives. In brief, the process had weak transformative dynamics.

From the perspective of peace as a process of transformation, this chapter focuses on two issues concerning the 2002 peace process in Sri Lanka. One is political and the other economic-developmental. The political issue relates to the form of the post-conflict state in the country as a whole and, particularly, the forms of governance in Sri Lanka's northern and eastern provinces, where the armed conflict has been concentrated for two decades. It examines governance in its macro-constitutional state reform dimension as well as its regional-local dimensions. The economic-developmental issue focuses on possibilities as well as contradictions in the process of economic reconstruction at both regional and local levels.

The ethno-political civil war in Sri Lanka began in 1983 against the backdrop of a profound crisis in Sri Lanka's postcolonial regimes of governance. At the centre of this crisis has been the claims made by the minority Tamil community that it had been subjected to discrimination and denied group rights in the processes of postcolonial political change. The Tamil nationalist insurgency, which was geographically concentrated in the island's northern and eastern provinces, sought the establishment of a separate Tamil ethnic state in those areas, which the Tamils viewed as their "traditional homeland." The trajectory of Sri Lanka's ethnic conflict has been interspersed with failed attempts at a negotiated settlement.[1]

One major reason for the recurring failure of peace attempts has been the enduring commitment of both sides to the conflict to a military approach to securing unilateral outcomes. The lack of clarity and/or consensus regarding what peace should entail and what its political outcomes should be has also blurred the distinction between war and peace. Some scholars have noted this continuing lack of distinction between war and peace in Sri Lanka to make the point that peace negotiations have been an "integral part" of the long, drawn out lifecycle of the country's ethnic conflict (Sahadevan 2006, 239). Both the government and the LTTE have often approached peace negotiations as war conducted by other means. Similarly, there have been contending views among the key political actors regarding what a settlement should constitute and what kind of peace would be desirable and acceptable.

Nor was there any unanimity over how to reach the goal of peace. The perspectives ranged from a complete military solution to a negotiated settlement with regional autonomy. Although the idea of a negotiated settlement has gained ground in recent years, a number of competing perspectives exist. "Negotiation from a position of military strength," "negotiation from a position of strategic parity," "negotiations combined with a military offensive," "negotiation under conditions of ceasefire," "negotiation without ceasefire," "negotiation with external assistance," "negotiation with no external assistance," "negotiation for an interim settlement," and "negotiation for a final settlement" are some of the contending approaches to peace through negotiation. Each of these positions has a constituency and is linked to competing political agendas. In brief, peace as an outcome and the path to peace have remained essentially contested.

Similarly, sharply divergent positions continue to exist on the nature of a possible peace settlement. The dominant perspectives in Sinhalese, Tamil, and Muslim societies in Sri Lanka do not have much in common. Even within each of these ethnic communities, intense debates continue on the positions concerning a peace settlement. In the Sinhalese society, reformist sections of the ruling elite have moved away from the old "military solution" approach. In recent years, some of them have begun to argue for power sharing within a federal framework. Although this position enjoys the support of the international community engaged in Sri Lanka's peace process, it has been resisted in Sinhalese society. Many Sinhalese nationalist forces continue to oppose a federal solution in the belief that it will bring peace only at the cost of Sri Lanka's territorial unity and state sovereignty. In the Tamil society, although there has been an increasing recognition of the need for a federalist alternative to secession, there is no clarity about how the federal option can best ensure what has been termed the "internal self-determination of the Tamil nation." Meanwhile, political forces in Sri Lanka's Muslim society have been demanding regional autonomy for Muslim-majority areas in the event of a political settlement between Sinhalese and Tamil elites.

Peace negotiations held in 2002-3 did not resolve any of these substantive disputes. Nor did they provide an effective forum within which to address these issues in a manner that might lead to civil war termination and political settlement. From a peacebuilding perspective, this constitutes the key failure of Sri Lanka's 2002-3 peace process. However, amidst these setbacks, two crucial gains were made in the 2002-3 peace process. The four-year suspension of the war between the Sri Lankan state and the LTTE is the first major gain. The ceasefire agreement, despite its many shortcomings, has demonstrated that it was possible to delink Sri Lanka's ethnic conflict from war and violence between the state and Tamil political actors. Second, the commitment made by the government and the LTTE to explore a federal solution to the ethnic conflict provides a useful, though unstable, basis for a historic compromise necessary to transform Sri Lanka's civil war into peace. The fact that the negotiations were suspended soon after the two parties made this unprecedented political commitment indicates that a settlement agreement, not just a ceasefire agreement, is necessary for the stabilization of the peace process. It also demonstrates that exploring a political solution as an alternative to both the unitary state and secession is actually easier said than done.

The role of the international community was a significant dimension of the 2002-3 peace process. Norway, as the facilitator, assisted the government and the LTTE to sign the ceasefire agreement in February 2002. In the six rounds of talks held thereafter, Norway, through its peace envoys, facilitated negotiations and assisted parties to find compromises to a variety of contentious issues. The international community also pledged direct economic assistance to the government as well as to the LTTE in order to promote peacemaking as well as peacebuilding. In order to coordinate international development assistance for peace in Sri Lanka, an international conference was held in Tokyo in June 2003, co-chaired by Japan, the United States, the European Union, and Norway. Even after the suspension of talks in April 2003, the international actors continued their engagement in Sri Lanka. The maintenance of the ceasefire agreement, particularly after the peace talks entered a stalemate, is largely due to the presence of international actors in the peace process. However, from a policy perspective, the role of the international community in strengthening the peace process in Sri Lanka was a relative failure. Its agenda placed a heavy emphasis on short-term success, and it approached negotiations as an exercise that should produce an early peace deal. The international community viewed its economic assistance program as an instrument to persuade the government and the LTTE to achieve a short-term breakthrough. This focus on short-term conflict management goals ignored the need to develop long-term, conflict-sensitive strategies to address such structural issues as poverty, governance, and economic development (Goodhand and Klem 2005, 11). Thus, the challenge of peacebuilding as disclosed in the 2002-3 peace attempt was to widen the actually existing limited peace towards a comprehensive peace settlement through a stable peace process.

Governance and Sustainable Transition to Peace

There were a number of dimensions that prevented the stabilization of Sri Lanka's 2002-3 peace process and arrested the transition from actually existing limited peace to a stage of peace settlement. Paradoxically, negotiations widened the gap between "desirable" peace and "possible" peace. Similarly, key political actors themselves attempted to unilaterally appropriate the peace process for partisan gains, thereby restricting the political space for the transition from limited peace to a peace settlement. In this section, I discuss some of the key barriers to the stabilization of the Sri Lankan peace process of 2002-3 under the following headings: (1) governance and state reform, (2) dilemmas of peace and democracy, (3) demilitarization and the transition from limited peace, (4) rights of the regional minorities and state reforms, and (5) unstable regime commitment to the peace process and its outcomes.

The Question of Governance as State Reform

In a very fundamental sense, Sri Lanka's ethnic conflict and the civil war are centred on the question of state power. Ethno-political conflicts are about the distribution of state power among ethnic groups. The starting point for building peace in such conflicts is more about addressing the political demands for recognition, autonomy, and self-determination and not so much about redressing economic and identity grievances. It presupposes altering the way in which state power is constituted, organized, and shared. Thus, the issues of governance in such a conflict may be both subordinate and intimately linked to the larger question of reforming the state. In Sri Lanka, if a state reform project is to promote peacebuilding, and a peacebuilding program is to leave the ground, it should possess the capacity to facilitate the Tamil nationalist project to effect one fundamental political transition – namely, reviewing and moving away from the maximalist goal of secession towards a non-secessionist compromise for power-sharing and regional autonomy. The LTTE, the dominant actor in Tamil nationalist politics, has not provided any unequivocal evidence of such a review or move being made.

Meanwhile, in the course of the civil war, a limited and fragile state reform agenda has also evolved in Sri Lanka. A discourse of power-sharing emerged during the early years of the civil war, in the 1980s. It rested on the concept of "devolution" of power. In Sri Lanka's context, it enunciated the idea that the central government should give to provincial units some of the powers it had earlier enjoyed under the unitary system. The creation of provincial councils in 1987 was essentially animated by this particular approach to power-sharing. Meanwhile, the autonomy idea, which the LTTE articulated in 2002-3, rested on a different premise: the periphery, backed by its military strength built up through an armed struggle for secession, should negotiate with the centre to construct a framework of extensive regional autonomy. For the LTTE, regional autonomy should be the political outcome of a "national liberation war," rather than a "concession," unilateral or negotiated, made to the Tamils by the Sinhalese political class. That is probably why the LTTE deployed the somewhat vague political concept of "internal self-determination" to refer to the goal that it sought through negotiation. The point, then, is that the outcome of negotiations that the LTTE envisaged in 2002-3 would have meant reconstituting the Sri Lankan state within a binational framework.

For the Government of Sri Lanka, which is run by the Sinhalese political class, it was extremely difficult to respond to this "two nations – one federated state" proposition. Thus, a wide gulf continued to separate the LTTE and the Government of Sri Lanka with regard to how they conceptualized the nature of the post-civil war state. Bridging this gulf was a necessary precondition for a constructive outcome of the government-LTTE political engagement. However, neither the Norwegian facilitators nor the international custodians of Sri Lanka's peacebuilding process seemed to have understood, or been sensitive to, this vital precondition for conflict settlement in Sri Lanka.

During the peace negotiations in 2002-3, there was an opportunity to overcome this conceptual gulf concerning the nature of the post-conflict state. During the talks held in Oslo in December 2002, the delegations of the Sri Lankan government and the LTTE agreed to "explore" a solution based on a federal structure within a united Sri Lanka. This was a significant advancement in the negotiation process, and it had the potential of producing a major political breakthrough towards a settlement agreement. However, there was no real exploration of the federal alternative beyond the agreement that appeared on paper. Negotiations came to a standstill after the Oslo Agreement of December 2002. In April 2003, the LTTE suspended its participation in the talks. In retrospect, one may now say that the negotiation stalemate in early 2003 was not an accident. It occurred in a context within which both the Sri Lankan government and the LTTE could take the peace process forward only by working together to craft a federalist political solution. There are two possible explanations for this deadlock. First, the two main protagonists to the conflict, although they had begun direct talks, were not yet ready to undertake that task. Second, they probably agreed on a federalist option too early in the negotiation process, when the conditions were not yet ripe for exploring the concrete details of a settlement.

In any case, the idea of federalism meant two different things to the government and to the LTTE. The wide gulf between these two federalist imaginings – minimalist and maximalist – came into sharp focus in mid- and late 2003, when the Sri Lankan government and the LTTE engaged in an exercise of developing proposals for an interim administrative framework for the northern and eastern provinces. This was a sequel to an understanding between the United National Front (UNF) government and the LTTE – an understanding that had been arrived at during the 2002 peace process and that concerned setting up an interim administrative structure in order to facilitate and expedite programs of rehabilitation, resettlement, and reconstruction in the conflict-affected areas. In April-June 2002, the UNF government produced two sets of proposals for an interim administration, which the LTTE rejected as inadequate. Indeed, the government proposals were framed merely as administrative arrangements, with no recognition of the political dimensions of the ethnic conflict. Nor did they seek to provide any degree of autonomy to the proposed interim institutions. While rejecting the government's two sets of proposals, the LTTE then undertook to draft its own proposals. In October 2003, it submitted proposals to the government for what was called an Interim Self-Governing Authority (ISGA) for the northern and eastern provinces.

The conceptual basis of the LTTE's ISGA proposals was federalism within a rather extended form of regional autonomy. In an interim solution, it put forward a political framework to provide "self-rule" to the Tamil people. It also presupposed the idea of shared sovereignty, or internal self-determination. Conceived within this unconventional framework, the LTTE proposals for an interim administration sought de jure recognition for the institutions and structures of governance and administration that the LTTE had established in areas under its control during the civil war. These included the police, the judiciary, education, taxation and revenue collection, law and order, and land administration. Quite significantly, the government could not respond to these proposals because they went far beyond the limits of *regional* autonomy that the Sinhalese political elite could endorse.

The contending approaches to state reform shared by the UNF government and the LTTE were grounded on two differing visions of the post-civil war state. The first rested on a "thin" version of federalism. The Sri Lankan ruling elites as well as the international actors involved in the peace process subscribed to this minimalist approach. On the other end, the LTTE articulated a "thick" version of federalism, approximating a confederal arrangement, based on the concept of sovereignty-sharing statehood for two "nations." It appears that the two sides were quite aware of the incompatibility of these two visions but were unable to address it either at or away from the negotiation table. Instead of reviving the stalled negotiations process, this controversy over the interim administration actually made the return to talks impossible. It also led to a major political crisis that resulted in the dismissal of the UNF regime. The day after the LTTE officially submitted its ISGA proposals, Sri Lanka's president, backed by the Sinhalese nationalist parties, took over the Ministry of Defence, arguing that national security and state sovereignty were facing an imminent threat from the LTTE. Three months later, the president dismissed the UNF government, dissolved Parliament, and called for fresh parliamentary elections. At the parliamentary elections held in April 2004, the UNF, which had initiated the negotiations with the LTTE, lost power. The new political coalition that replaced the UNF ran its election campaign on a Sinhalese nationalist agenda that promised to resume negotiations with the LTTE from a position of military strength and state supremacy. This, in a way, brought to an effective end Sri Lanka's peace process (which had begun in 2002) and its political reform potential.

Dilemma of Peace and Democracy

The question of governance as state power has a few other complexities that need to be examined in relation to the challenges of sustainable peacebuilding. The relationship between negotiated peace and democracy has been a recurring theme in this regard.

How can peace bring democracy to Sri Lanka's northern and eastern provinces? This question has assumed particular salience because of the differing perspectives on the possible link between peace and democracy. Among the contending perspectives on this question, the Sri Lankan government held two differing positions. The UNF government, which initiated direct talks with the LTTE, did not press for a clear link between peace and democracy. The UNF government leaders viewed "peace" in the limited sense of the absence of war between the state and the LTTE. On the other hand, President Kumaratunga and the People's Alliance, which she led, repeatedly emphasized that human rights and democracy should be central to the peace process and the UNF government's engagement with the LTTE. Many civil society groups also shared this approach. The link between peace, human rights, and democracy became a crucial issue in the 2002-3 peace process for one major reason. The LTTE administered a civilian population in areas under its control, and it sought, through the peace process, an opportunity to formalize its structures of administration and civilian control. However, the LTTE was not a political entity but, essentially, a military entity. In areas under its control it did not allow or practise human rights or democracy as understood in liberal terms.

The essentially militaristic character of the LTTE further complicated the democracy dilemma during 2002-3. Through its subordinate political wing, the LTTE, as a military entity, had been engaging the Sri Lankan state in negotiations. In a comparison with the situation that prevailed in Northern Ireland during negotiations, one might say that there is no Sinn Féin in Sri Lanka. Besides, the LTTE seemed to continue the practice of defining its political engagement in terms of military-strategic goals. Making the situation more complex, the LTTE had been behaving like a state in relation to the civilian population living in areas under its control.[2] Yet, the LTTE was not bound by international norms governing the behaviour of a state. The state-like behaviour of the LTTE is backed essentially by the movement's military-coercive power rather than by political institutions of democratic governance and domestic and international accountability. If one takes seriously the LTTE's claim that it represents the Tamil "nation" in the form of an "emerging state," then this "state" is no more than a regional ethno-political project engaged in the primitive accumulation of state power through military means. This, to a great extent, explains the absence of a strong political wing for the LTTE and its excessive reliance on military-coercive institutions in the conduct of politics.

Overcoming this contradiction between actually possible peace and democracy has not been easy. The transformation of the LTTE into a political party would, indeed, have strengthened that capacity of the peace process to produce democratic outcomes. It did not happen during the 2002 peace initiative. The Tamil National Alliance (TNA), the parliamentary party affiliated with the LTTE, was not the LTTE's political or parliamentary wing as such. Besides, the TNA has no political role independent of the LTTE. Even in this difficult situation, one policy option available during the negotiation crisis of 2003-4 was to broaden the peace process by making it inclusive and multi-partial (Ferdinands et al. 2004). This would have entailed, at an appropriate stage, including representatives of the Muslim community as well as Tamil parties other than the LTTE in the negotiation process. Critics of the 2002 peace process argued that broadening the participation would have made the peace process, as well as its outcomes, democratic and stable. Yet, this did not happen during the 2002-3 peace process. While the LTTE was opposed to any broadening of the range of Tamil, or even Muslim, participants at negotiations, the UNF government was not convinced about the outcomes of such broadening. Similarly, the People's Alliance (PA) party and its allies, who pushed for broad inclusivity in negotiations, had no real interest in a positive negotiation outcome. For them, the argument for inclusivity was, at best, a red herring.

Demilitarization in the Transition from Limited Peace

Linked to the dilemma of peace and democracy, which we explored above, was the equally difficult problem of demilitarization in the northern and eastern provinces, where the war had been concentrated for about two and a half decades. The developments during the peace process of 2002-3 suggested that the absence of a comprehensive demilitarization program weakened the stability of the entire peace process, even contributing to the eventual resumption of hostilities.

The 2002-3 peace process began with a plan for partial demilitarization. The ceasefire agreement, signed in February 2002, was the bedrock of that process. The ceasefire agreement (CFA) had a limited scope of demilitarization. It sought to manage the military relations between the state and the LTTE in a situation of no-war, supervised by an international monitoring group – the Sri Lanka Monitoring Mission. Beyond that, the CFA did not have any provisions for disarmament or demobilization. It thus left room for a negotiated agreement to address issues of comprehensive demilitarization.

The question of demilitarization surfaced in the negotiations in the second and third round of talks. The government and the LTTE agreed to set up a joint subcommittee on demilitarization and normalization. The subcommittee held some meetings, but in a few months it became defunct, when the LTTE decided not to participate. The LTTE appeared to view the subcommittee as a mechanism to compel it to initiate a demilitarization process before signing a peace agreement. In retrospect, it is clear that the LTTE was not ready for a demilitarization program that went beyond the limited framework of the CFA.

The failure of the demilitarization initiative in the 2002-3 peace process highlighted the actual difficulties in a disarmament, demobilization, and reintegration program during the civil war transition. The conventional approach to demilitarization is for the counter-state armed groups to demobilize their fighting units, decommission their weapons, and reintegrate their cadres. This model of DDR has worked under conditions in which the armed groups had either lost the civil war or decided to abandon the armed struggle. But, in Sri Lanka, the question of demilitarization had a different character. When it began negotiations with the government in 2002, the LTTE had neither lost the civil war nor abandoned armed struggle as a means to achieve political ends. It had been negotiating with the Sri Lankan state from a position of symmetrical power relations. Besides, the LTTE had taken up the position that it should maintain its military strength until a final settlement agreement was reached and the terms of such an agreement were fully and comprehensively implemented. This position was based on the argument that it was the military strength of the LTTE that had compelled the Sri Lankan government to abandon the project of a military solution and, instead, to seek a politically negotiated compromise. The LTTE had further argued that, once it decommissioned its weapons and dissolved its military structures, the "Tamil nation" would be "disarmed," with no guarantee that the Sinhalese leadership would honour its commitments to a political settlement.

The difficult question of DDR is also linked to the existence of a parallel, though primitive, state run by the LTTE in parts of the northern and eastern provinces. When fighting the war, the LTTE had also controlled civilian populations and had administered them by setting up institutions to tend to policing and law and order, customs, revenue and tax collection, and public health services (Stokke 2006). These institutions, which comprised a parallel administration, had also emerged in a context of war, in which the presence of governance institutions of the Sri Lankan state, in most areas of the northern and eastern region, was extremely weak and had been largely replaced by war machinery. From the militant Tamil nationalist perspective, war making had also been a process of state making. The resultant dilemma, which emerged during the 2002-3 peace process, was whether to allow the LTTE's institutions of governance to be accepted as legitimate – as something that could eventually be absorbed into a post-conflict governance structure – or whether to abolish them so that, in a postwar situation, the Sri Lankan state's institutions of governance could return to the entire region. The political engagement between the government and the LTTE in 2002-3 failed to address this key issue, which was central to civil war transition. In fact, the gradual collapse of the negotiation process occurred against the backdrop of this failure.

From a policy perspective, the failure of the short-lived demilitarization program in Sri Lanka's 2002-3 peace process raises the relevance of security and political guarantees, even in a pre-settlement phase of civil war transition. The scholarly literature on civil war settlement has extensively focused on the central importance of security guarantees in settlement stability (e.g., Stedman 1991; Walter 1999; and Hartzell 1999). The central point in this literature is that resolving the underlying issues upon which the civil war had been fought is enough to convince the combatants to accept and to implement a peace agreement. There still remains the higher hurdle of security guarantees in contexts where combatants are required to shed their partisan armies and hand over the territory as well as arms. These are issues that create among the combatants a condition of "fear of settlement"

(Stedman 1991)) and an "increased sense of vulnerability" (Walter 1999). The experience in Sri Lanka in 2002-3 demonstrates that security dilemmas surfaced in the pre-settlement phase of the peace process, during the transition from a ceasefire agreement to a political agreement. As such, the Sri Lankan experience also suggests that security guarantees must be implemented during the pre-agreement phase as well. In particular, it calls for exploring alternatives such as international guarantees, along with a solid post-conflict political framework, for settlement stability. These could be both security and political guarantees.[3] International political guarantees for settlement stability are particularly important in view of the possibilities of settlement instability in circumstances of regime change. Sri Lanka's recent experience shows that regime change tends to erode the commitment to agreements signed by previous regimes.

The Question of Regional Minorities: Inclusivity and Deep Federalization

One of the key sources of threat to the stability of the process during the 2002-3 peace initiative was the intensified majority-minority conflict over the consequences of the peace process itself. After the ceasefire agreement came into effect in February 2002 and the negotiations between the UNF government and the LTTE began a few months later, the Muslim as well as Sinhalese communities in the northern and eastern provinces became extremely apprehensive about the possible Tamil, and LTTE, domination of the region in a future power-sharing arrangement. The feeling of having been excluded from the negotiating process aggravated their skepticism about the peace process as a whole. There was a shared perception in these two communities that they had been losers and victims, rather than beneficiaries, of the peace process. The Muslim political parties demanded separate Muslim representation at negotiations. They also insisted that Muslim leaders should be a party to any agreement between the LTTE and the government. Meanwhile, nationalist political parties began to exploit the new sense of vulnerability felt by the Sinhalese community in the Eastern Province by mobilizing against the peace process. Their message to the Sinhalese people, who were a regional minority in the east, was that the particular peace process of 2002-3 was detrimental to their safety, security, and even existence.

Muslim and Sinhalese displeasure over the peace process of 2002-3 suggested two policy measures that were necessary for the stabilization of a future peace initiative. One was immediate and the other long-term. In the short run, ensuring the participation of Muslim representatives in negotiations, and providing guarantees to the Sinhalese community in the Eastern Province that their interests would not be endangered, is necessary in order to build the confidence of regional minorities in the negotiation process. From a long-term perspective, any settlement agreement, interim or final, needs to ensure that regional minorities will not become permanent and disempowered minorities in any post-civil war regional autonomy regime.

On the question of Muslim representation within a post-civil war political arrangement, there have been two sharply divergent views among Tamil nationalists and Muslim political activists in the Eastern Province. Tamil nationalists long held the view that, since the Sri Lankan Muslims were Tamil speakers, the political interests of all Tamil-speaking people, Tamils and Muslims alike, were identical. From this perspective, the Tamil parties were viewed as representing Muslim political interests as well as Tamil political interests. However, the Muslims began to oppose this view when, in the early 1980s, the Tamil national struggle became an armed civil war against the state. They began to assert their separate political identity on the basis of religion and to demand separate political representation. It was against this background that the Sri Lanka Muslim Congress was formed to project a separate Muslim political identity (Knoerzer 1998). The Congress became divided, and, as a result, there was no unified Muslim political leadership. Meanwhile, Muslims in the Northern Province, many of whom continue to live in displaced conditions, began to articulate the position that their needs and interests were substantially different from those of the Muslims in the Eastern Province.[4] They argued that regional autonomy was not a solution to their problems (such as the right to return to areas in the Northern Province where they had previously lived). In the context of these divisions and diversity of perspectives, the inclusion of Muslim representatives in the settlement process assumed greater salience.

The position taken by the LTTE with regard to the Muslim issue indicated that, during the civil war, a particular political complexity pertaining to Muslim-Tamil relations had emerged. The LTTE did not recognize the Muslim claim for separate representation at peace talks. Its argument was that the war had been between the Sri Lankan state and the Tamil community and that, therefore, the settlement agreement should be between the two principal parties to the conflict. The LTTE also claimed that, once it reached a peace agreement with the state, it (the LTTE) would sign a separate peace agreement with Muslim representatives of the northern and eastern provinces. The LTTE's notion of two-party talks and settlement ran counter to the Muslim notion of three-party talks and a tripartite settlement. Given the recent history of extreme violence in LTTE-Muslim relations, the LTTE position did not have much credibility in the Muslim polity. In fact, during the 2002 peace process, there emerged a new wave of radicalization among Muslim youth who felt excluded from and marginalized by the government-LTTE negotiations. A student at the predominantly Muslim South Eastern University in Olluvil, Amparai, stated in an interview: "For people living in Colombo, Sri Lanka's ethnic problem is a conflict between the Sinhalese and Tamils. Here in the Eastern Province, it is between Tamils and Muslims,

LTTE and Muslims. Muslims cannot forget all those killings, massacres, and violence." Another university student pointed to the increasing frustration as well as the tendency for radicalization among the Muslim youth in the Eastern Province: "There are no jobs for educated Muslim youth. The government does not listen to our peaceful voice. Our Muslim political leaders do not listen to us either. Tamils took to guns and that is why the government and the world powers have taken them seriously. Muslim youths feel that to be taken note of, they should also take up arms and fight. Then only will Tamils also learn how to treat Muslims with dignity."

Complaints coming from the Sinhalese community in the Eastern Province were not dissimilar. The Sinhalese there were a national "majority" that had to face the political reality of becoming a "regional minority." They did not have a regional political party to articulate their specific grievances and interests; rather, they were basically represented by national political parties. There was a growing fear among them that, during the peace process with the LTTE, the national political parties in power ignored their concerns about safety, security, and the future. In an interview, a Sinhalese woman shopkeeper in a village in the Amparai district in the Eastern Province vividly expressed this deep sense of insecurity: "We, the Sinhalese, are surrounded by them, the Tamils and Muslims. We have no way to escape when they attack next time." In interviews, many Sinhalese in the Eastern Province expressed the feeling of being surrounded by "hostile" Tamils, and to some extent Muslims. They viewed themselves as being in a situation in which they were a powerless regional minority. During one interview, a Sinhalese woman political activist from Trincomalee district asked about the right of the "minority" Sinhalese in the area when, under democracy, "Tamils and Muslims would begin to dominate the federal unit in the Eastern Province. We are the national majority, but a powerless minority under federalism." This is not an entirely unfounded fear. The Sinhalese people in the region are most likely to view a conflict settlement arrangement that would result in the LTTE's securing political and administrative leadership in the province as totally inimical to their interests.

These conditions in the Eastern Province highlight the question of the rights of the regional minorities, in interim as well as in post-conflict arrangements, with regard to regional autonomy. They also compel policy makers to re-examine some of the key assumptions about the policy of federalism. Regionalized, or territorial, power-sharing has the inherent problem of making a national minority a regional majority, often ignoring the rights of regional minorities. These rights concerns are issues that emerged during a violent and protracted war. The experience of violence and destruction during the time of civil war, including massacres and disputes over land and private property, has severely estranged intercommunity relations in Sri Lanka's conflict areas. As Rajasingham-Senanayake (1999) has noted, particularly in the Eastern Province, multiethnic and multicultural community co-existence among Tamil, Muslim, and Sinhalese peoples has disappeared against the backdrop of war, violence, ethnic cleansing, displacement, and the destruction of social infrastructure. The fact that the LTTE's own interim self-government proposals of 2002 did not elaborate upon any arrangement for Muslim rights has created further fears that the LTTE might practise regional ethnic majoritarianism in an authoritarian manner.

Sri Lanka's experience in ethnic relations shows that a meaningful arrangement for regional self-governance in Sri Lanka's north and east will need to address the following concerns of the three communities: (1) recognition as political communities with grievances as well as aspirations and rights, (2) security and safety of members of their communities and their property, (3) representation at all levels of regional and local governance, and (4) citizens' equal access to institutions of governance, notwithstanding the numerical or material, political or resource strength of the respective communities. Translated into the language of rights, they constitute four specific domains of rights that a new regional/local regime of self-governance should endure: recognition rights, security rights, representational rights, and governance rights. These indeed constitute self-determination rights of not one ethnic community but, rather, of all minorities. A commitment to guaranteeing self-determination rights of all minorities necessitates innovative policy options as, within its conventional framework, federalism is not adequate to address minority claims for autonomy within regional autonomy (or federalism within federalism). It also calls for broadening federalism at the centre as well as in the regions.[5]

Unstable Commitment to the Peace Process

Is peacebuilding through civil war termination by peaceful means possible in a fractured democratic polity? Sri Lanka's experience in 2002-3 does not provide an affirmative answer to this question. Both the CFA and the peace talks fell victim to interparty political competition and rivalry, eventually creating a situation in which undermining the peace process became a major part of "normal" politics.

Scholars have noted the role of the "politics of ethnic outbidding" in Sri Lanka's escalating ethnic conflict (Roberts 1978; DeVotta 2006). One key element has been the parliamentary opposition's mobilization of Sinhalese nationalist resistance against any step taken by the ruling party towards accommodating the Tamil minority's demand for regional autonomy. One ironic aspect of this politics of ethnic outbidding is that the very political party that initiated such accommodation while in power would undermine similar policy measures taken by the new government (which, when in opposition, had mobilized nationalist resistance). This has been a particular form of tit-for-tat politics.

In Sri Lanka's peace process in and after 2003, this politics of ethnic outbidding took a novel form. The UNF government, which initiated the peace process with the LTTE in 2002, did not have full control over the government structure since the leader of the parliamentary opposition continued to hold the powerful office of president of the country. With a history of intense interparty rivalry, the UNF government excluded the president and her powerful opposition coalition from the peace process. The president and her PA coalition, in turn, gave leadership of Sinhalese nationalist resistance to the UNF-LTTE peace process, portraying it as a threat to "national" security and state sovereignty. This rivalry between the UNF government (which had the majority in Parliament) and the president (who controlled the executive branch of the state) created a peculiar dual power situation in which the regime's responsibility (as well as capacity) to take the peace process forward was both uncertain and unstable. When the rivalry between the prime minister and the president reached a high point towards the end of 2003, President Kumaratunga dissolved Parliament and called for fresh parliamentary elections, in which the UNF lost power.

The April 2004 elections brought an essentially Sinhalese nationalist coalition into power. This coalition government, the United People's Freedom Alliance (UPFA), held the view that any peace process with the LTTE should be based on a position of military-strategic advantage for the state. The new government's agenda with regard to the peace process initiated by the UNF government in 2002 was to bring it to an end and then begin a new peace process from a position of military strength. However, a relapse into war did not occur until 2006. A new president belonging to the UPFA took over power after the presidential election held in November 2005. The new president, backed by Sinhalese nationalist forces, continued the policy of negotiating with the LTTE from a position of military strength. The LTTE, for its part, seemed to have made a similar decision during this period to pursue the negotiation option from a position of military advantage. With the regime change of April 2004, Sri Lanka's conflict seems to have entered a qualitatively new phase, in which a win-win outcome is no longer perceived as a desirable political goal either by the government or by the LTTE. Thus, both sides used the Geneva negotiations in early 2006 either to secure unilateral advantage or to gain international support, with no real commitment to advance the peace process. The relapse into war in the latter part of 2006 was, in a way, an inevitable outcome of the new approach to peace – peace as an essentially unilateral outcome defined by military-strategic interests – that the new Sri Lankan government and the LTTE developed during this period.

A complex political issue concerning peace, as revealed in the period after 2003, was the likelihood that electoral democracy could, under certain circumstances, undermine a peace process in an ethnically fractured society. Appealing to ethnic fears and the sense of insecurity arising out of a peace settlement were "legitimate" practices in the process of electoral politics. Yet, those practices made the government's commitment to the peace process unstable and weak, eventually paving the way for the resumption of war in 2006.

The Development Question

Parallel to the issues of governance and the politics of peace were the contradictory trajectories of economic development that emerged during the 2002-3 peace process, directly shaping the conflict and peace dynamics. The UNF government's 2002-3 peace process had a dual track – ceasefire and negotiations with the LTTE, along with economic recovery and reform. In the economic recovery and reform program, the UNF implemented what can be described as a textbook, liberal approach to peacebuilding, which was actively backed by the donor community. As we have already noted, the international community was involved in Sri Lanka's 2002-3 peace process at a variety of levels. Norway played the most direct role as facilitator, communicator, and mediator in negotiations. The American, British, Canadian, and Japanese governments and the European Union were closely involved in assessing the progress of negotiations so that international commitment and assistance for economic aid for reconstruction could be determined. In order to systematize the relationship between economic assistance and peace, the four key international actors in the Sri Lankan peace process – Norway, Japan, the United States, and the European Union – constituted themselves into what has been called "co-chairs" of the program for development assistance to strengthen Sri Lanka's peace process. They coordinated the Tokyo donor meeting of 17 June 2003.

The story of the link between peace and economic development in Sri Lanka in 2002-3 has three levels: the first involves the role of the international and donor communities in "promoting peace" and "assisting peacebuilding"; the second level involves the contradictory economic development visions shared by the UNF regime and the LTTE; and the third involves the electoral consequence of a liberal peace-dividend approach to civil war termination.

Negative Lessons of Peace Promotion through Development Assistance

The international engagement in Sri Lanka's peace process has a specific history. Earlier economic interventions have been largely in the form of humanitarian and development assistance. In the early period of civil war, the international economic assistance to Sri Lanka had no link with peace-building. Such assistance was essentially directed towards backing the Sri Lankan state, which, simultaneously, had engaged in an internal civil war as well as economic liberalization (Bastian 2003). For example, the Japanese government, the World Bank, and the Asian Development Bank had adopted an aid policy that was to "practically disregard the war and provide development assistance as if the war did not exist" (Ofstad 2002, 167). A significant shift in donor policy towards Sri Lanka occurred in the mid-1990s, when the government of the People's Alliance, headed by President Chandrika Kumaratunga, initiated a peace process with the LTTE in 1994 and later engaged in a major military campaign. This was a policy of "peace promotion." Direct international assistance, both political and economic, as well as the participation of international actors is a key distinguishing feature of the 2002-3 peace process. The UNF government, unlike the previous PA government, sought the active participation of the international community in the economic and political spheres for two strategic reasons. First, the UNF government leadership thought that the "internationalization" of the peace process was capable of providing the government with an "international safety net" while engaging in the peace process. Second, the government believed that a rapid process of rehabilitation, resettlement, and reconstruction, accompanied by a growth-oriented investment strategy and active support of the international community, would create tangible economic and social dividends for the people. At the Tokyo donor conference in June 2003, the donor community pledged US$4.5 billion over a four-year period (between 2003 and 2006). The donors viewed economic assistance of substantial proportions as a necessary strategic incentive to ensure that both parties to the conflict would work towards "a mutually acceptable final political solution" (Tokyo Declaration on Reconstruction and Development in Sri Lanka, 10 June 2003).

This brings us to the question of the "peace dividend" that has emerged in Sri Lanka's conflict resolution process. Political leaders in Sri Lanka who have changed their policies from waging war to pursuing peace have often rationalized their peace efforts by making the point that peace was a necessary condition for economic development and prosperity. They also argued that a reduction in the military and defence expenditure would enable governments to focus more on social welfare, growth, and infrastructure development.[6] For two main reasons, this "peace dividend" thesis re-emerged in 2001-2: First, the year 2001 recorded the worst economic growth rate in post-independence Sri Lanka, a negative figure – minus 1.4 percent; second, when the LTTE mounted a surprise attack on Colombo airport in September 2001, it became clear that the war had reached a stage at which the LTTE was targeting strategic economic installations. The attack on the airport resulted in the immediate collapse of the tourist industry and created great doubts in the minds of the external investor community about safety and security in Sri Lanka. Within this context of political and security uncertainty, the local business community organized itself to demand that the government and the LTTE resume peace negotiations through cessation of hostilities. The new UNF administration's approach to economic stability and development was to achieve that goal through a process of peace, the argument being that peace and economic development were intertwined. In this approach, the war-torn northern and eastern provinces were to be rebuilt through a program of rehabilitation, resettlement, and reconstruction (Triple R), while the economy in the rest of the country was to be developed by creating an atmosphere of peace and stability for the domestic and external business/investment communities.

However, the experience in 2003-4 showed that international economic incentives have not worked well in Sri Lanka (Kelegama 2004). The Tokyo pledge was made when peace talks remained suspended as a result of the LTTE's decision in March 2003 to boycott negotiations. The international community expected the LTTE to return to talks in response to the pledges of international economic assistance; however, the LTTE, ignoring both appeals and pressure brought by the donor co-chairs, boycotted the Tokyo donor conference too. It is quite pertinent to note that, as a policy tool, international economic assistance had its limitations. The LTTE clearly demonstrated that it accorded primacy to strategic objectives rather than to economic incentives for peace. The lesson to be learned from this experience is that incentives for rapid economic development were not sufficient to persuade a rebel movement committed to an autarchic development trajectory to return to the path of negotiation.

Contradictory Approaches to Economic Development

In the build up to the Tokyo donor conference of June 2003, a controversy emerged between the government and the LTTE regarding the priorities and the focus of international development assistance to Sri Lanka. In the development assistance program formulated by the former UNF regime (*Regaining Sri Lanka*), the focus was on the development agenda of the country as a whole. The LTTE objected to this position, arguing that, in peace-related international development assistance, the war-torn areas of the north and east should be given priority and precedence over the rest of the country. The LTTE's position on this argument was that, although there was generalized poverty and deprivation in Sri Lanka as a whole, the poverty in the war-affected north and east should be treated as being qualitatively different from that in the rest of the country. The basis for this argument was the claim that the poverty in the north and east was the result of the intensity of war, whereas the poverty in the south was largely a consequence of the government's economic mismanagement.

Sri Lanka's economic recovery agenda during 2002-3 had region-specific and country-specific dimensions. The region-specific aspects of the immediate development needs emanated from the reconstruction, rehabilitation, and development needs of the war-torn north and east region. Its country-specific aspects were linked to the overall economic crisis that Sri Lanka had experienced in 2001, and after, and the reform agenda implemented at the behest of the multilateral donor institutions. The UNF government, with a history of being the pioneer of free-market economic reforms, easily embraced the program of "liberal peace," the economic component of which promoted an agenda of further economic liberalization. Thus, the UNF government appeared to be quite at ease with the essentially "liberal" direction of peacebuilding under conditions of economic globalization, even welcoming and actively engaging with the donor agenda and conditions for peace promotion.

Sri Lanka's southern areas, administered by the Sri Lankan state, had gone through economic liberalization since 1978 and structural adjustment reforms since the mid-1980s. They had been closely integrated with the world economy. In contrast, the north, particularly the areas controlled and administered by the LTTE, had remained insulated from these economic reforms for about two decades. The economy there had some unusual characteristics. It had been devastated by the protracted war and, in fact, had been reduced to the status of a subsistence economy, supported by international humanitarian assistance and remittances from the Tamil diaspora. The market in the north had been almost entirely controlled and managed by the LTTE, which exercised strict state control. The economic activities in these areas had been largely confined to peasant agriculture, fishing, and trading within an acutely impoverished populace. In such an environment, the LTTE was unwilling to open up the economy of the north to market forces, unless the market functioned under its political and administrative control.

Thus, from a political economy perspective, a key challenge in the north involved consolidating the primitive accumulation of capital before embarking on market-led economic relations with either the southern areas of Sri Lanka or the global economy. However, the UNF government and the donor community were not adequately sensitive to the qualitative distinctions between the economies in Sri Lanka's war-torn north and the south. Whereas the southern parts of the Sri Lankan state had been subjected to major macroeconomic restructuring, the war-affected Northern Province had only a subsistence economy, supported by remittances from the Tamil diaspora and expatriate labour. Under these conditions, the LTTE appeared to prefer a path of "planned transition" to a market economy rather than an abrupt transition to an economy linked to the structures of globalization.[7] In this perspective, the best economic mechanism to facilitate the transition of the north's "war economy" to a "post-conflict" capitalist economy was a regional regime of "state capitalism" administered by the LTTE.

Reconstruction and Normalization before or after a Final Political Settlement

The LTTE, during all its negotiations with Sri Lankan governments, put forward the position that any peace process should accord primacy to the normalization of civilian life in the war-affected areas. The LTTE's interpretation of normalization included the return and resettlement of internally displaced people, the rehabilitation of all people affected by the war, and the reconstruction of economic and social infrastructure. This position stood in sharp contrast to the position held by the People's Alliance government (1994-2001 and 2004-5), which held that negotiations should address not only issues pertaining to the normalization of civilian life but also a final settlement to the ethnic conflict. The LTTE had consistently rejected this position. However, the UNF government's position on this issue in 2002-3 bore some similarity to the LTTE's stand. The LTTE claimed that the normalization of civilian life through a rapid rehabilitation, reconstruction, and resettlement process would create "conditions conducive to a permanent solution" to the ethnic conflict. In the LTTE's approach, the normalization of civilian life was a necessary prelude to discussions on a permanent solution. Similarly, the UNF government did not see that the idea of an early "final" political settlement with the LTTE was possible or even feasible. In the UNF's thinking, economic reconstruction and reforms under "no-war" conditions would eventually create an environment conducive to a settlement agreement. Therefore, emphasis in the short term would be on the ceasefire and an agenda for economic reconstruction.

But there was a great deal of skepticism over the LTTE's claim. Critics of the 2002-3 peace process saw in it the LTTE's avoidance of any commitment to negotiating a final settlement to the ethnic conflict. They also argued that the UNF government, by failing to press for an agenda for a final political settlement, had merely engaged in a futile exercise of "appeasement" of the LTTE that would eventually serve the latter's hidden agenda. Critics, including the powerful alliance of the PA, the Sinhalese nationalist party (Janatha Vimukthi Peramuna [JVP]), and the media, repeatedly emphasized this point in the intense public debate on the peace process. Eventually, this succeeded in reinforcing intense public doubt about the actual outcome of the UNF-LTTE negotiations. Yet, the issue about interim versus final peace is a contentious one that will surface in future peace processes as well. Both approaches have valid and formidable justifications. Combining the interim with the final peace within a framework of political transformation is perhaps one way to overcome the dichotomy.

Institution Building and Interim Governance for Reconstruction and Development

This is one of the major issues of contention that surfaced during Sri Lanka's peace process in 2002-3. When the UNF government and the LTTE agreed in September 2002 to initiate a Triple R program in the north and east, they also jointly agreed to set up new institutions to facilitate this process. Accordingly, the Subcommittee for Immediate Rehabilitation and Humanitarian Needs (SIRHN), a political affairs committee, and a gender subcommittee were set up. None of these subcommittees got off the ground since negotiations between the government and the LTTE reached a stalemate soon after they were set up. The LTTE's explanation of the SIRHN failure was that it became yet another government bureaucratic entity, operated by government officials who had no sensitivity to the special needs of the war-affected north and east. In contrast, the government claimed that the LTTE did not show much commitment to activating SIRHN. While both explanations may hold some truth, the real issue concerns the thin commitment of both sides to joint institution building during the transitional phase.

In the wake of the failure of the SIRHN experiment of institution building for development, the LTTE began to insist on setting up of an interim administrative structure to carry out reconstruction and development in the north and east. Thus, in October 2003, the LTTE proposed an interim self-governing authority, seeking extensive powers over economic development, administration, and political control of the region. The most striking point about the LTTE's proposals for an interim administration was that the LTTE sought full control over the entire reconstruction and development process in the north and east, quite independent of the central government. LTTE thinking on this issue appeared to be that, since it had led the Tamil nationalist armed struggle, it, not the state, should lead the reconstruction process in the north and east. However, the UNF government was extremely reluctant to grant such extensive powers and authority to the LTTE as it believed that this would erode the authority and sovereignty of the Sri Lankan state. The unwillingness of the UNF government to resume the stalled peace talks in order to discuss the LTTE's ISGA proposals was also largely linked to its position that discussions on contentious issues that impinged on a political settlement should be deferred.

The two sides failed to find a common ground that would enable them to break the deadlock. As a result, the reconstruction and development process, particularly in the north, was exceedingly slow, even within a context in which multilateral and bilateral donors had pledged considerable reconstruction support. One key lesson of this experience is that institution building for the transition to peace cannot take place outside the politics of the ethnic conflict. Even interim institutions are linked to the central question of reorganizing state power.

Economics and Politics of Post-Tsunami Rebuilding

The tsunami of 26 December 2004 devastated the coastal areas of Sri Lanka's northern, eastern, and southern provinces. It caused about 35,000 deaths and the complete destruction of most of the villages, towns, and livelihoods in the affected areas. Those who suffered were mostly poor communities belonging to Sinhalese, Tamil, and Muslim ethnic groups. Most of the affected areas in the Northern Province and some parts of the Eastern Province fell within territories that were under the military and administrative control of the LTTE. Because of this dual power situation, which was a consequence of the civil war, effective post-tsunami rebuilding called for cooperation between the Sri Lankan state and the LTTE. Meanwhile, the international donor community pledged about US$2.5 billion for Sri Lanka's post-tsunami rebuilding and reconstruction efforts. The donor community had also viewed the post-tsunami process as a window of opportunity for the Sri Lankan government and the LTTE to resume political engagement and to work together in post-conflict development efforts. The post-tsunami rebuilding task in the northern and eastern provinces had to be linked with the post-civil war recovery process. With regard to the latter, the government, with donor assistance and LTTE participation, had already implemented a Triple R process. Even when the government-LTTE negotiations were suspended, the Triple R programs continued, focusing on economic and social reconstruction.

When the tsunami struck Sri Lanka in December 2004, there had been a change in the political equation with regard to the peace process. The UNF government, which initiated political engagement with the LTTE, was no longer in power, having lost the power struggle with the president. President Kumaratunga, having dismissed the UNF government, held parliamentary elections in April 2004. At this election, the UNF lost its parliamentary majority. A new coalition, the UPFA, led by President Kumaratunga herself, formed the new government.

Even though the post-tsunami process opened up a new window of opportunity for the government and the LTTE to work cooperatively towards regional development, the two sides did not fully utilize this opportunity for peacebuilding objectives (Uyangoda 2005a). In fact, they had competing approaches and priorities regarding the post-tsunami recovery and rebuilding efforts. The government, while attempting to centralize all the processes involved in immediate, medium-, and long-term responses, also tried to prevent the LTTE from making use of the tsunami disaster to gain access to direct international assistance. The LTTE, on the other hand, saw the tsunami as an opportunity to initiate rebuilding and development programs in the tsunami-affected areas with direct international assistance, thus bypassing the Sri Lankan government, which they saw as ineffective in its responses to the humanitarian emergency. During the first few months after the tsunami, the government and the LTTE failed to achieve any progress towards cooperation.

Eventually, the slow materialization of international assistance for post-tsunami rebuilding compelled the two sides to negotiate and formulate a "joint mechanism" for planning and implementing the reconstruction programs. By June 2005, a draft of a possible joint agreement emerged. However, the draft generated Sinhalese nationalist resistance because the Sinhalese believed that a joint mechanism between the government and the LTTE for post-tsunami assistance would provide the LTTE political legitimacy as well as access to international economic assistance. The controversy eventually developed into a major political crisis when one partner in the government, the Sinhalese nationalist JVP, left the ruling coalition in July 2005, expressing strong opposition to the proposed agreement. When the government and the LTTE signed the agreement, Sinhalese nationalist groups, including the JVP, challenged its constitutionality before the Supreme Court. The Supreme Court, while accepting the overall validity of the agreement, invalidated some of its clauses. The outcome of the court determination was that the joint mechanism could not be implemented at all.

Governance and Development on the Ground

Some of the crucial issues concerning the governance and development challenges in the transition from civil war to peace in Sri Lanka can be highlighted in the experiences of the communities in Vavuniya (a district located in Sri Lanka's Northern Province) and Batticaloa, Trincomalee, and Amparai (districts located in the Eastern Province). The northern and eastern provinces are the regions in which the conflict and war have been concentrated for more than twenty-five years, with all that means in terms of destruction, population displacement, and violence. During the 2002-3 peace process, the LTTE also controlled a sizeable area of these two provinces, and this resulted in a dual power situation. The Eastern Province is ethnically mixed, with equal proportions of Sinhalese, Tamil, and Muslim communities. This ethnic diversity also provided the context for much of the inter-community violence in the province during the war as well as in recent years (under the conditions of the ceasefire).

In view of the specificities of the conditions in Vavuniya and the Eastern Province, and in an attempt to accommodate the different possibilities emerging from these varied conditions, we discuss the two cases separately.

Vavuniya

Vavuniya is a major town in the Northern Province. It is also the main town of the administrative district of the same name, and it has been under the dual control of the Sri Lankan state and of the LTTE for most of the past two decades. Even now, the political geography of the district reveals that it is divided into two entities. The northern area of the district is controlled by the LTTE, while the southern area is controlled by the state. In this sense, there is a "border" bifurcating the district. The state side of the border is maintained by the Sri Lankan military by means of a long line of military guard points, described as a "forward defence line." The LTTE also guards this border in a similar fashion. Civilian crossings of the border are strictly restricted by the government and the LTTE. The Vavuniya town is the main entry point to either side of the district.

The Vavuniya town is also a major military concentration, in terms of both men and war material belonging to the state. After the war began in the early 1980s, extensive military facilities were established in the Vavuniya town for the army, the navy, the air force, and the police. The presence of a huge military machine continued despite the ceasefire agreement between the government and the LTTE.

The economy of the Vavuniya town has, to a great extent, been militarized. In the context of economic embargo maintained by the state in the previous years, the Vavuniya town was the last location on the way to the Northern Province where the "normal" economy functioned and where commodities were available without restrictions. Beyond the town in the Vavuniya district were the areas under LTTE control, and there the war had subjected the economy to constant battering. Even today, the visitor who crosses the "border" is confronted with the visual evidence of two economies existing in the same district. The one in the southern part of the district is linked to the economy in the rest of the country, and there is evidence of relative economic prosperity; the one in the northern part of the district still remains no more than a subsistence economy, with evidence everywhere of absolute poverty and economic as well as social devastation.

The Vavuniya district had, in the past, been a multiethnic area with a Tamil majority and with Sinhalese and Muslim minorities living there. The war has altered the ethnic demography of the district. In the LTTE-controlled areas, the population is primarily Tamil, while in the government-controlled areas in the Vavuniya district, there are Sinhalese, Tamil, and Muslim communities. However, even in these multiethnic areas in the Vavuniya town, each ethnic community lives in its own ethnic "enclave," clearly separated from other ethnic communities. Consequently, there are Tamil villages, Sinhalese villages, and Muslim villages, but no multiethnic villages.

The ground conditions in Vavuniya during the 2002-3 peace process constituted a wide range of issues relating to peace, governance, and reconstruction in the transition from civil war. Concerning governance, Vavuniya
posed an unusual challenge, which arose out of the dual power situation in
the district between the Sri Lankan state and the LTTE. The Vavuniya district informally bifurcated into two military-political-administrative units,
one controlled by the Sri Lankan state and the other by the LTTE. In areas
under its control, the LTTE also functioned as a "parallel state." There were
informal "borders" defining and demarcating the two "territories." These
borders were essentially military demarcations frozen by the CFA as of February 2002. They reflected the ground situation of territorial control maintained by the Sri Lankan state and the LTTE, respectively, when they signed
the CFA. Against this backdrop, Vavuniya district represented the unusual
phenomenon of "two political systems" existing in one country.

How could a peace settlement deal with two political systems in one country, as exemplified in the district of Vavuniya? This was one of the key subtext
challenges inherent in the 2002-3 peace process. In a peace agreement with
the government, the LTTE would have insisted on extending its control to
the entire district, the argument being that areas of the district that were
under government control were part of the Northern Province of the Tamil
"homeland." It would have been extremely difficult for the Sri Lankan government to accede to such a demand because it would have been seen as
"surrendering" to the LTTE territories that were under state control. The
withdrawal of the huge military and administrative installations from the
district would have meant the transfer of territory that the state had managed to maintain during the war.

In a broad sense, this challenge was linked to the process associated
with the possible path of post-civil war state formation in Sri Lanka. Two
issues were at its centre: the question of two political systems and the
prospect of the transfer of territory. Thus, the management of the dual
power situation in Vavuniya required a great deal of constitutional and
political innovation with regard to institution designing in both the interim and post-interim phases of the transition from civil war. One option
would have been to recognize the existing ground reality of dual power
and to build institutions of governance to give expression to a specific
form of shared rule on the part of the government and the LTTE. The
creation of a joint district administrative council allowing the Sri Lankan
state and the LTTE to govern the district within a framework of "shared
governance" would have resulted in a concrete institutional form. Such
an institutional innovation would have necessitated the creation of a new
tier of power-sharing within the regional council of the north and east.
The resulting new institution could have been created as a second tier of

local federalization, in addition to the first tier of federalization at the regional level.

A second tier of federalization at the local level is also quite important for creating new institutions of governance in areas of dual power like Vavuniya. In this regard, one of the key assets that the communities in Vavuniya had was the presence of many civil society bodies that were actively engaged in development and reconciliation work. A large measure of relief and rehabilitation work had also been carried out by these organizations at the community level, where they addressed everyday issues confronted by the people. In the areas under government control, a vibrant network of civil society organization had developed. This had contributed to neutralizing the effects of the excessive degree of militarization on community life. Quite significantly, these civil society organizations had also developed close working links with the state agencies, the military, the LTTE, and the international donor agencies active in the area.

Vavuniya: Ground Conditions of Development

As we have already noted, the political economy of Vavuniya district had a bifurcated character. In the areas under the control of the government, market forces functioned with no hindrance. Vavuniya was the main trading city in the entire region. Outside the city were basically agriculture-based villages. The areas under LTTE administration provided a picture of a sharply contrasting political economy. Those areas had been subjected to a devastating war for about two decades. From 1996 to 2001, they remained a major theatre of concentrated war between the government and the LTTE. People in these areas have been surviving primarily on the relief services provided by the government as well as by international humanitarian agencies. Thus, in these subsistence and relief economies, people were living in chronic poverty. The priorities of development in these areas posed a fundamental challenge in a period of transition to peace: could the market economy and the private sector help these victims of war to emerge from a political economy marked by devastation?

It appears that the government and the LTTE have had two contrasting approaches to the question of development. The government's approach, which is, for the most part, supported by the international donor community, sought to link the war-affected areas with the country's market economy. The LTTE, on the other hand, saw a limited role for the market economy, in the sense that it believed that the state (which it represented) should play a leading role in economic reconstruction. There has not yet been a dialogue between the government and the LTTE, or even the LTTE and the international donors, regarding approaches to development. The donor approach involved donors' defining development priorities for the people in the north and east. The government had not questioned or even provided alternatives to donor prescriptions. Against this background, the LTTE faced a dilemma. It had to marshal international economic assistance for development in war-torn areas while, at the same time, resisting donor pressures and priorities. It appears that the LTTE opted for a strategy of unilateral isolationism – that is, it decided to insulate itself from international pressure to return to the negotiation table by rejecting international economic incentives.

The Eastern Province: Trincomalee, Batticaloa, and Amparai

The immediate and long-term challenges in governance as well as development in the three districts that comprise the Eastern Province are linked to four issues. The first involves the province's mixed ethnic demography. Sinhalese, Tamil, and Muslim populations have an almost equal presence in the Eastern Province, which also has areas in which there are ethnic concentrations. This ethnic demography stands in contrast to that of the Northern Province, where the Tamils are the dominant regional majority, with small minorities of Sinhalese and Muslims. The second issue involves the hostile relationship between Tamil and Muslim communities, which is exacerbated through general violence, killings, massacres, population displacement, and the appropriation of the property of those who were displaced during the war. The third issue is linked to the shadow war between the mainstream LTTE and its breakaway "Karuna faction" in the Batticaloa district. Since early 2004, this faction has created a state of continuing terror through killings, abductions, and the recruitment of underaged children. The military challenge that the Karuna faction mounted against the. mainstream LTTE undermined not only the latter's claim tõ having strategic parity with the Sri Lankan state but also the notion of a "unified Tamil nation." Colonel Karuna, who had been the military leader of the LTTE, claimed that his faction represented the political aspirations for autonomy of the Tamils in the Eastern Province. The fourth issue is linked to the complexities that emerged out of the politics of post-tsunami reconstruction.

The mixed ethnic composition of the Eastern Province had direct implications for regional autonomy arrangements. The Muslims and the Sinhalese, who are regional minorities in the Eastern Province, have resisted the Tamil nationalist claim that the province belongs to the unified political unit of the northeast. The Northern Province and the Eastern Province were temporarily merged in 1987. The Sinhalese and Muslims began to demand the "de-merger" of the two provinces in order to avoid what they referred to as potential Tamil domination under conditions of peace. This debate on the composition of the unit of autonomy for the north and east continued during the 2002-3 peace process, and it constitutes one of the most intractable problems with regard to power-sharing arrangements in Sri Lanka. While resisting possible Tamil domination in a merged unit of autonomy, Muslim political leaders have demanded a non-contiguous Muslim autonomy unit comprising Muslim-majority administrative divisions in the Amparai and Batticaloa districts.

The unresolved tension between the Tamil and Muslim communities in the Eastern Province also had a political-economic dimension, which emerged during the war. Population displacement led to disputes over land ownership and new commercial rivalries. Both communities made mutual allegations of "land grabbing" during the war as, when one community fled for safety or became displaced, members of the other community would come and occupy the vacated land and houses. Thus, during any peace process, it was not unusual for the restoration of land rights to original owners to become an immediate issue. Resolving land disputes, upon which the material conditions for community-level conflict had been built, was a priority for intercommunity reconciliation. In 2002-3, some civil society groups attempted to initiate a dialogue between the LTTE and Muslim community leaders in the Eastern Province in order to restore intercommunity peace. In September 2003, they reached an agreement that involved a series of decisions, which included the immediate return of the agricultural land in the Batticaloa and Amparai districts to its original Muslim owners (Mohideen 2005). The breakup of the LTTE and the resultant violence in the Eastern Province slowed this process of Muslim-Tamil reconciliation.

The continuing "war" between the mainstream LTTE and the breakaway Karuna faction became a major source of instability in the Eastern Province, threatening the ceasefire process. Colonel Karuna was the LTTE's military commander in the Eastern Province, and he had a regional militia of over 4,500 fighters. He justified his March 2004 rebellion against the mainstream LTTE by saying that the LTTE leadership, which was dominated by the Tamils from the Northern Province, was discriminating against the Tamils of the Eastern Province. The idea of a unified Tamil nation, the idea that the LTTE is its sole representative, and the idea that the northern and eastern provinces constitute a unified Tamil territory are the founding principles of the LTTE's version of Tamil nationalism. And it was this that the Karuna rebellion undermined. Although the two sides did not engage in a direct war for supremacy until early 2006, the killing of civilians, cadres, and even leaders continued, despite the ceasefire agreement. In fact, the ceasefire agreement did not cover violence between the LTTE and its breakaway groups. The LTTE's split, and the eventual violence between the two factions, demonstrates that even a condition of limited peace could sharpen those contradictions within the Tamil polity that, under conditions of protracted war, had remained hidden.

During the post-tsunami reconstruction process in early 2005, two major sources of complexity arose with regard to inter-ethnic group relations in the Eastern Province. First, the relationship between the Muslim community in the province and the Sri Lankan state became strained due to the inability of the state to provide adequate relief to Muslim victims. The Muslim community saw this particular "state failure" as a deliberate act of ethnic discrimination. The second source of complexity was linked to the fact that some areas affected by the tsunami were located in LTTE-held territory. This made it difficult for the state to engage in relief or reconstruction work. Further, the legal problems confronted by the post-tsunami joint mechanism, which the state and the LTTE formulated, made it extremely difficult to initiate any long-term or sustainable rebuilding initiatives.

In brief, the peacebuilding process in the Eastern Province is linked to a complex array of political, military, and humanitarian issues. The 2002-3 peace process proved itself to be incapable of addressing these issues. Against this backdrop was the ever-present possibility that the Eastern Province, under conditions of increasing ethnic enmity and escalating violence, might become the weakest link in the fragile chain of Sri Lanka's peace. If the chain were to break at this weakest link, the entire peace process would be at risk of collapsing.

This fragile chain of peace actually did break at its weakest link in 2006, when the new Sri Lankan government, led by President Mahinda Rajapakse, and the LTTE returned to war in the Batticaloa district of the Eastern Province. This occurred after the collapse of the Geneva Talks in January 2006. It should be noted that neither side formally withdrew from the ceasefire agreement; therefore, the war that began in mid-2006 can best be described as an "undeclared war."

Conclusion

This study demonstrates that Sri Lanka's 2002-3 peace process was deadlocked over the contradiction between a possible, limited, strategic peace and a desirable, long-term peace. For this reason, its transformative dynamics were weak and limited.

This analysis of what kind of peace was possible in Sri Lanka offers six major conclusions. The first conclusion is that the "actually existing peace" was fraught with instability and uncertainty because it was grounded in strategic considerations of the state and the LTTE. Nor did it enjoy the support of a strong domestic coalition for peace. Its ardent supporters have come from the international community. Yet, the policy options of the international community were limited by two factors: first, both the Sri Lankan government and the LTTE, the two principal parties to the peace process, ignored international pressure and persuasion whenever they decided that their strategic interests were at risk; second, the international community could not impose peace from outside because the principal as well as the secondary domestic actors were reluctant to take the peace process forward.

The second conclusion is that the political outcome of Sri Lanka's peace effort in 2002-3 was predicated on "process stability," which, in turn, was dependent on the concrete conditions available to facilitate the transition from the actually existing limited peace to a comprehensive peace settlement. According to this argument, "process stability" is the key variable in mapping out the way in which Sri Lanka's peace process moved towards relapsing into war and violence. The "conditions for process stability" that were lacking in the 2002-3 peace process included (1) the willingness and capacity of the parties to address the disputed issues, which were essentially about the sharing of state power, in a win-win framework, and (2) the political space and broad support available to enable the parties to take the negotiations to a higher political level in order to craft major and historic compromises so as to move towards settling political issues. The process stability in the 2002-3 peace initiative was also weakened by the excessive reliance on "negotiations" as a tool of conflict resolution. The international facilitators, the government, and the LTTE did not broaden the peace process beyond negotiations to initiate a substantial dialogue for conflict transformation. A key lesson to be learned from this experience is that elite-level negotiations are a necessary, but not a sufficient, tool for peacebuilding in societies torn by protracted ethno-political conflict.

Third, there was no creative link between "peacemaking from above" and "peacebuilding from below." Peacemaking from above requires negotiations, a monitored ceasefire, the signing and implementation of a peace agreement, international economic assistance, and state reforms. Peacebuilding from below presupposes the broadening of peace constituencies; the mobilization of popular support for a peace agreement; political reforms; effective popular participation in economic, social, and livelihood reconstruction; intergroup reconciliation; and solidarity with regard to the shared goal of peace. In order to forge a creative link between these two peace processes within a thoroughly divided polity, it is crucial to have a broad base of political and social support. The 2002-3 peace process could not overcome the absence of such a base.

Fourth, it was a mistake to view the development question as a *post-conflict* endeavour; rather, it should have been seen as a preliminary phase to stabilizing a pre-settlement negotiation process. There was a manifest risk in conceptualizing the economic reconstruction process in post-conflict, liberal, free-market terms. The 2002-3 experiments with a liberal, free-market reconstruction project were failures. The Sri Lankan electorate, particularly the voters in the low-income and poorer segments of majority Sinhalese society, rejected them in the April 2003 elections. Building social bases for peace, particularly among the low-income groups and the poor, is crucial for the democratic sustainability of the peace process. This requires economic policy strategies that can democratize and distribute the gains of the peace process to a broad base – the so-called peace dividend. The continuation of free-market economic policies, with no strategies for redistribution, in conjunction with a political reform agenda jeopardized the stability of the peace process.

Fifth, there was a continuing gulf between the economic visions of the government and the donor community, on the one hand, and the LTTE, on the other. While the former were committed to a project of rapid economic reconstruction in the war-torn areas through the intervention of private capital and market forces, the LTTE was justifiably cautious about such an approach. A creative dialogue between these two approaches was needed in order to achieve a viable development strategy that might have facilitated Sri Lanka's transition process.

And, finally, a narrow, peace-deal approach could not promote peacemaking and peacebuilding goals because its objectives did not go beyond achieving the short-term strategic goals of the parties to the conflict. Because it is grounded in the transformation of the country's politics, sustainable peacebuilding is a process that must be spread over a period of transition. Peace without political transformation can, at best, be only a limited, negative peace – one that is exceedingly vulnerable to shifting military balances and political calculations.

8

The Fate of Former Combatants in Guatemala: Spoilers or Agents for Change?

Wenche Hauge and Beate Thoresen

The focus of analyses of the disarmament, demobilization, and reintegration processes is often on the achievement of security and the return to normalcy. Even from a short-term perspective, a certain degree of success with regard to all three aspects of DDR is necessary if this is to happen. However, from a longer-term perspective, much more is needed. Even when armed groups are disbanded and former combatants are disarmed and reintegrated into civilian life, fighting may recur if little is done about the causes of the conflict. Combatants are often persons who have been fighting to change conditions with which they are discontent. If they do not become involved in processes of democratization, political participation, and socioeconomic policy changes, they may become frustrated, with the result that peace will not bring about these deeper changes. As pointed out by Baranyi (2005c, 8), minimalist approaches to peacebuilding tend to downplay these long-term challenges, while maximalist approaches tend not to look carefully at the obstacles facing the broader agenda of transformation. The discussion in this chapter takes up this challenge and, by focusing on the degree to which former combatants have been allowed and, indeed, empowered to become agents of change in post-conflict Guatemala, delves into one aspect of this agenda.

After thirty-six years of civil war, on 29 December 1996, the Guatemalan government and the insurgency movement – the Guatemalan National Revolutionary Unity (URNG) – signed a comprehensive peace accord, containing, among other things, the conditions for the demobilization of the URNG and the civil defence patrols (PACs) and the downsizing of the army. In Chapter 2 of this volume, Gabriel Aguilera deals with the bigger picture of peace implementation in the areas of democratic and economic development. This chapter focuses on the demobilization and reintegration of the URNG and the PACs as well as on the participation of ex-guerrilla soldiers and ex-PAC members after 1996. Being reintegrated into civil society and becoming active in social and political work are closely related issues. It is difficult to imagine former combatants having the capacity to become agents for change in the absence of a solid social and economic basis. Political activity requires both resources and a constituency. Bearing this in mind, the discussion in this chapter focuses on two interrelated issues: (1) the prerequisites for the successful reintegration of former combatants into civilian life and (2) the possibilities of former combatants becoming agents of change in a post-conflict peacebuilding process. In the academic literature, there is a substantial amount of research on DDR processes, but the bulk of this work focuses on the first of these two issues – the prerequisites for successful demobilization and the reintegration of former combatants into civilian life. There is less focus on political participation. Spear (2002, 142), for example, emphasizes five factors, which, she argues, are particularly important in determining the likelihood of successful disarmament and demobilization: "the feasibility of the peace agreement and its aims; the implementation environment; the capability and resources of the international implementers; the attitudes of the warring parties; and effective verification."

While Spear concentrates much of her focus on the framework for and context of demobilization (such as the character of the peace agreement and the implementing environment), other researchers put more emphasis on the combatants who are going to be demobilized. Who are they? To which kind of armed groups do they belong? What are their intentions? Stedman (1997, 5) warns that the greatest source of risk with regard to peace implementation comes from spoilers – "leaders and parties who believe that peace emerging from negotiations threatens their power, worldview, and interests, and use violence to undermine attempts to achieve it."

Jensen and Stepputat (2001) also draw attention to the combatants, but from a different perspective than Stedman. Jensen and Stepputat are concerned with the military-civilian dichotomy in DDR programs. They argue that the underlying assumptions of DDR programs are structured by a dichotomy between the civil and the military, two spheres that are seen as fundamentally different. While civilians are considered to be victims of armed conflicts, military personnel are considered to be responsible for the fighting. They argue that civilians can be victims, combatants, and beneficiaries at the same time and that "the 'military-civilian dichotomy' is normative rather than descriptive" (24).

Clearly, as emphasized by the different researchers referred to here, it is necessary to focus on who the combatants are – and what their intentions are – as well as on the framework for and context of successful demobilization. We do this in Part 2 of this chapter through a discussion of the armed actors' "embeddedness," understood as their local, social, and institutional background and their continued contact with this background during and after the war.

As Jensen and Stepputat point out, DDR programs are, in practice, no longer targeting regular troops alone. In addition to incorporating irregular insurgent armies, recently the programs have also incorporated paramilitary and other groups. This was the case in Sierra Leone, where paramilitary groups and civil defence patrols were mentioned in the peace accords and granted assistance upon demobilization (Jensen and Stepputat 2001, 16). It was also the case in Guatemala, although no assistance was granted to the civil patrols upon demobilization. The increasing emphasis on the need to demobilize different types of armed actors raises the need for a discussion about the appropriate responses to the different types of groups. We provide this in Part 3, which focuses on the URNG and the civil defence patrols.

However, increasing this focus a bit more, to take into account the potential of former combatants to become active agents of change in a post-conflict peacebuilding process, requires a somewhat wider theoretical framework. The solution to the challenge of engaging ex-combatants in political and development activities in a post-conflict reconstruction phase has, in several cases, been to transform former insurgent armies into political parties. This happened in Guatemala and in several other countries, like El Salvador and Mozambique, with varying degrees of success (Spear 2002). The legitimacy of such transformations depends on the record of the insurgent armies during the war, and their success also depends on the different movements' constituencies. Did they establish a broad network of contact with local communities during the war? Were they successful in mobilizing support, or were they mostly elitist movements?

In this chapter, we argue that three conditions are particularly influential when it comes to former combatants' potential for becoming participants in post-conflict peacebuilding. The first is their embeddedness: who they are; their ties to their social, institutional, or local background throughout the war; and the character of the armed group in which they participated during the war. The second factor is the framework for demobilization and participation set in the peace accord. This encompasses the different responses offered to different armed actors in the demobilization process, including issues of amnesty and human rights and, not least, issues related to the former combatants' economic livelihoods and social well-being. The third factor is the larger implementation environment – the juridical, political, and socioeconomic context. As explained by Gabriel Aguilera in Chapter 2 of this volume, in Guatemala, the uneven implementation of important peace agreements contributes to shaping the larger implementation environment, particularly through the lack of equitable socioeconomic development and insufficient democratization.

The method used in this case study combines semi-structured interviews, an analysis of selected primary documents, and a review of relevant secondary literature. The interviews are with key actors from the URNG –

including the leadership, intermediate, and grassroots levels – and with other key actors in the DDR process.

Armed Actors in the Guatemalan Conflict

The Conflict, the Armed Actors, and Their Embeddedness

The Guatemalan conflict broke out in 1960 and was brought to an end with the peace agreement between the government and the URNG signed in December 1996. It can be characterized as a war fought between a relatively small guerrilla force and a strongly superior military force. It was extremely bloody between 1980 and 1983, when the army carried out its major counter-insurgency campaign and slaughtered large numbers of the indigenous population in the western and central highlands. Among the insurgency movement's top goals were socioeconomic equity, land reform, democratization, and human rights.

On one side, the armed actors can be identified as consisting of several guerrilla groups that were formed during the thirty-six-year-long civil war. These joined forces, and from 1982 onwards the struggle took place under the united command of the URNG. On the other side was the army and groups linked to the counter-insurgency war. Those groups include the PACs, which, from 1981 onward, were organized and controlled by the army. A considerable number of indigenous men were forced to join the PACs. Finally, there were several paramilitary groups that operated during the war.

URNG

The first guerrilla organization in Guatemala, the Rebel Armed Forces (FAR),[1] was established in 1962, when the political space for reforms disappeared with a military coup in 1954. Consisting mainly of former soldiers, radical students, and intellectuals, FAR was active in the eastern part of Guatemala (Hauge 2003). It had some initial successes but was then decimated in a major anti-guerrilla campaign that started in the mid-1960s. In the 1970s, the depleted FAR regrouped and established new bases in the eastern highlands and northern jungles of the Petén, and it developed a strategy to work with the masses in labour and peasant unions. In the beginning, the Guatemalan Communist Party (PGT),[2] dating from 1949, had links to FAR and opted for a political armed struggle from 1969 onward (CEH 1999a).

The Guerrilla Army of the Poor (EGP) was established in 1972, and the Revolutionary Organization of the People in Arms (ORPA) in 1979.[3] The EGP and ORPA were both led by dissidents from FAR. Although controlled by *mestizos* (persons of mixed racial heritage), the EGP was based in indigenous highland areas and was able to recruit large numbers of Mayas. The EGP soon became the largest insurgent force and developed its strongholds along the northwestern border in Quiché and Huehuetenango. The

EGP's strategy of prolonged guerrilla war was influenced by Vietnamese experiences, and it directed its appeal to the masses and, particularly, to the indigenous population (ODHAG 1998b). One of the main reasons for its success was the relationship that it built up with some of the mass organizations, such as the Comité de Unidad Campesina (Committee for Peasant Unity). Thousands of peasants who were members of the committee joined the EGP in the northwest and on the south coast (201-01).

ORPA established its first significant guerrilla activity along the south coast and in western Guatemala, around San Marcos and Lake Atitlán. However, it also operated in the capital, Guatemala City. Among the guerrilla organizations, ORPA was the one that was most concerned about the issue of racism and how this was used as an instrument with which to oppress the indigenous population (Hauge 2003).

The guerrilla movement reached its peak in 1978-79, when, with six thousand to eight thousand fighters and up to half a million active supporters, it operated in most departments. In 1982, the guerrilla groups formed the URNG, a unified command with a platform for revolutionary government. As a result of the scorched earth repression during the regimes of General Romeo Lucas García (1978-82) and General Efraín Ríos Montt (1982-83), the movement was decimated. At the time of disarmament in 1997, after the peace agreement was signed, the combined membership of the guerrilla groups totalled 3,614 (Armon, Sieder, and Wilson 1997, 88). Of these, 1,812 had fought in the EGP, 1,025 in FAR, 307 in ORPA, and 470 in the so-called Unitary Front, a force dominated by ORPA but that also comprised combatants from the EGP and the PGT.

PACs

In 1981, under the García government, the first civil defence patrols were organized. These patrols were legalized in April 1982 as a part of the National Security and Development Plan put forward by Ríos Montt's military government. The patrol members were made up of indigenous men between the ages of fifteen and sixty – about 80 percent of the male population in the rural indigenous areas of Guatemala (ODHAG 1998a, 119). Although the civil patrols were referred to as voluntary civil self-defence committees from 1986 onward, human rights organizations have provided ample evidence that the patrol members were forced to render service, particularly in 1982-83 (Solomon 1994).

According to different sources, between 1 million and 1.3 million Guatemalans were organized in civil defence patrols at the peak of the armed conflict in 1982-83 (ODHAG 1998a; Solomon 1994). As part of Ríos Montt's strategy to militarize the country, the number of military zones in Guatemala increased from six to twenty-three in 1983. The PAC system constituted a cornerstone of the army's strategy to control the population and to expand the army into every corner of the country. A report on the civil patrols in Guatemala published by the Robert F. Kennedy Memorial Center for Human Rights in 1994 stated that the military was actively engaged in overseeing the patrols, that there were regular meetings held for patrol leaders at military bases, and that orders involving patrols were generated through the military chain of command (Solomon 1994, 11). During the war, the army also handed out weapons to the patrols, mostly old M1 rifles. According to General Vásquez, some twenty thousand weapons had been handed out to the PACs by 1994 (ibid.).

The most important part of the patrol members' work consisted of searching for and confronting guerrillas in rural areas, providing cover for the army during military actions, detaining and interrogating men and women who entered their communities, and informing the army of developments in the region. However, during the government of Vinicio Cerezo (1986-90), the number of patrol members declined to approximately 500,000 (ODHAG 1998a, 119). According to Solomon (1994, 26), "some patrollers have been able to leave the PAC system with great difficulty and danger, enduring threats and physical attack. Others have lost their lives for leaving the patrols, and some have been able to stop patrolling without problem." In 1994, President Ramiro de León Carpio formally dissolved the PACs through a presidential decree, and in 1995 – when the army made the decision to demobilize the civil patrols – there were 375,000 patrol members left (ODHAG 1998a, 119).

Embeddedness and Differences between the Armed Groups

From a comparative perspective, one important difference between the URNG and the PACs is that, while the PAC members were recruited from and stayed in their own communities during the war, the guerrilla members – also recruited from local communities – had to act clandestinely and moved around in different geographic areas of the country. The PAC members were openly and legally locally embedded. However, during the war, the URNG also relied on civilian support from friendly communities as well as on support from former combatants who had returned to their places of origin.

The PAC structure was inserted into – and changed – the power structures of local communities. While some supported the PACs, others, due to the forced nature of participation in the patrols and the unpaid labour they demanded, strongly opposed their presence (Procurador de los derechos humanos 1994).

The human rights records of the URNG and the PACs are also quite different. When the Commission for Historical Clarification – often referred to as the truth commission – published its report in 1999, it stated that the URNG was responsible for 3 percent of the human rights violations during the war, while the civil defence patrols were responsible for 18 percent and the army for 85 percent (subsuming some of the violations committed by the PACs) (CEH 1999b).

However, it should be added that most of the atrocities committed by the PACs were committed by the military commissioners or by other PACs with links to the army. The majority of the PAC members were poor, indigenous peasants, and many did not participate in human rights violations.

These differences between the URNG and the PACs have several consequences. As the URNG members had to act clandestinely during a war that lasted thirty-six years, they left their land, houses, and properties behind. Many guerrillas also completely cut ties with their families. When the war was over, they were therefore in dire need of shelter and income. They needed to be reintegrated in the traditional sense of this concept. This was not the case for the PAC members, who kept their properties and stayed with their families during the war.

Second, the issue of identity was important. Due to the length and character of the war, the members of the different organizations constituting the URNG developed strong group identities. Those recruited to the URNG during the period of extreme repression, 1981-83, and those recruited earlier who stayed on during this period, lived through a very difficult time together – something that contributed strongly to forming the combatants' common identity. Quite a few child and teenage survivors of the army massacres joined the URNG during this period, which meant that they spent most of the ten to fifteen formative years of their lives within the URNG. This explains, in part, why so many of the URNG members wanted collective reintegration.

The question of the group identity of the PAC members is more complicated. Many patrol members left the PACs in the late 1980s, and many have complained about the forced nature of their service in these patrols. What seemed needed and appropriate was some form of official excuse for the civil rights abuses of the patrol members. However, several patrollers were content with their work, and the military commissioners would have objected strongly to such an official excuse. For now, we focus more on the challenges of crafting appropriate responses for the different armed groups in Guatemala.

Different Actors, Different Responses

Demobilization, Reintegration, and Political Activity of the URNG

The emerging framework for the demobilization and reintegration of the URNG was a result of different factors, such as the power asymmetry between the URNG and the government/armed forces; the regional and international political context at the time of the negotiation process; the degree of the international community's economic support for the demobilization and reintegration process; and particular events, such as the kidnapping of Olga de Novella by ORPA members in the last and critical phase of the negotiation process, which weakened the URNG's position in the negotiations. The peace accord of December 1996 was the final compromise.

The content of the peace agreement is particularly important for the demobilization process. The agreement defines who or which groups are eligible for the demobilization and reintegration package, as well as the institutions responsible for the process.

The comprehensive peace accord of 1996 covers issues such as the agrarian situation and socioeconomic reforms, democratization, the indigenous population's rights, human rights, and the resettlement of the uprooted population, in addition to the issues directly related to the demobilization process and the downsizing of the army. In Chapter 2 (this volume), Aguilera discusses the different subsidiary agreements and their implementation in greater depth. Three subsidiary agreements are particularly relevant for this study: (1) the agreement on the final ceasefire, (2) the agreement on the basis for the reincorporation of the URNG as a legal entity, and (3) the agreement on the strengthening of civil society and the functioning of the army in a democratic society. Together, these three agreements deal with the function of the URNG, the army, the mobile military police (PMA),[4] and the civil defence patrols after December 1996.

The peace accord stated that the URNG should be disarmed and demobilized within sixty days of the signing of the final peace agreement. It further stated that the army should be downsized by 33 percent in 1997 in order to fit its new role in a democratic society. With regard to the military police and civil defence patrols, the accord is extremely brief. It says that the PMA should be demobilized within one year of the signing of the final peace accord and that the remaining PACs should be demobilized within thirty days of the signing of the accord. In the case of the PACs, it underlined that all relationships with the army should be ended and by no means re-established.

In the subsidiary agreement on the final ceasefire from 1996, ordinary guerrilla groups, locally organized groups, and groups operating in urban areas were included among those entitled to demobilization support (MINUGUA 1997, 341). Furthermore, combatants as well as those responsible for political work, intelligence, security, logistics, and health were covered by the agreement. The demobilization phase was set to last sixty days, and the main phase of the reintegration of the URNG as a legal entity was set for one year, starting immediately after the sixty days of demobilization. The agreement further contained a comprehensive set of measures in the juridical, security, social, and economic fields to assist this process.

The peace accord stated that a special commission should be established
to coordinate the work on programs related to the reintegration of the URNG
into legality. This commission should be made up of an equal number of
representatives from the URNG and the government, and it should have
representatives from donors and international organizations. This commission – the Special Commission for Reintegration – was established on 18
December 1997. The peace agreement gave the commission a mandate to
reach compromises with regard to financing the different programs and
projects. In addition, the peace accord stated that the URNG should establish its own foundation responsible for project implementation, which it
did through organizing the Fundación Guillermo Toriello (FGT).

Economic Framework and Overall Outcome

In December 1996, the envisaged amount of economic support for the demobilization and reintegration process from the international community
was US$85,272,000 (Corral 2005, 7). The prospect of such a considerable
amount of financial support for the process created high expectations within
the URNG. It was used to convince those within the movement who, for
reasons of lack of trust or worries about the future, doubted or were opposed
to the demobilization process (ibid; information obtained from interviews).

The demobilization process was financed by, among others, the United
Nations Development Program, the European Union, and USAID. The international community's support for the first phase was a well coordinated
effort, with active and direct participation of donors, and it included transport, establishment of provisional camps, activities in the camps, and verification. When the URNG left the transitional camps, the UNDP contributed
"exit grants" to the ex-combatants, while the European Union provided input packages containing equipment (e.g., for agriculture, services, and various types of production). For ex-combatants, this type of assistance served
as a transitional bridge from the provisional camps to a new life in communities. On arrival at the place of resettlement, ex-combatants received
support for education, health, and training. Also, a series of productive projects was started, again with the support of the UNDP, the European Union,
and USAID, although each of these donors directed its assistance to different target groups within the population of ex-combatants. Support for economic reintegration did not cover all of those demobilized, and a process of
selecting individuals and groups was undertaken.

The task of registering the URNG combatants and members of the logis-
tic, social, and political structures of the organization for the demobilization process presented quite a challenge to the URNG. The leader of the
FGT, as well as many others of those interviewed, admitted that quite a few
of those who should not have been registered were, while quite a few who
should have been registered were not (*ni son todos los que estan, ni estan*

todos los que son). Some external and very peripheral collaborators who, however, were already integrated into Guatemalan society, were included in the lists. Others were not, including those who lived at a distance, who lacked information about their residence, who had been supported by their families, or who had been staying in camps for refugees or internally displaced persons.

The difficulties were increased by a certain competition between the different guerrilla organizations that constituted the URNG – FAR, ORPA, the EGP, and the PGT – with regard to how many persons each of them could have on the list. Another problem was that several people came to the FGT after the registration process had been terminated. This resulted in an additional list of persons; however, these people did not receive any economic or reintegration support.

Three aspects of the external and institutional framework for the reintegration process proved to be of particular importance to its outcome: available economic resources in general, economic resources at the disposal of the FGT, and types of program and project assistance from international agencies and from the Guatemalan government.

In 1997, the URNG conducted a survey among the demobilized, asking, among other things, about each member's economic background and about what kind of work they wanted to do in order to sustain their livelihood after the demobilization. Altogether 2,109 of those interviewed had backgrounds in agriculture, only 1,101 of these expressed an inclination to continue this activity, and 514 of them demanded capacity building to develop their agricultural knowledge further in order to increase productivity (URNG 1997, 10). In general, the answers of those interviewed had a clear pattern: a decreasing interest in agricultural work and a strong interest in capacity building within service, technical, and professional activities. Altogether, 3,720 of those interviewed expressed an interest in continued education or studies (15).

Another clear tendency that came out of the survey was the preference to stay together and to work collectively after the demobilization. Of those interviewed, 41.3 percent expressed interest in carrying out their economic activity in a collective way, together with other *compañeros*, community, or family, and 18.5 percent expressed interest in working in a mixed way individually and collectively (URNG 1997, 10).

However, the framework for the reintegration process did not work according to the expectations of the URNG. At the end of 1998, the Special Commission for Reintegration was advised that only about US$27 million was available for the demobilization and reintegration process – around one-third of the originally anticipated amount (CEI 1998, 26). Of this sum, $21 million was directly available to the reintegration program, executed mainly by intermediary agencies, while the FGT only disposed of 15 percent (ibid.).

In general, the Guatemalan government wanted to close the reintegration chapter as quickly as possible and "convert the reintegrated into businessmen and normal citizens" (Corral 2005, 11). From the government's point of view, a very important argument for speeding up the process was that it did not want to create a basis for comparison – that is, it did not want the priority given to the demobilized combatants to draw attention away from the need to compensate other social sectors, nor did it want to be under increased pressure to provide such compensation. As pointed out by Aguilera in Chapter 2 of this volume, the government already had to face resistance from the business sector on tax reforms and economic policies geared towards fulfilling the peace accords.

The government gave institutional support and contributed social funds to the reintegration process, but the primary donor was the international community, which had considerable influence over the process. The URNG, through the FGT, played a more marginal role as it disposed of only a part of the funds. However, the FGT was important in terms of presenting information, maintaining the relationship with those who had been reintegrated, and formulating demands.

According to the URNG, there were differences between the international agencies. While USAID favoured and supported projects that were oriented towards individual development, the European Union and Spain had a "belligerent and progressive representation" that, from the perspective of democratic politics and pluralism, viewed social and economic reintegration as a condition for support (Corral 2005, 12).

The majority of demobilized combatants reintegrated individually in Guatemala City or in rural communities in fifteen different departments in the country. However, towards the end of the reintegration period, there was one particular group of ex-guerrillas whose members had long personal histories as combatants. These people expressed a strong preference for collective reintegration, and they lacked communities to which to return. This group consisted of 355 persons (CEI 1998, 8). For these people, three farms (*fincas*) were bought: El Horizonte in Petén, Las Tecas in Suchitépequez, and Santa Anita in Quetzaltenango. In addition, a larger area of land was bought in Chimaltenango for the purpose of constructing houses for another group of ex-URNG combatants. A common problem for those who reintegrated collectively, like the ex-combatants at El Horizonte, was that they became heavily indebted as the land they were offered had been negotiated under disadvantageous conditions. As an example, the debt of El Horizonte currently stands at 7 million quetzales, or about US$1 million.

Many of those who reintegrated individually ended up relying on family support for survival, which reveals the differences in opportunities for ex-combatants based on their social background. The support given to microenterprises was largely a failure, and the idea of converting *guerrileros* into entrepreneurs with a minimum of support did not work. Job opportunities and support for further education would have required more appropriate means of support for many of the ex-combatants.

In addition to external constraints, the FGT had to struggle with its own internal problems. There was internal rivalry between the former guerrilla organizations regarding the direction of the FGT. Ex-FAR combatants complained that ORPA had assumed the leadership and that FAR was only weakly represented in FGT (information obtained from interviews).

The URNG had many female fighters. Among its combatants, 766 women were demobilized and reintegrated. The FGT financed a project directly targeted at the women and their situation and at gender policy development within the FGT, and it also established a special team for the implementation of this project. As a result, twenty-nine women's committees were established, and nineteen of these gained legal status. Altogether, ninety women were trained as promoters of the project and 2,130 persons participated in gender-issue workshops.

Interviews revealed that several women experienced more gender equality during the war, when they lived in the mountains as guerrillas. At that time, men and women participated equally in all meetings and, for example, it was not considered good form for women to wash men's clothes.

Because of machismo, after demobilization, women came under pressure to return to their traditional roles, and some women complained that they were being demobilized into the kitchen. They also complained that there were too few women in the governing councils of the local communities of the demobilized. As many as 45 percent of the women claimed that women's needs were not taken into consideration to the same degree as were men's needs. During house constructions in Chimaltenango, women participated on an equal footing with men, but their need for babysitters while they worked was not taken into consideration. In spite of these difficulties, several women were and are active politically in the URNG and the Alianza Nueva Nación (ANN); and, for a period of time, one woman, Alba Estela Maldonado, was secretary-general of the URNG and is now a member of Congress for the URNG.

The most important observation of the reintegration process is that the URNG did not become a strong vehicle for development or for social and economic change, as many – particularly among its grassroots members – had to struggle for day-to-day survival. Two reasons for this are that much less economic assistance than had been originally promised by the international community was actually realized and that the micro-enterprise projects generally failed. Another reason is that some of the international donors' projects – particularly USAID's – were geared to individual reintegration, while many URNG members preferred collective reintegration. The attitude of USAID and the Guatemalan government on this issue made the process more difficult and less successful for those who wanted to reintegrate collectively.

However, the URNG's internal problems and division also contributed to making the reintegration process less successful. As a result, it can be said that the human and political resources that the URNG could have contributed to the peacebuilding process were largely lost or unrealized potentials.

There are also some very important positive aspects. In spite of the negative attitudes of USAID and the government, generally speaking, URNG members who reintegrated collectively seem to have managed better than those who integrated individually, at least in the sense that they have shown some capacity for wider social and political engagement. The community of ex-URNG combatants in Chimaltenango is, for example, well organized, with its own committees for health, education, and youth activities, and it has cooperated with surrounding communities through the Consejo Comunitario de Desarrollo (COCODES).[5] In Chimaltenango, women have taken a lead role: COCODES is headed by a woman, and women head the majority of the other committees in the community (information obtained from interviews).

The URNG complied with all its commitments – ceasefire, demobilization, reintegration, and, later, the formation of a political party. This was publicly recognized by MINUGUA (Corral 2005, 18). Another important result of the reintegration process, therefore, is that, except for one particular incident, ex-guerrilla members have not been involved in violence and criminality and, likewise, that the security situation of the former guerrillas has been good. No URNG members have been assassinated after having been demobilized. (In comparison, numerous ex-Farabundo Martí National Liberation Front members in El Salvador were killed.) Several ex-URNG combatants currently work or have worked as security guards for their own political leaders. These security guards are among the thirty ex-URNG combatants integrated into the national police (information obtained from interviews).

Thus, it can be concluded that the ex-URNG combatants did not become spoilers of the peacebuilding process. However, due to the design and implementation of the DDR programs, as well as to the incomplete implementation of the overall peace accords, they also did not realize their potential to become agents of change.

URNG as a Political Party

Several factors influenced the URNG's establishment and its work as a political party. Some of these factors are contextual – such as the juridical, political, and socioeconomic external environment within which they had to operate – while others are directly related to the different guerrilla organizations' history, identity, and visions of the future (and the dynamics that this caused between the different groups within the URNG). The DDR process was particularly important to the collective, socioeconomic basis for URNG survival.

In 1997, the URNG decided to establish one integrated structure and, thereby, to dissolve the four groups that constituted the organization (the EGP, FAR, ORPA, and the PGT). This decision came into effect in February 1997. Following the legal requirements for the constitution of a political party, a promoting group of one hundred persons initiated the process of legalization in June that same year and elected a provisional board of directors (Junta Directiva). The URNG was finally recognized as a political party in December 1998, two years after the signing of the peace accords (Sinchar 1999, 87). In 1999, the URNG participated in the elections as a part of the Alianza Nueva Nación. However, increasing tension within the URNG became evident in the second National Assembly in August 2001. Two competing tendencies were not able to reach a compromise, and, in the internal elections, ex-EGP members and ex-ORPA members gained, while the so-called "revolutionary tendency" led by ex-FAR members was left without participation on the board of the party. After that, the revolutionary tendency split and, prior to the elections in 2003, helped to establish the ANN as a political party participating independently in the electoral process.

In the 1999 elections, the URNG-supported alliance received 270,891 votes (12.36 percent) in the presidential election and 233,870 votes (11.04 percent) in the parliamentary election on the national list. In 2003, when the URNG participated without an alliance, the result was 2.56 percent of the votes for president and 4.2 percent of the votes for the national list for deputies to Congress. The URNG almost disappeared as a legal political party. However, if the votes for ANN were taken into account, the total number of votes for these two left-wing parties to the Congress is similar to the 1999 results (231,129) (Tribunal Supremo Electoral).

One of the first obstacles the URNG leaders met when they decided to register as a political party involved gathering enough signatures from their supporters. The legal requirement in 1996 was for at least two thousand signatures from supporters with identity papers. The URNG finally registered with 4,162 (Interview with Pablo Monsanto). The identity papers and the registration process were problems for many ex-combatants because they had to go through a costly bureaucratic process and because they had other and more pressing social and economic needs to look to first. In addition, a political party is only accepted as a national organization if it has a presence in fifty municipalities (with a minimum of fifteen members in each) in no less than twelve departments of the country. This required an enormous organizational effort on the part of a group that so recently had been living in a clandestine situation and lacked experience in dealing with the legal system.

In the process of becoming established as a political party, the URNG had to follow normal procedures in a situation that was not normal. The participants described this process as long and costly, and the URNG ended up spending most of its available economic resources on it.

The irony of the situation, which several of those interviewed pointed to, is that the URNG had access to external economic sources of support during the war – and received even more external economic support during the peace process. However, after the demobilization process, when the URNG became a legal political party, the external economic support almost dried up (information obtained from interviews).

The URNG does not have many sources of income. Its deputies have committed themselves to giving 30 percent of their salaries to the party, which represents the most important source of income, even if they only have two deputies (interview with Alba Estela Maldonado). In addition, the URNG receives support for specific events like seminars. The party is also entitled to two quetzales (US$0.30) per vote in presidential elections. During the last elections, a small Mexican party, Partido del Trabajo, offered the URNG assistance with its propaganda.

The differences between the financing resources of the URNG and ANN, on one side, and those of the established political parties, like the Guatemalan Republican Front (FRG), on the other, are large. It is estimated that the political parties spent 437 million quetzales (US$60.4 million) on the campaign in 2003, and at least 50 percent of this on propaganda (Mirador Electoral 2003a and 2003b). Of the funds used for advertising in the mass media, 89.2 percent was spent by the five traditional conservative parties. According to the URNG's own estimate, its electoral campaign expenditure in 2003 consisted of 5 million quetzales (US$700,000).

In addition to this, there is a problem of clientelism. According to Rodrigo Asturias,[6] who spoke to us during the election campaign, "the state was there, buying votes, offering positions." Several of those interviewed mentioned Quiché as a province in which the buying of votes took place, along with other occurrences, like the use threats and fear. "Having been subject to thirty-five years of psychological warfare also leaves traces" (interview with Rodrigo Asturias).

Lack of economic resources has many consequences, such as not being able to assure candidates adequate coverage in the mass media.[7] Another consequence was that the URNG could not offer its supporters payment for services during the election campaign. Some of those interviewed emphasized that, when people in Guatemala come to a meeting, they expect a meal or at least that their bus tickets will be paid. The URNG does not have the economic resources to offer this. However, external conditions alone did not determine either the URNG's or ANN's success as a political party. This must also be seen in light of their own strategies and priorities.

Prior to the establishment of the URNG as a political party, two possible organizational directions were discussed within its ranks: (1) to keep the structure of each of the former guerrilla organizations or (2) to dissolve these and form one unified party structure. The latter option was chosen, and the different guerrilla organizations were formally dissolved, although several ex-combatants claim that the structures were secretly kept in place because they were important to the identity of their members (information obtained from interviews).

The establishment of the URNG as a unified political party took place at a meeting in El Salvador. Although there were large differences in the size of the four guerrilla organizations, there was no quota system, and the composition of the party leadership was decided by secret ballot, resulting in the election of seven members from the EGP, four from FAR, three from ORPA, and two from the PGT (information obtained from interviews).

With a national leadership made up of members from four organizations with different philosophies and political visions, the URNG was seriously limited in its ability to establish organizational unity. As well, the leaders of ORPA (Rodrigo Asturias) and FAR (Pablo Monsanto)[8] had very different ideas and did not communicate well (information obtained from interviews). In addition, the political experience of the URNG came within a war context, and few members of the team had experience operating as a political party within the Guatemalan political system. According to some, the URNG was not able to work out an internally coherent strategy and was perceived by many outsiders as governing in alliance with the National Advancement Party (Plan por el Adelantamiento Nacional [PAN]), the governing party with whom the peace agreement was made. Some have questioned whether the URNG's actions comprised a strategy "to keep the peace" in order to gain the continued goodwill of the governing party.

The URNG is often compared to the Farabundo Martí National Liberation Front (FMLN) in El Salvador with respect to how the transition to a political party was managed:

In comparison to the URNG, FMLN had a political vision. They were able to convert soldiers into political activity and, in spite of divisions, they were able to reach some form of internal unity and create a strong party organization. The day after the peace accord was signed in El Salvador, the FMLN was established as a political party, and it proclaimed that the fight was not over and distanced itself from the government right-wing party, ARENA. In Guatemala, on the other hand, the URNG attended a social gathering together with PAN members to celebrate. (Interview with Cesar Montes)

The internal problems in the URNG intensified when the EGP leader, Rolando Moran,[9] died. Moran was a strong leader of the largest guerrilla organization, and he communicated well with the leadership of all four guerrilla organizations. When he died, the glue that held together the different groups was gone. No one could fill Moran's shoes. This led to the split in the URNG and the breakaway, mainly, of FAR members.

Some of the difficulties the URNG encountered in the process of transforming into a political party are related to the type of organization it was during the war. Unlike the FMLN in El Salvador, the URNG only had a military leadership, not a political one. Thus, the national organization of the URNG was directed by military criteria. The leadership went through the formalities necessary to create a legal political party but not to make it work (information obtained from interviews with ex-combatants in Guatemala City).

The URNG had problems developing organizational unity. Generally, the leadership was more developed in military and political-diplomatic work and less developed in work with the social organizations and the "masses," although to a certain degree it relied on their support during the war. It had difficulty changing its wartime relationship with organizations in the social movement into a peacetime relationship. In hindsight, some of its leaders have reflected on this and have realized that they should have looked for more opportunities "to use political work as a social movement work" (interview with Alba Estela Maldonado; Monroy 2005). However, the question of involving social organizations in political work has not been an easy one, particularly as the public does not have much trust in political parties in Guatemala and blames them for much of what went wrong in the past (information obtained from interviews).

Many ex-combatants at the grassroots level of the URNG have also lost a certain degree of confidence in their leaders. It was mentioned repeatedly in many interviews that this problem arose from the dissolution of the individual guerrilla organizations. According to some, there was agreement on this dissolution at the leadership level but not further down the ranks (information obtained from interviews with ex-combatants in Guatemala City). Many former supporters now feel orphaned and express great frustration over lack of information and contact (interviews with ex-combatants in Chimaltenango and Petén). Lack of information has created a distance between leaders and the grassroots former guerrillas. Many lower-ranking ex-combatants point out the need for a broader political process, with more focus on people's basic needs and on those issues with which people identify, such as the need for electricity (interviews in CPR-Petén; interviews in El Horizonte).

Shortly after demobilization, there was more support for the URNG among its grassroots members; however, currently many of those interviewed found it more useful to support non-governmental organizations, such as the Frente por la Vida y la Paz, which exerts pressure on the state to fulfill its responsibilities in the peace accord and protests against the mining activities of international companies as well as against the free trade agreement. Petén is the area where FAR mainly operated during the war and, in spite of frustrations with their leaders, many of those interviewed in Petén said that they voted for and supported ANN. However, they expressed strong discontent over the split in the URNG (Monroy 2005).

The URNG's transition to a political party and its later political activity was influenced by the same factors as was the reintegration process as a whole, and by some additional conditions. The first factor is the socioeconomic basis the URNG was left with as a result of the reintegration process. While parts of the reintegration process and some of its projects were successful, what clearly failed were the efforts to give the former combatants a proper source of income. This is reflected in the low level of political participation, particularly within the grassroots level of URNG ex-combatants as their capacity is almost completely absorbed by the struggle for survival. These effects have also been reinforced by the generally large socioeconomic disparities in Guatemalan society. While several of the more well-established and conservative political parties in Guatemala have developed strong ties to the economic elites, the URNG and ANN have few sources of financial support, which limits their ability to run effective election campaigns and to reach out more broadly though the media.

Clearly, political participation was highest in the areas where the URNG combatants had reintegrated collectively, such as in Petén and in Chimaltenango. Had the donors been more generous in supporting collective reintegration projects, there could have been much to gain from it, including greater political participation.

The second factor is the juridical framework within which the URNG had to operate in order to establish itself. The complexity of Guatemalan laws in this regard made the transition into a political party difficult and time-consuming. Lack of political and bureaucratic experience within the URNG added to this situation.

However, quite a few of the ex-combatants interviewed blamed the URNG's own strategy and internal split for the problems the URNG and ANN had in attracting support, particularly during the 2003 elections. The split has had a particularly negative effect, but the parties' inability to include and engage in a dialogue with civil society organizations is also considered quite important in this regard.

Demobilization of the PACs

DDR in the Peace Accord

The framework for the demobilization of the PACs was quite different from that for the demobilization of the URNG. As mentioned initially, the peace accord only briefly mentioned that the PACs should be demobilized, and it emphasized cutting the structural links between the patrols and the army.

No international economic assistance has been offered for the demobiliz-ation of the PACs. During the negotiation process, the URNG did not want the PACs to be given the same treatment as the URNG forces. Neither the army nor the government ever presented any real proposal on how to handle the PACs and the Guatemalan military police (PMA). The international com-munity opposed any support to the PACs, either in the form of funding their reintegration or in the form of state compensation (information ob-tained from interviews with former Guatemalan government officials). The reason for this was the PACs' human rights record. The negotiations on human rights and on the establishment of the Commission for Historical Clarification were already heated and tense. Bringing in the question of providing compensation to the PACs would have represented another very difficult and delicate issue for the government and the army to handle.

As a result, demobilization and reintegration of the PACs have been man-aged by only the government and the army. This includes some very small symbolic assistance offered by the government, which, in light of develop-ments after 1996, only seems to have provoked a strong demand for more assistance and follow-up.

Demobilization and Discontent

President Arzu began the demobilization of the PACs in late 1996, before the peace agreement came into effect. MINUGUA was invited to be present at some of the scenes of demobilization. However, it did not have sufficient information or the means to verify whether all the arms were collected or whether the organic links between the army and the rural communities were in effect broken. The army organized and supervised the disarmament procedures. The patrol members received a meal and a document thanking them for their service to their country (Jensen and Stepputat 2001).

Ex-patrol members were very discontent with the way they were treated. Their first demands for economic compensation were voiced already in early 1997, in the department of El Petén, where a group of ex-patrol members blocked access to gasoline stations. As a response to these events, Raquel Zelaya of the government's peace secretariat visited the area in 1997 and refused any possibility of such compensation but committed the govern-ment to provide socioeconomic projects to support former patrol members. However, the government's proposal was for large-scale projects, such as the construction of roads – also meant to be part of the response to the peace accord in general – which caused great discontent among the ex-combatants (information obtained from an interview with Catalina Soberanis).

During the electoral campaign in 1999, the FRG presidential candidate, Alfonso Portillo, promised the ex-PAC members economic compensation.

The ex-PAC members noted this, and it later surfaced as an important argument in their demand for compensation. Ex-PAC members in general constituted a solid social basis for the FRG and were an important factor in the party's electoral triumph (Sáenz de Tejada 2004, 73).

The issue of compensation came up again under the Portillo government as a reaction to the lack of fulfilment of the agreement with PAN and to Portillo's electoral promises. The Presidential Secretariat for Planning outlined a plan for 2000-1 to provide assistance packages to former PAC members. Another presidential secretariat (Secretaría de Coordinación Ejecutiva de la Presidencia) finally provided some support in the form of chickens and goats (information obtained from an interview with Catalina Soberanis). The recipients perceived this small symbolic assistance more as a provocation than as any real and dignified compensation. In June 2002 they began organizing, particularly in El Petén. The army veterans organization supported the former patrol members in their reorganization and demands.

Towards the end of 2002, individual applications for compensation from ex-PAC members were registered and piling up. By 13 October 2002, 250,000 applications had been registered, and, by early 2003, that number had reached 629,000. Originally, the former patrol members demanded compensation of 60,000 quetzales (US$8,286) per person. It then came down to 20,000 quetzales (US$2,762) and finally to 5,214 quetzales (US$720) per person (Sáenz de Tejada 2004, 76-77).

The government's first manoeuvre was to suggest levying a special tax to finance the PACs' demand, a plan announced by Minister of Finance Eduardo Weyman. However, confronted with a massive refusal from all sectors of society, Weyman then suggested taking loans on the international market (Eurobonos), selling the idea that the funds would be used for a national plan to aid the victims of the armed conflict. The suggested loans were for US$700 million, which, if realized, would increase Guatemala's foreign debt by 25 percent (Sáenz de Tejada 2004, 76-77).

The Portillo government paid the ex-patrol members a part of the compensation. Before, as well as after, this compensation was paid, human rights organizations protested strongly, as did the URNG, MINUGUA, and the association of business organizations known as CACIF. However, Guatemala's Court of Constitutionality later ruled that the cash payment to ex-PACs members was illegal. The Court's argument was that, since the former PAC members did not have any labour contract with the state during the war and their work was voluntary, the state could not pay them for it. Because of this, towards the end of 2005, the government switched to compensate the former patrol members with a reforestation program called "Trees for Peace." Under this program, 70 million trees will be planted by ex-PACs. With this initiative, the Guatemalan government has been quite innovative in trying to meet the ex-PACs' demand, but several ex-PAC members, wanting only cash compensation, have refused the work.

The most important implications of the failure of the ex-PACs demobilization to provide for the future of former patrol members were these members' reorganization, their demand for economic compensation, and their alliances with conservative political forces. Finally, but not least important, ex-patrollers have been involved in criminal activities and violence, although to a lesser degree than have ex-members of the military police. This means that, in both political terms and security terms, the civil defence patrols have become spoilers in the peacebuilding process.

Conclusion

From a comparative international perspective, and within traditional DDR thinking, the process in Guatemala has been quite successful. The URNG disarmed and demobilized without violence. The ex-combatants have, in general, not been involved in criminality and violence after their demobilization, and their own security has also been well taken care of. This achievement is – within the violent Guatemalan context – quite important on its own terms.

However, widening the security focus to former PAC members and the military police, the picture becomes different as both have been involved in criminal activities and violence. This is the point at which something went wrong in the process, both in providing former patrollers and PMAs with alternative employment and livelihoods and in providing public security. The ex-patrol members who had been subject to forced recruitment and suffering during the war became caught up in a campaign that was used by conservative political forces and military personnel who did not want justice for the violations of civil rights during the war but, rather, the legitimization of their participation in counter-insurgency warfare.

With regard to the URNG, the reintegration process was successful only in some respects, such as housing and education. In general, the reintegration projects did not properly reflect the needs of the URNG, which were rooted in the causes of the conflict and the longevity of the war. The extreme example of this failure may be observed in the groups of combatants who had fought for more than thirty years in an effort to move Guatemala in the direction of greater socioeconomic justice and the equitable distribution of land, only to end up at *fincas*, heavily indebted and almost completely absorbed by daily survival. This was not what they had been fighting for.

In his article published in *International Security* in 1997, Stedman (1997) emphasized that international actors who want to bring deadly, protracted civil wars to an end must anticipate violent challenges to peace processes, and, instead of thinking generally about threats to peace, they must ask, "Who are the threats to peace?" Our study not only confirms the need to focus on who the threats to peace are but also reveals the need to simultaneously look at *what* the threats to peace are. Because of the extraordinarily comprehensive character of the Guatemalan peace accord, the threats to peace are not found in weaknesses in the accord itself but, rather, in the implement environment and the overall failure to fulfill the accords.

In focusing first on *what* the threats to long-term sustainable peace in Guatemala are, the socioeconomic situation is key. First, during the DDR process, international donors did not deliver the amounts of economic assistance promised, which led to poorly financed projects and deprived many of the poor former URNG combatants of a proper basis of living.

Secondly, as pointed out by Aguilera in Chapter 2 of this volume, the failure to fully implement the subsidiary agreements of the 1996 peace accord – particularly on agrarian and socioeconomic reform – is an important reason why large socioeconomic disparities remain and negatively influence the ability of former URNG combatants, as well as of poor former civil patrol members, to rise out of poverty.

Third and most important, our study highlights how large socioeconomic disparities affect democratization. While well-established conservative political parties in Guatemala have continued to enjoy support from the economic elites, new and smaller political parties, like the URNG and ANN – with a support base among the poor – have almost no sources of income. These conditions represent a serious obstacle to further democratization and political participation.

Having focused on *what* the threats to sustainable peace are, it is now time to come back to *who* the threats to peace are. In doing this we must look at the differences between the armed groups and the implications of this for the peacebuilding process.

Different types of armed groups call for different types of responses. The Guatemalan war was particularly lengthy and violent. Many of the guerrillas developed a group identity. Their shared experiences of the war were psychologically important and led to a preference for collective reintegration. For those who managed it, collective reintegration eased their transition from life in the mountains to a normal civilized life. As well, ex-guerrillas had an urgent need to earn a living as many of them returned to absolutely nothing.

The government's and the international community's response to the URNG's reintegration needs was very much guided by traditional DDR thinking. As expressed by Spear (2002, 145), "reintegration is the most effective way to break former combatants' ties to their former fighting units and allows a means for them to provide for their dependents." However, collective reintegration is clearly not considered a potentially positive contributor to peacebuilding processes. The drive towards the individualization of the reintegration process in Guatemala, combined with badly planned and administered socioeconomic projects, served to diminish the ex--URNG combatants' ability to become an active social and political force.

However, when this did not happen, external factors were not the only reason for it. Another reason was that, to a certain extent, the URNG mirrors the authoritarian Guatemalan society, and it needs to work on its inclusiveness and dialogue with social organizations. The URNG and ANN suffer from Guatemalans' general level of distrust in political parties. This shows how important it is for the URNG and ANN to avoid reflecting the negative aspects of the society they have been trying to change and to allow more openness and inclusiveness in their own political activity, thus becoming an alternative to the traditional political parties.

The civil defence patrols did not require reintegration in the traditional sense, but the reorganization of the PACs between 2001 and 2004, and their demonstrations and demands for economic compensation, clearly revealed that this was an issue that the peace process had not solved. And, like a boomerang, it came back with great force.

The issue of the PACs was complicated by the fact that they had a very mixed composition, with military commissioners or other ex-army members as leaders and a huge number of civilians as members. The PACs issue is a good example of the difficulty of applying the civil-military dichotomy in practice. The most complicating factor is their human rights record. While the military commissioners and other former army members were responsible for many of the human rights atrocities, some civilians also contributed, while others did not. It should also be noted that many ex-patrol members still hold important positions in local communities.

An important aspect of the post-demobilization phase involves how conservative political forces took advantage of the discontent of the ex-patrol members and influenced their reorganization and demands in a direction that tended to legitimize what happened during the war rather than to deal with violations of their civil rights. It is possible that, if the issue of the civil defence patrols had been addressed during the peace process itself, this would have given those concerned patrol members a chance to flag the violations of their rights when they had been forced into the patrols during the war. This could also have opened space for a much needed public discourse on the extremely repressive character of the war. It could have contributed to making many of the ex-PAC members agents for change, particularly in the area of civil and human rights. However, that opportunity was lost.

There are several important lessons to be learned from the DDR process of ex-combatants in Guatemala. Some of these apply to donors and the international community, and others apply to the armed groups themselves. These lessons and their applications are formulated as propositions below.

Proposition 1: In 1997, the URNG conducted a survey among its ex-combatants, asking them about their backgrounds as well as their needs, desires, and aspirations for the future. The results of this survey were largely ignored by the donor agencies. Had they been listened to and used in the development of projects in the reintegration process, that process could have been much more sustainable. The creative approach taken by the URNG is an example of how DDR processes should be planned at an early stage. Indeed, it could take place even while ceasefire agreements are in effect.

Proposition 2: The URNG's survey also revealed that many former combatants would prefer to reintegrate collectively. The donors, particularly the USAID, did not take this into consideration and designed projects for individual reintegration. In future reintegration processes, the international agencies that are financially supporting them should seriously take into consideration group identity and the wishes of ex-combatants.

Proposition 3: Attention was paid to women's needs in the DDR programs aimed at URNG ex-combatants, and some female ex-combatants emerged as local or national leaders. Yet, many women feel that they have been "demobilized back into the kitchen." Clearly, programs for female ex-combatants need to be linked more systemically to national initiatives to advance the gender dimensions of overall peace implementation, especially with regard to political participation and sustainable livelihoods.

Proposition 4: At their peak, the civil defence patrols comprised between 1 million and 1.3 million members. Despite their numbers and their role in the war, the question of their future was largely neglected in the negotiation process that led to the 1996 peace accord. The PACs were considered to be represented by the army during the negotiations, but the army did not defend their interests. However, the PACs reorganized and made demands for economic compensation. This emphasizes the need to include all the most important armed groups in the peace process – not necessarily in the main negotiations – but alternatively, in other forums linked to the negotiation process.

Proposition 5: The URNG had ideological goals in its struggle, including socioeconomic equity, human rights, and democratization. However, it was not sufficiently vigilant to prevent negative aspects of Guatemalan society being reflected within its own organization. It is important that armed groups with political goals take up the challenges of inclusiveness, broad participation, and democratization in order to represent an alternative in deeply divided and undemocratic societies. At the same time, it is important that the political system be open to the inclusion of formerly excluded political options, like that of the Guatemalan left.

Proposition 6: Economic assistance from international agencies to the DDR process in Guatemala turned out to be much smaller than what had been promised. This led to poorly financed projects and disillusionment among ex-combatants. It is very important in the planning and implementation of future DDR processes that the international community stand by its promises of economic assistance.

Proposition 7: The large socioeconomic disparities in Guatemala and the failure to fulfill the subsidiary agreements aimed at changing these conditions have made it difficult for ex-combatants and for the poor in general to move out of poverty. This shows that, in armed conflicts in which socioeconomic inequality constitutes an important cause, long-term peacebuilding assistance and international pressure to implement socioeconomic reforms for more equity are necessary.

Proposition 8: This study of reintegration and political participation in Guatemala reveals that large socioeconomic disparities strongly hamper political participation and democratization. International assistance to peacebuilding has had a strong focus on institutional aspects of democratization. It is time now for the international community to focus on – and to do something about – one of the most serious obstacles to democratization: namely, socioeconomic inequity.

9
Fighting for Peace?
Former Combatants and the Afghan Peace Process
Arne Strand

As explained in Chapter 6 of this volume, Afghanistan harbours many peace-building challenges rooted in its own history and in the fact that it hosted the first post-9/11 intervention (which the United States and its allies presented as part of the War on Terror). Since the signing of the Bonn Agreement in late 2001, the country has undergone a deeply conflictual peacebuilding process (Suhrke, Harpviken, and Strand 2004; Rubin 2006). The formal democratization process has begun, and an Afghan president and parliament have been elected. The Afghans were made formally responsible for the peace process, supported by what was envisaged to be a "light footprint" United Nations Assistance Mission to Afghanistan and protected by the International Security Assistance Force (ISAF), both mandated by the UN Security Council.

Yet two different – but related – international military engagements have continued. One operation, under US command, has sought to eliminate remnants of terrorist networks and supporters, primarily the Taliban and al Qaeda. Meanwhile, the bulk of ISAF has adhered to its robust peace enforcement mission. In order to reduce military and political opposition to the peace process, a deliberate strategy has been adopted of co-opting military commanders into the new governance structure, excluding only those centrally placed in the militarily defeated Taliban. However, due to the sensitivity of the issue, the disarmament, demobilization, and reintegration process (the focus of this chapter) was not detailed in the Bonn Agreement.

The peacebuilding operation has taken place in a country that has seen continuous military conflict since 1978, in the course of which numerous military groups have been formed along lines of ethnicity, religion, and solidarity networks, the latter referred to as *quams*. These groups were mobilized and led by commanders and militia leaders who had highly diverse backgrounds and local support platforms. Many assumed command responsibility due to their religious stature or due to being local dignitaries or landlords, while others established their positions through their ability to fight and lead men. It was common for the majority of those terming themselves mujahideen – holy warriors – to locate their military resistance in their home areas. This happened even when fighting was being organized from neighbouring Pakistan and Iran; thus, they depended to a high degree on embeddedness and acceptance in the communities that they set out to defend.[1]

When the mujahideen later moved back to Afghanistan following the Soviet withdrawal in 1989, the trend of localized fighting remained, though some military groups that formed along ethnic lines, such as the Tadjik Shura-e Nazar, the Hazara Hezb-e Wahdat, and the Pashtun-dominated Taliban, were able to conduct warfare over larger geographical areas. The Afghan army, presently in the process of being reformed with US support and funding (Giustozzi n.d.), has historically been confined to the larger cities, and the forces were gradually merged with those of the mujahideen groups from 1993 onwards, as the latter groups defeated the Kabul-based government.

Tradition, low security, and a long history of conflict have left Afghans highly armed; most families have guns, and the different armed groups have kept huge stockpiles. Efforts made by the Taliban to disarm areas under their control and ban the use of landmines during the late 1990s were reversed by a massive US-supported rearmament in late 2001, which was part of the military strategy to defeat the Taliban and al Qaeda. It is estimated that there are between 8 and 10 million firearms in Afghanistan today (Sedra 2003), in addition to a range of heavy weapons and the possibility of purchasing new and old weapons from neighbouring states.

A number of researchers have addressed issues relating to the reform of the Afghan security sector, the DDR process, and strategies to address former warlords, who are feared as possible spoilers of the peace process. Most prominent is the research undertaken by Giustozzi (2003 and 2004), Sedra (2003), and Rubin (2005), who all debate different aspects of how to handle the warlords. Özerdem (2002) looks at DDR in a cross-cultural perspective, while Chrobok (2005) researches the demobilization and reintegration of young soldiers. There are, in addition, more general studies on the security situation, comparing Afghanistan with other postwar countries (Donini et al. 2004), while a report from the Feinstein International Famine Center (2004) presents an analysis of how rural Afghans perceive their security and livelihood situation. The lack of security is a topic in a range of reports from organizations such as Amnesty International and Human Rights Watch, and the disarmament concern is strongly voiced in a report from the Afghan-based Human Rights Research and Advocacy Consortium (2004) entitled *Take the Guns Away*.

Noteworthy, however, is the lack of attention paid to the relationships between the former (and present) commanders, the combatants, and the local communities. The main focus has been on commanders' attitudes towards the Afghan state and on what strategies might be applied to reduce their influence through processes run by the Afghan government or the external military or humanitarian actors. However, an issue of particular concern in this debate has been how best to reduce the influence of one particular group: the mid-level commanders who have not been fully co-opted by the Afghan government. And, while the weak reintegration aspect of the DDR process is discussed in passing, the main debate concentrates on the demobilization and disarmament of the former combatants, with the main aim being to reduce the potential for armed resistance against the new Afghan state, the administration, and the international actors involved in Afghanistan.

Addressing the armed actors' embeddedness – here understood as being their local, social, and institutional background and their continuing contact with these networks during and after the war – the literature provides limited insight. One general reference is the International Labour Organisation (1997), which states that it has found it more difficult to demobilize former combatants who have a strong ideological attachment to their group. As far as Afghanistan is concerned, Özerdem (2002) argues that many former combatants have maintained a civilian identity that will help them in their readjustment to society.

While the embeddedness option has lacked thorough research, the fear that former commanders and combatants might become spoilers of the peace process has received due attention. The work of Stedman (1997) is highlighted in the introductory chapter of this volume. He suggests three main strategies for addressing the problem of the spoilers, which I draw upon when presenting and discussing the Afghan case he outlines:

- socialization: the process of building a common normative foundation
- inducement: offering political positions or other alternatives
- coercion: the use of armed force (or the threat thereof).

Stedman's critics suggest that the emphasis placed on dealing with spoilers has led to a "security first" approach, in which demobilization and disarmament are prioritized, as is the emphasis on leadership by external rather than local actors (Baranyi 2005c).

The United Nations is assigned a central role in many peacekeeping operations, with UN agencies assuming different responsibilities in DDR processes. The Security Council (UNSC) had already addressed the DDR issue in 2000 (UNSC 2000), and a DDR working group in the Executive Committee on Humanitarian Affairs (ECHA) prepared a paper on the role and responsibility of the UN in DDR processes. This includes a suggestion for the division of responsibility between UN organizations and how these can best act in collaboration with national and international institutions (UN ECHA DDR Working Group 2000). The report acknowledges that the varying nature of the different conflicts, including social structures and political environment, makes it impossible to adopt one common strategy. ECHA underlines the importance of a holistic DDR approach, integrated in the overall peace process, and the necessity of allowing local government and NGOs to take lead roles in the process, with the United Nations and other international actors operating as facilitators.

Faltas, MacDonald, and Waszink (2001), whose article presents a comprehensive review of weapon collection programs, is foremost in addressing the disarmament component. In light of the recognition of the importance of parallel incentives for successful disarmament, the article presents the following lessons: the need for prior assessment, the need for coherence between initiatives, the need to target chosen incentives and sanctions, the need to acknowledge local conditions, and, not least, the need to recognize the fact that disarmament is most successful in combination with other efforts.

Moreover, Faltas, MacDonald, and Waszink point out an important security concern. They argue that, as the overall aim of practical disarmament is to (re)establish a government monopoly over violence, it must be accompanied by safeguards against the abuse of this monopoly. These safeguards involve linking demobilization measures to the broader peacebuilding efforts, including development programs. A successful means to this end, from their point of view, is recorded in Gramsh in Albania, where community-based development programs were offered in exchange for arms.

Kingma (2002b) has reviewed the role of the United Nations Development Program in reintegration processes, and he argues for a broad inclusion of actors. He suggests identifying the families of the demobilized soldiers, communities of resettlement, and other reintegrating groups, such as returned refugees and internally displaced persons, government agencies, security forces, NGOs, the United Nations, and donor agencies. He emphasizes the need for former combatants to establish new livelihoods where ensuring private job opportunities (due to the limited availability of formal-sector jobs) and/or access to land is important. He voices concern over the possibility of changing the social relations between former combatants and the communities, highlighting the difficulty female combatants have in being recognized by the wider society as well as the integration of child soldiers. Moreover, he is of the opinion that reconciliation and justice processes constitute a challenge, as do the numerous health concerns, including HIV/AIDS, with which many former combatants are affected.

Kingma brings up another important issue for discussion: the extent of targeting assistance to former combatants, who, in many cases, are regarded as part of the reason for civilian suffering. While arguing for the need to meet their special needs, as they have often sacrificed years of their lives to improve the situation of their compatriots, he recognizes that, in order to reduce tension and avoid conflicts, DDR processes should, as far as possible, be area- or community-based.

A common question emerges from this literature, which is that of individual-based versus community-based approaches to compensation, where most sources seem to agree that the latter have proved more effective. This would then, by its nature, be more long-term and development-oriented, providing larger roles for national institutions, organizations, and communities – a position supported by other studies in this research project (Hauge and Thoresen 2006; and Scholey and Shikaki 2006). Among lessons emerging, including those from the WKOP project, are the conclusions that armed actors should be regarded as possible agents of change; that DDR needs to be linked to the wider peacebuilding process in order to increase recognition and impact; and that there are varying degrees to which armed actors are socially embedded in their respective communities.

This chapter is based on a review of primary and secondary documentation on DDR processes, including a review of literature and reports in Spanish, combined with fairly extensive field research in different parts of Afghanistan conducted by an Afghan national NGO (the Cooperation for Peace and Unity) and my previous studies on the role of Mine Action for Peace in peacebuilding (Strand 2004).

Following a general introduction to Afghanistan, I discuss the formation and embeddedness of the different Afghan armed groups in more detail. I then present an outline of the Afghan government as well as of the international community's development of policy and organizational structures to handle the DDR process, which became Afghanistan's New Beginnings Programme (ANBP). I place a major emphasis on presenting and analyzing findings from field research. Finally, following a discussion of Stedman's spoiler theories, I provide a conclusion and recommendations as to how the DDR process can be improved through applying some of the suggestions presented by local communities.

The cautious response several informants had towards the research project underscores the high sensitivity of this issue. Many were hesitant to answer questions as they feared that information might be used against the commanders and the former combatants, whom the population either feared or depended on for their security. This illustrates well the Afghanistan of early 2006: a highly armed and insecure country, where smuggling and drug production provide the main income for large segments of the population, including centrally positioned government officials and those within the police force and the Afghan army.

The Afghan Context

Before entering into details regarding the armed groups and the DDR process, it is necessary to present a brief introduction to Afghan history, ethnic and tribal complexity, the role of Islam, and Afghanistan's development status. As noted above, and as detailed by Zakhilwal and Thomas in Chapter 6 of this volume, Afghans have experienced continuous war and conflict since 1978. Throughout Afghanistan's history, political, ethnic, and religious dividing lines have shifted. All the groups represented in the Northern Alliance as instrumental in defeating the Taliban in 2001 have, at some point, fought each other militarily.

The present Afghan border was drawn as a result of a British-Russian nineteenth-century compromise that created a buffer state between their respective empires; therefore, it does not reflect the regional distribution of the country's ethnicities. Southern Afghanistan is mainly populated by Pashtuns, who make up approximately half of the total population of some 23 million,[2] from the same tribes that live in the adjoining parts of Pakistan. Northern Afghanistan is inhabited by Turkmens, Uzbeks, and Tadjiks, and the central part of the country is populated by Hazaras. The latter have traditionally held an underprivileged position in Afghan society, partly due to their allegiance to Shia Islam rather than to the Sunni Islam followed by the majority of Afghans. Religious tension between these two main directions within Islam has been actively used to mobilize conflict.

The Pashtuns held a politically dominant role until 2001, when the Northern Alliance, with a more diverse ethnic and religious composition, came to power after joining Operation Enduring Freedom (OEF). The balancing of the ethnicities has been a major concern for the nation-building endeavours of the Karzai government, whose expressed aim has been to ensure a balanced representation in cabinet and the government administration.

Traditionally, Afghan society is male-dominated, with strong cultural and religious limitations on women's participation in public life, their employment opportunities, and their ability to hold political positions. The recent wars have been fought by men. Women were not actively engaged in armed conflict, although most of them shared men's religious and political convictions and assumed their share of responsibility for the family as men were enlisted or volunteered for the battlefield.

The 2005 Afghanistan Millennium Development Goals Report presents a worrisome picture of the development situation, pointing out that "nearly 40 percent of the rural population cannot count on having sufficient food to satisfy their most basic hunger; 57 percent of the population is under 18 years of age but with little hope of employment; in much of the country over 80 percent of the people are illiterate; life expectancy is under 45 years" (Government of Afghanistan 2005, xviii). The gravity of these problems has been reinforced by the fact that Afghanistan raised a mere 5 percent of its GDP as internal revenue in 2005 and that the drug economy is estimated to equal 50 percent to 60 percent of the legal economy.

Part of the international military intervention against the Taliban and al Qaeda in October 2001 involved the rearmament of the Northern Alliance. Former commanders were brought back from exile, and army units were re-established at the main battlefronts. These people and groups expected a peace dividend in addition to the political power they gained after capturing Kabul, the influence they secured in the Afghan Interim Authority, and their role in the following Afghan Transitional Authority. They maintained a major influence over the democratization process as participants in the Loya Jirgas (national councils) that sealed Hamid Karzai's position as interim president and that approved a new constitution, and later they cemented their influence through being elected to the Afghan Parliament. These developments took place despite a constitutional clause preventing leaders of armed groups from standing for any such elections.

A New Afghan Army, trained by the United States, was to replace former formal and informal military units, though excluding smaller militia groups engaged in OEF. As a consequence of this strategy, a need emerged for the disarmament and demobilization of Northern Alliance soldiers who had continued to receive a salary from the international community from late 2001. The UN Assistance Mission to Afghanistan estimated that, during 2002, some 75,000 men were in units under the control of the Ministry of Defence, while a further 100,000 belonged to private militias (Giustozzi n.d.).

When the international focus fell on security sector reforms and on how to best coordinate efforts, it was decided to divide the responsibility for the process between the main donors, establishing these as lead nations. Hence, by early 2002, Italy had assumed responsibility for judicial reform, the United States for rebuilding the Afghan army, Germany for the police, Japan for the DDR process, and the United Kingdom for drug eradication. Despite this formal division of responsibilities, it is evident that the United States has played a very dominant military and political role in Afghanistan. Based on its lead role in the War on Terror, the United States has attempted to engineer and direct the peace and democratization process, and this has included the very active involvement of the US Ambassadors to Afghanistan.[3]

Initially, the threat to the peace process was primarily associated with terrorist groups, such as those affiliated with the armed resistance of al Qaeda remnants, groups defined as "neo-Taliban," and other Afghan groups who opposed the government or the international forces. However, as the Afghan central state started to take shape during 2002, attention was gradually drawn towards commanders and even governors who resisted being governed by the central Afghan government or who were unwilling to transfer income from local taxation to the Ministry of Finance in Kabul. The "warlord" label was subsequently placed on a number of them, and they were increasingly seen as potential spoilers of the Afghan peace process and, thus, as a threat that needed to be addressed by both political and military means.

Concern for the consequences of the continued armed conflict and the presence of numerous armed groups caused the Government of Afghanistan to add a ninth Millennium Development Goal – Enhancing Security – stating that "lack of security is a principal obstacle to the education and public participation of women, as well as to long-term investment for development" (Government of Afghanistan 2005, xxi). The security concern is, moreover, noted in the Afghan Compact, which was approved in London in early 2006 and which established a joint vision shared by the Afghan government and the international community regarding the further development of the Afghan state. This included an emphasis on the need to achieve greater synergies between efforts on the security, governance, and development fronts.

Despite, or possibly because of, all the changes Afghanistan has gone through, Afghans have remained strongly influenced by their culture, traditions, and religion. Ethnic, tribal, and family networks have been safety nets and have provided security in the absence of a functional state. Nevertheless, Afghanistan is a very fragile and vulnerable society, where a dependency on external financing, extremely low education levels, high unemployment, regional interference, and unresolved disputes over land and water provide fertile ground for renewed conflict.

Early Formation of Armed Factions

In order to understand the present position of commanders, those termed "warlords," and the soldiers and volunteers, a historical recollection of Afghan-specific military formations and recruitment practices is required.

What needs to be acknowledged is that many of those still commanding authority and military resources became involved in political (and religious) activities and military operations as early as 1973. The then opposition to the Afghan kingdom was primarily based at Kabul University and mobilized against the lack of democratization and against nepotism within the ruling elite. It included personalities such as Professors Burhanuddin Rabbani and Abdul Raouf Sayyaf, and students such as Gulbuddin Hekmatyar and Ahmed Shah Masood, to name a few. These, all affiliated with the Muslim Brotherhood, were driven into exile in Pakistan, where political parties were formed, such as Jamiat-e Islami and Hezb-e Islami. Experiencing a political conflict with their neighbour, Pakistan provided the groups with military training and equipment to operate inside Afghanistan. Thus, a core group of Islamist militants was formed, and affiliations made with Pakistani, Western, and Islamic intelligence agencies – affiliations that would ensure them considerable financial support following the Soviet invasion.

The communist People's Democratic Party of Afghanistan (PDPA) gained control over Afghanistan through a coup d'état in 1978, utilizing its power base within the Afghan army (many officers had been trained in the Soviet Union). Different forms of resistance emerged inside Afghanistan; the major thrust, however, was from religious networks that opposed the PDPA government's reforms promoting land redistribution and co-education. Those involved included followers of religious leaders, such as the Mujadiddi family, and those associated with networks of mullahs and maulawis who had been educated in various madrassas (religious schools). Following the Soviet invasion in December 1979, millions of Afghans fled to Pakistan and Iran, there to join the various mujahideen parties. The fight was justified by the call for a jihad (holy war) by religious leaders, the first being the Pir of Tagab (Olesen 1995).

Until the Soviet withdrawal was completed in 1989, recruitment on the mujahideen side was largely voluntary. It was seen as a duty to join jihad for a period of time to defend a Muslim country against a communist invasion. With an increase in international military assistance from 1983 onwards, the Pakistan-based parties gained prominence over what might be described as the "internal resistance." Some salaries were paid to those joining one of the seven Pakistani-based Islamic parties; however, probably more important was the fact that, if they enlisted in one of the parties, families could have access to humanitarian assistance in the refugee camps. The recruits were largely drawn from the countryside, where they based their resistance, while the Afghan government, continuing the traditional army conscription system – and with Soviet military backing – controlled the cities, major roads, and airports. Later on, different militia groups were included in the government structure, the best known at present being Rashid Dostum's group, called *Gillam Jam* (carpet thieves) in acknowledgment of the fact that the foot soldiers earned their income from plundering the areas they captured.

Throughout the 1980s a very large number of Afghans underwent basic military training in Pakistan, while religious education was provided in the party camps or in the large number of madrassas established with funding from Islamic countries, groups, and charities. The party structures had significant differences as the Sunni parties were divided along religious and ethnic lines. The Shia Muslims, with one exception, located their parties in Iran and received military training and equipment there, where some of the fighters gained experience fighting in the Iraq-Iran War.[4]

Afghan tribes and families took a pragmatic approach to the parties. They often ensured that they had commanders in all the parties and that family members held a range of party cards so as to allow for the highest possible yield in military supplies and humanitarian assistance.

It is important to note that the commanders' local support varied considerably. Some assumed their responsibility as commanders due to requests made by their communities, including the religious leaders; others did so because of the responsibility implied in their social position, their army background, or their demonstrated courage or fighting skills. Another group became commanders due to their family affiliations and access to weapons and money rather than due to popular support. Thus, those who did not misuse their positions and who performed jihad in compliance with communal expectations maintained their positions after the jihad period came to an end. The other commanders largely lost their local standing, although they could continue to receive support through the party system or directly from various external intelligence groups.[5] It appears from observations that many members of the first group reverted to their former occupations, while those in the second group continued their military or related activities.

Changes Following the Soviet Withdrawal

With the Soviet withdrawal in 1989 and the fall of the Kabul government in 1992, a number of changes occurred as parties influenced the authority of the mujahideen groups. First, the high degree of voluntary return to Afghanistan drained the parties of "free" recruits, and, when combined with a sharp reduction in external funding (especially after the 1991 Gulf War), their influence was reduced. This was followed by a sharp increase in conflicts between mujahideen parties, mainly over influence, where, notably, Jamiat-e Islami and Hezb-e Islami (Hekmatiar) were engaged in a large number of internal battles. The attempts to form an Afghan interim government in Pakistan in 1989 illustrated how divided the mujahideen were. Commanders changed their affiliations, moving to the parties that were presumed to have the strongest financial backing, and the end result was a leadership compromise that failed to attract public support.

The consequent fall of Kabul to the mujahideen was engineered along ethnic lines: the Pashtun army officers sought to join Hezb-e Islami, while the Tadjiks and other minorities established a dialogue with Jamiat-e Islami and, in particular, Commander Masood. The latter came first to Kabul, having secured the support of Dostum's militia and some important Pashtun commanders, and could then set the terms for the first mujahideen government. This ethnic/military divide also illustrates how weakened the smaller parties had become, not least as a reduction in external support had limited their ability to provide substantial financial assistance to their commanders and supporters.

That being said, many of the commanders, from all parties, who had gained control over the countryside and smaller towns, used their financial and military resources to ensure themselves further income to maintain their personal power and influence. Cross-border smuggling, drug production, road taxing, and plundering were some of the ways in which this was done. The more sophisticated invested largely in property and land (at times acquired through force), while influential commanders continued to be paid handsomely by various external actors. What they had in common was a need for a continued source of income to maintain their power and, not least, to pay their soldiers as the party system could no longer be used to fund their influence.

The formation of the coalition mujahideen government in 1993 proved to be a new source of income for the commanders. With the ministry portfolios divided along party lines, each attempted to maximize its international financial (and military) support and to ensure employment for its former soldiers and followers. The political struggle between Pakistan and India was fully exploited, as was Iran's interest in gaining further influence in Afghanistan. During this period, which lasted until the Taliban took control, Afghanistan was effectively carved up into smaller "commanderdoms," with some provinces (such as Nangarhar) coming under the control of a commander council or a strong commander (such as Ismael Khan in Herat). Travelling or trading was a nightmare, checkpoints charged "travel tax" or simply robbed travellers and apprehended cars and trucks.

The Afghan army and intelligence agencies, which could have played a stabilizing role, were merged into the Tadjik military machine under the control of the first mujahideen minister of defence, Ahmed Shah Masood. Most of the higher-ranking army officers with formal army training had, by then, long since left the country, notably to Russia and India, although some went to Europe (or, if their financial resources were exhausted, ended up in Pakistan or Iran).

The battle between mujahideen groups that then commenced over control of Kabul took on a strong ethnic dimension, again allowing commanders to recruit (either voluntarily or by force) on the basis of historical ethnic enmity. Moreover, forced recruitment took place not only behind the battle lines in Kabul but also in the countryside, often targeting boys as young as twelve or thirteen.[6] Over a period of time, there emerged two distinct ethnic military/political groups that fought for control over Kabul. A subgroup of Jamiat-e Islami, called Shura-e-Nezar, was formed in northern Afghanistan sometime in the 1990s under the leadership of Ahmed Shah Masood, and it assumed de facto military and administrative command in areas under its control. By 1989, the numerous Iran-based Shia groups had come under pressure from Iran to merge with the Hezb-e Wahdat. While the party later split into two factions, it effectively assumed control over central

Afghanistan and parts of Kabul and the northern town of Mazar-e-Sharif. Both these minority groups developed standing armies of permanent soldiers that were able to move and fight over large areas. With Dostum proclaiming himself an Uzbek military and political leader both in the north and in Kabul (and by assassinating internal opponents), the Pashtuns emerged as the least unified group. However, that changed when the Taliban emerged as a military force in southern Afghanistan in early 1994.

The Rise and Defeat of the Taliban

The Taliban recruited its armies from a range of sources. Its most devoted fighters were the religious students – *talibans* – but they were joined by former mujahideen commanders and fighters, predominantly from the traditionalist groups. In addition, personnel from the Afghan army (such as pilots) were recruited, and later different groups of foreign fighters joined in, as they had previously done with the more radical Islamic parties. When the Taliban had established a degree of national control, it introduced a forced recruitment system. A village had to provide it with either a number of soldiers related to the size of the village or an agreed financial contribution. All of those in the top Taliban leadership were mullahs or maulawis, with a mix of mullahs and former commanders forming the commanding ranks. Although there were a number of non-Pashtuns in the Taliban ranks, and many areas were left to be controlled by local commanders of other ethnicities, the core political rank was Pashtun and was based in Kandahar, where Mullah Omar had established his base. The city became the main religious and administrative power centre, while Kabul became an administrative hub.

The Northern Alliance was formed as a coalition of groups in opposition to the Taliban, and it formed a joint standing army, including tank brigades, which then set the defensive lines against the Taliban advance. While the core group under Masood's command remained in Afghanistan, a majority of the commanders left the country from 1996 onwards for exile in neighbouring countries, to do business in Dubai, or to establish themselves in Europe or the United States. With a substantial funding base, and in many cases relatives who looked after their investments in Afghanistan, they suffered no hardship, and many maintained their political affiliations.

As a result, while the international military response to the 11 September 2001 attack in the United States was being planned, many of these commanders were brought back to Afghanistan. They were supplied with guns and satellite phones and were heavily funded to re-establish their former military groups. As the attack commenced in Afghanistan on 8 October 2001, the Northern Alliance provided the main military force in the north, while smaller groups were active in the south. All of these groups were directed by international military advisors and operated under heavy air support. After a brief period of resistance and heavy losses, the majority of the Taliban returned quietly to their villages and mosques, if they had not already shifted their allegiance to the winning side or been jailed at the battlefront.

The Northern Alliance continued to press its victory on all fronts. It cemented the political victory and secured a majority of ministerial posts through the Bonn Agreement, assuming military control over Kabul, and it again ensured its control over the Afghan military forces and the intelligence services. During the first Afghan Interim Authority, a large number of party associates were shifted to jobs in ministries.

Part of the peacebuilding policy agreed upon by the United States, the United Nations, and the Afghan government was to include in the new administration anyone who had fought on the allied side, had changed their position in time, and/or were regarded as a major military threat to the new government. Commanders, of whom many had been out of Afghanistan since the Taliban took power, were (re)installed as governors and district administrators, and many of these belonged to the Islamist parties. The police force was built on the previous mujahideen forces, with commanders ending up as chiefs. The military force was set at 100,000 soldiers in early 2002, which, according to the ANBP, was a randomly set number of people who were to be rewarded with salaries from the international community for their military efforts. The number of soldiers was later set at sixty thousand when the target for demobilization was reduced and it became apparent that many of the payment lists were incorrect.

The DDR Process and Emerging Challenges
To facilitate the DDR process, the ANBP was established in 2002 as a joint program between the Government of Afghanistan and the United Nations Development Program (UNDP).[7] Soldiers were to hand in their guns in exchange for financial compensation, making them eligible for a reintegration program based on either a farming package or skills and literacy training. Special programs, including business training, were established for those commanders who had not been drawn into government positions. The UNDP had a slow start but was intensified in advance of the presidential elections in 2004 in an attempt to increase security by reducing the number of arms in circulation and by reducing the ability of armed groups to influence the elections. The collection of heavy arms was prioritized, partly as a strong symbolic gesture but also in order to pressure some of the major commanders (and the then minister of defence) to indicate their willingness to disarm.

What should be noted, however, is that the DDR process was only partially applied to the armed groups and that it was not properly conducted. Armed groups involved in OEF were excluded, and reports and interviews from several parts of Afghanistan indicate that many commanders handed in their older guns and put forward "non-essential" soldiers to be demobilized, maintaining their best guns and men. Moreover, reintegration was not prioritized. In fact, it was even postponed in order to get as many people as possible through the demobilization and disarmament parts of the process in advance of the presidential election.

To summarize, a large number of mobilization arguments have been used over time, including ideology, religion, ethnicity, and, certainly, economic interests. There has been strong popular support, on the part of men and women from all ethnic and religious groups and social classes, for the religious argument that propounds the defence of homeland and religion. Thus, there was equally strong support for those leaders, here termed "commanders," who led this struggle.

Still, it should be noted that there is a large difference between party leaders, mid-level commanders, and smaller commanders. Within the first group, emerging from the Islam-based struggle at Kabul University in the early 1970s, the majority are still alive and actively involved in the present political and military power game. With the exception of Ahmed Shah Masood (who was assassinated in 2001) and Gulbuddin Hekmatyar and his Hezb-e Islami (now labelled terrorists), the other leaders have maintained a high degree of influence for their respective groups over Afghan society and polity. More mid-level commanders have been killed over the years, but those who survived have been able to secure major influence in the present Afghan state either as police chiefs, governors, and district administrators or through their affiliation with armed groups involved in illegal activities.

The group suffering the largest losses, and that has only managed to secure limited influence today, consists of the smaller commanders. If not rewarded with lower positions in the army or the police force (or through illegal activities), they have generally had no other option than to return to their home communities to take up their previous occupations. Arguably, the members of this latter group will be those who have the highest degree of embeddedness within their societies, while there is a larger variation among the mid-level group and the party leaders who have become rather distanced from their societies. However, many of them do still hold major command over areas under their influence, such as Sayaff in the Paghman district north of Kabul, and they might use this (and financial rewards) to mobilize political and military pressure, as witnessed during the presidential and parliamentary elections.

One can further argue that the dependency relationship between the commanders and the combatants might be influenced by a number of other factors, both internal and external. There is certainly a varying degree of economic dependency, patronage, and tribal or family relationships between the combatants and the commanders. The increased ethnic and religious polarization of society, including the impact of ethnic cleansing, that has been brought about by the war might lead to strengthened protective relationships within these groups. The War on Terror has complicated matters further, as commanders who are part of OEF receive financial assistance and protection that allow them to continue to exploit and to use force against civilians in order to maintain their position and "business" interests. While they can continue to pay their combatants, and ensure their loyalty, they are at the same time likely to offend and use violence against persons within their own solidarity network and, thus, replace positive embeddedness with forced embeddedness.

The use of guns for aggressive purposes, including revenge killings, has traditionally been fairly well regulated through the family and tribal networks. However, a combination of a weak central state that remains unable to protect its citizens and a large surplus of arms has led almost every family to possess at least one gun for self-protection. A survey undertaken in 2006 showed alarmingly high numbers of murders in some districts, primarily over land, water, and heritage,[8] and indicates that the networks might no longer hold as much influence over the use of armed force as they once did.

However, in order to achieve a better understanding of relations between the commanders and the former combatants, and of the extent to which communities might have influence over conflicts and the use of violence, one does need to seek the views of different groups. In the following section, I present the understandings and views of the different national stakeholders in the Afghan peace process.

Voices from the Field
The field research was undertaken in nine districts of five Afghan provinces – Badakhshan, Ghazni, Kabul, Kunduz, and Wardak – allowing for a fair degree of geographic, ethnic, and religious representation. A total of 89 former combatants, 26 former commanders (ranging from smaller to mid-level ones), 23 community councils, 24 local government administrators, and 37 women/women's groups were interviewed.

The questionnaire focused on five main clusters of questions: (1) those dealing with the general peace, (2) those dealing with the DDR process, (3) those dealing with the influence and role of the commanders, (4) those dealing with the influence and role of the community councils, and (5) those dealing with the peace process and who various actors relate to when managing conflicts. Also included were questions addressing the relationship between the commanders and the former combatants, the commanders' relationships with the community and the government, and how the commanders and the combatants had been mobilized for fighting and whom they would consult if they were to give up their arms.

It should be noted that, among the combatants, 44 out of 89 were illiterate and 25 out of 89 were unemployed at the time of the interviews. Among the commanders, the literacy level was higher: only 8 out of 26 were illiterate, but as many as 50 percent (13) were unemployed. Certainly, the high degree of unemployment in both groups is a major concern; moreover, that joblessness is found almost equally in all nine districts.

The two groups had the following employment pattern (in number):

	Combatants	*Commanders*
Farmer	13	4
Shopkeeper	9	2
Government	7	4
Student	2	0
NGO	1	0
Skilled labour	32	2
Teacher	0	1

Interestingly, when former combatants and commanders were asked why they had initially formed their relationship, the majority cited their religious obligation to join in jihad in defence of Afghanistan, followed by mobilization undertaken by their quam (solidarity group). Here, a majority of the former combatants referred to jihad, while a large majority of the commanders referred to the quam, the latter a possible indication that the commanders' responsibility had been bestowed on them by their quam. Only five of the combatants said that they had joined due to fear of the commanders or that they had been forcibly recruited, and only one commander and one combatant said that money had been the primary reason for their joining. Interestingly, none of the informants mentioned political affiliations or associations as a reason for recruitment. The main conclusion is that the majority of those who joined in the conflict acted of their own free will but as defined within the framework of their larger responsibility towards their religion (and country) and their quam.

When the former combatants were asked why they joined an armed group, the majority referred to jihad, to the need to defend Afghanistan from the Soviet invasion, and to the need to protect human and religious rights. Further down the list came ethnic tension, forced recruitment, personal enmity, and vulnerability. Only one person provided no reason for why he had joined an armed group, which may indicate a high degree of communal and personal understanding of the recruitment process.

Equally interesting, then, are the responses to questions about why and when the former combatants chose to disengage from the fighting. The majority referred to the Bonn Agreement and subsequent establishment of the Afghan Interim Authority, some mentioned the Taliban surrender, and some said that the defeat of the communist regime had left many without any justification for continued warfare. Some mentioned being tired of warfare, improved local security, the DDR process, and the negative effects of an imposed war, infighting among groups and commanders, and war injuries. These influences reflect a mix of factors: progress in the overarching peace process, progress in addressing the initial justification for taking up arms, and personal war weariness.

The DDR Process

Turning to the DDR process, a minority of both combatants and commanders stated that they had received any benefit from the process – only twenty-four of the combatants and ten of the commanders. The responses to the question about the DDR process can be grouped into three main categories. The first comprises those who believe that the aim of the process is to ensure peace and security and to allow for improved justice, reconstruction, development, and "freedom"; the second comprises those who have a positive understanding of how DDR could reduce the power of the warlords and distance the commanders from their armies; the third comprises those who believe that the DDR process is part of a "hidden agenda" meant to reduce the power of the people and Afghanistan and "a strategy for foreign powers to legitimize their presence and earn money." Some also mentioned the fact that promises to former combatants had not been fulfilled. Nevertheless, only a small majority of combatants found the DDR process unjust, while half of the commanders did so. The local council, local authorities, and women had more mixed views, although a majority were of the opinion that the DDR process was unjust. Many responded that powerful commanders had been excluded, that only a small portion of the arms had been collected, and that there was a geographical and ethnic imbalance in areas selected for disarmament.

Influence over Commanders

A central issue for this research – the level of embeddedness of commanders and former combatants in their communities – was addressed through questions on the influence of local communities over the commanders. A number of signs of reduced commander influence were noted, and, beyond general statements, several people pointed out that forced recruitment had stopped and that the community councils had increased their influence. Others downplayed the general influence of commanders but thought that they could exert influence through ethnic connections, indicating that they remained dependent on their solidarity networks. More worrying, however, are the views that the commanders have been legitimized by the current DDR process and, not least, that the communities hold very limited influence over commanders who have been allowed to occupy governmental positions. Not only are commanders protected in such positions, but they have also been provided with access to funding and connections that might increase their influence.

Addressing this matter from a different angle, one question asked whether the government could have an influence over the commanders. Here the response was unanimous – and negative. The argument was that, as the commanders were employed in key positions, often after a compromise between them and the government, the government had very limited influence over them. This view was supported by statements that the widespread degree of corruption within the government limited its ability (and will) to influence the commanders and that these commanders, through their positions, were excluded from the rule of law. It was also thought that there was a general culture of impunity. One person observed that many commanders were involved in drug production and trafficking and that the government had no means (or will) to stop them. The only positive influence noted was that enforced through the presence of international forces.

With few exceptions, a follow-up question that asked whether the role of the commanders had changed after Hamid Karzai assumed the role of president had negative responses. But it provided further indications as to how the population views the symbiosis between the government and the commanders: "Mr. Karzai's government supports the commanders." Also mentioned was the fact that the already rich and powerful commanders had increased their influence, that they had managed to strengthen their links with the international (drug) mafia, and that, through their positions, they had gained legal authority.

Failed Co-optation

The general conclusion is that the policy of co-optation has not reduced the influence of all the commanders; rather, those co-opted have been able to strengthen their position and influence within the government and, more worryingly, to reduce the ability of their communities and solidarity networks to influence them. And, while some see the international peacekeeping military forces as the only corrective influence over the commanders, others note that international military recognition of and collaboration with the commanders has reduced government and communal influence over them. If anything, it has led to a clearer division between the commanders – between (1) those who were already rich and influential and who have been able to further their position and influence through the government's co-optation strategy and (2) those who did not have the necessary influence to be co-opted. Meanwhile, the smaller commanders, who did not have enough power to be offered government positions, have ended up jobless within their communities – and very dissatisfied with their present roles. Combined with a generally high unemployment rate among former combatants and an incomplete DDR process, these commanders remain a major possible destabilizing factor in Afghanistan, as do the co-opted commanders. This will remain the case so long as the DDR process does not increase governmental or communal influence over them.

The vulnerability of the current peacebuilding and DDR process is clearly exposed through responses to the questions asked regarding the possibility of renewed fighting. Of the commanders, fifteen stated that they had considered going back to fighting, while eleven stated that they would not go back. Among the former combatants, thirty-nine thought that they would consider resuming fighting, although fifty said that they would not do so. However, among these were groups that had undergone more active peace education than others. The local councils confirmed that they knew that persons within their communities had considered resuming fighting. The local authority explained that such sentiments prevailed in the population due to the fact that there had been no major improvements in general living conditions, while women pinpointed the lack of jobs as the main reason for a willingness to again take up arms.

The question that has to be asked is: are there any alternatives to such a centrally (and externally) driven DDR process? Fortunately, this research project was able to identify several suggestions from Afghans.

DDR Improvement
Those interviewed had clear opinions regarding how the DDR process could be improved. The most important seems to be ensuring public support for the process through the application of a non-discriminatory system in the selection of areas and commanders to be "DDR-ed." And, as one person explained, "this requires firmness of the government." Others mentioned the need for a proper mechanism to ensure that the process was just.

More practical suggestions were also offered: a proper survey prior to the DDR process and the involvement of religious leaders, women, and local people because "we know where the guns are." Others suggested that combatants be paid directly rather than through commanders and that there should be a more elaborate system for the purchase of weapons. And, naturally, given the high rate of unemployment, people were concerned about the reintegration aspect of DDR and suggested improving skills training to increase job security and to secure sustainable livelihoods.

The ANBP has been central in developing and implementing the DDR process, and it has been heavily criticized for how the program has been managed. The decision to stop paying for guns handed in when it became known that the combatants had to pay a share of that money to the commanders caused an uproar among the former combatants. The ANBP management side was regarded as weak, a concern raised by several donor countries.

In 2003, interviews conducted with the central ANBP management in Kabul and regional managers in two northern locations left the impression of an organization that was not up to such a challenging task as negotiating a sensitive DDR program with seasoned commanders. For one thing, most Afghans in the organization were very young, and, although managing English well, they did not have the necessary seniority to gain respect from the commanders and the former combatants. The two expatriate regional managers interviewed had very limited knowledge about Afghanistan in general and the Afghan army system in particular. This might have been due to their military background or to their frustration with the lack of progress in the DDR process, but the attitudes they expressed towards the Afghans and their suggested ways of handling commanders did not seem to benefit the ANBP. One manager suggested using military means to force the commanders to comply with the DDR program: "If we bomb their house and kill their wives and children, I am sure they will be more willing to collaborate."

If such attitudes are allowed to develop and to be publicly expressed, the ANBP will never be able to gain the necessary trust among commanders for them to hand in their weapons. Similarly, in the north, the different parties refused to be disarmed until the commanders they regarded as their enemies were included in the DDR program.

Security and the Role of Commanders

When the different groups were asked if the influence held by commanders had been reduced, there was general agreement that that had been the case. Among the commanders, seventeen stated that they felt their influence had been reduced, four were of the opinion that there had been a minor reduction, while five did not see any reduction in their influence. This view was supported by the former combatants, with fifty-three seeing their power reduced, ten agreeing that there had been a minor reduction, and twenty-six not seeing any significant reduction in influence. While the local councils stated that the DDR process had had a minimal effect on reducing commanders' influence, the local authorities, on the contrary, thought that it had had a major influence. Among women, the views were more mixed: some emphasized the people's increased ability to express their views, while others observed that the same commanders still yielded considerable power in their communities.

Asked if security had improved in their areas after the DDR process, the informants expressed the general view that there had been a major improvement. As many as sixty-four of the former combatants and twenty-one of the commanders supported this view, while fourteen former combatants saw a minor improvement and only five commanders and eleven former combatants did not see any improvement. The local councils noted that there were considerable variations in different areas, the local authorities expressing a concern over the government's limited control, while women felt that there had been a considerable improvement in their security. They noted their access to education, participation in elections, and ability to seek work, and they said that fighting and the threat level had been reduced.

The primary role of ISAF has been to improve security in Afghanistan, though the answers received indicate that the population takes the entire military engagement into consideration when responding to the question about its role in improving security. In some of the areas where interviews have been conducted, there had not been any ISAF presence and only scant representation of OEF troops. The majority within all groups believe that the ISAF presence has improved security. This is supported by seventy-one of the former combatants and twenty-three of the commanders, although seventeen former combatants and three commanders felt that security had been reduced. The local council was worried that security forces promoted their own interests, while local authorities underlined sensitivity around having foreign troops in Afghanistan and stated that such troops had committed atrocities. Women presented more diverse views, some fearing that the violence would increase if the international forces withdrew, others feeling that their presence was only symbolic and that "in reality they reduce security." It is thus apparent that Afghans are confused about what roles the different military contingents play. This is possibly made more difficult to comprehend by the fact that each of ISAF's provincial reconstruction teams has adopted different strategies and degrees of involvement in the provision of humanitarian assistance.

Building the Peace

As argued above, disarmament and disengagement from fighting must be seen in connection with the national peace and DDR process. Such a comparison is, moreover, deemed necessary in order to measure, at least to a degree, what support there is in the population for national policies and for securing a more permanent peace process. The findings are worrying. A large majority of the commanders (eighteen out of twenty-six) and a small majority of the former combatants find the peacebuilding process unjust, although, in the latter group, there are larger geographical variations. A small majority of the local councils also find it unjust, while a majority among local authorities and the women/women's groups find it just.

Reasons given for why they regard the process as unjust are diverse, but prominent is the lack of job opportunities and their understanding that it has been an unfair process. This is reflected in statements such as "all people have not been equally disarmed" and "good jihadis have been forgotten and criminals are given good posts." Others mention widespread corruption and insecurity, external interventions in Afghan affairs, continued power struggles, the unfair distribution of reconstruction efforts, and "no real peace." Those who argued that the process had been just drew attention to job and training opportunities and the fact that people had been given a chance to participate.

In sum, these responses are a strong indication of a lack of public support for the peace process. Clearly, many regard it as an externally engineered process, which they can easily distance themselves from – or mobilize against.

Three further questions were asked to seek deeper insight into people's understanding of and support for the democratization process. One question asked about their knowledge of the new Constitution; the second asked whether they felt they had any influence over the present development of Afghanistan; and the third asked whether they planned to vote in the upcoming parliamentary elections.

A large majority of the former combatants, the local councils, and the local authorities said that they were familiar with the new Constitution – although control questions indicated that there was no in-depth understanding of it. Those least familiar with the Constitution were the commanders and the women. Several commanders complained about a lack of information about the Constitution, while women who were familiar with it highlighted the importance of women's rights.

When asked about their possible influence on the development process, as many as twenty-four of the commanders and sixty-five of the former combatants felt that they had influence. Local authorities shared that view, regarding themselves as part of the governmental process. Local councils were of the view that they had limited influence, albeit recognizing the potential of their councils for conflict resolution and social recovery. Women generally felt that they held very little influence: "We have the rights, but we are not given the chance and opportunity to work." Among several groups a concern was voiced that "development is in the hands of foreigners."

Given the above answers, it might come as a surprise that seventy-five out of eighty-nine former combatants and twenty-five out of twenty-six commanders stated their intention to vote in the parliamentary election. These answers could, however, be interpreted as their perceived need to secure parliamentary seats for persons they regarded as supportive of their interests, not least given that the former combatants and commanders felt that they had received limited benefit from the peace and development process. Nor can one underestimate the impact of active campaigns by influential figures to mobilize their former followers to vote for them. If this were a general trend in Afghanistan, it might help to explain the high number of people with links to and command over armed groups elected to Parliament.

Responses to a question asked to help us better understand interviewees' perceptions of what they regarded as major threats to a permanent peace revealed a wide variety of concerns. What most informants mentioned was a fear of foreign military intervention, international terrorism, and general insecurity, which is understandable given Afghanistan's recent history. However, the second most cited cluster of threats related to their perception of the present political and development situation, in which they listed injustice, corruption, discrimination, lack of job opportunities, and poverty as the major concerns. Moreover, many feared that a lack of education, limited participation in the development process, and a general lack of trust in society would have a negative influence on securing a permanent peace. Other important threats were the presence and continuous supply of arms, the way Afghan culture was being dishonoured by the international actors, and what they labelled as "double standard politics."

Taking the conflict dimension down to the local community level, the groups were asked who they would call upon to solve problems in their communities. Highest on their list were community councils, community elders, and religious leaders, followed by influential individuals and teachers. Then came the district and provincial administration and the peace councils, where these had been established. Thus, the elders and religious leaders, often organized in a community council and traditionally entrusted to solve communal conflicts, still hold a high degree of authority, despite an increase in the number of commanders and guns.

When former combatants and commanders were asked whom they would consult before going back to fighting, their answers confirmed the above findings. The majority mentioned community elders, religious leaders, and community councils, followed by their parents, family members, and friends. Only a very few stated that they would not consult anyone but would decide on their own. In interviews conducted in the spring of 2004, several of the demobilized soldiers emphasized seeking advice from their mothers. As one explained: "She was the one that told me to join jihad. If she tells me to stop fighting, I will have to obey."

These statements, in which they all refer to traditional communal authorities, indicate that former commanders and combatants maintain a high degree of embeddedness in their communities. In addition, it opens up a range of untapped opportunities for local mobilization of the DDR process and how it might be improved as well as for ways of seeking a more permanent peace, or at least a respected conflict-handling mechanism at the communal level.

People are well aware of these opportunities. When asked how the Afghan people can influence development, the first suggestion offered is to ensure the people's and women's participation and involvement. This is followed by suggestions for awareness raising in the communities, education and capacity building, and for the government to support local councils and to encourage the development of more democratic entities. A number emphasized the need for improved security and the promotion of peace and the need for decision makers to share plans and decisions with people in order to encourage and ensure ownership. Also mentioned were the fact that people's basic needs must be met, that ethnic tensions must be reduced and trust built, and that corruption needs to be stopped.

An interesting observation is that, even if the rural development process described in Chapter 6 in this volume, the National Solidarity Process, has not achieved its envisioned potential, many recognize the community councils that have been formed as bodies that might have a positive influence on local conflicts. Given the fact that the plan is for the NSP to become nationwide and that at least one facilitating partner (which is implementing the program) has added a conflict resolution component to capacity-building for the councils, the NSP could help to prevent violent conflicts.

However, one might suggest that a major weakness of the Afghan DDR process, and peacebuilding in general, is that it has made itself dependent on, and vulnerable to, the commanders, who are regarded as the largest military threat to the peace process. The process would have benefited largely from acknowledging and drawing on the traditional strengths of the local communities for democratization, development, and the DDR process. That should have been done not only to improve the process but also to ensure wider support for and understanding of its complexity and, thereby, a higher degree of ownership.

Conclusion

This research project has attempted to take a more holistic approach to the Afghan DDR process, recognizing that, before giving up military power, dismantling organizations, and handing in their guns, commanders and combatants need to see a clear link to overall peacebuilding. Former combatants and commanders need to have enough trust in the DDR process and the wider peace process to be convinced to give up their arms and influence, and they also need to be backed by their local communities. In the Afghan case, neither process has generated enough trust for the commanders to give up their powers. Opportunities for using the influence of local communities and leaders to influence commanders' and former combatants' decision making have been missed. The embeddedness option has not been recognized; rather, it appears that the fear of commanders as the potential spoilers of the peace process has overshadowed a deeper understanding of the mechanisms at play in Afghan communities.

Moreover, the picture that emerges shows an undue reliance on the use of military means in peacebuilding processes and, thus, a limitation of other options. From the military point of view, some armed groups are labelled as necessary allies and are excluded from the DDR process, while others necessarily end up as foes and are thus subject to being "DDR-ed." This further illustrates the analysis, given in several other chapters in this volume, of the limitations of a minimalist approach to peacebuilding. Here the priority placed on the demobilization and disarmament component has primarily functioned to limit the number of arms and soldiers rather than to emphasize the reintegration that could have created more permanent livelihood options and, thus, possibilities for a more permanent disengagement from the conflict.

This brings us back to Stedman's theory, which seems to have informed policy and practice. Recall his suggestion that there are three basic ways of addressing spoilers: socialization, inducement, and coercion. The socializing aspect, the building of a common normative foundation, seems primarily to have centred on establishing Hamid Karzai as the Afghan president (and as a reliable partner to the military and the international actors) rather than on building a vision of a unified Afghanistan based on knowledge of the new Constitution and the common rule of law. The choice of using DDR to reduce tension in advance of the presidential election rather than to increase security in the communities underscores the symbolic (rather than normative) foundation of the new Afghan state. Relations are to be established between the president (and the military and international force supporting him) and individual commanders rather than between the president and the people.

Inducement is heavily drawn upon. As one interviewee observed: "To keep the big commanders satisfied they offer them the high government positions, their subcommanders are offered mid-level positions and the smaller commanders minor positions, as in the district administration." The consequence of this bonding process neither increases stability nor adds to the positive image of the government. Those holding governor positions are not dismissed, even if they are performing their job poorly. They are either transferred to other provinces (where they remain governors) or to a position in the central government. This allows them continued influence on (and access to resources from) the government, while they can maintain, through their subcommanders and networks, a high degree of influence in their home areas, thereby securing their national and local political, military, and financial interests. Thus, the inducement does not necessarily break their links to and power over their constituencies but, rather, rewards them for their loyalty to the president. While this seems to have ensured a degree of stability (at least when compared to Iraq), it has reduced the government's ability to be reformed, to advocate for the rule of law, and to improve the human rights situation. As a result, the necessary safeguards against the government's (and co-opted commanders') abuse of monopoly over violence are not in place, as Faltas, MacDonald, and Waszink (2001) predicted.

In addition, as the commanders have been allowed to use government positions and resources to strengthen their influence, as many of them did while in the mujahideen government during the early·1990s, this could end up as a prolonged national ceasefire rather than as a more permanent peace. Ironically enough, this process is then guaranteed (and protected) by the presence of international peacekeeping forces, while, at the same time, being continuously fuelled by the actions of the forces operating under OEF.

This brings us to coercion, and to the very mixed signals being sent by the international community and the Afghan government. The use of force is selectively directed towards the Taliban, while the threat of the use of force is also directed towards commanders seen as disloyal to the central government. Governor Ismael Khan in Herat is a good example. When he was reluctant to pay a larger share of the official tax income to the Ministry of Finance rather than utilize it in Herat (thus maintaining his power base), he was put under military pressure from Afghan and OEF forces. And this pressure was increased when he stated his intention to support Karzai's main opponent for the presidency. Other commanders, such as Hazrat Ali in Nangarhar, who allegedly secured substantial income from cross-border smuggling, were allowed to continue to increase their influence as they are regarded as being (at least temporarily) loyal to President Karzai.

This underscores the problematic way in which Stedman's approach has been put into practice in Afghanistan. Another concern is that the DDR process has not been pursued in a nationally unifying manner; rather, the population sees the selective approach towards different commanders as being unjust without really addressing or influencing their real power base. Moreover, this approach has been narrowly focused on the power relations between the central state (which, in the case of Afghanistan, is backed by international force and funding) and the commanders (due to their spoiler potential), and it does not acknowledge the influence and power that is held by other parts of Afghan society (not least being the former combatants, religious leaders and elders, and the local community councils). This lack of understanding of the Afghan context, the social fabric and the specificities of the different armed groups, and, thus, their possible role as peacebuilding rather than peace-spoiling agents, prevents any alternative approaches. What seems a preoccupation for identifying individuals and groups as potential spoilers, then, easily gets in the way of searching for alternative actors, and groups of actors, that could be instrumental in building sustainable peace. The spoiler discourse seems to limit the debate, as is noted in other chapters in this volume, rather than to facilitate a deeper understanding of the context and its complexities.

Returning to the DDR process, there are a number of arguments underlining the failure of conventional DDR processes within complex and politicized contexts such as that of Afghanistan. These arguments also show how it is only partially linked to (and used) in the democratization process. The most alarming finding involves the effect of the low priority given to the reintegration aspect of DDR: 50 percent of the commanders are unemployed, as are a high number of former combatants. When unemployment is combined with humanitarian need, a feeling that the peace and DDR processes are unjust, external interference, and a high willingness among commanders and former combatants to resume fighting, the outlook for a peaceful future remains bleak. The "R" part must not be regarded as an add-on to the "D" parts; rather, it must be seen as an important component of the wider economic, social, and political development process.

Nevertheless, there are ways to counter these alarming trends. One is to place increased importance on reintegration, starting with that element and then letting demobilization and disarmament follow, once jobs have been secured. There are, in fact, such a large number of weapons in circulation that, beginning the process by handing in guns is only of symbolic interest. What is required is a total change of strategy and the replacement of the current military-trained ANBP management staff with people who have a background in rehabilitation and development. At the very least, it is necessary to obtain a better skills balance among management staff (combined with hiring older and more senior Afghans).

A second approach, and one in line with a more developmental approach to the DDR process, would be to increase and institutionalize consultation with the local communities. Their knowledge about where weapons are kept (and where power is vested) is one reason for this. But such knowledge will only be conveyed to international actors (and the national actors associated with them) if there is genuine support for peace and disarmament in these communities. My research indicates that networks and religion matter, both for mobilizing and for discouraging fighting. Therefore, those belonging to these networks and practising this religion need to be engaged, informed, and encouraged to use their influence. This strengthens the arguments for a communally rather than an individually oriented process, in line with recommendations from ECHA; Faltas, MacDonald, and Waszink; and Kingma. This finding also converges with those of other chapters in this book.

In addition, recognizing the strong solidarity networks and loyalty that characterize many postwar countries, DDR processes need to be more collective, more group- and network-oriented, rather than singling out individual commanders and former combatants. This finding seems to be strongly supported by the Guatemala DDR case discussed in Chapter 9 in this volume. And it should not come as any surprise, given that people function as part of a solidarity network in daily life, that lasting solutions will need to address collective as well as personal needs. This goes for planning for jobs, capacity building, and education. It is about securing communities and livelihoods rather than only individuals, be these commanders or former combatants.

Third, all findings point towards the importance of the DDR process being part and parcel of a national strategy, ideally outlined in a peace agreement and carefully sequenced. If DDR is only emphasized in connection with specific events (such as the presidential election) or for targeting the power of some of the groups, it will raise suspicion rather than support.

If these concerns are not properly analyzed and addressed in each conflict context, there is a danger that DDR will only serve as a very expensive way of symbolically addressing one of the major challenges with which most peace processes are confronted: the overarching challenge of finding more permanent ways of disengaging combatants from conflicts and providing alternative lifestyles and incomes for the majority of the commanders and former combatants who have used arms to defend their rights, their religion, and their societies. It is still not too late. Another lesson that needs to be emphasized is that peacebuilding processes need to be flexible and adjusted in order to meet changing realities on the ground. However, this will certainly demand a willingness to "demilitarize" DDR planning and implementation processes. Otherwise, combatants will continue seeing their guns and networks as the only way to defend their interests and those of their communities.

Acknowledgments
The field research was conducted in collaboration with the Afghan-based Cooperation for Peace and Unity, which implemented the field survey, while the introductory section draws on research on DDR literature undertaken by Ragnhild Berg.

10

Considering the International DDR Experience and Spoiling: Lessons for Palestine

Pamela Scholey and Khalil Shikaki

At the time of writing, the Israel-Palestine situation was an extreme manifestation of incomplete peacebuilding and resultant failed disarmament, demobilization, and reintegration. We examine DDR through the lens of peacebuilding that has been constructed in this volume. We use the example of Palestine to illuminate and interrogate the lessons and failures of DDR generally as well as, in this case, prospectively.

The chapters in this volume investigate the experience of peacebuilding, including how DDR is an integral part of building peace in postwar contexts. Stephen Baranyi opens with a review chapter on the record of peacebuilding, its challenges, and the lessons we can derive from its experiences. In particular, through an examination of the discourses and practices of several generations of peacebuilding, fragile states, and conflict prevention, Baranyi highlights (and this is echoed in the various national chapters) the necessarily multifaceted nature of *durable* peacebuilding, including inclusive peace negotiations, the governance and socioeconomic development at its core, and the (re)establishment of the rule of law and strong institutions, accompanied by sensitive attention to inter- and intragroup politics, vulnerabilities, and interests.

The chapters on DDR by Wenche Hauge and Beate Thoresen on Guatemala (Chapter 8) and by Arne Strand on Afghanistan (Chapter 9) highlight the issue of embeddedness of combatants and the challenges and opportunities this poses to DDR and to peacebuilding. While Hauge and Thoresen focus on the positive potential contributions ex-combatants can make to peace processes and peacebuilding, as well as on the determining nature of the juridical, political, and socioeconomic context of the overall process of DDR, Strand emphasizes that reintegration is as important as demobilization and disarmament. He also stresses the need for holistic and community-based approaches to DDR.

This chapter revisits the literature on DDR and on spoilers to draw lessons for a possible model of Palestinian DDR. It also draws on interviews with members of armed groups, the Palestinian Authority (PA), international experts, and policy makers that were conducted during the second half of 2005. These interviews enable us to explore non-state armed group structures, capacities, and roles in Palestinian national resistance and to interrogate existing thinking on DDR and spoiling in Palestine. We end by offering tentative conclusions regarding a possible plan for effective DDR in Palestine.

We argue for a comprehensive link between DDR and holistic peacebuilding in Palestine. This needs to be premised on the political inclusion of all groups and inclusive socioeconomic development. Equally important, durable peacebuilding in the Middle East requires a rejection of the normative premises and practices of the current War on Terror – which serves to demonize and exclude important actors in the Israeli-Palestinian conflict and implies the prominence of a military-led peacebuilding as well as a coercive approach to DDR. Our review of the DDR literature, and Baranyi's review of the peacebuilding record, suggests that there are significant problems with military-led peacebuilding and with coerced DDR. The Palestinian case serves to illuminate some of the reasons why this might be so, as explained in this chapter and in Khalil Shikaki's chapter (Chapter 5) in this volume.

The Political Context of DDR in Palestine

The Palestinian security sector (PSS) is an outcome of the Palestinian-Israeli peace process that started in 1993 with the signing of the Oslo Agreement. As the chapter on the Palestinian study shows, the dynamics of the state-to-state process of peacemaking had a far-reaching impact on the intrastate process of state building and vice versa. Indeed, the two processes have been highly interdependent. Failed peacemaking increased dissent within the political system and gradually increased the power of opposition forces that were already excluded from the political system, such as Hamas and the young guard nationalists. The exclusion of these groups had already pushed them to seek alternative informal means to influence public policy, such as violence.

The Oslo Agreement set the parameters for the PSS in terms of doctrine, mission, size, armaments, branches, movement, command and control, supervision and accountability, and relations with Israel (see Strategic Assessments Initiative 2005). Since ensuring Israeli security was a cornerstone of the Oslo Agreement, the PSS's mission was framed in the context of fighting terror and violence and not merely in terms of performing normal functions of internal security and policing. The PA's security services undertook this mission against a background of protracted, and only partially resolved, conflict with Israel and highly charged domestic political opposition to the Oslo Agreement.

In contrast to most situations of post-conflict peacebuilding, the Oslo Accords provided for the establishment and development of an armed PSS, where none had previously existed in the Israeli-occupied Palestinian Gaza Strip and West Bank. The PSS – along with the Palestinian civil service – was used as an instrument of patronage and loyalty maintenance by Yasir Arafat, and this resulted in the oversizing of both. As a result, there was no process of DDR during the 1993-2000 period but, rather, a process of arming and equipping Palestinian security services to carry out their mission of guaranteeing Israeli security and repressing forces opposed to the peace process. Moreover, there was no provision for an international monitoring and verification mission to oversee the implementation of the Oslo process. This absence allowed room for frequent disputes between the PA and the Israeli government on adherence to the Oslo Accords, which contributed to heightened tensions between the two parties that eventually culminated in the second intifada, which began in 2000.[1]

The most immediate outcome of the PA's mandate to protect Israeli security was the tension created in Palestinian society between the PA security services and those in the Palestinian opposition who refused to acknowledge the legitimacy of the Oslo Agreement and insisted on their right to resist occupation by force if necessary. Another outcome was the tendency of the political system to give priority to "security" rather than to good governance and human rights in the service of preserving Israeli security.

Failure of peacemaking to deliver an end to occupation created incentives to go back to violence. Failure of state building to deliver good governance and an inclusive politics gradually diminished the legitimacy of the PA while empowering its opposition. The eruption of violence in the second intifada, which started in September 2000, and the subsequent Israeli decision to target Palestinian security forces for destruction, significantly weakened the ability of those forces to deliver security or to enforce the law. This provided Islamists and young guard nationalists with the opportunity to assert themselves and their agenda by forming their own militias and building their own arms-production capacity. By early 2001, three armed wings of existing political factions (Fateh, Hamas, and Islamic Jihad) and a new armed group (Palestinian Popular Committees) were created. While the goal of the militias was to fight Israeli occupation, the net effect was the creation of a state-within-a-state, the near collapse of order, and the marginalization of the Palestinian security services.

With the rise of large and well-armed militias and warlords and the continued Israeli onslaught on the Palestinian security services and territories, the ability of the PA to carry out the simple and routine tasks of enforcing law and order grew weaker by the day. With the Israeli army reoccupying most of the West Bank in 2002, service delivery could no longer be guaranteed.

Indeed, the PA was on the verge of collapse. These developments confronted the Palestinian political system with a serious challenge. The ability to deliver basic and social services, build a viable economy and state institutions on the way to independence, and bring an end to Israeli occupation all depended on the ability to ensure the nascent state's monopoly over violence. By early 2003, public demand for more PA control over law and order was greater than ever. Despite efforts and promises by various PA governments since 2002 to clamp down on violations of law and order and to put an end to the growing anarchy and social disorder, at least 176 people were killed and thirty-six were kidnapped due to lawlessness during 2005. In March 2007, approximately three-quarters of Palestinians stated that they and their families were not safe or secure.[2]

It was not until after the death of Yasir Arafat that the new president, Mahmud Abbas, deemed a Palestinian DDR program essential to effectively address the near collapse of law and order. To do that, however, the PA needed to confront the challenge of how to deal with existing armed militias (at a time when the PA lacked legitimacy in the eyes of its public, in part due to the exclusion of these groups from the formal political process) and at the same time to rebuild and reform the destroyed security sector – all while Israeli occupation persisted. At the same time, plans for and implementation of Israeli redeployment from Gaza produced an impetus for PSS reform on the part of both the PA and the donors. In the second half of 2005, the impending redeployment created a more positive environment in Gaza, where Palestinian factions were more willing to contemplate issues of disarmament in the post-redeployment period.[3]

Yet President Abbas soon discovered that he lacked the capacity to enforce law and order, let alone implement a DDR program. Attempts to confront well-armed groups, warlords, and gangs could have led to civil strife. To avoid such a bleak future, the new president sought the approval of all major factions for every important step he took leading to the March 2005 Cairo Declaration. The Palestinian domestic political system was to be made inclusive, with Hamas integrated into it and into the PLO, and, in return, Hamas would agree to a ceasefire and to endorse the establishment of a Palestinian state within the framework of a defined Israeli-Palestinian peace.[4] It was understood by all factions, however, that the issue of arms collection and disbanding of militias would be subject to discussion only after the holding of the parliamentary elections. Abbas hoped the legitimacy gained by the upcoming parliamentary elections would give a future cabinet the political will to deal effectively with all of the PA's ills, including the collection of arms and disbanding of militias.

While the concept of DDR was by then acceptable to the mainstream nationalist movement, Fateh, the sequence envisaged in the concept was not. Palestinians viewed the idea of starting with disarmament as a non-starter.

PA forces lacked the capacity to force factions to disarm before full political and military integration took place. In other words, even after elections, Palestinians wanted to integrate members of the militias into the security services first, before disarming and disbanding them. Integration into the security services would provide assurances to the factions about their role in the political system and about jobs for their members. Once integrated, militias would then be disarmed, and members would be gradually demobilized as part of a package of gradual economic and social integration.

It was fully understood that any DDR program would be constrained by the status of the peace process with Israel. What made a quick DDR program in 2005 even more difficult was the lack of progress in the peace process, despite the death of Arafat and the election of Abbas. Moreover, the only instrument of the peace process that was accepted by the two sides, the Quartet Road Map, insisted that the PA must not only put an end to violence against Israelis but also that the greatly weakened PA security services must "dismantle the infrastructure of terror" by disbanding the militias, destroying their infrastructure, and collecting their arms. Under prevailing conditions in 2005, these Road Map demands were simply unattainable.

The added difficulty introduced by the Road Map was made even more challenging by the fact that, while the overwhelming majority of Palestinians would have supported the goal of disarming the militias for the sake of law and order, Palestinian society was divided on the goal of disarming "resistance groups," or groups whose arms are perceived as essential in helping to end the Israeli occupation. In reality, however, the militias and the "resistance groups" are one and the same.

In the aftermath of the January 2006 Hamas electoral victory, doubts increased about the ability of the PA to quickly embark on a comprehensive DDR program. The formation of a national unity government composed of Fateh and Hamas and committed to the restoration of law and order created a rare opportunity for the PA to embark on a DDR program. Still, given Hamas's refusal to renounce the right to resist occupation by force, the road to a successful program is not straightforward. Moreover, in the absence of serious progress in the peace process towards a negotiated end of occupation, it is highly unlikely that the Palestinian public would be willing to give significant support to disarming "resistance groups," even as the demand for law and order becomes ever greater. Progress in the peace process could reduce the demand for armed "resistance" and increase the demand for enforcement of law and order and, therefore, facilitate the implementation of a far-reaching DDR program.

Palestinian Armed Groups

Four armed groups were created by the end of 2000 and early 2001: al-Aqsa Martyrs Brigades, belonging to the Fateh "young guard"; Izz Eddin al-Qassam, a Hamas armed wing; Saraya al-Quds, the armed wing of Islamic Jihad; and al Nasir Salah ed Din Brigades, the armed wing of a new group called the Palestinian Popular Committees, a coalition of independents as well as groups and individuals previously belonging to Fateh, Hamas, and the PSS. Over the years of the second intifada splinter groups emerged, mostly composed of disgruntled members of al-Aqsa Brigades or independent Fateh groups such as the Abu al-Reesh Brigades.

Most of the members of the various militias are young men in their twenties, with twelve to sixteen years of education, who live in refugee camps. While the core groups of the nationalist militia of al Aqsa Brigades came from full-time members of security services or the Tanzim of Fateh, most of the members of this group were unemployed before joining the militia. In fact, many joined with the hope of receiving a monthly stipend in the range of US$100 to US$300. Members of Islamist militias tend to have a history of association with those groups before actually joining their armed wings.

While political factions have used these militias to mobilize public support and to launch armed attacks on Israelis, they have also used them to:

- illegally take control of public land, facilities, and other resources to establish headquarters, camps, and training bases
- establish occasional and permanent check points and other barriers to protect headquarters and bases, establish presence and assert control over neighbourhoods, prevent citizens and rival groups from entering closed areas, and, at times, kidnap foreigners and members of rival groups
- enforce political directives and social codes (such as forcing merchants to close their shops during declared strike days) or, as in the case of Hamas, to deter flagrant violation of Islamic dress code or "immoral" behaviour
- blackmail merchants and investors to "contribute" money to the "cause"
- force public institutions, such as ministries and local councils, to employ militia members or their family and friends
- block public roads, institutions, and services to protest PA policies or to force PA institutions to provide their members services denied to them
- use violence to settle accounts with opponents in the same militia or in different ones.

In early 2007, it was estimated that the total size of the militias exceeded forty thousand men and that most of them were armed. During the second half of 2005, about twenty thousand of those (mostly members of al-Aqsa Brigades) were listed as part of the PA security services and were receiving a monthly stipend, even though they were neither integrated into the services nor disarmed. There are essentially three sources of arms for the militias: the PSS, the Israeli black market and other criminal sources, and smuggling into the Gaza Strip through tunnels underneath the Egyptian-Palestinian border in Rafah.[5] Estimates of the number of automatic and semi-automatic guns in the hands of the militias range between fifteen thousand and twenty thousand, mostly in the Gaza Strip, with less than 25 percent of those in the West Bank.[6]

Most of the militias in the Gaza Strip have also acquired the capacity to build locally manufactured explosives, hand grenades, anti-armour rockets, and primitive short range (six- to nine-kilometre) surface-to-surface rockets with little accuracy or firepower. By comparison, it is estimated that the size of the PA security services is about fifty thousand (including civilian police, preventive security, national forces, and intelligence) with about thirty thousand deployed in the Gaza Strip and the rest in the West Bank. The number of arms in the hands of the security services is estimated to be fewer than ten thousand, with about 80 percent of the security personnel being without arms.

For members of the militias, attitudes regarding DDR are framed mostly in terms of its effect on Israeli policy rather than the impact it could have on the domestic balance of power. Arms collection is accepted as long as it positively affects efforts to end Israeli occupation and to release Palestinian prisoners jailed in Israel. Nonetheless, it is clear that, even when Israeli policy changes – as indeed was the case with regard to the Gaza Strip when the Israeli army and settlers were withdrawn in September 2005 – domestic imperatives remain high on the agenda of these groups. None of the Gaza militias voluntarily gave up arms or offered to do so in the aftermath of the Israeli withdrawal. However, the victory of Hamas in the January 2006 elections and the formation of a Hamas government strongly affected that group's views of DDR. For example, under the control of Hamas, in May 2006 the Ministry of the Interior started a process of integrating about 3,700 armed men from Izz Eddin al-Qassam Brigades and from the armed wing of the Popular Committees in the Gaza Strip into the PA security services. In other words, once Hamas was included in the political process and once the status of the Israeli occupation changed, DDR became (partly) feasible. The formation of the national unity government is likely to reinforce this trend.

Al-Aqsa Martyrs Brigades

The al-Aqsa Martyrs Brigades belong to Fateh and were the first militia to be established at the start of the intifada around the end of 2000. They have the largest number of recruits, with most of their members coming from the security services or the Tanzim, which represents the organized Fateh's young guard. It is estimated that about twenty-five thousand persons, essentially men in their twenties, belong to this group. The brigades are the most decentralized and indeed fragmented of all the militias. They lack discipline as well as a unified political or military leadership, with members in different parts of the Palestinian territories enjoying a great deal of independence in their decision making. Most of the arms in the hands of the brigades came originally from sources in the PA security services, but arms are also bought on the black market, normally through Israeli sources, or smuggled from abroad through tunnels, as in the case of the Gaza Strip.

The al-Aqsa Brigades were established by local decisions of Fateh activists rather than by an official directive from Fateh's top decision-making body, the Fateh Central Committee. Indeed, most members of that central body, who belong to the old guard, do not approve of their establishment, and some, like Mahmud Abbas, publicly oppose their activities. Fateh's old guard view the brigades as the coercive arm of the young guard, not only in resisting occupation but also, and most important, in domestic and internal party political competition. Therefore, they see them as a threat to their dominant role in Fateh. The most popular Fateh leader, Marwan Barghouti, currently in an Israeli jail, played a central role in the formation of the brigades and was perceived as a direct threat to the top leadership of Fateh's old guard, including Yasir Arafat. However, Arafat saw a certain advantage in keeping the brigades active as a means of pressuring Israel to yield concessions at the negotiating table. To prevent the emergence of a cohesive and centralized leadership of the group, he sought to buy the loyalty of some of them by funding some of their activities and maintaining personal contact with some of their field commanders.

The brigades were originally envisaged as a defence force aimed at protecting Palestinian civilians engaged in non-violent demonstrations against the Israeli army during the onset of the second intifada. However, soon enough they were involved in attacks on Israeli soldiers and settlers in the occupied Palestinian territories, and, by early 2002, in response to Israeli assassinations of their top military leaders, they also became involved in suicide attacks against Israeli civilians inside Israel.

Gradually, the undisciplined nature of the al-Aqsa Brigades led them to fall victim to the manipulation of various ambitious commanders and party leaders. As a result, most violations of law and order in the Palestinian areas have been carried out by this group. Attacks on public property and PA institutions aimed at forcing favourable decisions from the government went unpunished as a consequence of dual membership, with most of the attackers coming from the same security services that were supposed to stop and arrest them. By the second half of 2005, in an attempt to put an end to the emerging anarchy and to ensure the continued adherence of the brigades to an existing ceasefire with Israel, the newly elected president allowed the Ministry of the Interior to "enlist" members of this group, wanted by the Israeli army, into the PSS. As mentioned earlier, these men were now paid a monthly stipend by the Ministry of Finance, even though the PA was never able to force them to show up for work or disarm them. Instead of reducing the incidence of violations of law and order, this practice led to a worsening of the situation. While this practice of "insertion" was to apply to a limited group of about seven hundred men, it was soon applied to thousands more. By the end of 2005, it is estimated that about twenty thousand may have been added to the public payroll, with thousands more seeking similar treatment. It became clear from the outset that the integration of armed men into the security services would be futile if it were not part of a larger package that addressed the issues of the peace process and a Palestinian-Israeli ceasefire, reforming and rebuilding the PSS, and economic development and job creation.

Izz Eddin al-Qassam Brigades

In its early days in the 1970s and 1980s, the Islamist group Hamas, originally part of the Muslim Brotherhood, focused more on socioeconomic matters, building mosques, schools, hospitals, and a huge socioeconomic network that provided jobs and services to the poor. Hamas's armed wing, Izz Eddin al-Qassam Brigades, was established in the early 1990s during the first intifada as a small secret group that carried out occasional armed attacks against Israelis and Palestinian collaborators and, later, suicide attacks inside Israel. During the second intifada, this group was transformed into a large militia with various public and secretive activities. No reliable data are available regarding the number of armed men in this group, but estimates range between five thousand and seven thousand, mostly in the Gaza Strip. Units of the Qassam Brigades provide protection to Hamas leaders and institutions, while others engage in efforts to promote and to enforce Hamas's social agenda. In places where the PA security services are too weak to enforce law and order, the group seeks to play that role, particularly in terms of fighting drug dealers, apprehending criminals, and ensuring domestic stability. Al-Qassam arms are smuggled from Egypt into Gaza through tunnels, but the group also has its own local workshops that produce various types of explosive charges as well as rockets.

Currently headed by Mohammad Daif, one of Hamas's legendary figures, the Qassam Brigades exhibit the utmost level of cohesion and discipline. While al-Qassam is separate from the political leadership of Hamas, it is believed that the armed wing views itself as an operational arm of the movement, with complete loyalty to its political leaders. Since early 2005, the group has been strict in implementing its commitment to refrain from attacks on Israelis. With the exception of a few incidents, members of the group have rarely attacked public or private property. The role of al-Qassam Brigades in the prevailing anarchy in the Palestinian territories is limited, indeed minor. The main concern lies in the possibility that this group might use force against PA security services and Fateh's militias. This concern has recently been intensified in the aftermath of the January 2006 parliamentary elections, in which Hamas won most of the seats.

Relations between al-Qassam and the PA security services have never been amicable. While Hamas's armed wing never targeted PA security officials, the PA did occasionally, as in March 1996, arrest hundreds of al-Qassam members and leaders and kept many of them in jail without charge for long periods. Occasionally, however, al-Qassam attacked police stations and senior security officials in retaliation for actions taken by the Palestinian police. In contrast, this group enjoyed close cooperation with Fateh's al-Aqsa Brigades during most of the years of the second intifada. However, tensions between the two groups emerged in the aftermath of Hamas's election victory. Before the formation of a national unity government in March 2007, these tensions escalated into serious armed clashes in late 2006 and early 2007, with dozens killed on both sides.

Saraya al-Quds

Palestinian Islamic Jihad (PIJ), established in the early 1980s, was the first Islamist group to engage in armed attacks against Israelis. PIJ is a small group with little popular support and a limited socioeconomic infrastructure. It has a special relationship with Iran and has established bases in Lebanon and Syria, where its top leadership resides. While the group has been willing to participate in local elections in the occupied territories, it has refused to take part in parliamentary elections, seeing them as the means to legitimize the Oslo peace process, which the group opposes. However, PIJ did take part in the Cairo dialogue and agreed to the ceasefire that followed. Unlike Hamas, however, the group was unwilling to forgo revenge attacks on Israeli targets in response to Israeli assassinations of its military wing leaders.

With the eruption of the second intifada, Saraya al-Quds became the armed wing of PIJ, carrying out attacks against Israeli soldiers and settlers in the West Bank and the Gaza Strip as well as suicide attacks inside Israel. This armed group is very small, perhaps with fewer than one thousand persons, and is located mostly in the Gaza Strip. Like al-Qassam, Saraya al-Quds has not contributed significantly to lawlessness and anarchy in the occupied Palestinian territories.

Al Nasir Salah ed Din

At the start of the second intifada, a mixed group of Fateh and Hamas activists, as well as members of the security services, established the Popular Resistance Committees, which have since involved mainly armed activities carried out by its armed wing, al Nasir Salah ed Din Brigades. Established in the Gaza Strip in early 2001, the group is small and known mostly for its rocket attacks on Israeli targets. However, it has also been reportedly involved in the assassination of political foes, armed attacks on foreigners –

including American diplomats – and the kidnapping of aid workers and diplomats, all in the Gaza Strip. The group has also sought to find jobs for its members in the PA bureaucracy and security services and, when it failed, has resorted to occupying public offices or seeking to disrupt vital normal activities at critical facilities, such as the international crossing at the Rafah terminal. Like other groups, it produces some of its own explosives and smuggles arms though tunnels.

Lessons from More Than a Decade of Global DDR Programming

The United Nations Security Council (UNSC) describes DDR as "vital to stabilizing a post-conflict situation; to reducing the likelihood of renewed violence, either because of relapse into war or outbreaks of banditry; and to facilitating a society's transition from conflict to normalcy and development" (UNSC 2000, 1). Indeed, the results from a recent review project undertaken by the International Peace Academy and the Center for International Security and Cooperation at Stanford University suggest that demobilization of soldiers and demilitarization of politics (i.e., "transformation of soldiers into civilians and warring armies into political parties") are the two most important tasks in peacebuilding (Stedman 2002, 3).

Many authors suggest different initials for DDR – from DDRRR (disarmament, demobilization, reinsertion, rehabilitation, and reintegration) to DR (to stand in for all possible Ds and Rs) (ICG 2003) – and posit various definitions for the components of DDR, but most are in accord with the UN definitions that follow here. Disarmament is "the collection of small arms and light and heavy weapons within a conflict zone. It frequently entails the assembly and cantonment of combatants; it should also comprise the development of arms management programmes, including their safe storage and their final disposition, which may entail their destruction" (UNSC 2000, 2). Demobilization is "the process by which parties to a conflict begin to disband their military structures and combatants begin the transformation into civilian life ... It may be followed by recruitment into a new, unified military force" (ibid.). Finally, reintegration is "the process which allows ex-combatants and their families to adapt, economically and socially, to productive civilian life. It generally entails the provision of a package of cash or in-kind compensation, training, and job- and income-generating projects" (ibid.).

According to some analysts, DDR has a very mixed record of success (Berdal 1996, 5; Kingma 1997, 184-85; Muggah 2005), despite numerous UN-led missions and other modes of implementation since 1989.[7] Furthermore, although the goal of disarmament is to create a secure environment, Mats Berdal (1996, 24) asserts that there is "no automatic or inherent relationship between the process of disarmament and the creation of a secure environment ... [U]nder certain circumstances, disarmament is likely to aggravate

rather than enhance the security required for demobilisation and reintegration to proceed." Kees Kingma (2002a, 182) echoes Berdal by suggesting
that, in some instances, DDR can result in new social and political conflicts,
an issue to which we return below.

At its core, DDR is a political and socioeconomic set of interlinked processes. Treating DDR as a set of mere managerial or administrative tasks
runs the risk of failure, particularly in contexts where there is not a clear
victor to a conflict and where, as in the Palestinian case, resolutions of root
causes to the conflict are still being negotiated or resolved (Berdal 1996, 5-6).
On the political level, DDR's success relies on – and is part of – national reconciliation processes, particularly those that aim at improving civil-military
relations and where the responsiveness of the military to democratic controls is ensured – in other words, security sector reform.[8] This is especially
the case as successful DDR creates or reinforces the state government's monopoly over the use of force. For this to be feasible and successful, DDR
must be coupled with establishment of the rule of law and respect for human rights and civil liberties. Otherwise, disarmament will fail as people
will be reluctant to give up arms, or they may pick them up again, in the
absence of power-sharing and governmental transparency and accountability (Berdal 1996, 55-57; Kingma 1997, 159; Faltas, MacDonald, and Waszink
2001, 3, 8; GTZ 2001, 14, 35; Babiker and Özerdem 2003, 222).

To address this challenge, as with most peacebuilding and development
approaches, DDR needs to be tailor-made to the political, economic, historical, and cultural context within which it is to be implemented (Berdal
1996; GTZ 2001; Spear 2002). Robert Muggah (2005) argues that DDR needs
to be more soundly positioned, conceptualized, and designed to be part of
the postwar reconstruction and development trajectory, with a broader vision of security that encompasses human security and development objectives and indicators.[9] Some researchers even suggest that the conventional
and linear DDR sequence needs to be rethought in order to put reintegration first in specific contexts, such as in Afghanistan (Özerdem 2002; Knight
and Özerdem 2004), as will be suggested later in this chapter.[10]

When it comes to the Palestinian case, three features require special attention. First, since Palestinian-Israeli efforts to put an end to the violence
and to revive the peace process during the last decade have essentially failed,
a Palestinian DDR program that meets state-building requirements will most
likely have direct implications for the Palestinian-Israeli conflict, adding to
its existing challenges. Second, since many of the groups needing to be
disarmed reject basic elements of any conceivable Palestinian-Israeli permanent settlement, efforts to disarm such groups must first assure them
that, despite their disarmament, they would still be able to influence public
policy by peaceful means. Third, since most of these groups have already

been mostly excluded from the political process since the start of the peace process – a process that essentially sought to delegitimize them – it is important that the DDR sequence occurs in such a manner as to postpone disarmament until after integration is successful. This clearly precludes forced disarmament. Given existing weaknesses of the Palestinian security services and their total demoralization in the absence of progress in the peace process, forced disarmament would be tantamount to calling for civil war. This section examines what the literature on DDR might tell us about how to approach the Palestinian case, particularly through inclusive governance and socioeconomic development, and through alternatives to military-led peacebuilding.

Most analysts draw attention to the economic, security, and political dimensions of DDR and the opportunities these dimensions pose for non-compliance, spoiling, and criminality. While all of these dimensions are important, the DDR literature tends to emphasize the economic and social integration issues, leaving security and political dimensions – not to mention cultural and ideological ones – as secondary concerns. This stands in contrast to recent work done on spoilers and armed non-state actor groups and dynamics, which tends to put much more focus on political issues and dynamics. Such concerns are likely to prove critical in the Palestinian case and are explored later in this chapter.

In the Palestinian case, socioeconomic considerations are a significant piece of the overall framework for peaceful resolution of the conflict with Israel and are a key component of Palestinian state building, which must accompany any durable peace. Years of closure and conflict – now manifested in the separation wall and "roads and tunnels system" constructed by Israel on occupied Palestinian land, enabling the consolidation of the Israeli settlement of most Palestinian land in the West Bank – have wreaked havoc on the Palestinian "state" and society, not to mention the peace process and its prospects (World Bank 2005). Thus, DDR's socioeconomic component will need to be tied to a reversal of Israel's closure and settlement policies, and it will be a powerful demonstration of an end to conflict between Palestine and Israel. Moreover, given the embedded nature of Palestinian non-state militias, as well as the considerable sacrifices made by Palestinian civilians (enduring Israeli shelling in civilian areas, house demolitions, infrastructure destruction, conflict and closure-related poverty, invasions and destructions of refugee camps, etc.), the socioeconomic reintegration and rehabilitation of militants will require a community-based approach. Nonetheless, socioeconomic considerations do not stand apart from political issues. Armed militants acquire a certain amount of power and prestige – particularly in embedded situations – but with those political rewards come obligations and expectations to deliver community/national rights and protection.

Successful DDR, then, is tied to the delivery of self-rule and/or inclusive governance. This section explores these dynamics in relation to Palestine in order to demonstrate the tight links between these issues.

In an early review of DDR, Berdal (1996, 16) pointed out that "weapons always have an *economic* as well as a *security* value for those who possess them" (emphasis in original). Through the World Bank, Paul Collier (Collier 2000; Collier and Hoeffler 2001) introduced an analysis of economic incentives for civil war through the "greed and grievance" debate, which pointed to the interplay and connections between criminal economic activity and conflict.[11] These understandings of civil war and non-state combatants' interests and their implications receive much attention in the DDR literature (Berdal 1996, 16-17, 40, 46; Faltas, MacDonald, and Waszink 2001, 5; GTZ 2001, 37-38; Babiker and Özerdem 2003, 225, 226; Nitzschke and Studdard 2005, 226-28). At its most simplistic, analysts suggest that economic incentives for disarming and demobilizing need to be sufficient to replace the short-term monetary value of war-related criminal activity, particularly in the context of a war-ravaged economy, where legitimate economic opportunities are few (e.g., Weinstein 2002, 3-4). Others point out that, if DDR fails, ex-combatants may (re)enter a criminalized existence (Kingma 1997, 157). While the Israeli-Palestine conflict concerns late colonization and military occupation – a nationalist struggle – as mentioned earlier, this is not to say that criminal elements that benefit from the conflict (e.g., through arms smuggling, political extortion, etc.) have not emerged in the occupied Palestinian territories as a result of deep impoverishment and weak governance. Palestinian DDR will require attention to this aspect of the armed groups' dynamics, with careful attention to the mix of community power and material interest involved.

Nonetheless, several researchers bring to bear more nuanced and sophisticated analyses to DDR's economic problems, which are tinged with social, political, and security considerations. For instance, some writers discuss how war fundamentally reshapes a country's economy, polity, and society, indicating that this potentially repositions winners and losers in a post-conflict setting. Within such a context, and as noted above, individual and group choices and decisions to visibly lay down arms can be less than attractive for a variety of reasons, where expectations of return for years of fighting and fears of adjusting to civilian life can be considerable (Berdal 1996, 15, 39-40; Babiker and Özerdem 2003, 221). During the second intifada, Palestinian young guard nationalists managed to weaken and marginalize the old guard's institutions and leadership. It is highly unlikely that they will lay down arms before the old guard's relinquishment of formal dominance is ensured. In this case, the holding of Fateh's Sixth Convention,[12] with the aim of setting new rules and electing a new leadership, would likely be a precondition for any successful Palestinian DDR program. Similarly, while

the elected Hamas leadership in the West Bank and the Gaza Strip is showing willingness to begin merging some of Hamas's armed men into the Palestinian security services, it is doubtful that the leadership of Hamas,
stationed in Damascus, would be willing to endorse such integration.

Others point to the importance of senior officers when it comes to DDR
as they have the potential to remobilize combatants and, therefore, must be
carefully managed. Incentives must be sufficiently attractive to draw them
to DDR programs (Berdal 1996, 48; Nitzschke and Studdard 2005, 228). Indeed, participation in war economies makes room for subsets of actors to
fragment from larger factions if they disagree with a peace process, and it
may also make it difficult to enforce discipline in armed forces. Sometimes,
dual loyalties are at play, where actors are "sobels": soldiers by day, rebels by
night. There is also the phenomenon of police involvement in predatory
activities that the government may actively or tacitly encourage. In the
Palestinian case, the second intifada witnessed the rise of warlords, particularly in the Gaza Strip, who built fortunes and militias based on the smuggling of arms and other scarce products. Some of those warlords headed
important families or were current or former commanders in the Palestinian security services. Both our research and a recent study on the Palestinian security forces and armed non-state opposition groups (Strategic
Assessments Initiative 2005) cited the phenomenon of actors in each of
these organizations holding dual loyalties to the other (e.g., a Palestinian
police officer may also have sympathies for al-Aqsa Martyrs Brigades or participate in their activities). In fact, our research revealed that most members
of al-Aqsa Brigades were active members of one or another Palestinian security service. As in many other international contexts (see Nitzsckhe and
Studdard 2005, 225, 229), a troika composed of a "nouveau riche 'criminal
elite'" class (i.e., the Palestinian warlords mentioned above) with close ties
to government and nationalist political parties has emerged, with a vested
interest in blocking reform and establishing civilian control and budgetary
oversight over security forces and national budgets.

Failure of peace accords to address a conflict's root causes and combatants' expectations can pose challenges for durable DDR and set conditions
for criminality and renewed political violence. A return to the status quo
ante is hardly desirable for ex-combatants as it is these conditions that often motivated conflict in the first instance (Spear 2002, 150; Babiker and
Özerdem 2003, 227). Failure of the state to provide services that are often
provided by non-state actors and their networks undermines the creation
of the "social contract" necessary for democratic, accountable government
to take root – something that must go hand in hand with DDR. Peacebuilding efforts need to address the criminalized informal economy while
retaining its socially beneficial aspects (e.g., provision of services, economic
support of civilians, etc.) (Nitzschke and Studdard 2005, 224, 230). In the

Palestinian case, continued Israeli settlement activities, land confiscation, economic siege, and mobility restrictions make it difficult for the PA to effectively implement a far-reaching DDR program, not to mention a protection of citizens and social services and welfare provision. PA corruption only compounded the difficulties. Hamas filled some of these gaps quite handily through its social services programs. Moreover, the failure of the peace process to put an end to the Israeli occupation and find a solution to the refugee problem – root causes of the conflict – triggered the second Palestinian intifada. Combined with meaningful Palestinian governance reform and performance, these issues will be critical for the durability of any DDR programming in the West Bank and Gaza.

One set of debates on DDR centres on whether ex-combatants should be treated as a special group when it comes to reintegration. In contexts in which many segments of the population are war-ravaged (e.g., refugees, internally displaced persons, civilian victims of physical violence and war-related losses of property, etc.), such an approach risks igniting postwar tensions and appears to privilege combatants who have victimized civilians (Kingma 1997, 154; Lodgaard 1997, 148; GTZ 2001, 13-14; Kingma 2002a, 193-94; Farr 2003, 33). In the Palestinian case, many farmers, merchants, and homeowners have been victims of Israeli military attacks on their property. Any DDR program would have to be situated within a context in which other compensation programs ensured that such groups receive appropriate compensation as well. In particular, Palestinian prisoners in Israeli jails, currently numbering about ten thousand, are likely to feel cheated by any DDR program that keeps them in jail and denies them the benefits of socioeconomic integration. Some argue that ex-combatants need special treatment during disarmament and demobilization, but reintegration support should be more generalized (Kingma 1997, 162). Others justify treating ex-combatants as a special group as reintegration programs benefit a wide circle of persons around the ex-combatant (their families and immediate communities) (Babiker and Özerdem 2003, 220), but this is contested by others who claim that there is no evidence that reintegration benefits filter down to women and families (Farr 2003, 31). One analyst suggests that it is dangerous to treat ex-combatants as a special group – he cites Zimbabwe as a contemporary example of the result of this approach – arguing that all citizens make sacrifices and are victimized during wartime and that "history" rather than individuals should be cast as the "hero of the struggle" (Mashike 2000, 6-7).

Nonetheless, there is no dispute that ex-combatants require assistance to facilitate their transition from fighters to civilians. Most ex-combatants in postwar contexts have lost skills or are unskilled for a civilian workforce – as well as uneducated. Most low-income, war-torn countries are agricultural economies, in which that sector has been hard hit by war and by land mines (Berdal 1996, 45-46). Ex-combatants may suffer psychological and trauma effects from years of fighting (Kingma 1997, 155; GTZ 2001, 37; Knight and Özerdem 2004, 502-03), and they may also experience "returning hero syndrome," where they experience significant pressure to improve their families' fortunes upon their return (Spear 2002, 146). Years of being part of fighting forces (and, in some contexts, away from family and community) may pose significant social and cultural challenges to reintegration and result in conflicts between civilians and ex-combatants as a result of attitudes that make it difficult for former fighters to fit into civilian life (Kingma 2002a, 191-92).[13] In the Palestinian case, as in the Afghanistan and Guatemalan cases discussed in this volume, combatants are embedded in their communities. Many leaders of armed groups came from impoverished backgrounds and saw their status elevated when they joined the militias. They are likely to resist attempts to go back to their old status. Moreover, the conditions of continued conflict with Israel, closure, and settlement expansion in Gaza[14] and the West Bank have undermined the Palestinian economy (PCBS and World Bank 2004; World Bank 2005), posing a real challenge for any planners and implementers of a DDR strategy in Palestine. As well, the Palestinian community at large has expectations of political and economic return from years of intifada-related sacrifice and violent resistance.

Another layer of challenge noted in the DDR literature concerns the fact that many governments are unwilling to work directly with armed non-state actor groups for fear that they will be seen as rewarding or engaging with "terrorists." Anti-terrorist legislation sometimes blocks third parties from taking constructive approaches when it comes to engaging armed non-state actor groups, and those trying to work constructively with these groups sometimes run the risk of being labelled terrorist sympathizers (Berdal 1996, 67-68; Capie 2004, 11; CR 2004, 14; Philipson 2005, 3-4). For instance, in Palestine the categorization and listing of several Palestinian armed non-state actor groups, such as Hamas and PIJ, as "terrorists" means that donors have boxed themselves into a position of being unable to work constructively with such groups – a necessary prerequisite for effective Palestinian DDR and security sector reform. The current War-on-Terror approach to resolving Middle East conflict has, in fact, debilitated Western governments' abilities to successfully negotiate with groups with which it holds normative and political differences in favour of military-led strategies to deal with such parties.[15]

One review of UN peacekeeping-led disarmament and demobilization exercises reveals a record of problems with establishing sufficient ground-level authority to implement DDR (Gamba 2003). Although some analysts identify two types of DDR – coerced and cooperative – the former approach is dismissed as ineffective and counterproductive based on the experiences of the United States in Somalia in 1992-93 and India in Sri Lanka in 1987 (Berdal 1996, 24-32; Spear 2002, 142).[16] Mohammed Babiker and Alpaslan Özerdem (2003, 221) characterize coerced disarmament as a "commitment to combat" that can destroy a peace process. In the absence of a peace agreement, such an approach constitutes the conduct of war rather than the implementation of a disarmament initiative as part of a larger peacebuilding and reconstruction process. This experience stands counter to the current demand on the PA by Israel and the internationally backed Road Map to disarm armed Palestinian groups, forcibly if necessary, as a precondition to the resumption of peace negotiations. The PA has thus far refused to systematically and forcibly confront and engage armed Palestinian factions on the ground, fearing, as indicated above, that this would thrust Palestine into a civil war. It prefers negotiating with these groups.

Even with cooperative approaches, larger political problems remain with DDR. First, vague peace agreements without detailed provisions can lead to problems in implementation and verification (Spear 2002, 148-49). More important, weak post-conflict states and dispersed political authority – particularly in contexts in which no clear victor has emerged at the end of conflict – make DDR implementation a challenge (Berdal 1996, 20-21; Kingma 1997, 158, 159; Kingma 2002a, 188; Spear 2002, 151-52). In the Palestinian case, where there exist internal power splits and contests between various armed factions as well as a broken-down peace process with Israel, the challenges associated with fragile states and DDR are writ large. It goes without saying that any successful Palestinian DDR program must envisage efforts to reform and rebuild the destroyed Palestinian security services in order to ensure its ability to manage the process and to deter violations. A necessary component would be independent external monitoring and verification forces for any Israeli-Palestinian peace agreement struck (including the now defunct Road Map) as well as for a DDR program.

The above mentioned challenges point to issues at the political, economic, and social levels that lend potential for spoiling peace agreements and their implementation as well as continued or heightened criminality. As demonstrated, the DDR literature makes many references to this phenomenon, but there is also an emergent literature on spoiling and armed non-state actor groups that we examine below in order to gather further insight, again using the Palestinian case as an illustrative example.[17]

DDR, the Security Dilemma, and Spoilers

The previous section elaborates on debates in the DDR literature that have particular resonance in the Palestinian case as well as on this volume's wider perspective on durable peacebuilding. This section goes into greater detail on links between DDR and spoiling that are especially pertinent when it comes to negotiating with Islamist and other armed non-state actors. In particular, it deals with the issues of political inclusion in, and the conduct of, peace processes, peacebuilding, and political (re)integration as an aspect of DDR.

As mentioned above, the political, security, and socio-cultural dimensions of DDR have received far less attention than they merit. Most analysts simply point to the need for political trust and guerrilla concerns to retain their mobilizational capacity should it prove politically necessary (e.g., Berdal 1996, 21, 43). Some argue that disarmament is a "social contract," thus injecting some dynamism into DDR analysis. If this contract is unfulfilled due to the failure of ex-combatants to find a place for themselves in the postwar order, spoiling or criminality appear as viable choices (Knight and Özerdem 2004, 506-07, 513). In interviews with Palestinian "foot soldiers" conducted for this research, most emphasized the need for social integration to become a critical element in a successful DDR program. As many of the armed men were in fact students and unemployed, they needed assurances that they would be accepted in universities and public institutions. Some analysts point out that partial disarmament in contexts in which central authority is weak can pose actual dangers for those complying with DDR programs, leaving them vulnerable to groups and individuals who remain armed and engaged in combat or criminal activity (Berdal 1996, 28-29; Faltas, MacDonald, and Waszink 2001, 3; Spears 2002, 146) and leading to a black market in arms. Research on the relationship between guns, identity, and masculinity – and their connections to DDR and compliance failure, spoiling, and violence – is in its infancy (Berdal 1996, 36; Kingma 1997, 157-58; Spear 2002, 145; Myrttinen 2003; Knight and Özerdem 2004, 505). One good example of this kind of analysis in South Africa examines how militant identity conferred authority and prestige on the subject – authority and prestige that is not easily abandoned after the conflict, particularly in contexts that offer few other opportunities for personal status and power (Gear 2002). As indicated earlier, many commanders in the Palestinian case told us they feared loss of status once they surrender their guns and return to their normal occupations.

The emerging debate on spoilers and new research on armed non-state actors can shed some further light on compliance failure when it comes to DDR.[18] Stephen Stedman (1997, 5) opened the debate with an article that offered a case-based typology of spoilers and the following definition: "[Spoilers are] leaders and parties who believe that peace emerging from negotiations threatens their power, worldview, and interests, and use violence to undermine attempts to achieve it. By signing a peace agreement, leaders put themselves at risk from adversaries who may take advantage of a settlement, from disgruntled followers who see peace as a betrayal of key values, and from excluded parties who seek either to alter the process or to destroy it." Nonetheless, he later refers to RENAMO as a spoiler, even though he cites no violent dimension in its behaviour, just resistance (e.g., it stalled implementing commitments it had made regarding the peace process and threatened to boycott elections and return to war) (Stedman 1997, 6).[19]

The literature brings out three main issues relevant to DDR: motivations for spoiling and spoiler behaviour, various uses and meanings of violence vis-à-vis peace processes (voice, entry, exit, destruction), and the security dilemma. Before discussing these issues, it is perhaps instructive to point out that armed non-state actors frequently grapple with the issue of asymmetry at the negotiating table, shaped in part by the existing state-centric international system that grants legitimacy over the use of force to the state and therefore leads to the assumption that armed non-state groups are illegitimate in their use of force. States assume that other states comply with the rule of law and human rights while armed non-state groups do not. Further, international norms privilege states over non-state groups. As a result, armed non-state groups feel like second-class parties and perceive themselves as victims and as less powerful players on an uneven playing field (CR 2004, 13-14; Philipson 2005, 2-3). This has real implications for motivations, meanings, and behaviour. In addition, anti-terrorist legislation cultivates a rhetoric of demonization of armed non-state groups that disconnects their cause(s) from any real and legitimate set of grievances, which only entrenches exclusion and asymmetry (CR 2004, 14; Philipson 2005, 3-4). This latter dynamic can be seen in full play in the Palestinian situation, where much of the international community – including three of the four parties to the Quartet – have refused to deal with Hamas in its new role as the fairly and democratically elected leaders of the Palestinian government on the basis that it is a "terrorist" organization. However, an additional layer is also at play in the Palestinian case, where a former armed non-state actor is now at the helm of Palestinian government – now a "state" power – yet Western democracies remain intent on its exclusion. While it could be argued that this exclusion is based on Hamas's previous actions, it is also clearly premised on Hamas's ideology and political aims as Israel and Western governments retain the unprecedented privilege of refusing to negotiate peace with anyone other than friendly parties. This hallmark of the Western- and Israeli-led War on Terror seems to demand complete capitulation of its Islamist enemies – a desire for asymmetry writ large.

There are various opinions and explanations for why actors enter into peace agreements and why they spoil them. Referring to Hamas and other Islamist groups, Alastair Crooke (2005, 3) draws on understandings of "fourth-generation" warfare, where he posits that "fluid asymmetrical insurgency ... is aimed at undermining the psychological steadfastness of the opponent. Its deliberately uneven tempo also affords the irregular forces more flexibility to test the political waters without experiencing adverse political consequences from their supporters. A change in an already un-even tempo does not imply concessions or defeat." This explanation is some-what echoed by Caroline Hartzell, who suggests that adversaries sometimes enter unsustainable peace processes as a means of learning about their op-ponent and testing their will, which sometimes contributes to a learning curve that eventually leads to successful negotiations. She also offers a sec-ond explanation, which is less laudatory but just as credible, where she suggests that weak settlements are concluded under international or third party pressure to sign an accord (Hartzell 1999, 19). This latter explanation goes well with Marie-Joëlle Zahar's (2003, 116, 117) observation that some peace agreements are more vulnerable to spoiling than are others. A poten-tially aggravating factor is the difference between the timelines of govern-ments and armed non-state groups for negotiations, where governments' timelines may be determined by the electoral calendar while armed non-state groups typically have a long-term time frame committed to social/political change (Philipson 2005, 5) and, thus, can prolong the conflict and/or the peace process through the selective use of violence.

Several instances of Israeli-Palestinian negotiations serve to illustrate these points. A review of accounts of the Camp David negotiations of 2000 re-veals the inordinate pressure on Arafat and the Palestinian team to agree to unfavourable Israeli proposals on the negotiating table – proposals justified by Israeli prime minister Ehud Barak's need to satisfy his electorate (and based on the assumption that Arafat, conveniently being an autocrat, had no need to satisfy his constituency). This was an extension of the trajectory of the Oslo process to that date (Hanieh 2001; Malley and Agha 2001; Sontag 2001). In the end, the second intifada resulted, which some analysts argue was manipulated by Arafat in an attempt to force better terms to the table, as was done during the "tunnel intifada" in 1996 (Sayigh 2001). Addition-ally, in 2003 and 2005, Hamas and the PIJ agreed to unfavourable ceasefire terms under pressure from Egypt and the PA. One possible interpretation for this, in support of Hartzell's first point, is that both organizations agreed to those terms believing that the other side, Israel, would not honour them anyway and that the public, in such a case, would demand a return to vio-lence (or would at least view a return to violence as justified). However, another, more intriguing, interpretation goes to intranational politics, where Hamas was seeking to gain political hegemony with the purpose of deliver-ing inclusive governance within the Palestinian polity, its longer-term goal being to deliver an agreement with Israel (Usher 2005b).

Aside from learning motivations and managing pressure, there are other reasons, apart from outright destruction of peace itself, for adversaries to enter into a peace agreement and to spoil it. Stedman argues that "inside" spoilers only enter into agreements for tactical reasons in order to gain advantage over their opponent. They comply – and spoil through stealth by minimizing the amount of violence they use in order to stay inside the process – but not enough to weaken their offensive military capacity. Sometimes these actors are afraid for their security, or they are greedy and want a better deal. Other times spoilers have absolute goals that are incommensurate with a negotiated peace based on compromise or leaders may not be able to bring their followers along in the peace process (Stedman 1997, 8, 17-18). Armed Palestinian groups opposed to the peace process recognize fully that they cannot defeat the Israelis on the battlefield, but they hope to maintain enough violent pressure to pre-empt peace negotiations. One could also argue that the Israelis use insider spoiler violence to avoid the need to make the sacrifices necessary to conclude a durable peace with the Palestinians. However, Zahar contests the claim that spoilers enter into peace processes for devious reasons and, instead, suggests that motivations for peace and spoiling are contingent upon circumstances and fluid commitment to peace processes and are therefore subject to change. Frequently, these changed motivations will manifest themselves in difficulties implementing DDR (Zahar 2006, 2-3). This is clearly illustrated in the failure of the Oslo peace agreements to put an end to the conflict by postponing all the important issues of borders, refugees, Jerusalem, settlements, and statehood that prevented the Palestinian national movement, Fateh, from making a full and irreversible commitment to war termination or the end of violence. When doubts about Israel's ultimate intention of fully ending its occupation accumulated (e.g., when Israel doubled the size of its Jewish settlement construction in the occupied Palestinian territories), many in Fateh's young guard demanded a return to violence.

However, there are gaps in the spoilers literature that are illustrated by the Palestinian case and that have real implications for conduct of the War on Terror in Palestine. These gaps are related to social psychology and identity, and they are embedded in a set of historical, political, and socioeconomic relations, which donors and peacebuilders ignore at their peril. Stedman tends to represent spoilers in a two-dimensional typology that implies a rather static and innate – rather than dynamic and relational – interaction with conflict and peace processes on the part of spoilers. Zahar injects a more useful organizational change perspective into spoiler dynamics. For instance, Stedman characterizes some sets of spoilers as "absolute" and/or "greedy," ignoring the fact that there may be quite legitimate or reasonable motives for not compromising and that armed non-state actor groups' motivations and goals can change during the lifetime of a conflict and peace process. The sum total of this kind of analysis is to contribute to a demonization of certain types of groups, which leads opponents to conclude that there is no other approach but to seek their total capitulation or annihilation, which Stedman himself advocates as the only solution when it comes to absolute spoilers. We can see this analysis taken up in the current approach to both Hamas and Hezbollah on the part of Israeli and Western governments.

On the other hand, Zahar suggests that there are a number of possible purposes for violence within a peace process, including to protest non-compliance on the part of "insiders" to the process or to seek inclusion in the process on the part of "outsiders." Zahar further argues that exit from a peace process may be premised on few incentives to stay within it, particularly pertaining to power-sharing. In other words, "thick" peace agreements provide more reasons to stay within a peace process, and for outsiders to desire entry, than do "thin" peace agreements (Zahar 2005, 2006).[20] If non-state combatants cannot deliver political goods to their constituencies, they may be unable to carry their cadres' compliance (see McCartney 2005 for a discussion of this aspect). In the Palestinian case, as Shikaki (2002) has argued elsewhere, the second intifada was as much about protesting failure in the peace process as it was about protesting autocratic governance in the PA. Moreover, Palestinians saw a glimpse of how political incentives work when both Hamas and Islamic Jihad agreed to a unilateral cessation of violence in March 2005 as part of the larger package of the Cairo Declaration. That declaration opened the way to the effective integration of these groups into the PA and the PLO, and it set the broad terms of a possible peace agreement with Israel. Until recently, Hamas held its end of the ceasefire despite numerous violations on Israel's part. Failure to ensure a joint nationalist-Islamist ownership of a political framework, of which DDR is only one component, would create impulses on the part of those excluded to delay or destroy the process, as is consistent with one analysis of the incident involving the kidnapping of an Israeli soldier in July 2006. Moreover, and as mentioned earlier, our research clearly shows that armed factions view Israeli refusal to release Palestinian prisoners as a significant impediment to any comprehensive disarmament, and this is also consistent with the July 2006 abduction.[21]

Some analysts point to the "security dilemma" faced by armed non-state actors when it comes to peace processes and DDR. We argue that this goes beyond the obvious dimensions of physical and political survival. To begin with physical and political security dilemmas, Hartzell (1999, 5) writes that the security dilemma is particularly vexing for opponents in intrastate conflicts as they must continue to engage with each other in the post-conflict context as partners in a single state, while interstate adversaries can erect security guarantees (monitoring and verification systems, defence systems, alliances, and sanctions) that are not available to intrastate adversaries. Ironically, while these mechanisms have been available to the Israelis, they have not been available to Palestinians with regard to their interstate conflict with Israel. Moreover, traditional mechanisms offered by third parties to reassure adversaries as they disarm and demobilize – insertion of peacekeepers and guarantees of punishment by third parties if ceasefires are violated (which were also absent from the Oslo peace process) – do not mitigate security concerns as they are out of the control of the adversaries themselves. Armed non-state groups continue to struggle in arrangements where they feel they can only rely on themselves while their opponents, who will try to destroy or undermine them and their friends, do not share their commitments and will be willing to compromise on core issues. Therefore, the coercive forces of the state must be neutralized or balanced through inclusion of competing groups and/or integration of antagonists' forces (Hartzell 1999, 7; McCartney 2005, 5; Philipson 2005, 5).

Moreover, DDR programs are much less likely to be successful if they are designed according to a short time frame with limited goals when one is dealing with an ideology-based armed non-state group. Instead, DDR programming and peace settlements for this type of group need to address the political landscape (by including ex-combatants in political, military, and police institutions) as well the conflict's root socioeconomic causes (Weinstein 2002). Given that almost the entire Palestinian security forces are made up of Fateh members and supporters,[22] Hamas requires two main reforms coupled with DDR: (1) security sector reform that depoliticizes the security services and (2) the integration of many of Hamas's armed men into those services.

However, other research suggests more deeply rooted reasons for a Palestinian security dilemma, which, perhaps in some ways, echoes Israeli psycho-social concerns. Our research revealed that most armed Palestinian combatants are in their twenties, meaning that they were children during the first intifada of 1987-93. Research investigating trauma effects on Gazan children during this time is illuminating when it comes to possible interpretations of the current militants' collective psychology vis-à-vis armed resistance. This research demonstrated high rates of exposure to Israeli violence,[23] and it showed that the more exposure to this violence these children had experienced, the more likely they were to take risks and the more likely they were to suffer low self-esteem. Current studies on adolescents in the West Bank during the second intifada found preliminary evidence to suggest that exposure to trauma may be a causal factor in political engagement (Qouta et al. 1995; Giacaman et al. 2004). While these studies are important in and of themselves, and because of what they say about child and adolescent development, they also offer preliminary clues as to the emotional and socio-political needs of armed actors in Palestine. Engagement in violent politics is possibly a way to psychologically "master" violent traumatic acts suffered in one's past.[24]

While this is not to pathologize armed militants, various scholars have theorized on political violence, and here it is instructive to return to Frantz

Fanon's writings on the colonial and anti-colonial experience as well as to Johan Galtung's writings on structural and cultural violence. These writers relate the violence of colonization to the violence in resistance, as those who are colonized internalize the violence of colonization and refract it back in confrontation with the colonizers (Fanon 1963; Bulhan 1980; Galtung 1990; and Srivastava 2005). For the Palestinians, their nationalist struggle is an anti-colonial one against Israeli occupation and, for armed militants, this will sometimes require the use of violence. For instance, as one Hamas leader has stated, "Armed resistance is not simply a tool that we use to respond to Israeli aggression ... It gives our people confidence that they are being defended, that they have an identity, that someone is trying to balance the scales" (Perry and Crooke 2006b). As Mark Perry and Alastair Crooke note, "The West's seeming abhorrence of violence is derived from its deeply rooted belief that political change is possible without it. But defending this proposition requires an extraordinary exercise in historical amnesia" (ibid.). In recounting their dialogue sessions with Hamas, which included former US officials of various types, they relay the response of one of their participants: "Their [Hamas's] description of terrorism ... convinced me that we are not dealing with genetically encoded monsters, but hard-headed – albeit brutal – political actors who carefully choose their tactics and attempt to manage the effects of their actions" (Perry and Crooke 2006a). Hence, while armed militants in Palestine might be survivors of trauma, they retain control over their actions and think about their meanings.

When it comes to Palestinians and Israelis, DDR, and the existential security dilemma, it is critical that negotiations promote and rest on foundations that respect and protect the other's dignity. Perry and Crooke are clear about these essentials – as well as the need for the West and Israel to listen to Islamist groups' messages – as derived from their numerous discussions with Hamas and Hezbollah leaders. This has clear implications for the West's current War-on-Terror goal of capitulation of the enemy or its total annihilation. Palestine is the smallest and weakest battleground in this war, its major terrain of engagement being in Iraq and Afghanistan and, beginning in July 2006, in Lebanon. At the time of writing, the West and Israel had not succeeded in winning or gaining the upper hand in even one of these conflicts. Nawaf Mousawi, chief of Hezbollah's foreign relations department, has reflected, "It may be that some day we will have to sit down across from our enemies and talk to them about a political settlement. That could happen ... But no political agreement will be possible until they respect us. I want them to know that when they're sitting there across from us that if they decide to get up and walk away, they'll have to pay a price" (Perry and Crooke 2006b). Perry and Crooke (2006c) relate Hamas's narration about a meeting they had held with Americans and Europeans in 2004:

The meeting had featured presentations by American and European scholars that emphasized that the West would enter a dialogue with political Islam only if three prior conditions were met – that Islamist groups renounce violence, recognize Israel, and disarm.

"We wondered, if we met those conditions, just exactly what there would be to talk about," a Hamas official said. The meeting became a lecture … [and] the Islamist delegates walked from the room.

Nonetheless, according to Perry and Crooke (ibid.) as well as our own research, DDR could be attained given the right conditions, beginning with integrating militias into the PSS and embedding the process within a framework of dignity, inclusion, and justice.

A Proposed Approach to Palestinian DDR

The DDR and spoilers literature point to several considerations when it comes to DDR programming. Although the immediate aims of such programming are to achieve security and stability, a broader approach needs to be taken towards understanding DDR. DDR does not exist in a vacuum. It is situated within a larger peacebuilding context that needs to be taken into account in order to design and ensure successful DDR programming. DDR is normally envisaged within a political context that seeks to address the causes of conflict. It (re)establishes the state's monopoly over the use of force. However, if the taking up of arms again is to be avoided, this must be balanced by the rule of law, respect for human rights, and security guarantees for both ex-combatants and civilians. Many analysts emphasize the need for sufficient economic incentives and socioeconomic reintegration support for ex-combatants. Some of them also highlight the requirement for adequate incentives for senior officers and the political and economic classes who benefit from the war economy and who may block moves to establish state budgetary transparency and security sector reform. To meet these broad-ranging needs, detailed peace agreements must be negotiated with provisions for institutionalized power-sharing, resource distribution, and sharing in coercive state powers (e.g., integration in police and military) as well as neutral monitoring and verification systems. A developmentalist approach must be taken to DDR that articulates it with more general economic and political reconstruction and reforms. In addition, in some contexts, such as Afghanistan and Palestine, consideration must be given to reordering the DDR sequence.

We believe that conditions in the Palestinian case allow for a DDR program even after the election of a Hamas government and despite the lack of a permanent Israeli-Palestinian agreement. This view has been strengthened with the formation of the Fateh-Hamas national unity government. Nonetheless, we fully recognize that one of the main reasons for the failure to implement a credible and comprehensive DDR program in the aftermath of the Oslo agreement was that discussion of all major issues to the conflict was deliberately postponed until the end of the peace process. This interim nature of the Oslo Agreement created incentives for both sides to give away as few "assets" as possible and to maintain and, indeed, strengthen their capacity to inflict pain and suffering on the other side. As a result, the Israelis gave the Palestinians much less land and jurisdiction than was called for in the agreement, while the Palestinians refused to abandon the right to resort to arms if negotiations failed. Progress made in Palestinian-Israeli final status negotiations in 2000-01 and Israel's withdrawal from the Gaza Strip as part of its policy of "disengaging" from Palestinian territory have helped to reduce the gap in Palestinian and Israeli expectations regarding the ultimate nature of the permanent settlement.

Another lesson of the past thirteen years of Palestinian-Israeli peacemaking has been the recognition that only a broad coalition of nationalists and Islamists, coexisting in an inclusive and democratic political system, is capable of sustaining successful peacebuilding. The agreement reached in June 2006 between Fateh and Hamas on a national conciliation document, which was originally drafted through an inclusive process of consultation among Palestinian prisoners in Israeli jails, provides a basis for a successful DDR effort. The formation of the current governmental coalition of Fateh and Hamas provides yet another opportunity for Palestinian factions to examine the potential for a comprehensive program of DDR. Steps should now be taken in three directions: (1) Hamas's inclusion into the PLO, (2) a more explicit commitment by Hamas to respect and observe agreements and international obligations made by the PLO, and (3) a comprehensive DDR program.

The DDR approach we propose has four elements. First, security sector reform and DDR cannot be seen in terms of counter-terrorism as viewed by the Quartet Road Map; instead, it should be envisaged as part of the larger question of Palestinian peacebuilding, with its two main components of peacemaking and state building. Therefore, DDR programming must first be embedded within a larger political framework that builds on the updated Cairo Declaration by providing for an internationally negotiated package of stabilization, including a long-term mutual ceasefire agreement ensuring the end of Palestinian violence and Israeli targeting of militants, a timetable for the release of prisoners, and a return to bilateral Palestinian-Israeli negotiations. Needless to say, this political framework should also build on the relevant parts of the Road Map that seek to stabilize Israeli-Palestinian relations, such as the commitment to the two-state solution, cessation of settlement activities and land confiscation, and the reopening of Palestinian public institutions in occupied East Jerusalem. This framework should also give assurances to Hamas and other armed factions that the domestic political system will remain inclusive and democratic and that all factions must be committed to periodic elections and to respecting the outcomes of those elections. The opportunity to influence public policy through political means must be guaranteed to all factions.

Second, DDR is not a technical solution. It requires serious and collective efforts at the legal, judicial, and security levels. A Palestinian DDR program should contain three basic supporting systems:

- a clear legal framework for the PSS and related issues that might arise from an implementation of the DDR program
- a functioning justice system that has credibility and acceptance from all factions
- meaningful security sector reform that would depoliticize the PSS and facilitate rather than complicate DDR program implementation.

Given the existing tension between the PA security services and their allies in the militias associated with Fateh, on the one hand, and Hamas's al-Qassam Brigades, on the other – and that tension has escalated greatly since Hamas's election victory – the institution of these supporting systems, particularly the depoliticization of the PSS, becomes critical for the success of a Palestinian DDR program. Similarly, PSS reform should ensure that the mission of the security services is stated first and foremost in terms of Palestinian state-building needs (i.e., the rule of law, protection of civil society, economic prosperity, etc.). While the mission is also expected to refer to the defence of the PA as one of its objectives, it is obvious that the goal of external defence will only become viable in the context of Palestinian sovereign statehood.

Third, our approach reorders the sequence of DDR. Any attempt to start by disarming the militias is likely to be met by the forcible objection of most of them; instead, it should start with the integration of all armed groups into the security services. We estimate that the total number of those subject to integration is likely to reach thirty thousand, including those already "inserted" during the second half of 2005. Once integrated, the collection of arms and ending arms production could proceed. The decommissioning of armed men could take place in two phases: those who agree to immediate decommissioning could be helped to find jobs and to socially integrate if required. However, most of the armed men integrated into the security services would have to be decommissioned over a long period of time, perhaps three to five years, as part of a larger socioeconomic and developmental plan. Integration alone provides little law and order, as demonstrated by the first PA attempt to integrate armed men into the security services during the second half of 2005. To avoid a repeat of this experience, a future Palestinian integration plan must be part of the larger political process that reduces incentives to keep or return to arms, and it must be accompanied by socioeconomic development beyond a purely job creation scheme.

This is not an unprecedented approach. Other countries have integrated armed non-state groups into national security forces as part of a larger DDR process, as in post-apartheid South Africa and post-1980 Zimbabwe and Ethiopia (Rupiah 1995; Berdal 1996, 52; Lodgaard 1997, 143; Babiker and Özerdem 2003, 218-19). Nonetheless, this can be an expensive approach – one fraught with challenges having to do with command and control, harmonizing doctrines, demilitarizing public security, and so on – but it also goes to the heart of political power-sharing and the security dilemma faced by opposing armed groups. Thus, its long-term costs may be lower than the social and political costs ultimately incurred by quick and incomplete DDR (Kingma 1997, 154).

Fourth, the integration of armed factions should be comprehensive (viewed as socioeconomic, not merely military) and long term, taking several years to fully implement. Different analysts offer various ways of articulating successful socioeconomic DDR approaches. Realistic needs assessments and local market (including labour market) assessments should be conducted to identify aspirations and capabilities of ex-combatants and potential matches with the local socioeconomy (Berdal 1996, 45). More important, ex-combatants and their communities should be involved in the design and implementation of reintegration programs (49-50). In particular, this approach would positively enhance ex-combatants' embeddedness in their communities and the whole community's investment in DDR and post-conflict reconstruction as well as promote a developmentalist approach to DDR (Muggah 2005, 245). In the Palestinian case, it will be particularly important to help members of armed groups find study spaces in schools and universities, to provide compensation to armed groups for rifles and other pieces of military hardware given up as part of the program, to convert military workshops (used by armed groups to manufacture arms and explosives) into civilian uses, to gradually decommission former members of the armed groups based on job opportunities, and so on. Without assurances of long-term sustainable economic development – obtainable only in the context of a permanent peace agreement – it is doubtful that a DDR program would be sufficient to permanently end the violence in domestic Palestinian politics or in Israeli-Palestinian relations.

Palestinians may find a close parallel with Afghanistan when considering their own case. Like Palestine, Afghanistan is fractured along regional, cultural, and ideological lines. Warlordism has found fertile ground, allegiances to formal command structures are fluid and subject to other competing identities, the central government is weak, and armed conflict is ongoing (Özerdem 2002; ICG 2003, 1-3, 5; ICG 2004d). Many combatants are "part-time" in both contexts and fully integrated into their communities. While

DDR is usually premised on negotiated peace agreements, no such thing exists in either Afghanistan or Palestine, where the Bonn Agreement was not a negotiated peace settlement, the Oslo Accords never contained DDR provisions in the first instance,[25] and the Oslo process has now collapsed. The Bonn Agreement does state that armed groups should be integrated into the national army, according to national security needs. Both contexts are those in which armed conflict still shapes local and national life, where Afghanistan is occupied by NATO troops and Palestine remains occupied by Israel. Yet DDR needs to be undertaken in both contexts for reasons of public security, and, if success is to have any chance, it will need to begin with reintegration, including into the respective security forces,[26] and a long-term commitment to inclusive, community-led, and comprehensive socio-economic development.

Our argument rests, in part, on linking Palestinian DDR to the larger Israeli-Palestinian peace process. It also rests on the belief that, the more inclusive and consultative the internal process, the greater the chances for a successful Palestinian DDR. However, the way Israel and the US-led international community have responded to the electoral victory of Hamas and the formation of the national unity government raises doubts about this optimistic assessment. Indeed, the US and Israeli policy of political isolation and financial sanctions that seeks to strangle or bypass the Hamas government could lead to the collapse of the PA and internal strife. This policy intensified Fateh-Hamas rivalry and led to a greater arms race in the Palestinian territories before the unity government was finally struck. As the international community continues to grapple unsuccessfully with Palestinian-Israeli peacemaking and peacebuilding, it becomes more apparent than ever that, given the nature of the international system in the post-9/11 environment, it might not be possible to reconcile the short-term needs of peacemaking with the long-term expectation of sustainable peacebuilding.

11
Conclusion

Stephen Baranyi and Kristiana Powell

.

Peacebuilding requires national ownership, and must be home-grown. Outsiders, no matter how well-intentioned, cannot substitute for the knowledge and the will of the people of the country concerned. It is the latter who best know their own history, culture and political contexts. It is they who will live with the consequences of the decisions taken. And it is they who must feel that peacebuilding is their achievement, if it is to have any hope of lasting.

– UN Secretary-General Kofi Annan, June 2006

Every day, as the What Kind of Peace Is Possible? (WKOP) project drew to a close in 2006, television viewers could see dramatic images of failed or failing peacebuilding efforts across the world. Newspaper headlines were equally disturbing:

Iraq's killing fields

Afghan MPs face massacre claim

When the UN left East Timor violence broke out ...

Israel attacks office of Palestinian Prime Minister.[1]

Naturally, the media focus on crises, but research confirms that there are deeply worrisome trends in contemporary peacebuilding. One of these is the oft-quoted statistic that 50 percent of post-conflict situations now relapse into armed conflict after five years (Annan 2005). The other is equally disturbing, though less mentioned in polite conversation. It is the shift, especially since 11 September 2001, away from peacebuilding based on negotiated processes and towards military-driven stabilization operations.

Research also reminds us that there is good news out there, even if it seldom makes the headlines. Peacebuilding has been relatively successful in some countries. Mozambicans celebrated the tenth anniversary of their peace accords in 2002. In December 2006, Guatemalans celebrated the tenth anniversary of their final peace accord. Citizens in both countries have cause to celebrate the fact that war ended over a decade ago.

Why have certain peacebuilding efforts been somewhat successful? Why have others been mixed, while some have been dramatic failures? What do contemporary trends mean for the possibility of sustainable peace, particularly since 9/11? What can be done to stretch the limits of the possible, despite contemporary constraints?

This chapter addresses these questions by returning to the propositions presented in Chapter 1 and reformulating them as conclusions based on the final case studies. We begin by sketching the shift from negotiated multilateral peacebuilding in the early 1990s to stabilization operations even before September 2001. We then offer some considerations for assessing peacebuilding efforts at different points in time. This provides a basis for synthesizing conclusions on multidimensional peacebuilding in Guatemala and Mozambique, and in the Palestinian territories until 2001. We also synthesize conclusions about more robust peacebuilding and stabilization operations in Haiti and Afghanistan as well as in the Palestinian territories since 2001. Then we revisit three major challenges of postwar peacebuilding: democratic governance; economic development; and the disarmament, demobilization, and reintegration of ex-combatants. In each instance, we focus on peacebuilding at the national and local levels, with a particular concern for national agency and political inclusion.

In late 2005, the international community decided to establish the UN Peacebuilding Commission, Support Office, and Fund to coordinate selected peacebuilding efforts over time. The commission's mandate is to:

- propose integrated strategies for post-conflict peacebuilding and recovery
- help to ensure predictable financing for early recovery activities and sustained financial investment over the medium- to longer-term
- extend the period of attention by the international community to post-conflict recovery
- develop best practices on issues that require extensive collaboration among political, military, humanitarian, and development actors.[2]

This mandate reflects some WKOP insights and other learning processes. Through our governments and through the Global Partnership on the Prevention of Armed Conflict (GPPAC), WKOP partners fed our conclusions into debates on the UN Peacebuilding Commission in 2004-5. The partnership's final statement in July 2005 underscored the importance of national ownership, long-term international engagement linking post-conflict recovery to sustainable peacebuilding, and the importance of involving civil society in peacebuilding at several levels (GPPAC 2005). It is encouraging to see how certain governments, the UN, and other bodies have taken some of these recommendations on board.

Most of those involved in establishing the Peacebuilding Commission recognize that putting these ideas into practice will be difficult. Some also acknowledge that long-standing challenges have been compounded by post-9/11 shifts from negotiated peacebuilding to more unilateral stabilization operations. This underlines the importance of the commission's mandate to foster learning about best (and worst) peacebuilding practices. We hope that the WKOP studies will feed into such learning processes.

From Negotiated Peacebuilding to Stabilization Operations

In the introductory chapter, we suggest that there has been a major shift from multidimensional peacebuilding in the early 1990s to more robust peacebuilding in the late 1990s and stabilization operations post-9/11. Second-generation, or multidimensional, peacebuilding is characterized by a sequenced approach to peace negotiations, followed by verification operations that lay foundations for complex peacebuilding efforts – typically under the aegis of multilateral organizations like the United Nations. Third-generation, or robust peacebuilding, often follows military, or "peace enforcement," operations, based on fairly legitimate multilateral mandates, which evolve into peacebuilding efforts. What we term "fourth-generation peacebuilding" operations in the introductory chapter are more accurately called "stabilization operations" by their managers. These often start with international military interventions that enjoy less multilateral and host country support and, therefore, end up combining war-fighting and "peacebuilding." We can now conclude that "peacebuilding" is a misnomer for stabilization operations.

The WKOP project reminds us of Max Weber's insight that ideal types are useful but that reality is messier than they would indicate. Clearly, the 1994 intervention in Haiti was a third-generation operation before that term was even coined. Similarly, the Oslo peace process in Israel and Palestine was crafted as a second-generation effort but did not benefit from many instruments available in other contexts at the time, such as on-site international verification. Shortly after that process collapsed with the second intifada, the Israeli state backed away from peacebuilding and attempted to impose stability through force. The experience of Sri Lanka also reminds us that stabilization operations existed before 2001 (e.g., the Indian peacekeeping force in the 1980s).

Despite these nuances, this chapter uses the image of a movement from negotiated peacebuilding to more robust peacebuilding to stabilization operations to illustrate a major trend over the past fifteen years. We also use this metaphor to juxtapose different approaches to peacebuilding, their consequences, and the possibilities or constraints embedded in contemporary trends. As such, we can reformulate this image as a first conclusion from the WKOP project:

1   Since 1989 there has been a movement from second-generation peace-building efforts, based on negotiations and overseen by multilateral verification, to more robust third-generation efforts in the late 1990s, to the emergence of more unilateral stabilization operations post-9/11. These ideal types shade into and overlap with each other.

Assessing Peacebuilding Efforts

In the introductory chapter, we argue that, over the past decade, there has been an unproductive dialogue of the deaf between minimalist and maximalist analysts of peacebuilding. Minimalists like Stephen Stedman and William Durch insist on the primary importance of assessing peacebuilding efforts according to whether they have ended wars and have led to several free and fair elections. Maximalists like Alejandro Bendaña and Rita Manchanda insist that such measures are insufficient and can even be counterproductive if they do not lead to the more profound institutional and structural changes required to consolidate peace and to prevent the re-emergence of armed conflict.

The case studies in this book confirm the validity of assessing short- and medium-term peacebuilding outcomes based on minimalist benchmarks. Clearly, ending long-lasting wars and holding relatively free elections have been enormous achievements in Guatemala and Mozambique. In contrast, Afghans, Israelis, and Palestinians, as well as Sri Lankans, are well placed to know just how valuable even "negative peace" can be.

The studies in this book also confirm the importance of implementing peace agreements over the long run and of assessing that implementation from the standpoint of its sustainability. They confirm the importance of tracking peace implementation beyond the departure of UN blue helmets in order to see whether commitments that stakeholders deemed essential for conflict resolution have been put into practice. They suggest that, while it is unrealistic to assess peacebuilding in the first years according to whether all major reforms have been implemented, it is fair to use more ambitious benchmarks over a five-to-twenty-five-year period. They confirm that it is possible to assess steps taken in the first years according to whether they are laying foundations for more profound changes over the long run. The issue is not whether minimalist or maximalist benchmarks are more valid. Both are important and should be used in sequence to understand the accomplishments and challenges of sustainable peacebuilding over the short, medium, and long term.

Finally, the case studies show how the analysis of sustainability can and should look beyond major urban centres, by canvassing the views of local authorities, the poor, rural women, indigenous peoples, and ex-combatants – persons whose perspectives are rarely central to assessments of peacebuilding. In sum:

2   It is fair to assess postwar peacebuilding efforts in the first five years primarily according to whether they have helped end wars. Yet it is important to assess peacebuilding efforts over periods of five to twenty-five years according to whether they are addressing the causes of conflict and are leading to sustainable peace. It is also essential to assess the impacts of peacebuilding beyond major cities and from the viewpoint of historically excluded populations such as women, the poor, and indigenous peoples.

Let us apply this logic to the second-generation peacebuilding efforts examined in the case studies: Guatemala, Mozambique, and the Palestinian territories from 1993 to 2001.

Multidimensional Peacebuilding

Despite their enormous differences, peacebuilding efforts in Guatemala and Mozambique have been quintessential second-generation efforts. In Mozambique, peacebuilding took root in a context in which the socialist FRELIMO government had already initiated market-oriented economic reforms out of necessity, and where the RENAMO guerrilla movement's publicly stated demand was the institutionalization of liberal democracy. In Guatemala, the civilian governments that emerged from the military-controlled democratic opening espoused programs combining market-oriented economic policies with social reforms and the consolidation of liberal democracy, while the URNG guerrillas advocated more equity-oriented economic, social, political, and cultural reforms. This was in a context in which indigenous peoples, comprising about 50 percent of the population, had historically been excluded from welfare and power. Yet, despite these contrasting starting points, both countries ended their long-standing wars through internationally assisted negotiations leading to comprehensive peace agreements, multi-functional UN peacekeeping and verification, as well as major security, economic, and other reforms partially financed and otherwise supported by the international community.

In their case studies, Eduardo Sitoe and Carolina Hunguana (Mozambique, Chapter 3) and Gabriel Aguilera (Guatemala, Chapter 2) argue that these efforts have been quite successful, perhaps even more than our concept of "relative success" suggests. The fairly definitive termination of long and socially devastating armed conflicts; the disarmament, demobilization, and reintegration of thousands of official and irregular ex-combatants; the repatriation and resettlement of hundreds of thousands of refugees and internally displaced persons; the legalization of banned opposition parties and the celebration of several free and fair elections; the establishment of new public institutions (such as the Indigenous Women's Secretariat in Guatemala) – all these were huge steps towards peace in both countries. The authors credit a confluence of national and international factors for these historic achievements: from the end of the Cold War and a strengthening of reformist elements within each country's political and economic elites, to the persistent, multidimensional engagement of the UN and other international agencies.

Yet, in both cases, the authors cogently argue that the glass is half full and fragile. Indeed, the move towards liberal democracy, as a mechanism for the peaceful management of differences, remains limited by the determination of current political elites to maintain their grip on the levers of power. In Mozambique, this is manifested in FRELIMO's preference for administrative deconcentration over democratic decentralization. The move towards more sustainable peace also remains stunted by the opposition of economic elites to deeper reforms, such as the tax and land reforms codified in the Guatemalan Accords. The enduring weakness of opposition parties and of civil society organizations representing historically excluded populations, and the persistent difficulties of forging coalitions linking the efforts of reformists in parliament, the state, the private sector, and civil society, also remain an obstacle to the consolidation of more sustainable peace. The wave of postwar criminal violence, particularly in Guatemala, reflects the fragility of peace and further undermines that ultimate goal.

The authors conclude that, notwithstanding these limitations and difficulties, in both countries the normative and political foundations have been laid for deeper reforms that could lead to more sustainable peacebuilding. It is up to networks of reformists traversing the state, the private sector, and civil society, nationally and locally, to generate a greater buy-in for more inclusive, equity-oriented reforms. And it is up to the international community to continue supporting those efforts to help consolidate peace over the long run instead of rushing off to the next "crisis state." In this connection, it is worth recalling Kenneth Bush's (2004, 24) deceptively simple but profound insight that "peacebuilding takes a long, long time." The experiences of Guatemala and Mozambique suggest that peacebuilding requires both time and depth and that, without deeper changes, sustainability will be a cruel mirage – always on the horizon but never reached in time.

As explained in the case study by Khalil Shikaki (Chapter 5), in Palestine the Oslo Accords also laid the foundations for a second-generation peace-building and state-building effort. Major changes were registered in the first years: the withdrawal of Israeli military forces from parts of the occupied territories and the decrease of violence on both sides, the establishment of the Palestinian Authority and Legislative Council (and elections for the latter), the reactivation of the Palestinian economy. Yet, by 2000, several factors converged to destroy this limited peace. These included the inability to negotiate a final status agreement as promised in Oslo, the lack of on-site international verification, the authoritarianism of PLO leaders, their acquiescence to repression against Islamic and other militants in the name of "security," the election of a right-wing government in Israel, and US support for its positions. In the context of the second intifada, the government of Ariel Sharon backed away from the Oslo process, reoccupied the West Bank, and attempted to impose a military solution.

We return to this approach and its recent variants in the section on third- and fourth-generation operations. For now, let us simply conclude with two points. First, though the Oslo peace process led to significant advances in the areas of peace and state building, the inability to secure more profound agreements and reforms – for example, on a reversal of Israeli settlements from the occupied territories or the opening of Palestinian politics to Islamic and other armed movements – fostered an environment in which Prime Minister Sharon's visit to the Temple Mount triggered the al-Aqsa intifada. Second, the political coalitions that underpinned the Oslo Accords were insufficient to move the process towards more permanent, balanced, and inclusive peace agreements. It is hardly surprising that peace could not be sustained under those conditions.

As discussed at the WKOP international conference in 2005, Middle East peace processes also highlight the trade-offs between negotiating interim agreements between a few parties and investing in more consultative but lengthy peace talks. Closed peace processes can be negotiated quickly and may help bring an immediate end to violence. Yet, the risk of negotiating quick, minimalist agreements is that they often generate spoilers because they put critical issues for sustainable peacebuilding aside. More broadly consultative processes may help ensure that peace agreements take into account diverse concerns and set up mechanisms for addressing the root causes of conflict (Powell and Baranyi 2006).

These dynamics highlight the complexities of nurturing national actors that are genuinely committed to durable peace throughout the negotiation and peacebuilding processes. The process of selection is an inherently political one. Who decides which local or national agents of change should be supported? Who decides which and whose demands are legitimate and which are not? What can actors who accompany negotiation and peacebuilding processes do in situations in which different groups have equally legitimate yet contradictory claims? Who adjudicates (and how) between these competing claims? These challenges are manifested in many sectors from truth and justice to land and economic development. They underscore the need to build institutions that are capable of peacefully mediating competing claims in any society.

This rereading of relative success in Guatemala and Mozambique, and of failure in Israel and Palestine, confirms and enriches the propositions about second-generation peacebuilding advanced in the introductory chapter. The relevant propositions can be restated as additional conclusions from the comparative synthesis:

3   Multidimensional peacebuilding has contributed much to ending wars since 1989, due to a convergence of domestic stakeholders' interests with those of major international actors. Multidimensional peacebuilding offers an enabling framework for transnational coalitions – or "peace infrastructures," in John Paul Lederach's words – linking agents of change from the local to the international levels through negotiated processes. Nurturing broad coalitions from the negotiations stage onward can be crucial for long-term sustainability.

4   Yet, even such efforts have rarely secured the deeper reforms required to sustain peace beyond the initial decade. It has been difficult to forge the transnational coalitions required to underpin more profound changes – such as deepening democratic practices at the local level – over the long term. In Guatemala and Mozambique, the foundations may have been laid for national actors to secure deeper reforms and to attain sustainability over the long run. In Israel and Palestine, changes fell far short of stakeholders' expectations, peace collapsed, and violence escalated with a vengeance.

5   That being so, stakeholders could invest much more to build domestic and transnational coalitions in order to deliver the reforms required to sustain peace over the long run. A negotiated, comprehensive approach to peacebuilding, including a substantial international verification presence on the ground, appears crucial to the emergence of such coalitions for sustainable peace.

Robust Peacebuilding and Stabilization Operations

Haiti has the dubious distinction of having experienced two international interventions since the end of the Cold War, in 1994 and again in 2004. The first aimed to restore President Jean-Bertrand Aristide to power and was conducted on the basis of solid mandates from the UN and the Organization of American States (OAS). The second aimed to seal his removal from power and stabilize the situation in Haiti and was initially based on dubious normative foundations. The first intervention enables us to look at the outcomes of a third-generation intervention over the time frame of ten years, while the second enables us to understand how even an initially problematic stabilization operation can be turned around through a more inclusive approach.

As explained in the case study by Hérard Jadotte and Yves-François Pierre (Chapter 4), the return of constitutionally elected president Aristide in 1994, on the heels of the UN- and OAS-mandated international intervention, generated enormous expectations of change in Haiti. The Lavalas government initially cooperated with the international community to disband the army and to create a new national police, to implement far-reaching market-oriented economic reforms, to extend basic social services to the poor, to open the political system to popular participation, and to bring the majority language, Creole, into public discourse.

Yet, within a year, the relationship between the government and the international community had deteriorated dramatically. According to Jadotte and Pierre, this was due to the convergence of two trends: first, the inability or unwillingness of the government to nurture truly democratic electoral processes in 1995 and 1997; second, disagreements over the structural adjustment program negotiated with the IMF. Though the adjustment program initially stabilized the economy in aggregate terms, it generated huge dislocations in public-sector and agricultural employment, endangering Lavalas' electoral base. Disagreements over economic policies and turmoil over the elections led the international community to decrease its assistance, further aggravating the crisis. Most parties boycotted the elections in 2000, which Lavalas won with landslide majorities. Several civil society coalitions advocated a peaceful way out of the crisis, but, in early 2004, in a context of increased political violence, former army personnel reorganized, with US assistance, and moved towards the capital.

We will return to the ensuing international intervention in a moment. The key for now is to understand how this first intervention presaged two problems that third- and, especially, fourth-generation interventions would encounter later on. First, Haiti showed that it is extremely difficult to build democratic institutions and habits once you have installed political leaders through international military intervention.[3] Second, it showed that the attempt to build democracy and peace could be undermined by economic reforms that generate dislocation in the short run. As noted in the introductory chapter, at the same time, in the mid-1990s, UN officials, who had experienced a similar contradiction in El Salvador, challenged the IMF and World Bank on their orthodox approach to structural adjustment in war-affected economies. Haiti was unable to benefit from those insights in the 1990s due to the escalation of internal and external conflicts.

Yet, Haiti and the international community did apply some lessons the second time around. Though the military intervention that began in February 2004 led to the installation of a transitional government of dubious legitimacy, the international community and the transitional authorities cooperated to lay foundations for democratic change. Former army personnel who led the uprising against President Aristide were not brought into the transitional government. The promised national dialogue did not materialize, and violence escalated in the poorest areas of Port-au-Prince, with the involvement of national police and UN forces. Yet, despite these mixed beginnings, the elections in 2006 were free and fair. The international community and most political parties recognized the victory of Lespwa candidate René Préval in the first round of the presidential elections, despite initial confusion over the count and despite Lespwa's links to the Parti Lavalas. When Lespwa did not win a majority in either chamber of the National Assembly, it and other political parties committed themselves to work together to ensure legislative progress and to consolidate democracy.

An innovative approach to "adjustment for peace" was also applied in the domain of economic and social policy. The Cadre de coopération intérimaire (CCI), which provided the framework for economic recovery during the transitional period, clearly moved beyond earlier orthodoxies. Indeed, it combined measures to stabilize prices and restore a balance in public finances with measures to address urgent needs in urban and rural areas, steps to rebuild infrastructure as well as public-sector capacities in areas like health, education and public security. The international community put huge resources behind the implementation of the CCI. Although the CCI could not meet pent-up demands for an immediate improvement in Haitians' conditions, its utility was confirmed by President Préval's request that it be extended to late 2007 to allow his government to prepare a poverty-reduction strategy on the basis of wide consultation.

This still leaves huge challenges for Haiti in the areas of economic and democratic development, especially at the local level. It is also too early to pass definitive judgment on the results of the 2004 intervention or the 2006 elections. Yet, in contrast to the outcome after 1994, developments since March 2004 suggest that it is possible for committed national leaders and the international community to open the door to sustainable peacebuilding even on the heels of a stabilization operation. Taking the time needed to organize free and fair elections, respecting the outcomes of those elections and fostering cooperation among political parties, jointly formulating policies that revive markets while renewing public-sector capacity and focusing on poverty reduction – all seem crucial to the relatively positive outcomes of the 2004 intervention to date.

Yet, Haiti may be the exception to post-9/11 trends. Developments in Afghanistan seem more symptomatic of current stabilization operations. As explained by Omar Zakhilwal and Jane Thomas (Chapter 6), the October 2001 military intervention in Afghanistan certainly opened the door to many positive changes. These include the widely consulted formulation of a new constitution, relatively free and fair elections, repatriating over 3 million refugees, major rural development initiatives like the National Solidarity Program, the recognition of women's rights in areas like education, building a new national army, police forces, and judiciary, and so on. The decision by the UN to adopt a "light footprint" in Afghanistan, in partnership with reformers such as President Hamid Karzai, have been at the root of the positive outcomes they have achieved together.

Nonetheless, Zakhilwal and Thomas show how the NSP has been undermined by hasty design, underfunding, and poor implementation. In his chapter on DDR in Afghanistan (Chapter 9), Arne Strand confirms that similar problems have hampered demobilization efforts. Strand also argues that coalitions formed during the US-led invasion and refashioned under Operation Enduring Freedom have entrenched the power of elites that do not share the aims of consolidating liberal democracy. The inability or unwillingness of OEF commanders to support serious negotiations with Taliban leaders, and the way some of their forces have conducted themselves in the field, have alienated parts of the population and fuelled warfare. The eruption of violence in Kabul in May 2006, in response to excessive use of force by US troops, was almost bound to happen in that context.

Despite profound differences, what Afghanistan and Palestine have in common post-9/11 is the failure of regime change and stabilization underpinned by military occupation. Soon after Israel reoccupied most of the Palestinian territories in 2002, the Bush administration signalled its intent to remove president Yasir Arafat, and it allowed Israel to crush Islamic and other militants by force. That approach failed to achieve its aims, but, as explained by Shikaki, the death of Arafat and the change of leadership in the PLO converged with demands to hold free and fair legislative elections in January 2006. Shikaki convincingly argues that Hamas' electoral victory opened the door to its incorporation into peaceful politics since Hamas had already taken major steps towards this goal. Yet by rejecting the results of those elections – officially to press Hamas to renounce violence and accept the Oslo Accords, including recognizing Israel's existence – the United States, the European Union, and their allies made it extremely difficult to advance towards democratic politics in Palestine and serious peace negotiations with

Hamas. The full implications of the West's rejection of election results in Palestine are addressed in more detail in the section on democratization and decentralization.

This comparison between stabilization operations in Haiti, Afghanistan, and the Palestinian territories enables us to enrich the propositions advanced at the outset of the WKOP project. We can now conclude the following:

6   Though robust peacebuilding and stabilization operations appear to give the international community more room to reshape institutions as they see fit, from the standpoint of sustainable peacebuilding, those efforts tend to be much less effective than do second-generation operations. This is partly due to the contradictory international motives that tend to drive such operations. It is also due to the many problematic national and local partners that the international community tends to cultivate in situations in which key stakeholders are excluded by warfare or by limited negotiations.

7   Even in such situations, peacebuilding can move towards a more solid footing by engaging a broader range of stakeholders, including leaders of groups that have been excluded from transitional arrangements. Addressing these groups' legitimate – though sometimes conflicting – political, socioeconomic, or cultural demands through innovative re-forms could help reposition peacebuilding efforts. Movement towards the use of force as a last resort, based on the rule of law, is also necessary to recover ground lost during deeply contested interventions.

Democratization and Decentralization

In the first half of this chapter, we reviewed the overall record of selected multidimensional and robust peacebuilding efforts as well as of several stabilization operations. We now look at their track record in three areas: democratization, economic development, and DDR. We pay particular attention to local realities as a hard test against which to examine the sustainability of peacebuilding in these areas.

Earlier we summarized our Guatemalan and Mozambican partners' views that the extension of liberal democratic norms and institutions has been central to peacebuilding in their countries. In Guatemala, this trend converged with a revival of decentralization efforts in the 1970s and 1980s, which had established a network of urban and rural development councils that were supposed to link structures for multi-stakeholder participation from communities and municipalities to departments, regions, and, finally, to the national level. In 2002, Congress passed three new laws updating the normative framework for the councils, municipal affairs, and decentralization. The new peace implementation strategy launched in 2005 gave the councils the additional responsibility of promoting compliance with the peace accords from the local to the national level. However, the research conducted by Aguilera and his colleagues shows that, in practice, several structures contemplated in the new legislation have not yet been established; the councils tend to focus on infrastructure projects and provide little space for policy debate (they hardly touch on issues of peace implementation); and the decision-making power of women, indigenous people, and other civil society representatives remains limited.

In Mozambique, decentralization and democratization were conceived as mutually reinforcing dimensions of peacebuilding when the first decentralization bill was tabled in 1994. However, as Sitoe and Hunguana explain in Chapter 3, disagreements between the government and the RENAMO opposition – on the timing and scope of decentralization – blocked the adoption of this law. Over the following years, FRELIMO managed to secure the adoption of new laws that codified the quite different strategy of gradual administrative deconcentration. Within that framework, twenty-three cities and ten district towns, out of a possible 128 major municipalities, have been accorded municipal status and endowed with democratic processes. In municipalities in which RENAMO has been elected to office, FRELIMO has taken steps to ensure that its appointed governors hold the reins of power at the district level. Nonetheless, in Mozambique, as in Guatemala, the authors conclude that democracy and peacebuilding could be extended further at the local level if parts of the central government, municipal authorities, key civil society organizations, and donors work together to promote genuine democratic decentralization.

Democratization has also been central to peacebuilding in Afghanistan, Haiti, and the Palestinian territories, yet, as noted earlier, the outcomes to date have been mixed. So have the outcomes of each society's experiments with local democracy. In Afghanistan the National Solidarity Program has been a vehicle for extending democratic participation to communities across the country. By 2006, ten thousand villages had elected community development councils to design and administer NSP projects. In theory, these councils should lay foundations for local democracy and peacebuilding. Yet Zakhilwal and Thomas' research suggests that many CDCs tend to reproduce traditional power relations and do little to extend decision-making power to groups like women and the poor. This reflects a trend observed by Strand on DDR issues – namely, powerful local and regional military leaders tend to reinvent themselves as democratic leaders through nominally free and fair electoral processes.

In Haiti, the 1987 Constitution codified the architecture of a new democratic order. It envisaged decentralizing democracy through elected councils and assemblies running from the local level to the national level. Yet, the 1987 Constitution remained *une lettre morte* due to the protracted crisis of governance. Moreover, Jadotte and Pierre's research suggests that, while some local development projects initiated in recent decades did promote democratic participation, few linked into structures of municipal governance and none connected with broader peacebuilding efforts (partly because that process had ground to a halt).

In the Palestinian territories, the establishment of the Palestinian Authority was supposed to proceed in tandem with a strengthening of elected local councils and other municipal institutions. Yet, in reality, the research conducted by Shikaki and his colleagues shows that the PLO's practice of appointing local councils and controlling their finances undermined the councils' legitimacy and effectiveness. The phased local elections that began in December 2004 hold the promise of transforming municipal institutions into spaces for democratic participation, the inclusion of women and of Islamists in peaceful politics, and, therefore, for peacebuilding. Yet, as the Palestinian study concludes, the PLO's decision to delay the last local elections after a string of Hamas' victories and the West's reluctance to accept Hamas' victory in the January 2006 legislative elections could close the door to an experiment in democratization and peacebuilding from below.

Although Sri Lanka has not yet experienced a major peacebuilding effort, its peace process provides a novel prism through which to view the possibilities and constraints of contemporary peacebuilding. In the area of governance, Jayadeva Uyangoda (Chapter 7) shows how, despite Sri Lanka's liberal democratic credentials and the steps taken towards administrative devolution in the late 1980s, the inability of key parties to creatively address the question of state power has undermined the peace process since 2002 and, more recently, generated renewed violence. In contrast to this situation, Uyangoda sketches the contours of a possible solution based on three pillars: a recognition of the LTTE-controlled state in the north and east through federal arrangements providing more autonomy for those provinces, the entrenchment of minority rights and democratic institutions there, and real respect for minority rights in the rest of the country.

Grappling with the difficulties of getting from here to there, Uyangoda suggests that Sinhalese political parties and Buddhist leaders could mobilize their social bases behind a new dispensation rather than playing the ethnic card merely to win elections. The LTTE could recognize that it will not secure the support it requires in the north and east (and beyond) until it accepts ethnic and political diversity in areas under its control. Civil society organizations could intensify their pressure to gain access to the peace talks. Once there, they could press for deeper transformation. The international community could support such changes by promoting the negotiated construction of a uniquely Sri Lankan brand of democratic federalism as a vehicle for conflict transformation.

This is perhaps what should happen, but its low probability underscores the paradoxical links between democracy and peacebuilding. The demand for democratic governance, the protection of minority rights and of broader human rights, are central demands by key parties in the south, north, and east of Sri Lanka. Not surprisingly, given its tradition of militarized governance and totalizing nationalism, the LTTE is unsympathetic to this discourse. Yet, liberal democracy has not always been favourable to peace either. It is majoritarian democracy, and its discriminatory consequences in the postcolonial period, that underpinned violence and war in the first place. More recently, an elected president dismissed an elected UNF government in 2004 on the grounds that its concessions to the LTTE threatened national unity. The electorate then voted in a government that further backed away from the peace process. The Tamil Tigers' tactics and the War on Terror have complicated these dynamics and further justified the isolation of the LTTE.

The complicated relationships between democracy, peacemaking, and peacebuilding in Sri Lanka pose enormous challenges for stakeholders. How can international and other actors strike the right balance between supporting the outcomes of democratic processes while counteracting the undemocratic tendencies of the governments these processes sometimes bring to power? How can international and other actors forge constructive relationships with democratically elected governments that may not fully support peace processes, while engaging with social forces that are more committed to durable peace?

Similar tensions between democracy and peacebuilding have appeared in the other countries. As WKOP advisor Rubén Zamora noted at the Vilankulo international conference in 2005, these experiences underscore the paradoxes of combining liberal democracy with peacebuilding, despite the apparent necessity of doing so. This tendency has been refracted by the post-9/11 War on Terror and its emphasis on tolerating less-than-perfect democratic practices by friendly governments, excluding from peaceful politics those movements that use political violence, and pushing for regime change in states that have fallen out of favour.

Before looking at how similar paradoxes play out in the realm of economic development, let us summarize some conclusions on the dilemmas of democracy and peacebuilding:

8   Democracy is seen by many, in the north and in the south, as essential for peacebuilding. Broader inclusion and the institutionalization of conflict management mechanisms from the local to the national level seem central to the sustainable transformation of conflicts. Other entry points for democratic development in postwar contexts include: fostering national

legal and institutional reforms, strengthening governments' capacities for participatory policy making, and building the capacities of historically excluded stakeholders to influence policy processes.

9 Yet, democratic processes have been limited in many postwar contexts. They have sometimes led to the election of governments or parliaments that have blocked peace implementation. At other times they have generated governments that have been rejected by major powers. In general, increases in participation – for example, by women, the poor, and historically excluded ethnic minorities or majorities – have not led to major increases in these groups' influence on decision making, even locally.

10 Even relative successes like those in Guatemala and Mozambique have not been immune to these tendencies. Yet, these limitations are more pronounced in robust peacebuilding and stabilization operations such as in Afghanistan or in the Palestinian territories, where post-9/11 local-to-global power alignments trump democratization and peacebuilding.

Economic Aspects of Peacebuilding

Several studies in this book confirm that there have been successes and much innovation in the domain of economic policies for peacebuilding since the early 1990s. Mozambique has experienced consistent rates of economic growth, averaging 8 percent per year since the mid-1990s. Guatemala's growth has been less impressive, averaging just over 3 percent per year during the same period. Yet, its peace accords were perhaps the first to codify the idea of "adjustment for peace," with provisions in areas like tax increases, shifts in public spending, and the resolution of land claims to ensure that economic policies served peacebuilding instead of pulling the other way.

In Mozambique, stakeholders negotiated a new poverty reduction strategy paper that places an even stronger emphasis on the reduction of poverty and regional imbalances through rural development and local development at the district level. In Haiti, the Cadre de coopération intérimaire struck a balance between reviving markets and infrastructure and developing public-sector regulation and service delivery capacities in key areas like education, health, and public security. There has also been considerable innovation in Afghanistan, for example, the initiation of participatory rural development through the National Solidarity Program.

These are all significant achievements. They confirm that there has been much learning at the policy level in many quarters, including some international financial institutions and Southern governments, as well as some business and civil society actors. Yet the case studies also highlight enduring and disturbing gaps between policy and practice.

In Afghanistan, Zakhilwal and Thomas (Chapter 6) note that the National Solidarity Program has reached over ten thousand villages; however, they also note that many projects were badly designed, do not reflect the needs of marginalized groups such as women, are disconnected from larger national development initiatives, and are often unsustainable, financially and otherwise. These weaknesses are due to hasty planning driven by the schedules of international agencies, short-term international financing, the excessive use of foreign executing agencies, capture by local elites, and limited capacities for participatory rural development among Afghan governmental and non-governmental agencies. The authors suggest that this situation can be turned around on the basis of the Afghanistan National Development Strategy, which was adopted in 2006. Yet, it seems far from clear that key national and international actors will be able to do this, particularly given the steady resurgence of violence in recent years.

In Guatemala, Aguilera (Chapter 2) shows how certain business elites worked with their allies in conservative political parties and the media to block fiscal reforms that could have laid the financial foundations for sustainable peace. A similar coalition blocked the legislation required to redress dramatic inequities in land tenure and to broaden the basis for rural development. Yet, Aguilera optimistically argues that growing indigenous peoples' and women's movements could work with more liberal elements in the private sector and political elite to counterbalance this resistance to change over the long run. In Mozambique, it remains to be seen whether the equity-oriented PRSP will be fully supported by the government and international agencies, despite the favourable alignment of forces around this approach. In Haiti, we will see whether the Préval government and other stakeholders are able to formulate and implement a PRSP that builds on the strengths of the CCI while addressing major gaps in areas like rural development.

Uyangoda's chapter on Sri Lanka (Chapter 7) highlights enduring obstacles to crafting pro-peace economic policies. One challenge is that of bridging the government's market-oriented policies and the LTTE's statist approach. Uyangoda suggests that the international community sided with the government on this matter without giving due consideration to the specific needs of the north and the east. Yet, he also shows how the international community's leverage over both parties has decreased in recent years, despite pledges of reconstruction assistance and the attempt to use post-tsunami reconstruction to foster cooperation between the parties. He builds on analyses by Kelegama and others who argue that the United National Front's liberal economic policies weakened its social base and contributed to its electoral defeat in 2004. This is one factor that, since then, has led to the deepening impasse in the peace process. Though Uyangoda flags the importance of greater imagination and civil society involvement to break this impasse, it is not clear whether these elements will come together over the coming years.

Although more research is required to understand the possibilities of crafting economic policies that reinforce long-term peacebuilding in different postwar situations, three conclusions can be drawn from this comparative synthesis:

11 Over the past decade, much has been learned about harmonizing macroeconomic policies and sustainable peacebuilding, jointly devising conflict-sensitive economic and social policies/programs, investing more to strengthen the capacities of national and local governments, and linking community-based projects with broader development strategies.

12 Yet, it is proving inordinately difficult to apply this learning. Some national economic elites still prefer macroeconomic orthodoxy over redistributive policies that could contribute to more sustainable peacebuilding. Donors still tend to support this approach and invest too little in strengthening national capacities for conflict-sensitive development. Together, they still tend to inadequately reinforce local development initiatives. Meanwhile, local elites often resist economic changes that could empower rivals or traditionally excluded stakeholders, such as women.

13 Only a local-to-international realignment of forces, specific to each society, could turn these trends around. Currently, there are openings for such realignment in Haiti, Mozambique, and perhaps Guatemala. It seems unlikely that this will occur soon in the other societies examined in this book, partly because of their positions in the global War on Terror.

DDR and Spoilers

The case studies of DDR in Guatemala, Afghanistan, and the Palestinian territories suggest several trends common to post-Cold War DDR efforts. They have benefited from huge international investments. They have included innovations ranging from surveying combatants to assess their needs prior to demobilization to converting their arms into memorable works of art and using community-based approaches to reintegration. DDR programs have been relatively successful where broader peace processes have also been relatively successful (for example, in Guatemala).

Yet, even there, as shown by Wenche Hauge and Beate Thoresen in Chapter 8, reintegration programs received too little attention and financing compared to demobilization and disarmament efforts. Certain international donors' emphasis on individual approaches to DDR undermined the potential of ex-combatants to fully contribute to peacebuilding, economically and politically. Hauge and Thoresen also show how the blanket demonization of the civil defence patrols, and key parties' unwillingness to develop appropriate DDR programs for some ex-PACs, also came back to haunt the peace process years later.

These tendencies are magnified under stabilization operations. As explained by Arne Strand in Chapter 9, the Afghanistan's New Beginnings Programme has been severely undermined by the exclusion of armed groups deemed crucial to Operation Enduring Freedom. Disarmament and demobilization have been emphasized at the expense of reintegration efforts, and the latter have often been disconnected from wider economic, social, and political development initiatives. Yet, without a socioeconomic environment that offers sustainable income-generating options for former combatants, these individuals risk remaining armed groups, being recruited again or engaging in criminal activity to meet their basic needs. Finally, the ANBP has failed to carefully examine and tap the potential of ex-combatants, and the communities in which they are embedded, as agents of peacebuilding – partly, as Strand argues, as a result of an excessive emphasis on blunting their potential to spoil peacebuilding.

Chapter 10, in which Pamela Scholey and Khalil Shikaki discuss DDR in Palestine, suggests that the inability to implement DDR is rooted in the failure to apply lessons from other post-Cold War contexts. The first lesson is that coercion is insufficient and often counterproductive, particularly with regard to dealing with broadly based armed movements. Armed groups require sufficient incentives to lay down their arms for good: security guarantees from neutral third parties and/or incorporation into reformed security services; the replacement of labels like "terrorists" or "spoilers" by more grounded understandings of armed actors' specific characteristics; space for them to participate in peaceful politics and take office through elections; and adequate programs to facilitate long-term integration into the economy and society. By resisting many Palestinians' demand for UN peacekeepers, by demonizing Islamists and excluding them from peaceful politics, by insisting on their disarmament before reintegration programs had been developed or linked to advances on larger issues like the end to Israeli military occupation, Israel and the United States undermined DDR, sometimes with the collusion of the mainstream PLO. The tragedy is that these same actors missed a historic opportunity to reposition DDR (as reintegration followed by disarmament) in a new peace process when they rejected the results of Hamas's election in January 2006. If Scholey and Shikaki are correct, the current attempt to disarm (and decapitate) the Islamists by force is destined to fail too.

This comparison of three very different DDR efforts enables us to reformulate the relevant introductory propositions as conclusions:

14 There have been successes with regard to the disarmament, demobilization, and reintegration of ex-combatants in some peacebuilding

processes. DDR has tended to work when broader peace processes have been relatively successful. Success at both levels has been facilitated by security guarantees from neutral third parties and reformed security services; the replacement of labels like "terrorists" or "spoilers" with more grounded understanding of different armed actors' characteristics; space for them to participate in peaceful politics; and adequate programs to facilitate long-term integration into the economy and society. Even in promising contexts such as Guatemala, it has been difficult to apply these lessons, especially with regard to the long-term reintegration of ex-combatants.

15 DDR is much more challenging during stabilization operations, given the character and multiplicity of armed groups in those situations. However, it is also due to an overemphasis on military instruments, an underemphasis on long-term socioeconomic reintegration, selectivity in the application of DDR programs, as well as an insufficient consideration of ex-combatants and their communities as potential agents of peacebuilding.

Conclusion

The case studies in this book, written mostly by analysts and practitioners in the South, confirm that there is profound cause for concern about the direction that the enterprise of peacebuilding has taken in the past decade and, especially, since 11 September 2001. They highlight the contradictions of stabilization operations in Afghanistan, Haiti, and the Palestinian territories. They explain the enormous difficulties caused by the way these efforts began – as military interventions based on contested international mandates or on unilateral action. They also highlight the potential trade-offs between negotiating exclusive but quick peace processes that produce minimalist peace agreements, on the one hand, and pursuing more inclusive processes that are much slower but may lay more durable foundations for peace, on the other. They show how it is difficult to construct democracy under such conditions, given the tendency to exclude certain broadly based movements while turning a blind eye to the undemocratic practices of other national partners. They underscore the related challenge of striking the right balance between developing a constructive relationship with elected governments that may not support peacebuilding processes, while also supporting other agents of change. They show that it is difficult to revive a legitimate economy, and promote community-based development, under conditions of protracted violence. They explain why it is almost impossible to secure the full disarmament, demobilization, and reintegration of combatants when some become allies in the new war, when others are excluded from peaceful politics, and when reintegration programs receive inadequate investment and are poorly woven into broader economic, social, and political reforms. The studies of Afghanistan and Israel-Palestine, in particular, suggest that these societies are likely to relive the fate of Sisyphus rather than to break the shackles of historical repetition.

Yet, the chapter on Haiti suggests that it is possible to turn some stabilization operations around through a different approach. Indeed, experiences in Haiti since March 2004 indicate that even contested international interventions can be reoriented through:

- the early multilateralization of peace enforcement operations based on a clear mandate from a legitimate international organization
- strict control over the use of force by international and national security forces, and strategic interventions to transform the composition and practices of the latter
- steadfast efforts to bring a wide range of political forces into free and fair electoral processes, and rigorous respect for the outcomes of those processes
- the joint development of an economic recovery strategy that combines necessary market-oriented reforms with a strengthening of key public-sector capacities and the promotion of an enabling environment for sustainable development.

The Responsibility to Protect norms discussed in the introductory chapter could provide useful tools to reorient certain stabilization operations and, especially, to prevent the counterproductive repetition of such operations in the future. The Haiti chapter also reminds us that shifting the approach to stabilization is only a new beginning and that consolidating peace, democracy, and generating inclusive economic development are long-term challenges that require much more innovation and patience.

The studies on Guatemala and Mozambique confirm that even after the more promising openings created by negotiated peace accords and their international verification, even with national leadership and international engagement in the implementation of peace accords, it is extremely difficult to secure the deeper changes required to sustain peace beyond the first ten years. Even under such conditions, they show how the reintegration elements of DDR programs tend to be inadequate, how democratization and decentralization processes are limited, and how difficult it is to implement the economic reforms needed to redress historical inequities like major regional imbalances, discrimination against ethnic minorities or majorities, and gender inequality.

Yet, these two case studies are insightful because they also identify openings for deeper reforms, agents of change, and reasons for hope within their societies. Hope rests on the research-based conclusion that there is a critical mass of national actors emerging within the state, in the private sector, at the municipal level, and in civil society that could push the agenda of sustainable peacebuilding much further over the coming decades. One challenge is to strengthen institutions that can adjudicate between the equally legitimate but sometimes conflicting priorities of stakeholders. In each case, all the authors ask of the international community is that it supports those actors, and their exploration of creative policy/institutional alternatives, more consistently.

The chapter on Sri Lanka reminds us that such a relatively promising alignment of forces is rare. The ceasefire agreement fell apart because it did not lead to accords on institutional and structural changes that could end armed violence on the island. The government, the LTTE, and the international community have not shown the flexibility required to negotiate the governance and economic reforms that could open the door to conflict transformation. Uyangoda suggests that including minority communities and civil society in the search for peace could break this stalemate. Yet, the dominant trend has been to remilitarize decision making on both sides. Sri Lanka also seems on the path to reliving the fate of Sisyphus in the coming years. Whether violence leads to all-out war or whether it leads the parties to pull back from the brink, one can only hope that it will remind all those concerned that they need to negotiate more far-reaching peace agreements, through more inclusive processes, in the next round.

At the WKOP conference in Mozambique, WKOP advisor Dyan Mazurana summarized an overarching paradox of contemporary peacebuilding with the following observation: "What is desirable is not possible, and what is possible is not desirable."[4]

On the basis of the final case studies and of further reflection, we can now provide a more fine-grained answer to the question of what kind of peace is possible post-9/11. It is true that the type of peace being attempted through stabilization operations, as in Afghanistan and Iraq, is not desirable because (among other things) it is not sustainable. Yet, recent experiences in Haiti show that some stabilization operations can be turned around through a fresh approach to the use of force, economic reform, and democratic change. It is also true that even peace constructed through negotiated processes in countries like Guatemala and Mozambique has not delivered the deeper changes seen by many stakeholders as key to sustaining peace. Yet, negotiated processes have laid foundations for national actors to drive the implementation of deeper reforms over the long run.

The fate of Sisyphus is not inevitable. There are alternatives in the future. As such, we can reformulate Mazurana's paradox as three final conclusions from the WKOP project:

16 What seems possible – namely, stabilization – is not sustainable and, therefore, not desirable. What seems impossible – namely, sustainable peace – may be possible with more imagination and innovation on the part of national actors as well as greater humility and long-term engagement on the part of international actors.

17 In the post-9/11 era, it is much more difficult to join the desirable with the possible in contexts such as Afghanistan, as well as Israel and Palestine, given their positions in the War on Terror. Even in Sri Lanka, the global war on terror has converged with divisive national dynamics to undermine fragile peace.

18 More is possible, maybe even sustainable peace, in less geopolitically burdened contexts such as Guatemala, Haiti, and Mozambique. The interests of key stakeholders on the ground and in the North should underpin continued efforts to consolidate peace in those societies, even if they do not make the current shortlist of "crisis states."

The United Nations Peacebuilding Commission (PBC) could help stakeholders address some of the conclusions drawn from the WKOP studies. The commission could focus the attention of international and national actors on bridging gaps between immediate post-conflict recovery and the deeper reforms required to consolidate peace. It could help direct resources towards priorities that tend to be underfunded, including the reintegration elements of DDR processes. Given its small budget and short project time frame, the commission's energies should continue focusing on coordinating national and international stakeholders' strategies for peacebuilding in selected contexts.

Yet two experiences, since its inauguration in June 2006 (UN Security Council 2006), illustrate the commission's ambiguities. In Burundi, the PBC has contributed to the transition from the large UN Peacekeeping Operation (ONUB) to a smaller integrated bureau (BINUB). The commission and BINUB have used their mandates to convene a range of official and civil society interlocutors, in New York and on the ground, in partnership with the Government of Burundi. The commission and BINUB helped broker a package of fresh UN assistance to bridge short- and medium-term peacebuilding (information obtained from interviews with UN Peacebuilding Support Office officials in New York, 30 January 2007).

In contrast, at the behest of the Government of El Salvador (which chaired the PBC Operational Committee), in January 2007 the commission helped convene an event to mark the fifteenth anniversary of that country's peace accords. The event was attended by important personalities from the UN, the region, and El Salvador, but it was largely celebratory in tone. A parallel event organized by Salvadoran civil society organizations was largely ignored by officials. This was despite (or perhaps because of) the fact that the comprehensive report on fifteen years of peace implementation presented at that meeting highlighted many pending reforms required to secure sustainable peace. Civil society attempts to discuss these issues with government officials in San Salvador and in New York were rebuffed.[5]

Will the PBC be able to act on its mandate to foster the inclusion of stakeholders beyond the official world? Will it use only minimalist criteria – such as war termination and two elections – to decide that peace has been achieved? Or will these be combined with benchmarks linked to reforms addressing the causes of armed conflict over time? What will happen to countries, like Guatemala and Mozambique, that do not make the PBC shortlist but still require reforms for sustainable peace? Will the commission offer a platform to bring failed stabilization efforts into a multilateral fold? Will the commission use its mandate to identify best practices in such processes?

It is important in this connection for the UN to reach out beyond experts in the North when drawing lessons from experience. The WKOP studies underscore the value of research by analysts and practitioners in the South, and the importance of supporting their efforts to canvass the voices of those often excluded from peacebuilding processes and the assessment thereof. These studies are modest contributions to the national ownership of peacebuilding called for by former UN secretary-general Kofi Annan at the first meeting of the Peacebuilding Commission. We hope that our insights will not fall on deaf ears in New York, in our capitals, and beyond.

Notes

Chapter 1: Introduction

1 For a different but compatible categorization of UN peace operations, see Woodward (2002a).
2 This sketch is based on the WKOP case study by Shikaki (2005).
3 This sketch is based on the WKOP case study by Aguilera (2005).
4 Despite this blockage on R2P at the global level, the African Union and subregional entities such as the Economic Community of West African States (ECOWAS) have codified commitments on R2P and are currently establishing the machinery to give effect to those norms. See Powell (2005).
5 This sketch is based on the WKOP case study by Jadotte and Pierre (2006).
6 See Baranyi (2005a, 2005b) for a more detailed analysis of these trends in Canada. See Maas and Mepham (2004) for German and UK perspectives, and US Commission (2004) for a US perspective. For a Norwegian counterpoint to this trend, see Norwegian Ministry of Foreign Affairs (2004).
7 This sketch is based on the WKOP case study by Sitoe and Hunguana (2005).
8 This sketch is based on the WKOP case study by Zakhilwal and Thomas (2005).
9 This sketch is based on the WKOP case study by Uyangoda (2005b).

Chapter 2: Peace in Guatemala

1 I use these terms as defined in the United Nations "Peace Agenda," understanding peacemaking "as diplomatic action to bring hostile parties to agreement, essentially through such peaceful means as those foreseen in Chapter VI of the Charter of the United Nations" and peacebuilding as "action to identify and support structures which will tend to strengthen and solidify peace in order to avoid a relapse into conflict" (Norwegian Ministry of Foreign Affairs 2004, 14).
2 Among the studies on the issue of the military in Guatemala, I would mention those of Héctor Rosada, Bernardo Arévalo, Jennifer Schirmer, and Alejandro Gramajo. In terms of proposals for new parameters on security, I would mention the collective work of the Democratic Security and FOSS projects, as well as the works of Edgar Gutiérrez and Miguel Angel Reyes.
3 Unidad Nacional Revolucionaria Guatemalteca.
4 Misión de Verificación de las Naciones Unidas en Guatemala.
5 These goals are set forth in the *Programación de Metas Mínimas Indicativas 1997–2000* and in the annex of the Schedule Accord.
6 CONADES is the Consejo Nacional de Desarrollo [National Development Council].
7 COREDES is the Consejo Regional de Desarrollo [Regional Development Council].
8 CODEDES is the Consejo Departamental de Desarrollo [Departmental Development Council].
9 COMUDES is the Consejo Comunitario de Desarrollo [Municipal Development Council].
10 COCODES is the Consejo Comunitario de Desarrollo [Community Development Council].

11 This research was directed by Carmen Lucía Pellecer.
12 The Program for Participation and Democracy, an entity that follows up the recommenda-tions of International-DEA (International Institute for Democracy and Electoral Assistance) in regard to the fulfillment of the peace accords.
13 Braulia Thillet de Solórzano directed this project.
14 The PPD-FLACSO project worked with the COMUDES of Sumpango, Santa Cruz Balanyá, Patzún, El Tejar, San Antonio Palopó, Santa Catarina Pinula, Santiago Atitlán, Comitancillo, San Antonio Sácatepequez, San Lorenzo, San José Ojetenam, Tejuela, San Felipe, San Martín Zapotitlán, Zunilito, San Miguel Panán y Pueblo Nuevo. The PPD-FLACSO project was designed to provide the following: support for civil society groups attempting to meet the legal requirements to gain a seat in the councils; support for the development of council regulations; support and lobbying for the set-up and operation of council work-ing committees.
15 Analysis developed by the Participation and Democracy Program/FLACSO: *Evaluation Work-shop of the 2004 Operational Plan*, photocopy of documents and verbal reports, evaluation workshop, Guatemala, 21 October 2002.
16 Interview with Sister Isabel Can, director of Radio Quiché and coordinator of Indigenous Organizations in the Department of El Quiché. Interview from a study entitled "From the Conclusion of War to the Consolidation of Peace – What Kind of Peace Is Possible?" (Pellecer Arellano 2004, 12).
17 One example is the violent eviction of peasants from the Nueva Linda farm in the depart-ment of Retalhuleu in August 2004, which resulted in the death of several peasants and police. See the Human Rights Ombudsman's report on this case: Procuraduría de los Derechos humanos. *Resolución sobre el desalojo en la finca "Nueva Linda," Champerico, Retalhuleu.* Expediente EIO.REU. 23-2004/D.I., 12 October 2004.
18 In one significant move, the Human Rights Ombudsman organized a consultative council for the peace accords in August 2005. One of this council's most prominent members is Cardinal Rodolfo Quezada Toruño.

Chapter 3: Decentralization and Sustainable Peacebuilding in Mozambique
1 Frente de Libertação de Moçambique (FRELIMO) and Resistência Nacional Moçambicana (RENAMO).
2 On 20 January 2005, the Constitutional Council validated the results of the 2004 general elections exactly as the National Electoral Commission had declared them. It did not vali-date RENAMO's appeal to have the results invalidated and the electoral process repeated. Interestingly – and with a certain degree of surprise – RENAMO accepted the final decision of the Constitutional Council without further considerations. Indeed, its leader, Afonso Dlhakama, announced the following day that all RENAMO elected MPs would take up their seats in Parliament and that he himself would take up his seat on the State Council.
3 Ministério de Administração Estatal.
4 Bernhard Weimer in an interview with Carolina Hunguana in April 2001, included in her master's thesis in political science (Weimer in Hunguana 2000, 42).
5 Interview with Custódio dos Mucudos, Coordinator of the Decentralized Planning and Finance Project, 28 January 2005.
6 The policy of consistently requiring that all ward committees be proportionally composed of men and women is an attempt to work towards gender-oriented development and democratization.
7 These growth rates are significant, particularly when one takes into consideration the fact that the population growth rate of Mozambique is 2.4 percent.
8 In some years, GDP growth rates presented by the Bank of Mozambique tend to be slightly different from those presented by the UNDP (1998, 2000b) and the Instituto Nacional de Estatística (2006). Thus, in the graph in Figure 1, only the former indicators are considered. This is because of their consistency and the fact that they are more widely used in macro-economic analyses of Mozambique.
9 Plano de Acção para a Redução de Pobreza Absoluta.

10 Mozambique uses standard World Bank poverty measures, according to which a family with an income of less than one US dollar per day is considered extremely, or absolutely, poor. About 60 percent of the households in Mozambique have a monthly income equal to or lower than US$20 and, therefore, live below this poverty line (UNDP 1998 and 2000).
11 *Noticias* (2004).
12 This expression belongs to Gustavo Krauze (cited in Mazula 2002, 2), the former Brazilian Minister of the Treasury and the Environment.

Chapter 4: Local Governance and Sustainable Peace in Haiti

1 Mission des Nations Unies pour la stabilisation de Haïti.
2 Chapter VII of the UN charter links social pacification in Haiti to the "threat for peace and international security, and for stability in the Caribbean." See Hector (2007, 12).
3 There are essentially two approaches to local governance and economic interventions in Haiti: first, there are programs that aim to reduce poverty through the creation of several short-term infrastructure works in urban and/or rural areas; second, there are community development projects that enable communities to define their needs and to manage their development processes, while implementing the basic principles of good governance. See ARD (1996) for the basis of this distinction. One of the authors of this chapter (Yves-François Pierre) participated in the research that was used to produce that report.
4 Mission internationale civile d'appuien Haïti.
5 This salary varies between seventy-five and one hundred gourdes. Approximately forty-two gourdes are equivalent to one American dollar.
6 This is a deconcentrated state service that works to provide safe drinking water to rural areas.
7 However, within this consortium, the Pan American Development Foundation is managing disaster preparedness and conflict mitigation. We were unable to document whether or not any technical transfers were made to local institutions.
8 As opposed to traditional groups organized to exchange agricultural work, the gwoupman reflects a type of collective movement oriented towards socioeconomic development. Interviews in the field reveal that the gwoupman can also be attached to traditional work groups.
9 This section benefited from comments by agronomist Pierre Jacques Vil, an expert in the participatory approach taken in this project (Institut Haïtien de statistiques et d'informatique, DARD, 1999-2007).
10 Four levels of participation – the collection of information from residents, consultation with residents, the active participation of residents in project activities, and technical capacity building – were attempted in this project. See Inter-American Development Bank (2003).
11 Comité communal de concertation et de planification.
12 Comités de développement local.

Chapter 5: Palestine, 1993-2006

1 The Quartet is an international coalition comprising the United States, the United Nations, the European Union, and Russia.
2 Article 18, paragraphs 4 and 6 of the Israeli-Palestinian Interim Agreement on the West Bank and the Gaza Strip, Ministry of Foreign Affairs, 1995.

Chapter 6: Afghanistan: What Kind of Peace?

1 Co-author Jane Murphy Thomas represented an international NGO in the World Bank/NSP meetings with NGOs in Kabul from November 2002 to March 2003. She also acted as one of the facilitators in the mentioned workshops.

Chapter 7: Transition from Civil War to Peace in Sri Lanka

1 There have been four previous attempts to negotiate a resolution to the ethnic civil war in Sri Lanka: in 1985, 1987, 1989, and 1994. For details see Loganathan (1996), Rupesinghe (1998), and Uyangoda (2005a).

2 The state-like thinking and acting of the LTTE is explored in some detail in a separate section below.

3 For a useful discussion on the question of security and political guarantees in managing civil war transition, see Walter (1999).

4 Since 2002, Dr. M.S. Anees, a university academic, and some of his Muslim colleagues from the Northern Province have begun to articulate this stand. This position has received sympathetic responses from the internally displaced Muslim communities in the Northern Province, although, for understandable reasons, it has troubled national Muslim political parties.

5 There is an emerging body of thinking in Sri Lanka in this regard (see Devaraj 2004). Representation for multiple minorities can be ensured at both national and local levels. At the national level, the principle of non-territorial federalism offers Sri Lanka an option worth exploring. The composition of the Second Chamber could combine both territorial and non-territorial principles, with weightage to the latter, or exclusively on the non-territorial principle since the House of Representatives provides representation on the basis of territoriality. A slightly different option would be to establish separate community councils at the national level for the main ethnic communities, with specific powers over group-specific domains such as culture, language, education, religion, and social welfare. It would also provide an institutional mechanism to address the group rights claims of the ethnic communities.

6 Lal Jayawardena argued, as far back as 1994, that drastic reduction in military expenditure, backed by a matching, dollar for dollar contribution by the donor community and a rise in domestic and foreign savings, could raise the investment target to 30 percent of the GDP. Jayawardena (1994) asserted that, on this basis, Sri Lanka's economic growth in the decade between 1994 and 2005, would rise to 8 percent.

7 These observations are based on my interactions with the officials of the LTTE's Planning and Development Secretariat.

Chapter 8: The Fate of Former Combatants in Guatemala

1 Fuerzas Armadas Rebeldes.
2 Partido Guatemalteco de los Trabajadores.
3 Ejército Guerrillero de los Pobres and Organización Revolucionaria del Pueblo en Armas.
4 Policía militar ambulante.
5 A development council. See Chapter 2, this volume, for a comprehensive description of the work and organization of the development councils.
6 Rodrigo Asturias was the leader of ORPA. His nom de guerre was Gaspar Ilom, but since in Guatemala he is better known by his real name, that is what we prefer to use.
7 In Guatemala, a *campo pagado* costs 35,000 quetzales (US$4,834) (interview with Rodrigo Asturias).
8 Pablo Monsanto is the nom de guerre of Jorge Soto. In Guatemala, he is best known by the former.
9 Rolando Moran is the nom de guerre of Ricardo Ramirez. In Guatemala, he is best known by the former.

Chapter 9: Fighting for Peace?

1 There are only a very few examples of women holding command or engaging in fighting.
2 This is the official figure of the Central Statistics Office. However, the exact size of the population, influenced by migration patterns, is unknown. Estimates vary between 23 million and 28 million.
3 Most notable here is the influence of US ambassador Zalmay Khalilzad, an Afghan by birth.
4 I interviewed a number of disabled Afghans in Herat in 1994 while they were undergoing skills training.
5 When the Taliban captured Jalalabad in 1995, many of the mujahideen commanders fled to Pakistan, where they were lodged in guesthouses run by the Pakistani intelligence agency, Directorate for Inter-Services Intelligence (ISI).

6 In Baghlan in 1994, I witnessed a recruitment process organized by Shura-e Nezar, and in 1995 I noted that trucks packed with lightly armed youths were driven towards Taliban frontlines south of Kabul.

7 A web page is established to present the program and to provide updates on progress. It is available at http://www.undpanbp.org.

8 The survey was conducted by the Afghan Women's Network (AWSDC), Coordination for Peace and Unity (CPAU), and Sanayee Development Foundaton (SDF) in late 2005.

Chapter 10: Considering the International DDR Experience and Spoiling

1 See the "Cambridge Forum's" second report on track 2 negotiations to establish a third-party intervention force in Palestine in order to help bring an end to hostilities between Israel and Palestine on the eve of the Roadmap in April 2003. http://www.strategic assessments.org/ ontherecord/sai_publications/planning_considerations_part_2.pdf.

2 All data on Palestinian public opinion is taken from surveys conducted by the Palestinian Center for Policy and Survey Research (PSR). For details, see http://www.pcpsr.org/survey/index.html. At the time of writing, PSR's most recent and specific data on the public perception of insecurity could be found at http://www.pcpsr.org/survey/polls/2007/p23e1.html#domesticissues2.

3 Interviews conducted by PSR with leaders and members of various Palestinian militias in the second half of 2005.

4 For Hamas's Politburo head Khalid Masha'al, the Cairo Declaration was aimed at "ending the monopoly on decision making and widespread corruption within the Palestinian Authority." For an excellent analysis of the Cairo Declaration, see Usher (2005a).

5 It should be noted that, at least until Israel's redeployment from Gaza, the tunnels were mostly used for smuggling cigarettes, drugs, and pornography, with arms coming in at a distant fourth place (Peter Bartu, former military advisor to UNESCO, May 2004).

6 Information obtained from interviews with militia leaders and heads of security services. These interviews were conducted during the second half of 2005.

7 The UN Secretary-General's report to the Security Council on DDR identifies the UN Observer Group in Central America (ONUCA) in 1989 as the UN's first DDR exercise (UNSC 2000, 2-3).

8 Security sector reform is also an inherently political process, but, like DDR, it is usually treated as a technocratic exercise. See Jones and Riley (2004) for a technocratic discussion of Palestinian security sector reform that neglects to mention armed non-state groups but, rather, focuses on reform, law, and order.

9 Kingma (1997, 154) argues that reintegration schemes should include employment programs that would enable ex-combatants to secure employment and contribute to economic reactivation in areas such as infrastructure, agriculture, and industry.

10 Knight and Özerdem (2004) also challenge the need for cantonment in demobilization, but this issue is not addressed here as it is of limited relevance to the Palestinian case.

11 It should also be noted that this analysis is contested. See Nitzschke and Studdard (2005, 223) and Ballentine and Sherman (2003).

12 Yasir Arafat had successfully managed to prevent the holding of Fateh's conventions since 1989, leading inevitably to the exclusion of young activists. One of the critical demands of the Fateh's young guard is the holding of its Sixth Convention. After the death of Arafat, Fateh's old guard, which controls its Central Committee, agreed to hold the convention in the second half of 2005. The date was later postponed until after the holding of the parliamentary elections and was expected for late 2006. No serious steps have been taken by Fateh since the January 2006 elections to prepare for that convention.

13 Few of the typical challenges faced by combatants in other contexts are relevant in Palestine, where armed non-state actors reside with their families and communities and where levels of Palestinian literacy and education are among the highest in the region.

14 Israel redeployed its military and evacuated all of its settlements from the Gaza Strip in August 2005. However, almost all Israeli settlements and military forces remain in the West Bank. All Gaza and West Bank borders are controlled and/or monitored by Israel. The experiment of having the European Union monitor the Gaza-Egypt border (with Israel

playing a secondary monitoring role) has proven successful – with the exception of Israeli-imposed closures of the border since July 2006 – but it is still only used for passenger crossing. See World Bank (2007) for a discussion of using the Rafah crossing for trade purposes.

15 For a fascinating discussion of this, see Mark Perry and Alastair Crooke's five-part series in the *Asia Times* from 31 March to 8 June 2006.

16 See also Bose (2002) for an extended treatment of the Indian mission in Sri Lanka in 1987.

17 This is not meant to be a full review of the spoilers literature and related material; rather, we mine a small selection of this literature for its value to our arguments for Palestinian DDR.

18 This chapter offers a selective treatment of work on spoilers and armed non-state actors. See the work of Conciliation Resources, including its reading guide, at http://www.c-r.org. See also Geneva Call's work on armed non-state actors and their adherence to international law at http://www.genevacall.org/home.htm; the Berghof Centre's program on the transition of armed non-state actors to mainstream political actors at http://www.berghof-center.org/english.htm; and the Armed Groups Project at University of Calgary at http://www.armedgroups.org.

19 This chapter is not meant as a critical review of the spoilers debate. It should be noted that both Stedman (1997) and Zahar (2003, 2005, 2006) neglect to examine in any deep way the dynamics within, and viewpoints of, armed non-state actor groups. Keeping this observation in mind, see Strand (Chapter 9, this volume) with regard to research on DDR in Afghanistan and the dearth of information on armed actors' perspectives. Indeed, Clem McCartney (2005, 1) argues that the "assumption that violence is a tactic that can be replaced by another tactic reflects a partial analysis of the nature of armed groups." He also argues that one must take into account the communities that support these groups as their attitudes have a significant influence on armed actors.

20 See also Hartzell (1999) on how power-sharing agreements strengthen commitments to peace processes.

21 See International Crisis Group's report on the crisis precipitated by Hamas' and Hezbollah's kidnapping of Israeli soldiers in July 2006.

22 Within the Palestinian security forces, 82 percent voted for Fateh and only 12 percent for Hamas in the January 2006 elections.

23 The article cites high rates of exposure among Gaza children: 92.5 percent had been teargassed, 85 percent had been subjected to night raids on their homes, 55 percent had witnessed assaults on family members, 42 percent had themselves been beaten, 23 percent had been injured, and 19 percent had been detained (Qouta et al. 1995, 291).

24 See McCann and Pearlman (1990) for a discussion of how violent trauma survivors attempt to "master" the event by engaging in risk and violence.

25 In fact, until the arrival of the Palestinian Authority in 1994, Palestinians in the West Bank and Gaza were almost entirely unarmed. The Oslo Accords contained provisions to build up Palestinian security forces by allowing the transfer of most of the forces of the Palestinian Liberation Army from Egypt, Jordan, Syria, and other places (about twenty-five thousand armed men) to the Palestinian territories.

26 It should be noted here that the UN's Afghanistan New Beginnings Programme (ANBP) DDR program also entails conventional sequencing. Nonetheless, the Afghan state has no capacity to enforce regulations on carrying arms, and the Afghan political, economic, and security climate and cultural norms reinforce the value of owning and using guns – all factors that militate against a conventional DDR program. See Strand (Chapter 9, this volume) as well as Özerdem (2002), ICG (2003), and Rubin (2003).

Chapter 11: Conclusion

1 These titles and subtitles were selected from the *Guardian Weekly* and *Granma* in June-July 2006.

2 UN Security Council (2006). This succinct formulation of the commission's mandate is adapted from UNSC Resolution 1645 (20 December 2005) and UNGA Resolution 60/180 (30 December 2005).

3 We are grateful to Michèle Oriol for making this point at the forum enitled "Haïti: Quelle sorte de paix est possible?" Hotel Montana, Port-au-Prince, 26 May 2006.
4 The Mazurana quote was noted verbatim by Stephen Baranyi at the WKOP international conference in 2005.
5 Presentations by Salvadoran civil society leaders at the Seminario Internacional sobre Paz, Seguridad y Prevención de Conflictos Armados en América Latina y el Caribe, Santo Domingo, Dominican Republic, 17-18 April 2007. For the report, see Espacio de Concertación (2007).

References

Abirafeh, Lina. 2005. *Lessons from Gender-Focused International Aid in Post-Conflict Afghanistan ... Learned?* Bonn: Friedrich Ebert Stiftung, Division for International Co-operation, Department for Development Policy.

Abrahamsson, Hans, and Anders Nilsson. 1994. *Moçambique em Transição: Um estudo da história de desenvolvimento durante o período 1974-1992* [Mozambique in transition: A study of the history of development during the period 1974-1992]. Maputo: Pagrigu and CEEI-ISRI.

Afghanistan National Human Development Report. 2004. *Security with a Human Face*. New York: United Nations Development Program.

Agency Coordinating Body for Afghan Relief. 2003. *Policy Brief: Provincial Reconstruction Teams and the Security Situation in Afghanistan, Agency Coordinating Body for Afghan Relief*. http://www.careusa.org/newsroom/specialreports/Afghanistan.

Aguilera, Gabriel. 1988. "The Hidden War: Guatemala's Counterinsurgency Campaign." In *Crisis in Central America: Regional Dynamics and US Policy in the 1980s*, ed. Nora Hamilton, Jeffrey A. Frieden, Linda Fuller, and Manuel Paster Jr., 153-72. Boulder and London: Westview.

–. 2003. *Construyendo un imaginario: El proceso de paz en Guatemala* [Constructing the imaginary: The process of peace in Guatemala]. Guatemala: FLACSO.

–. 2005. *Guatemala: Entre la paz posible y la paz deseable* [Guatemala: Between possible peace and desirable peace]. WKOP working paper. Guatemala: Programa de Participación y Democracia.

Annan, Kofi, United Nations Secretary-General. 2005. "Explanatory Note by the Secretary-General on the Proposed Peacebuilding Commission," 17 April.

ARD (Associates in Rural Development). 1996. *La démocratie locale en Haiti: Evaluation du statut-quo et perspectives sur le développement des capacités de gouvernance locale*. Vol. 1. [Local democracy in Haiti: Evaluation of the status quo and perspectives on the development of local governance capacities, Vol. 1]. Port-au-Prince: USAID.

Armon, Jeremy, Rachel Sieder, and Richard Wilson. 1997. "Negotiating Rights: The Guatemalan Peace Process." *Accord* 2. http://www.c-r.org/our-work/accord/guatemala/contents.php.

Atallah, Amjad, Jarat Chopra, Yaser Dajani, Orit Gal, and Jim McCallum. 2003. *Planning Considerations for International Involvement in the Israeli-Palestinian Conflict, Part II*. Report on the second session of the "Cambridge Forum," Cambridge University, UK, 25-26 April. http://www.strategicassessments.org/ontherecord/sai_publications/planning_considerations_part_2.pdf.

Atmar, Mohammad Haneef, and Jonathan Goodhand. 2001. "Coherence or Co-option? Politics, Aid and Peace-Building in Afghanistan." *Journal of Humanitarian Assistance*. http://www.jha.ac/articles/a069.htm.

Azpuru, Dinorah, Carlos Mendoza, Evelyn Blanck, and Ligia Blanco. 2004. "Democracy Assistance to Post Conflict Guatemala." Working paper 30, Democratic Transition in Post-Conflict Societies Project. Conflict Research Unit. Guatemala: Netherlands Institute of International Relations "Clingendael" in cooperation with ASIES.

Babiker, Mohammed Hassan, and Alpaslan Özerdem. 2003. "A Future Disarmament, Demobilisation and Reintegration Process in Sudan: Lessons Learned from Ethiopia, Mozambique and Uganda." *Conflict, Security and Development* 3, 2: 211-32.

Baechler, Guenter. 2004. "Conflict Transformation through State Reform." In *Berghof Handbook for Conflict Transformation*, ed. David Blomfield. Berlin: Berghof Research Center for Constructive Conflict Management. http://www.berghof-handbook.net/articles/baechler_handbook.pdf.

Ballentine, Karen, and Jake Sherman, eds. 2003. *The Political Economy of Armed Conflict: Beyond Greed and Grievance*. London: Lynne Rienner Publishers.

Banco de Guatemala. 2006. *Algunas variables macroeconómicas: Años 1950-2004* [Some macroeconomic variables: Years 1950-2004]. http://www.banguat.gob.gt.

Baptista Lundin, I. 2004. "An Analytical Reading of Social Spaces that Mozambique Has Opened to Accommodate and Cultivate Peace." In *Mozambique Ten Years of Democracy*, ed. Brazão Mazula, 96-139. Maputo: CEDE.

Baranyi, Stephen. 2005a. "Canada and the Peace and Security Pillar of the Millennium Declaration." *Towards 2015: Meeting Our Millennium Commitments*. Ottawa: The North-South Institute.

–. 2005b. "Quel avenir pour le Canada et la consolidation de la paix? Innovation et efficacité dans une periode de turbulences" [What future for Canada and peacebuilding? Innovation and efficiency in a period of turbulence]. In *Faire la Paix* [Make peace], ed. Yvan Conoir and Gérard Herna, 422-65. Québec: Les Presses de l'Université de Laval.

–. 2005c. *What Kind of Peace Is Possible in the Post-9/11 Era? National Agency, Transnational Coalitions and the Challenges of Sustainable Peace*. WKOP working paper. Ottawa: The North-South Institute.

Bastian, Sunil. 2003. "Foreign Aid, Globalization and Conflict in Sri Lanka." In *Building Local Capacities for Peace: Rethinking Conflict and Development in Sri Lanka*, ed. Markus Mayer, Darini Rajasingham-Senanayake, and Yuvi Thangarajan, 132-51. Delhi: Macmillan India.

–. 2004. "How Development Can Undermine Peace." *Polity* 2, 2: 9-12.

Bastian, Sunil, and Robin Luckham. 2004. *Can Democracy Be Designed? The Politics of Institutional Choice in Conflict-Torn Societies*. London and New York: Zed Books.

Bastos, Santiago, and Manuela Camus. 2004. *El Movimiento Maya en perspectiva: Texto para reflexión y debate – Mesa intersectorial de diálogo sobre Pueblos Indígenas* [The Mayan movement in perspective: Text for reflection and debate – Intersectorial dialogue table on Indigenous Peoples]. Guatemala: FLACSO.

Bendaña, Alejandro. 2003. "What Kind of Peace Is Being Built? Critical Assessments from the South. A Discussion Paper." What Kind of Peace is Being Built? Working paper 7. Ottawa: IDRC.

Berdal, Mats R. 1996. *Disarmament and Demobilisation after Civil Wars*. Adelphi Paper 303. Oxford: IISS and Oxford University Press.

Berdal, Mats, and David M. Malone, eds. 2000. *Greed and Grievance: Economic Agendas and Civil Wars*. London: Lynne Rienner Publishers.

Boesen, Inger E. 2004. *From Subjects to Citizens: Local Participation in the National Solidarity Programme*. Kabul: Afghanistan Research and Evaluation Unit.

Bonini, Roberto, ed. 2005. *La Comunidad de San Egidio y el proceso de paz en Guatemala: Ponencias del foro de diciembre de 2004* [The community of San Egidio and the process of peace in Guatemala: Communications of the forum of December of 2004]. Guatemala: Colección Cultura de Paz. (FLACSO, UNESCO, Cooperación Italiana.)

Bose, Sumantra. 2002. "Flawed Mediation, Chaotic Implementation: The 1987 Indo-Sri Lankan Peace Agreement." In *Ending Civil Wars: The Implementation of Peace Agreements*, ed. Stephen John Stedman, Donald Rothschild, and Elizabeth Cousens, 631-59. Boulder, London: Lynne Rienner Publishers.

Boyce, James K. 2002. *Investing in Peace: Aid and Conditionality after Civil Wars*. Adelphi Paper 351. London: IISS.

Brown, Nathan. 2003. *Palestinian Politics after the Oslo Accords: Resuming Arab Palestine*. Berkeley: University of California Press.

–. 2005. *Evaluating Palestinian Reform*. Washington: Carnegie Endowment for International Peace, Middle East Series, Democracy and Rule of Law Project.

Bulhan, Hussein Abdilahi. 1980. "Frantz Fanon: The Revolutionary Psychiatrist." *Race and Class* 21, 3: 251-71.

Burgos, Amilcar. 2004. "Institucionalización de los Consejos de Desarrollo" [Institutionalization of the Councils of Development]. Paper presented at the workshop "Construyendo la democracia desde abajo: Descentralización, iniciativas locales y ciudadanía" [Constructing democracy from·below: Local decentralization, initiatives and citizenship], 8 April 2005, Guatemala. Guatemala: Woodrow Wilson Center for Scholars, FLACSO, Fundación Interamericana.

Bush, Kenneth. 2004. *Building Capacity for Peace and Unity: The Role of Local Government in Peacebuilding*. Ottawa: International Centre for Municipal Development/Federation of Canadian Municipalities.

Cabaço, José Luis. 1995. "A longa estrada da democracia moçambicana" [The long road to Mozambican democracy]. In *Eleições, democracia e desenvolvimento* [Elections, democracy and development], ed. Brazão Mazula, 78-113. Maputo: Inter-Africa Group.

Cabrita, Joao. 2000. *Mozambique: The Tortuous Road to Democracy*. New York: Palgrave.

Capie, David. 2004. *Armed Groups, Weapons Availability and Misuse: An Overview of the Issues and Options for Action*. Briefing paper. Geneva: Centre for Humanitarian Dialogue.

Carbonnier, Gilles. 1998. "Conflict, Post-War Rebuilding and the Economy: A Critical Review of the Literature." WSP occasional paper. Geneva: War-Torn Societies Project.

CARE/Center on International Cooperation. 2003. "Good Intentions Will Not Pave the Road to Peace." Policy brief. http://www.care.org/newsroom/specialreports/afghanistan/09152003_afghanistanbrief.pdf.

Carlin, Anne. 2003. *Rush to Reengagement in Afghanistan: The IFI's Post-Conflict Agenda with Special Focus on the National Solidarity Program*. Washington, DC: Bank Information Center.

Carnegie Commission. 1997. *Preventing Deadly Conflict: Final Report*. New York: Carnegie Corporation.

Castelo-Branco, Carlos N., ed. 1994. *Moçambique: Perspectivas económicas* [Mozambique: Economic perspectives]. Maputo: Imprensa Universitária.

–. 1995. "Opções económicas de Moçambique, 1975-95: Problemas, lições e ideias alternativas" [Economic options of Mozambique, 1975-95: Problems, lessons and alternative ideas]. In *Eleições, democracia e desenvolvimento* [Elections, democracy and development], ed. Brazão Mazula, 581-636. Maputo: Inter-Africa Group.

CEH (Comisión para el Esclarecimiento Histórico). 1999a. *Guatemala: Memoria del silencio – Conclusiones y recomendaciones del Informe de la Comisión para el Esclarecimiento Histórico* [Guatemala: Memory of silence – Conclusions and recommendations of the Report of the Commission for Historical Elucidation]. Guatemala: Litoprint.

–. 1999b. *Guatemala: Memoria del silencio*. Tomo 1. *Mandato y procedimiento de trabajo, Causas y orígenes del enfrentamiento armado interno* [Guatemala: Memory of silence. Vol. 1. Mandate and work process, causes and origins of internal armed conflict]. Guatemala: UNOPS.

CEI (Comisión Especial de Incorporación). 1998. "Incorporación." Report from CEI. Guatemala: CEI.

Centro de Estudios de Guatemala. 2002. *La reorganización de las PAC* [The reorganization of the PAC]. Guatemala: CEG.

Chambers, Robert. 1983. *Rural Development: Putting the Last First*. Harlow, UK: Longman.

Chataigner, Jean-Marc, and François Gaulme. 2005. "Agir en faveur des acteurs et des sociétés fragiles: Pour une vision renouvelée des enjeux de l'aide au développement dans la prévention et la gestion de crises" [Acting in favour of the actors and the fragile societies: For a renewed vision of the stakes of development assistance in the prevention and management of crises]. Working paper. Paris: Agence Française de Développement.

Chesterman, Simon, Michael Ignatieff, and Ramesh Thakur, eds. 2005. *Making States Work: State Failure and the Crisis of Governance*. Tokyo: UN University Press and the International Peace Academy.

Chrobok, Vera. 2005. *Demobilizing and Reintegrating Afghanistan's Young Soldiers*. Bonn: BICC.

Coalición para la CICIACS. 2004. *Comisión de Investigación de los Cuerpos Ilegales y Aparatos Clandestinos de Seguridad: Acuerdo entre las Naciones Unidas y el Gobierno de Guatemala* [Commission of Investigation of the Illegal Bodies and Clandestine Apparatuses of Security: Agreement between the United Nations and the Government of Guatemala]. Guatemala: SE.

Cojti Cuxil, Demetrio (Waqi'Q'anil). 1995. *Configuración del pensamiento político del pueblo Maya* [Configuration of the political thought of the Mayan people]. Guatemala: Cholsamaj.

–. 2005. *La difícil transición al estado multinacional: El caso del estado monoétnico de Guatemala, 2004* [The difficult transition to the multinational state: The case of the monoethnic state of Guatemala, 2004]. Guatemala: Cholsamaj.

Colegio de Abogados y Notarios de Guatemala, and UNESCO. 1996. *Acuerdos de Paz* [Peace accords]. Guatemala: SE.

Collier, Paul. 2000. "Doing Well out of War: An Economic Perspective." In *Greed and Grievance: Economic Agendas in Civil Wars*, ed. Mats Berdal and David Malone, 91-112. Boulder: Lynne Rienner Publishers and IDRC.

Collier, Paul, and Anke Hoeffler. 2001. "Greed and Grievance in Civil War." http://econ.worldbank.org/programs/conflict/library/doc?id=12205.

Collier, Paul, V.L. Elliott, Håvard Hegre, Anke Hoeffler, Marta Reynal-Querol, and Nicholas Sambanis. 2003. *Breaking the Conflict Trap: Civil War and Development Policy*. Washington and Oxford: World Bank and Oxford University Press.

Comisión de acompañamiento del cumplimiento de los acuerdos de paz. 2000. *Cronograma de implementación, cumplimiento y verificación de los acuerdos de paz, 2000-2004* [Timeline of implementation, fulfillment and verification of the peace accords, 2000-2004]. Guatemala: SE.

Comisión económica para América Latina y el Caribe (CEPAL). 1997. *Estudio económico de América Latina y el Caribe, 1996-97* [Economic study of Latin America and the Caribbean]. Santiago de Chile: United Nations.

–. 2007. *Anuario estadístico de América Latina y el Caribe, 2006: Estadísticas económicas* [Statistical yearbook of Latin America and the Caribbean, 2006: Economic statistics]. http://www.eclac.org/publicaciones/xml/3/28063/LCG2332B_2.pdf.

CONGCOOP and CNOC. 2002. *FONTIERRAS: El modelo de mercado y el acceso a la tierra en Guatemala* [FONTIERRAS: The market model and access to land in Guatemala]. Guatemala: CONGCOOP.

Constant, Jean-Robert. 2003. *Gonaïves, berceau du dechoukaj: Témoignages et compilations pour l'histoire* [Gonaïves, cradle of uprooting: Testimonies and compilations for history]. Port-au-Prince: Ateliers des Presses Nationales d'Haïti.

Constitución Política de la República de Guatemala [Political constitution of the Republic of Guatemala]. 2001. Guatemala: Editorial Serviprensa. (Aplicada en fallos de la Corte de Constitucionalidad [Applied in the judgments of the Court of Constitutionality].)

. Corral, Enrique Alonso. 2005. "Análisis del proceso de incorporación de URNG en Guatemala" [Analysis of the process of incorporation of URNG in Guatemala]. Unpublished paper.

CR (Conciliation Resources). 2004. "Engaging Armed Groups in Peace Processes: Joint Analysis Workshop Report." http://www.c-r.org/our-work/accord/engaging-groups/workshop-report.php.

–. 2005. "Engaging Armed Groups in Peace Processes: Accord Reading Guide." http://www.c-r.org/accord/engage/resources/reading.shtml.

Crooke, Alastair. 2005. "In Search of Respect at the Table: Hamas Ceasefires, 2001-3." In *Choosing to Engage: Armed Groups and Peace Processes, Accord*, ed. Robert Ricigliano, 16. http://www.c-r.org/accord/engage/accord 16/18.shtml.

Cullather, Nick. 1999. *Secret History: The CIA's Classified Account of the Operations in Guatemala, 1952-1954*. Stanford: Stanford University Press.

Darby, John. 2001. *The Effects of Violence on Peace Processes*. Washington, DC: United Institute of Peace Press.

Daudelin, Jean. 2002. "Agrarian Structures, Agrarian Policies and Violence in Central America and Southern Mexico." Unpublished paper for the North-South Institute. http://www.nsi-ins.ca.

Devaraj, P.P., ed. 2004. *Power-Sharing and the Rights of Non-Territorial Minorities*. Colombo: Centre for Community Transformation.

Development Alternatives Inc. 2000. *Political Will for Decentralization in Haiti*. Port-au-Prince: USAID.

DeVotta, Neil. 2006. "From Ethnic Outbidding to Ethnic Conflict: The Institutional Bases for Sri Lanka's Separatists War." In *Politics of Conflict and Peace in Sri Lanka*, ed. P. Sahadevan and Neil DeVotta, 3-29. New Delhi: MANAK Publications.

Donini, Antonio, Larry Minear, Ian Smillie, Ted van Baarda, and Anthony C. Welch. 2004. *Mapping the Security Environment: Understanding the Perception of Local Communities, Peace Support Operations, and Assistance Agencies*. Medford, MA: Feinstein International Famine Center, Tufts University.

Downs, George, and Stephen Stedman. 2002. "Evaluation Issues in Peace Implementation." In *Ending Civil Wars: The Implementation of Peace Agreements*, ed. Stephen Stedman, Donald Rothchild, and Elizabeth Cousens, 43-69. Boulder and London: Lynne Rienner Publishers.

Doyle, Michael W., and Nicholas Sambanis. 2000. "International Peacebuilding: A Theoretical and Quantitative Analysis." *American Political Science Review* 94, 4 (2000): 779-801.

Dunham, David, and Sisira Jayasuriya. 2000. "Equity, Growth and Insurrection: Liberalization and the Welfare Debate in Contemporary Sri Lanka." *Oxford Development Studies* 28, 1: 97-110.

Espacio de concertación por la paz, la dignidad y la justicia social. 2007. *Evaluación de 15 años después de la firma de los Acuerdos de Paz en El Salvador* [Evaluation of 15 years after the signing of the peace accords in El Salvador]. San Salvador: Espacio de concertación por la paz, la dignidad y la justicia social.

Falcoff, Mark. 1996. "What 'Operation Restore Democracy' Restored." *Commentary* 10, 5: 45-48.

Faltas, Sami, Glenn MacDonald, and Camilla Waszink. 2001. *Removing Small Arms from Society: A Review of Weapons Collection and Destruction Programmes*. Occasional Paper 2. Geneva: Small Arms Survey.

Fanon, Frantz. 1963. *The Wretched of the Earth*. Trans. Constance Farrington. New York: Grove Press.

Farr, Vanessa. 2003. "The Importance of a Gender Perspective to Successful Disarmament, Demobilisation and Reintegration Processes." *Disarmament Forum* 4: 25-35.

Fearon, James, and David Laitin. 2003. "Ethnicity, Insurgency and Civil Wars." *American Political Science Review* 97, 1: 75-90.

Feinstein International Famine Center. 2004. *Human Security and Livelihoods of Rural Afghans, 2002-2003*. Boston: Feinstein International Famine Center.

Ferdinands, Tyrol, Kumar Rupesinghe, Paikiasothy Saravanamuttu, Jayadeva Uyangoda, and Norbert Ropers. 2004. *The Sri Lankan Peace Process at a Crossroads: Lessons, Opportunities and Ideas for Principled Negotiations and Conflict Transformation*. Colombo: Berghof Foundation for Conflict Studies.

Fitoussi, Jean-Paul. 2004. *La démocratie et le marché* [Democracy and the market]. Paris: Grasset.

Fleiner, Thomas, and Lidija R. Basta Fleiner. 2002. "Federalism, Federal States and Decentralization." In *Federalism and Multiethnic States: The Case of Switzerland*, ed. Thomas Fleiner and Lidija R. Basta Fleiner, 1-40. Fribourg: Institute of Federalism.

Foro Nacional de la Mujer. 2002. *Avances en la participación de las mujeres Guatemaltecas, 1997-2001* [Advances in the participation of Guatemalan women, 1997-2001]. Guatemala: Artgrafic de Guatemala.

Galtung, Johan. 1969. "Violence, Peace and Peace Research." *Journal of Peace Research* 6, 3: 167–91.

–. 1990. "Cultural Violence." *Journal of Peace Research* 27, 3: 291-305.

Gálvez, Victor. 2002. "Condiciones para la participación ciudadana y comunitaria: A propósito de las leyes recién emitidas que pretenden impulsarse" [Conditions for citizen and community participation: On the recent laws being promoted]. In *Participación social y poder local en Guatemala* [Social participation and local power in Guatemala], ed. V. Gálvez, L. Linares, and R. Velásquez, 9-25. Guatemala: MINUGUA and FLACSO.

Gamba, Virginia. 2003. "Managing Violence: Disarmament and Demobilization." In *Contemporary Peacemaking: Conflict, Violence and Peace Processes*, ed. John Darby and Roger MacGinty, 125-36. New York: Palgrave Macmillan.

Gamboa, Nuria, and Barbara Trentavizi. 2001. *La Guatemala posible: La senda del pacto fiscal* [The possible Guatemala: The path of the fiscal pact]. Guatemala: Hombres de Maiz, FyG Editores.

Gear, Sasha. 2002. *Now That the War Is Over: Ex-Combatants and the Question of Violence – A Literature Review*. Violence and Transition Series. Johannesburg: Centre for the Study of Violence and Reconciliation. http://www.csvr.org.za/papers/papvtp9.htm.

Giacaman, Rita, Hana Saab, Viet Nguyen-Gillham, Anita Abdullah, and Ghada Naser. 2004. *Palestinian Adolescents Coping with Trauma, Initial Findings*. Institute of Community and Public Health, Birzeit University, Occupied Palestinian Territory/Social Program Evaluation Group, Faculties of Education and Health Sciences, Queen's University, Kingston, Ontario, Canada. http://icph.birzeit.edu/.

Gills, Barry, Joel Rocamora, and Richard Wilson. 1993. *Low-Intensity Democracy*. London: Pluto Press.

Giustozzi, Antonio. 2003. *Respectable Warlords? The Politics of State-Building in Post-Taliban Afghanistan*. London: DESTIN, LSE.

–. 2004. *"Good" State vs. "Bad" Warlords? A Critique of State-Building Strategies in Afghanistan*. London: DESTIN, LSE.

–. N.d. *Re-Building the Afghan Army*. London: Development Research Centre, LSE.

GOA/MRRD/NSP (Government of Afghanistan, Ministry of Rural Rehabilitation and Development, National Solidarity Program). 2003a. *1383: Project Document for National Solidarity Program, Livelihoods and Social Protection Program*. Kabul: Ministry of Rural Rehabilitation and Development.

–. 2003b. *National Solidarity Program Operations Manual, March 1, 2003*. Kabul: Ministry of Rural Rehabilitation and Development.

–. 2005a. *National Solidarity Program after 2006: A Proposal for an Exit Strategy for the Oversight Consultant, .Working Draft, May 2005*. Kabul: Ministry of Rural Rehabilitation and Development.

–. 2005b. *Program Profiles*. Kabul: Ministry of Rural Rehabilitation and Development.

–. 2006a. "Results of the NSP CDC Conference, Kabul, 2005." Unpublished report. Kabul: Ministry of Rural Rehabilitation and Development.

–. 2006b. NSP Website. http://www.nspafghanistan.com/March_2006.

Gobierno de Guatemala. 1997. *Invirtiendo en la reconciliación nacional, democracia y desarrollo sostenido: Informe de la reunión de seguimiento del Grupo Consultivo de Bruselas* [Investing in national reconciliation, democracy and sustained development: Report of the follow-up meeting of the Brussels Consultative Group]. Antigua, Guatemala: SE.

–. Grupo Consultivo de Seguimiento. 2003. *Caminando a la paz con reconciliación y desarrollo* [Walking toward peace with reconciliation and development]. Guatemala: Ministerio de Finanzas Públicas.

–. Vicepresidencia de la república. Secretaría de la paz. 2004. *Gestión de fortalecimiento de la sociedad civil en el marco del relanzamiento de los acuerdos de paz* [Managing the reinforcement of civil society and relaunching the peace accords]. Guatemala: SE.

Goodhand, Jonathan. 2002. "Aiding Violence or Building Peace? The Role of International Aid in Afghanistan." *Third World Quarterly* 23, 5: 837–59.

Goodhand, Jonathan, and Bart Klem. 2005. *Aid, Conflict and Peacebuilding in Sri Lanka, 2000-2005*. Colombo: The Asia Foundation.

Government of Afghanistan. 2005. *Vision 2020 – Millennium Development Goals: Islamic Republic of Afghanistan Country Report, 2005.* http://www.ands.gov.af/src/src/MDGs_Reps/MDGR%202005.pdf.

Government of Afghanistan, United Nations, and International Community. 2006. *Afghanistan Compact.* http://www.unama-afg.org/news/_londonConf/_docs/06jan30-AfghanistanCompact-Final.pdf.

Government of Sri Lanka. 2002. *Regaining Sri Lanka: Vision and Strategy for Accelerated Development.* Colombo: Government of Sri Lanka.

GPPAC (Global Partnership for the Prevention of Armed Conflict). 2005. *People Building Peace: A Global Action Agenda for the Prevention of Violent Conflict.* Utrecht: ECCP.

Granma [English language edition of the newspaper of Cuba's Communist Party]. 2006. Vol. 42, no. 157: 7.

Green, Leslie. 1995. "Internal Minorities and their Rights." In *The Rights of Minority Cultures,* ed. Will Kymlicka, 256-72. Oxford: Oxford University Press.

Gross, Jean-Germain. 1996. "Towards a Taxonomy of Failed States in the New World Order: Decaying Somalia, Liberia, Rwanda and Haiti." *Third World Quarterly* 17, 3: 455-71.

GTZ. 2001. *Demobilisation and Reintegration of Ex-Combatants in Post-War and Transition Countries.* Eschborn, Germany: GTZ.

Guardian Weekly. 2006. Vol. 174, no. 25 (June 9-15); Vol. 174, no. 26 (June 16-22); and Vol. 175, no. 1 (June 23-29).

Gutierrez, Edgar. 2004. "Minugua y el regateo de la historia" [MINUGUA and the abandonment of history]. *Informe Guatemala* [Guatemala report] 1, 6: 1-3.

Hagman, Lotta. 2002. *Lessons Learned: Peacebuilding in Haiti.* New York: International Peace Academy.

Hampson, Fen Osler. 1996. *Nurturing Peace: Why Peace Settlements Succeed or Fail?* Washington, DC: United States Institute of Peace.

Hanieh, Akram. 2001. "Camp David Papers." *Al-Ayyam Newspaper,* 29 July-10 August. Reprinted as "The Camp David Papers." *Journal of Palestine Studies* 30, 2 (2001): 75-97.

Hanlon, Joseph. 1984/90. *Mozambique: The Revolution under Fire.* London and New Jersey: Zed Books Ltd.

–. 1996. *Peace without Profit: How the IMF Blocks Rebuilding in Mozambique.* Oxford: James Currey and Heinemann.

Harnecker, Marta, 2000. *La izquierda en el umbral del siglo XXI* [The left on the threshold of the 21st century]. Spain: Siglo Veintiuno Editores.

Hartzell, Caroline. 1999. "Explaining the Stability of Negotiated Settlements to Intrastate Wars." *Journal of Conflict Resolution* 43, 1 (1999): 3-22.

Harvard Law Students Advocates for Human Rights and Centro de Justiça Global. 2005. *Keeping the Peace in Haiti?* Cambridge: Harvard University.

Hassan, Minoz. 2002. "Finanças municipais" [Municipal finances]. In *Jornalística do processo de descentralização* [Journal of the decentralization process], ed. A. Cobertura, 40-52. Maputo: Fundação Friedrich Ebert-Moçambique.

Hauge, Wenche. 2003. "Causes and Dynamics of Conflict Escalation: The Role of Economic Development and Environmental Change – A Comparative Study of Bangladesh, Guatemala, Haiti, Madagascar, Senegal and Tunisia." PhD diss., University of Oslo.

Hauge, Wenche, and Beate Thoresen. 2006. "The Fate of Former Combatants in Guatemala: Spoilers or Agents for Change?" Unpublished WKOP working paper.

Hector, Cary. 1985. "Des 'prises de démocratie' de la société civile au renouvellement des pratiques répressives du pouvoir, 1975-1983" [The "grips of democracy" of civil society in the renewal of repressive practices of power, 1975-1983]. *Collectif paroles* [Collective words] 32: 8-15.

–. 2007. "L'intervention multinationale de 2004 en Haïti: Antecedents, resultats et perspectives" [The multinational intervention of 2004 in Haiti: Antecedents, results and perspectives]. *Pensamiento propio* [Own thought] 25: 11-46.

Human Rights Research and Advocacy Consortium. 2004. *Take the Guns Away.* Kabul: HRRAC.

Human Rights Watch. 2007. *The Human Cost: The Consequences of Insurgent Attacks in Afghanistan.* http://www.hrw.org/reports/2007/afghanistan0407/afghanistan0407web.pdf.

Hunguana, Carolina. 2001. "Decentralisation et pouvoir urbain au Mozambique: Le cas de Maputo et Matola" [Decentralization and urban power in Mozambique: The case of Maputo and Matola]. MA thesis, Université de Lyon II.

Huntington, Samuel P. 1991. *The Third Wave: Democratization in the Late Twentieth Century*. Norman: University of Oklahoma Press.

ICG (International Crisis Group). 2003. *Disarmament and Reintegration in Afghanistan: ICG Asia Report 65*. Kabul/Brussels: ICG.

–. 2004a. *Dealing with Hamas: ICG Middle East Report 21*. Amman/Brussels: ICG.

–. 2004b. *Iraq's Transition: On a Knife Edge, Middle East Report 27*. Baghdad/Brussels: ICG.

–. 2004c. *A New Chance for Haiti?* Port-au-Prince/Brussels: ICG.

–. 2004d. *Who Governs the West Bank? Palestinian Administration under Israeli Occupation: ICG Middle East Report 32*. Amman/Brussels: ICG.

–. 2005. *Enter Hamas: The Challenge of Political Integration: ICG Middle East Report 49*. Amman/Brussels: ICG.

–. 2006. *Israel/Palestine/Lebanon: Climbing out of the Abyss: ICG Middle East Report 57*. Amman/Beirut/Brussels/Jerusalem: ICG.

ICISS (International Commission on Intervention and State Sovereignty). 2001. *The Responsibility to Protect: Report of the International Commission on Intervention and State Sovereignty*. Ottawa: IDRC.

Ignatieff, Michael. 2003. *Empire Light: Nation Building in Bosnia, Kosovo, Afghanistan*. London: Minerva.

Institut Haïtien de statistiques et d'informatique, DARD (Division d'analyses et de recherches démographiques). Conversations. 1999-2007. Port-au-Prince. (DARD typically provides information orally rather than through publications.)

Instituto Nacional de Estatística [Mozambique]. 2006. *Agenda Estatística 2006* [Statistical agenda 2006]. Maputo: INE.

Inter-American Development Bank, Regional Operations Department II, Country Division 3. 2002. *Guatemala: International Assistance, Summary of Internationally Financed Projects*. Washington: IADB.

–. 2003. *Community-Driven Rural Development: What Have We Learned?* Washington, DC: IADB.

International Labour Organisation. 1997. *ILO and Conflict-Affected People and Countries*. Geneva: International Labour Organisation.

International Monetary Fund. 2001. *West Bank and Gaza, Economic Performance, Prospects, and Policies: Achieving Prosperity and Confronting Demographic Challenges*. Washington, DC: IMF.

International Network for the Availability of Scientific Publications. 2004. "Rural Development Directory, International Network for the Availability of Scientific Publications from 435 International, Regional and National Networks and Organisations in Rural Development around the Globe." http://www.inasp.info/pubs/rd/html/introd.htm.

IRIN. 2005. "Progress on Disbandment of Illegal Armed Groups." IRIN News. http://www.irinnews.org/report.aspx?reportid=28724.

Israeli Ministry of Foreign Affairs. 1995. *Israeli-Palestinian Interim Agreement on the West Bank and the Gaza Strip*. Jerusalem: MFA.

–. 2004a. *The Disengagement Plan: General Outline*. Jerusalem: MFA.

–. 2004b. *Israeli-Palestinian Interim Agreement on the West Bank and the Gaza Strip, September 28*. Jerusalem: MFA.

Jadotte, Hérard. 2005. *Le Carnaval de la révolution: De Duvalier à Aristide* [The carnival of the revolution: From Duvalier to Aristide]. Port-au-Prince: Éditions Fardin.

Jadotte, Hérard, and Yves-Francois Pierre. 2006. "Haiti: Transition inachevée et consolidation de la paix" [Haiti: Incomplete transition and peacebuilding]. WKOP working paper. Port-au-Prince: Université de Notre Dame d'Haïti.

Jayawardena, Lal. 1994. *Sri Lanka: The Outlook for Employment and Economic Growth during the Next Decade, 1995-2005*. Colombo: N.p.

Jensen, Steffen, and Finn Stepputat. 2001. *Demobilizing Armed Civilians*. CDR policy paper. Copenhagen: Centre for Development Research.

Jonas, Susan. 2000. *De centauros y palomas: El proceso de paz Guatemalteco* [Of centaurs and doves: The Guatemalan process of peace]. Guatemala: FLACSO.

Jones, Seth, and K. Jack Riley. 2004. "Law and Order in Palestine." *Survival* 46, 4: 157-78.

Karim, Farahnaz, and Gregory Hess. 2001. *Thinking about Aid Management and Peacebuilding in Afghanistan*. Rome: Peacepath Consulting.

Karzai, Hamid. 2007. "Corruption Not Only in Government Says Karzai." *Afghanistan Times*.

Keating, Tom, and Andy Knight, eds. 2004. *Building Sustainable Peace*. Edmonton: University of Alberta Press.

Kelegama, Saman. 1999. "Economic Costs of Conflict in Sri Lanka." In *Creating Peace in Sri Lanka: Civil War and Reconciliation*, ed. Robert I. Rotberg, 71-88. Washington, DC: Brookings Institution Press.

–. 2004. "Economic Dividend of the Post-War Period in Sri Lanka: Problems and Prospects." IPS working paper. Colombo: Institute of Policy Studies.

Kingma, Kees. 1997. "Demobilization of Combatants after Civil War in Africa and Their Reintegration into Civilian Life." *Policy Sciences* 30: 151-65.

–. 2002a. "Demobilization, Reintegration and Peacebuilding in Africa." *International Peacekeeping* 9, 2: 181-201.

–. 2002b. "Improving External Support for Reintegration of Combatants into Civilian Life." Paper presented at IPA-UNDP Conference entitled "A Framework for Lasting Demobilization, Disarmament and Reintegration of Former Combatants in Crisis Situations," New York, 12-13 December.

Knight, Mark, and Alpaslan Özerdem. 2004. "Guns, Camps and Cash: Disarmament, Demobilization and Reinsertion of Former Combatants in Transitions from War to Peace." *Journal of Peace Research* 41, 4: 499-516.

Knoerzer, Shari. 1988. "Transformation of Muslim Political Identity." In *Culture and Politics of Identity in Sri Lanka*, ed. Mithran Tiruchelvam and C.S. Dattathreya, 136-67. Colombo: International Centre for Ethnic Studies.

Kruij, Dirk, and Rudie Van Meurs. 2000. *El guerrillero y el general: Rodrigo Asturias y Julio Balconi – Sobre la guerra y la paz en Guatemala* [The guerrilla and the general: Rodrigo Asturias and Julio Balconi – On war and peace in Guatemala]. Guatemala: FLACSO.

Kumar, Chetan. 1999. "Sustainable Peace as Sustainable Democracy: The Experience of Haiti." *International Politics and Society* 4: 380-91.

Lakshman, W.D. 2002. "Cease-Fire Agreement and Beyond." *Pravada* 8, 4: 17-20.

Lederach, John Paul. 1997. *Building Peace: Sustainable Reconciliation in Divided Societies*. Washington: United States Institute of Peace.

Ley de los consejos de desarrollo urbano y rural y su reglamento [Law of the councils of urban and rural development and its regulation]. 2002. Decreto número 11-2002 [Decree number 11-2002]. Guatemala: Librería Jurídica.

Lodgaard, Sverre. 1997. "Managing Arms in Peace Processes." *Policy Sciences* 30: 143-50.

Loganathan, Ketesh. 1996. *Sri Lanka: Lost Opportunities, Past Attempts at Resolving Ethnic Conflict*. Colombo: University of Colombo.

Maas, Gero, and David Mepham. 2004. *Promoting Effective States: A Progressive Policy Response to Failed and Failing States*. London: Friedrich Ebert Stiftung and the Institute for Public Policy Research.

Maley, William. 1998. *Fundamentalism Reborn? Afghanistan and the Taliban*. New York: NYU Press.

Mallaby, Sebastian. 2002. "The Reluctant Imperialist: Terrorism, Failed States, and the Case for American Empire." *Foreign Affairs* 81, 2: 2-7.

Malley, Robert, and Hussein Agha. 2001. "The Palestinian-Israeli Camp David Negotiations and Beyond." *Journal of Palestine Studies* 31, 1: 62-85.

Maloney, Sean M. 2004. "Afghanistan: From Here to Eternity?" US Army Professional Writing Collection, US Army Home Page. http://www.army.mil/professionalwriting/volumes/volume2/october_2004/10_04.html.

Manchanda, Rita, ed. 2001. *Women, War and Peace in South Asia: Beyond Victimhood to Agency*. London: Sage Publications.

Manning, Carrie. 2003. "Local Challenges to Post-Conflict Peacebuilding." *International Peacekeeping* 10, 3: 25-43.

Martínez, Miguel. 2003. *Palabras de clausura del presidente del Grupo Consultivo para Guatemala: 13 y 14 de mayo de 2003* [Closing address of the president of the Consultative Group for Guatemala: 13 and 14 May 2003]. Guatemala: Ministerio de Finanzas. (Photocopy of transcribed version.)

Mashike, Lephophotho. 2000. "Standing Down or Standing Out? Demobilising and Reintegrating Former Soldiers." *African Security Review* 9, 5/6. http://www.issafrica.org/pubs/ASR/9No5And6/Mashike.html.

Mayer, Markus, Darini Rajasingham-Senanayake, and Yuvi Thangarajah, eds. 2003. *Building Local Capacities for Peace: Rethinking Conflict and Development in Sri Lanka*. Delhi: Macmillan India, Ltd.

Mazula, Brazão. 2000. *A construção da democracia em África: O caso moçambicano* [The construction of democracy in Africa: The Mozambican case]. Maputo: Ndjira.

–, ed. 2002. *Mozambique: Dez anos de paz* [Mozambique: Ten years of peace]. Maputo: CEDE.

Mazurana, Dyan, Susan McKay, Khristopher Carlson, and Janel Kasper. 2002. "Girls in Fighting Forces and Groups: Their Recruitment, Participation, Demobilisation and Reintegration." *Peace and Conflict: Journal of Peace Psychology* 8: 97-123.

McCann, I. Lisa, and Laurie Anne Pearlman. 1990. *Psychological Trauma and the Adult Survivor: Theory, Therapy, and Transformation*. NYC: Brunnel/Mazer.

McCartney, Clem. 2005. "From Armed Struggle to Political Negotiations: Why? When? How?" In *Choosing to Engage: Armed Groups and Peace Processes, Accord 16*, ed. Robert Ricigliano. http://www.c-r.org/accord/engage/accord 16/07.shtml.

Milton-Edwards, Beverley, and Alastair Crooke. 2004. "Waving, Not Drowning: Strategic Dimensions of Ceasefires and Islamic Movements." *Security Dialogue* 35, 3: 295-310.

MINUGUA (Universidad Rafael Landívar and Misión de Verificación de las Naciones Unidas en Guatemala). 1997. *Acuerdos de paz: Firmados por el gobierno de la República de Guatemala y la Unidad Revolucionaria Guatemalteca (URNG)* [Peace accords: Signed by the government of the Republic of Guatemala and the Guatemalan Revolutionary Union (URNG)]. Guatemala: Universidad Rafael Landívar and MINUGUA.

–. 2004a. *Informe del secretario general de las Naciones Unidas sobre verificación de los acuerdos de paz de Guatemala* [Report of the Secretary-General of the United Nations on the verification of the Guatemalan Peace Accords]. Guatemala: Oficina de información de MINUGUA.

–. 2004b. *Situación de la mujer: Retomando el camino – Tareas pendientes en la construcción de la paz* [The situation of women: Retaking the way – pending tasks in the construction of peace]. Guatemala: Oficina de Información Pública de MINUGUA.

Mirador Electoral. 2003a. *Informe de observancia 6* [Observation report 6]. Guatemala: Mirador Electoral.

–. 2003b. *Informe de observancia 7* [Observation report 7]. Guatemala: Mirador Electoral.

Mohideen, M.I.M. 2005. "Sri Lanka Peace Process and the Muslim Question." Unpublished paper.

Molketin, Gudrun. 2001. *Los difíciles senderos de la paz en Guatemala* [The difficult paths of peace in Guatemala]. Guatemala: FLACSO.

Mondlane, Eduardo. 1969. *The Struggle for Mozambique*. London: Penguin Books.

Monroy, Alfonso. 2005. *Los acuerdos de paz: Resultados y perspectivas desde el punto de vista de miembros de las comunidades populares en resistencia del Petén (CPR-P)* [The peace accords: Results and perspectives from the point of view of members of the popular communities in resistance of Petén (CPR-P)]. Guatemala City: N.p.

Monteforte Toledo, Mario. 1997. *Vinicio: Entrevista de Mario Monteforte Toledo* [Vinicio: Interview of Mario Monteforte Toledo]. Guatemala: Artemio Edinter.

Moore, David. 2000. "Levelling the Playing Fields and Embedding Illusions: 'Post-Conflict' Discourse and Neo-Liberal 'Development' in War-Torn Africa." *Review of African Political Economy* 27, 83: 11-28.

Morrell, James, Rachel Neild, and Hugh Byrne. 1999. "Haiti and the Limits to Nation-Building." *Current History* 98, 626: 127–32.

Muggah, Robert. 2005. "No Magic Bullet: A Critical Perspective on Disarmament, Demobilization and Reintegration (DDR) and Weapons Reduction in Post-Conflict Contexts." *The Round Table* 94, 379: 239-52.

Munslow, Barry. 1983. *Mozambique: The Revolution and Its Origins*. London, New York, and Lagos: Longman.

Murphy, Alexander. 1995. "Belgium's Regional Divergence: Along the Road to Federation." In *Federalism: The Multiethnic Challenge*, ed. Graham Smith, 73-100. London and New York: Longman.

Myrttinen, Henri. 2003. "Disarming Masculinities." *Disarmament Forum: Women, Men, Peace and Security* 4 (2003): 37-46.

Narayan, Deepa, and Jennifer Rietbergen-McCracken. 1998. *Participation and Social Assessment, Tools and Techniques*. Washington, DC: World Bank.

Nathan, Laurie, 2001. "The Four Horsemen of the Apocalypse: The Structural Causes of Crisis and Violence in Africa." *Track Two* 10, 2: 1-13.

Newitt, Malyn. 1995. *A History of Mozambique*. London: Hurst and Company.

Nitzschke, Heiko, and Kaysie Studdard. 2005. "The Legacies of War Economies: Challenges and Options for Peacemaking and Peacebuilding." *International Peacekeeping* 12, 2: 222-39.

Norwegian Ministry of Foreign Affairs. 2004. *Strategic Framework: Peacebuilding – A Development Perspective*. Oslo: Utenriksdepartmentet.

ODHAG (Oficina de Derechos Humanos del Arzobispado de Guatemala). 1998a. *Guatemala nunca mas II: Los mecanismos del horror – Informe proyecto interdiocesano de recuperacion de la memoria historica* [Guatemala never again II: The mechanisms of horror – Report of the Inter-Diocesan Project on the Recuperation of Historical Memory]. San José: Litografia e Imprenta LIL, S.A.

–. 1998b. *Guatemala nunca mas III: El entorno historico – Informe proyecto interdiocesano de recuperacion de la memoria historica* [Guatemala never again III: The mechanisms of horror – Report of the Inter-Diocesan Project on the Recuperation of Historical Memory]. San José: Litografia e Imprenta LIL, S.A.

OECD. 2001. *The DAC Guidelines: Helping Prevent Violent Conflict*. Paris: OECD.

OECD DAC/DCD. 2005. "Principles for Good International Engagement in Fragile States." Draft Note by the Secretariat. Paris: OECD DAC/DCD.

Ofstad, Arve. 2002. "Countries in Violent Conflict and Aid Strategies: The Case of Sri Lanka." *World Development* 30, 2: 165-80.

Olesen, Asta. 1995. *Islam and Politics in Afghanistan*. Surrey, UK: Curzon Press.

Oriols Prats, J. 2000. *Concepto de gobernabilidad* [Concept of governability]. Barcelona: Instituto de Gobernabilidad.

Özerdem, Alpaslan. 2002. "Disarmament, Demobilisation and Reintegration of Former Combatants in Afghanistan: Lessons Learned from a Cross-Cultural Perspective." *Third World Quarterly* 23, 5: 961-75.

Pain, Adam. 2004. *Understanding Village Institutions: Case Studies on Water Management from Faryab and Saripul*. Kabul: Afghanistan Research and Evaluation Unit.

PCBS (Palestinian Central Bureau of Statistics). 2003. *PCBS Selected Statistics*. Ramallah: PCBS.

PCBS (Palestinian Central Bureau of Statistics) and World Bank. 2004. "Deep Palestinian Poverty in the Midst of Economic Crisis." Working paper. Ramallah and Washington: PCBS and World Bank. http://www-wds.worldbank.org/servlet/WDSContentServer/WDSP/IB/2004/11/24/000112742_20041124092935/Rendered/PDF/307510Eng.pdf.

Paris, Roland. 1997. "Peacebuilding and the Limits of Liberal Internationalism." *International Security* 22, 2: 54-89.

–. 2004. *At War's End: Building Peace after Civil Conflict*. Cambridge: Cambridge University Press.

Pásara, Luis. 2003. *Paz, ilusión y cambio en Guatemala: El proceso de paz, sus sctores, logros y límites* [Peace, illusion and change in Guatemala: The peace process, its actors, achievements, and limits]. Guatemala: Instituto de Investigaciones Jurídicas, Universidad Rafael Landívar.

Patel, Seema, and Steven Ross. 2007. *Breaking Point: Measuring Progress in Afghanistan*. Washington, DC: Center for Strategic and International Studies Press.

Pearce, Jenny. 1999. "Peace-Building in the Periphery: Lessons from Central America." *Third World Quarterly* 20, 1: 51-68.

Pei, Minxin. 2002. "Implementing the Institutions of Democracy." *International Journal on World Peace* 19, 4: 3–29.

Pellecer Arellano, Carmen Lucía. 2004. "Estudio: De la conclusión de la guerra a la consolidación de la paz – Que clase de paz es posible?" [Study: From the conclusion of the war to the consolidation of peace – What kind of peace is possible?]. Guatemala: Informe de consultoría, Programa Participacion y Democracia (PPD).

Perry, Mark, and Alastair Crooke. 2006a. "How To Lose the 'War on Terror,' Part 1: Talking with the 'Terrorists.'" *Asia Times* 31 March. http://www.atimes.com/atimes/Middle_East/HC31Ak02.html.

–. 2006b. "How to Lose the 'War on Terror,' Part 2: Handing Victory to the Extremists." *Asia Times*, 1 April. http://www.atimes.com/atimes/Middle_East/HD01Ak02.html.

–. 2006c. "How to Lose the 'War on Terror,' Part 3: An Exchange Of Narratives." *Asia Times*, 3 June. http://www.atimes.com/atimes/Middle_East/HF03Ak01.html.

Pershing, Timothy. 2004. "Transitions from Authoritarian Rule and Regime Consolidation: Leaving Democracy Out." *Brandeis Graduate Journal* 2: 67-81.

Philipson, Liz. 2005. "Engaging Armed Groups: The Challenge of Asymmetries." In *Choosing to Engage: Armed Groups and Peace Processes, Accord 16*, ed. Robert Ricigliano. http://www.c-r.org/accord/engage/accord 16/16.shtml.

Powell, Kristiana. 2005. "The African Union's Emerging Peace and Security Regime: Opportunities and Challenges for Delivering on the Responsibility to Protect." NSI working paper. Ottawa: North-South Institute.

Powell, Kristiana, and Stephen Baranyi. 2006. *Closing the Gaps between Desirable and Possible Peace: A Conference Report*. Ottawa: The North-South Institute.

Presidencia de la República. Coordinación de la Crónica Presidencial. 1997. *De las palabras a las obras: Crónica de la paz 1996* [From words to works: Chronicle of peace, 1996]. Guatemala: Editorial del Ejército.

President of the United States. 2002. *The National Security Strategy of the United States of America*. Washington, DC: President of the United States.

Pretty, Jules N., Irene Guijt, John Thompson, and Ian Scoones. 1995. *Participatory Learning and Action: A Trainer's Guide*. London: International Institute for Environment and Development.

Procurador de los derechos humanos. 1994. *Los Comités de Defensa Civil en Guatemala* [The civil defence committees in Guatemala]. Guatemala: Procuraduría de los derechos humanos.

–. 2004. *Resolución sobre el desalojo en la finca "Nueva Linda," Champerico, Retalhuleu* [Resolution on the evacuation of the "Nueva Linda" property, Champerico, Retalhuleu]. Guatemala: Procuradoria de los derechos humanos.

Putnam, Robert D. 1988. "Diplomacy and Domestic Politics: The Logic of Two Level Games." *International Organization* 42, 3: 427-60.

Qouta, Samir, Raija-Leena Punamaki, and Eyad el-Sarraj. 1995. "The Relations between Traumatic Experiences, Activity, and Cognitive and Emotional Responses among Palestinian Children." *International Journal of Psychology* 30, 3: 289-304.

Rajasingham-Senanayake, Darini. 1999. "The Dangers of Devolution: The Hidden Economies of Armed Conflict." In *Creating Peace in Sri Lanka: Civil War and Reconciliation*, ed. Robert Rotberg, 57-87. Washington, DC: Brookings Institution Press.

–. 2003. "The Economics of Peace: The World Bank, Information Asymmetries and the Post-Conflict Industry." *Polity* 1, 1: 17-20.

RAND Corporation. 2005. *Building a Successful Palestinian State*. Santa Monica: RAND Corporation.

Reilly, Benjamin, Peter Harris, and Michael Lund. 1998. *Democracy and Deep-Rooted Conflict*. Sweden: Institute for Democracy and Electoral Assistance.

Reimann, Cordula. 2004. "Assessing the State of the Art in Conflict Transformation." In *Berghof Handbook for Conflict Transformation*, ed. David Bloomfield, Martina Fischer, and Beatrix Schmelzle. Berlin: Berghof Research Center for Constructive Conflict Management. http://www.berghof-handbook.net/articles/baechler_handbook.pdf.

République d'Haïti. 2004. Câdre de coopération intérimaire: Rapport de synthèse [Interim cooperation framework: Summary report]. http://haiticci.undg.org/uploads/ReportVersion8%20Fre%20FINAL%20Low%20Res.pdf.

Roberts, Michael. 1978. "Ethnic Conflict in Sri Lanka and Sinhalese Perspectives: Barriers to Accommodation." *Modern Asian Studies* 12, 5: 353-76.

Roberts, Nigel, and Stefano Mocci. 2005. "Palestinian Economic Revival." *bitterlemons-international.org* 3, 15. http://www.bitterlemons-international.org/previous.php?opt=1&id=81.

Robinson, William. 1996. *Promoting Polyarchy: Globalization, US Intervention and Hegemony*. Cambridge: Cambridge University Press.

Rocca, Roberto Morozzo della. 1998. *Moçambique da guerra a paz* [Mozambique: From war to peace]. Maputo: UEM-Livraria Universitária.

Rosende, Raul. 2002. "La descentralización y la construcción de la paz" [Decentralization and the construction of peace]. In *Participación social y poder local en Guatemala* [Social participation and local power in Guatemala], ed. V. Gálvez, L. Linares, and R. Velásquez, 53-64. Guatemala: MINUGUA and FLACSO.

Rotberg, Robert. 2002. "The New Nature of Nation-State Failure." *Washington Quarterly* 25, 3: 85-96.

Rothstein, Robert, Khalil Shikaki, and Moshe Ma'oz. 2002. *The Israeli-Palestinian Peace Process: Oslo and the Lessons of Failure*. East Sussex: Sussex Academic Press.

Roy, Sara. 1999. "De-Development Revisited: Palestinian Society and Economy since Oslo." *Journal of Palestine Studies* 27, 3: 64-82.

–. 2004. "Religious Nationalism and the Palestinian-Israeli Conflict: Examining Hamas and the Possibility of Reform." *Chicago Journal of International Law* 5, 1: 251-70.

Rubin, Barnett R. 2002. *The Fragmentation of Afghanistan: State Formation and Collapse in the International System*. New Haven, CT: Yale University Press.

–. 2003. "Identifying Options and Entry Points for Disarmament, Demobilization, and Reintegration in Afghanistan." In *Confronting Afghanistan's Security Dilemma: Reforming the Security Sector, Brief 28*, ed. Mark Sedra, 40-44. Bonn: Bonn International Center for Conversion-BICC.

–. 2005. *Afghanistan 2005 and Beyond: Prospects for Improved Stability*. New York: Center on International Cooperation, New York University for the Clingendael Institute.

–. 2006. *Afghanistan's Uncertain Transition: From Turmoil to Normalcy*. New York, Council on Foreign Relations.

–. N.d. "Afghanistan and Threats to Security." Social Sciences Research Council Essay. http://www.ssrc.org/sept11/essays/rubin.htm.

Rupesinghe, Kumar. 1995. *Conflict Transformation*. Houndmills, UK: Macmillian.

–, ed. 1998. *Negotiating Peace in Sri Lanka: Efforts, Failures and Lessons*. London: International Alert.

–. 2003. "Redesigning the Peace Process." *Polity* 1, 1: 9-11.

Rupiah, Martin. 1995. "Demobilisation and Integration: 'Operation Merger' and the Zimbabwe National Defence Forces, 1980-1987." *African Security Review* 4, 3. http://www.iss.co.za/pubs/ASR/4No3/Demobilisation.html.

Sáenz de Tejada, Ricardo. 2004. *Victimas o vencedores? Una aproximacíon al movimiento de los ex PAC* [Victims or winners? An assessment of the ex-PAC movement.] Guatemala: FLACSO.

Sahadevan, P. 2006. "Negotiating Peace in Ethnic Wars." *International Studies* 43, 3: 239-66.

Salahuddin, Sayed. 2005. "Afghanistan Seeks to Become Master of Its Own Aid." *Reuters*, 4 April. http://www.adf.gov.af/2005/press_review_2.asp#15th.

Saldomando, Angel. 2002. "Diagnóstico de la paz en América Central" [Diagnostic of peace in Central America]. IDRC working paper 6. Ottawa: IDRC.

Sarti, Carlos, ed. 2005. "Paz y democracia en Guatemala: Desafíos pendientes" [Peace and democracy in Guatemala: Pending challenges]. Report of the MINUGUA International

Conference entitled "Construyendo la paz desde un enfoque comparado" [Constructing peace from a comparative approach], 27-29 October. Guatemala: Propaz, MINUGUA.

Sayigh, Yezid. 2001. "Arafat and the Anatomy of a Revolt." *Survival* 43, 3: 47-60.

Sayigh, Yazid, and Khalil Shikaki. 1999. *Strengthening Palestinian Public Institutions*. New York: Council on Foreign Relations, Report of the Independent Task Force.

Schnabel, Albrecth, and David Carment, eds. 2004. *Conflict Prevention: From Rhetoric to Reality*. Toronto: Lexington Books.

Scholey, Pamela, and Khalil Shikaki. 2006. *Considering the International DDR Experience and "Spoiling": Lessons for Palestine*. Ottawa: The North-South Institute.

Secretaría de la Paz. 2005. *Agenda pública hacia los pueblos indígenas en el marco de los acuerdos de paz, 2005-2012 (SF): Resultado de los talleres de Antigua I, II y III, junio-julio 2005* [Public agenda towards the indigenous towns within the framework of the peace accords, 2005-2012 (SF): Result of the factories of Antigua I, II and III, June-July 2005]. Guatemala: SEPAZ.

Sedra, Mark. 2003. "New Beginning or Return to Arms? The Disarmament, Demobilization and Reintegration Process in Afghanistan." Paper presented at the conference entitled "State Reconstruction and International Engagement in Afghanistan," 30 May-1 June, Bonn.

Sedra, Mark, and Peter Middlebrook. 2004. "Afghanistan, the Problematic Path to Peace: Lessons in State Building in Post September 11th Era." *Foreign Policy in Focus*. http://www.fpif.org/indices/topics/terrorism/index.php.

SERJUS. 2005. "Desinstitucionalización del sistema de consejos de desarrollo en Guatemala" [Deinstitutionalization of the system of development councils in Guatemala]. Paper presented at the seminar entitled "Construyendo la democracia desde abajo: Descentralización, iniciativas locales y ciudadanía" [Constructing democracy from the bottom up: Decentralization, local initiatives and citizenship]. Guatemala: Woodrow Wilson Center for Scholars, FLACSO, Fundación Interamericana.

Shamsie, Yasmine. 2006. "International Political Economy Considerations for Democracy Promotion in Latin America: The Cases of Haiti and Guatemala." Paper presented at the Canadian Political Science Association Annual Meeting, 3 June, York University, Toronto.

Shikaki, Khalil. 2002. "Palestinians Divided." *Foreign Affairs* 81, 1: 89-105.

–. 2003a. *Building a State, Building a Peace: How to Make a Roadmap That Works for Palestinians and Israelis*. Washington DC: The Brookings Institution, Saban Center for Middle East Policy.

–. 2003b. *Reforming the Palestinian Authority: An Update*. Report of the Independent Task Force. New York: Council on Foreign Relations.

–. 2004a. "The Future of Palestine," *Foreign Affairs* 83, 6: 45-60.

–. 2004b. *A Palestinian Perspective on the Failure of the Permanent Status Negotiations*. Ramallah: Palestinian Center for Policy and Survey Research.

–. 2005. "What Kind of Peace Is Possible? The Case of Palestine: 1993-2005." WKOP working paper. Ramallah: Palestinian Center for Policy and Survey Research.

–. 2006. *Willing to Compromise: Palestinian Public Opinion and the Peace Process*. Washington DC: United States Institute of Peace.

Sieder, Rachel, ed. 1998. *Guatemala after the Peace Accords*. London: Institute of Latin American Studies, University of London.

Sinchar Moreno, Gonzalo. 1999. *Historia de los partidos políticos Guatemaltecos: Distintas siglas de (casi) una misma ideología, 2 edición* [History of the Guatemalan political parties: Different abbreviations from (almost) the same ideology, 2nd edition]. Guatemala: Editorial Nojib´sa.

Sitoe, Eduardo J. 2004. "Making Sense of the Political Transformations in Angola and Mozambique from 1984 to 1994." PhD diss., Essex University, UK.

Sitoe, Eduardo, and Carolina Hunguana. 2005. "Democratic Decentralization Is Needed to Keep the Mozambican Miracle Alive." WKOP working paper. Maputo: Centro de Estudios de Democracia y Desenvolvimento.

Smith, Dan. 2003. *Getting Their Act Together: Towards a Strategic Framework for Peacebuilding – Overview of the Joint Utstein Study of Peacebuilding*. Oslo: PRIO.

Smucker, Glenn. 1983. *Credit among Haitian Peasants*. Port-au-Prince: USAID.

Snow, John. 2001. "Chapter IV: Food for Work, an Evaluation Report of the Enhanced Food Security II Program." Project Report USAID Haiti Mission. Port-au-Prince, USAID.

Soberanis, Catalina. 2004. "La participación de los partidos políticos en el proceso de paz en Guatemala y su papel en el fortalecimiento del Organismo Legislativo" [The participation of political parties in the peace process in Guatemala and its place in the reinforcement of the legislative body]. Paper presented at the MINUGUA International Conference, 27-29 October, Guatemala.

Soiri, Lina. 1999. *Moçambique: Aprender a caminhar com uma bengala emprestada? Ligações entre descentralização e alívio à pobreza* [Mozambique: Learning to walk with a borrowed cane? Linkages between decentralization and poverty reduction]. http://www.ecdpm.org/Web_ECDPM/Web/Content/Download.nsf/0/527E6F32B78CC3BEC1256CAA0052727A/$FILE/99-013P-Soiri_ff_..pdf.

Solomon, Joel A. 1994. *Institutional Violence: Civil Patrols in Guatemala, 1993-1994*. Washington, DC: Robert F. Kennedy Center for Human Rights.

Solórzano, Braulia Thillet de, ed. 2004a. Los Consejos de Desarrollo frente al desafío de la transición hacia la democracia [The Development Councils facing the challenge of the transition to democracy]. Guatemala: PPD, FLACSO.

–. 2004b. *Memoria del foro descentralización y participación ciudadana* [Report of the forum on decentralization and citizen participation]. Guatemala: PPD, FLACSO.

Sontag, Deborah. 2001. "Quest for Middle East Peace: How and Why It Failed." *New York Times*, 26 July. Reprinted as "The Palestinian-Israeli Camp David Negotiations and Beyond." *Journal of Palestine Studies* 31, 1 (2001): 75-85.

Soto, Alvaro de, and Graciana del Castillo. 1995. "Implementation of Comprehensive Peace Agreements: Staying the Course in El Salvador." *Global Governance* 1, 2: 189-203.

Spear, Joanna. 2002. "Disarmament and Demobilization." In *Ending Civil Wars: The Implementation of Peace Agreements*, ed. Stephen John Stedman, Donald Rothschild, and Elizabeth Cousens, 141-82. Boulder, London: Lynne Rienner Publishers.

Srivastava, Neelam. 2005. "Anti-Colonial Violence and the 'Dictatorship of Truth' in the Films of Gillo Pontecorvo, An Interview." *Interventions* 7, 1: 97-106.

Stedman, Stephen. 1991. *Peacemaking in Civil War: International Mediation in Zimbabwe, 1974-1980*. Boulder and London: Lynne Rienner Publishers.

–. 1997. "Spoiler Problems in Peace Processes." *International Security* 22, 2: 5-53.

–. 2002. "Introduction." In *Ending Civil Wars: The Implementation of Peace Agreements*, ed. Stephen Stedman, Donald Rothschild, Elizabeth Cousens, 1-40. Boulder and London: Lynne Rienner Publishers.

Stedman, Stephen, Donald Rothschild, and Elisabeth M. Cousens, eds. 2002. *Ending Civil Wars: The Implementation of Peace Agreements*. Boulder and London: Lynne Rienner.

Stokke, Kristian. 2006. "Building the Tamil Eelam State: Emerging State Institutions and Forms of Governance in LTTE-Controlled Areas in Sri Lanka." Unpublished paper.

Strategic Assessments Initiative. 2005. "Planning Considerations for International Involvement in the Palestinian Security Sector: Operational Assessment." Washington, DC, and Jerusalem: SAI. http://www.strategicassessments.org/ontherecord/sai_publications/SAI-Planning_Considerations_for_International_Involvement_July_2005.pdf.

Strand, Arne. 2004. "The 'Mine Action for Peace' Programme, Afghanistan." Workshop report. Kabul: PRIO.

Strickland, Richard, and Nata Duvvury. 2003. *Gender Equity and Peacebuilding: From Rhetoric to Reality – Finding the Way, a Discussion Paper*. Washington, DC: International Center for Research on Women.

Suhrke, Astri, Kristian Berg Harpviken, and Arne Strand. 2004. *Conflictual Peacebuilding: Afghanistan Two Years after Bonn*. Bergen: CMI/PRIO.

Suhrke, Astri, and Arne Strand. 2005. "The Logic of Conflictual Peacebuilding." In *After the Conflict: Reconstruction and Development in the Aftermath of War*, ed. Sultan Barakat, 141-54. London and New York: I.B Taurus.

Suhrke, Astri, Espen Vilanger, and Susan Woodward. 2004. "Economic Aid to Post-Conflict Countries: Correcting the Empirical and Theoretical Foundations of Policy." Paper presented at the WIDER conference entitled "Making Peace Work," Helsinki, Finland, 4-5 June.

Tandon, Yash. 1999. *Globalization and Africa's Options*. Harare: International South Group Network.

Thillet, Braulia, and FLACSO Guatemala. 2003. *Tierras municipales en Guatemala: Un desafío para el desarrollo local sostenible* [Municipal lands in Guatemala: A challenge for sustainable local development]. Guatemala: FLACSO.

Thomas, Jane. 1990. *Afghanistan: A Forgotten War – An Overview for Canadians*. Ottawa: Human Concern International.

Torres-Rivas, Edelberto. 1998. "Construyendo la paz y la democracia: El fin del poder contrainsurgente" [Constructing peace and democracy: The end of counterinsurgency power]. In *Del autoritarismo a la paz* [From authoritarianism to peace], ed. Edelberto Torres-Rivas and Gabriel Aguilera, 9-111. Guatemala: FLACSO.

Transitional Islamic State of Afghanistan. 2004. "Afghanistan's National Priority Programs – An Overview." Kabul. http://www.af.

Tschirgi, Neclâ. 2004. *Post-Conflict Peacebuilding Revisited: Achievements, Limitations, Challenges*. New York: International Peace Academy.

UNCTAD (United Nations Conference on Trade and Development). 2002. *Report on UNCTAD's Assistance to the Palestinian People*. Geneva: UNCTAD.

–. 2003. *Report on UNCTAD's Assistance to the Palestinian People*. Geneva: UNCTAD.

–. 2005. *Report on UNCTAD's Assistance to the Palestinian People*. Geneva: UNCTAD.

UNDP (United Nations Development Program). 1998. *Mozambique: Human Development Report*. UNDP: Maputo.

–. 2000a. *Haiti: Bilan commun de pays* [Haiti: Common country assessment]. Port-au-Prince: UNDP.

–. 2000b. *Mozambique: Human Development Report*. Maputo: UNDP.

–. 2003. *Agenda Nacional Compartida: Un esfuerzo multipartidario para la Guatemala del siglo XXI* [Shared National Agenda: A multiparty effort for a Guatemala of the twenty-first century]. 2003. Guatemala: UNDP, Instituto Holandés para la Democracia Multipartidaria, Magna Terra Editores.

United Nations Economic Commission for Africa. 1989. *South African Destabilization: The Economic Cost of Frontline Resistance to Apartheid*. Addis Ababa: United Nations.

UN ECHA DDR Working Group (United Nations Executive Committee on Humanitarian Affairs DDR Working Group). 2000. *Harnessing Institutional Capacities in Support of the DDR of Former Combatants*. New York: United Nations.

United Nations General Assembly. 2005. *Resolution 60/180. The Peacebuilding Commission*. A/Res/60/180. 30 December.

United Nations Office of the Special Coordinator in the Occupied Territories. 2000. *Report on the Palestinian Economy*. Jerusalem: UNSCO.

United Nations Secretary-General. 2001. *Prevention of Armed Conflict: Report of the Secretary-General*. Fifty-fifth session. New York: United Nations.

UNSC (United Nations Security Council). 2000. *The Role of the United Nations Peacekeeping in Disarmament, Demobilization and Reintegration: Report of the Secretary-General*. New York: United Nations.

–. 2006. *Security Council Report: Special Research Project – Peacebuilding Commission, No. 3*. New York: United Nations.

United States Commission on Weak States and National Security. 2004. *On the Brink: Weak States and US National Security*. Washington: Center for Global Development.

URNG (Unidad Revolucionaria Nacional Guatemalteca). 1997. *Diagnostico socio-economico: Personal incorporado* [Socio-economic diagnostic: Incorporated personnel]. Unpublished study by Fundacion Guillermo Toriello carried out with support from the European Union. Guatemala: URNG.

Usher, Graham. 2005a. "The Calm before the Storm?" *Al-Ahram Weekly* 735 (24-30 March). http://www.miftah.org/Display.cfm?DocId=6993&CategoryId=5.

–. 2005b. "The New Hamas: Between Resistance and Participation." *Middle East Report Online*. http://www.merip.org/mero/mero082105.html.

Uvin, Peter. 2002. "The Development/Peacebuilding Nexus: A Typology and History of Changing Paradigms." *Journal of Peacebuilding and Development* 1, 1: 5-24.

Uyangoda, Jayadeva. 2003. *Beyond Mediation, Negotiation and Negative Peace: Towards Transformative Peace in Sri Lanka*. Colombo: Social Scientists' Association.

–. 2005a. "Ethnic Conflict, the State and the Tsunami Disaster in Sri Lanka." *Inter-Asia Cultural Studies* 6, 3: 341-52.

–. 2005b. "Transition from Civil War to Peace: Challenges of Peacebuilding in Sri Lanka." WKOP working paper. Colombo: Social Scientists' Association.

Uyangoda, Jayadeva, and Morina Perera, eds. 2003. *Sri Lanka's Peace Process 2002: Critical Perspectives*. Colombo: Social Scientists' Association.

Valdez, J. Fernando, and Tania Palencia Prado. 1998. *Los dominios del poder: La encrucijada tributaria* [The dominions of power: The fiscal crossroads]. Guatemala: FLACSO.

Velásquez, Alvaro. 2003. "Aproximación a una sociología del proceso de paz Guatemalteco" [Approaching a sociology of the Guatemalan peace process]. *Perfiles Latinoamericanos* [Latin American Profiles] 22: 137-58.

Vines, Alex. 1996. *RENAMO: From Terrorism to Democracy in Mozambique?* York, UK: Centre for Southern African Studies, University of York.

Walter, Barbara. 1999. "Designing Transition from Civil War: Demobilization, Democratization and Commitment to Peace." *International Security* 24, 1: 127-55.

Watteville, Natalie de. 2003. "Demobilisation and Reintegration Programs: Addressing Gender Issues." New York: World Bank.

Weimer, Bernhard. 2002. "Autarcização em Moçambique: Alguns critérios de avaliação para o balanço das primeiras experiências" [Establishing local governments in Mozambique: Criteria for assessing first experiences]. In *Jornalística do processo de descentralização* [Journal of the decentralization process], ed. A. Cobertura, 30-39. Maputo: Fundação Friedrich Ebert Stiftung.

–. 2004. "Mozambique: Ten Years of Peace – Democracy, Governance and Reform Interrogations of a Privileged Observer." In *Mozambique: Ten Years of Democracy*, ed. Brazão Mazula, 61-86. Maputo: CEDE.

Weinstein, Jeremy. 2002. "The Structure of Rebel Organizations: Implications for Post-Conflict Reconstruction." Dissemination notes, 4. New York: World Bank.

Williamson, John. 1994. *The Political Economy of Policy Reform*. Washington, DC: Institute for International Economics.

Wood, Elizabeth Jean. 2001. *Forging Democracy from Below: Insurgent Transition in South Africa and El Salvador*. Cambridge: Cambridge University Press.

Woodward, Susan L. 2002a. *Economic Priorities for Peace Implementation: International Peace Academy Series on Peace Implementation*. New York: IPA.

–. 2002b. "Local Governance Approach to Social Reintegration and Economic Recovery in Post-Conflict Countries." Discussion paper for the IPA/UNDP workshop, New York, 8 October.

World Bank. 1999. *Development under Adversity: The Palestinian Economy in Transition*. Washington, DC: World Bank.

–. 2002. *Work in Low-Income Countries under Stress: A Taskforce Report*. Washington, DC: World Bank Group.

–. 2004a. *Four Years: Intifada, Closure and Palestinian Economic Crisis – An Assessment*. Washington, DC: World Bank.

–. 2004b. *Stagnation or Revival? Israeli Disengagement and Palestinian Economic Prospects*. Washington, DC: World Bank.

–. 2005. *The Palestinian Economy and the Prospects for Its Recovery: Economic Monitoring Report to the Ad Hoc Liaison Committee, No. 1*. Washington, DC: World Bank. http://siteresources. worldbank.org/INTWESTBANKGAZA/Data/20751555/EMR.pdf.

–. 2006. *Economic Update and Potential Outlook, West Bank and Gaza.* Washington, DC: World Bank.

–. 2007. *Potential Alternatives for Palestinian Trade: Developing the Rafah Trade Corridor.* Washington, DC: World Bank. http://siteresources.worldbank.org/INTWESTBANKGAZA/ Resources/RafahCorridorMarch07.pdf.

Wuyts, Marc. 1980. "Economia política do colonialismo" [Political economy of colonialism]. *Estudos Moçambicanos* [Mozambique studies] 1: 9-22.

York, Geoffrey. 2006. "Canadian Program Presents Alternative to Taliban," *Globe and Mail,* 22 May. http://www.theglobeandmail.com/servlet/story/LAC.20060522.AFGHAN22/ TPStory/.

Zahar, Marie-Joëlle. 2003. "Reframing the Spoiler Debate in Peace Processes." In *Contemporary Peacemaking: Conflict, Violence and Peace Processes,* ed. John Darby and Roger MacGinty, 114-24. New York: Palgrave Macmillan.

–. 2005. "Political Violence in Peace Processes: Voice, Exit and Loyalty in the Post-Accord Period." In *Violence and Reconstruction,* ed. John Darby, 33-52. Southbend: Notre Dame University Press.

–. 2006. "Understanding the Violence of Insiders: Loyalty, Custodians of Peace, and the Sustainability of Conflict Settlement." In *Challenges to Peacebuilding: Managing Spoilers during Conflict Resolution,* ed. Edward Newman and Oliver Richmond, 40-58. Tokyo: United Nations University Press.

Zakhilwal, Omar. 2002. "Reconstructing Peace in Afghanistan." *Human Rights Tribune* 8, 3. http://www.hri.ca/tribune/viewArticle.asp?ID=2642.

–. 2005. *State Building in Afghanistan: A Civil Society Approach.* Feature service article. Washington, DC: Center for International Private Enterprise.

Zakhilwal, Omar, and Jane Thomas. 2005. *Afghanistan: What Kind of Peace? The Role of Rural Development in Peacebuilding.* WKOP working paper. Kabul: Afghanistan Centre for Policy and Development Studies.

Zeeuw, Jeroen de. 2004. "Projects Do Not Create Institutions: The Record of Democracy Assistance to Post-Conflict Societies." Paper presented at the 45th Annual Convention of the ISA, Montreal, Canada, 17-20 March.

Interviews

Chapter 2 (Guatemala: Aguilera)

Burgos, Amilcar, former member of the Peace Commission of the Government of Guatemala, 2005.

Calí, Francisco, Coordinador de la Comisión Presidencial contra el Racismo y la Discriminación, Ciudad de Guatemala, 2004.

Chávez, Aura Lolita, Integrante del Consejo Departamental de Desarrollo del Quiché, 2004.

Cordón, Nuria, Foro Nacional de la Mujer, 2004.

Carpio, Violeta de, Secretaria Presidencial de la Mujer. 2004.

Lux de Cotí, Otilia, Presidenta del Comité Directivo del Programa Participacion y Democracia (PPD), 2004.

Tomasa Bulux, Maria, Integrante del Consejo de Desarrollo Departamental de El Quiché, 2004.

Zapeta, Teresa, Directora de la Defensoría de la Mujer Indígena, Ciudad de Guatemala, 2004.

Chapter 3 (Mozambique: Sitoe and Hunguana)

Ali, Buana, member of the Municipal Assembly, Nacala, 15 November 2004.

Aly, Ibraimo Achimo, student, Public Administration Department, Universidade Eduardo Mondlane, 8 September 2004.

Amade, Zeca, member of the Municipal Assembly, Nacala, 15 November 2004.

Armando, Carlitos, member of the Municipal Forum and an environment association, Dondo, 18-19 October 2004.

Atumane, Estevão, councillor and member of the Municipal Forum, Angoche, 18-19 October 2004.

Bacar, Taquidir, Officer of Monitoring and Evaluation of District Planning and Decentralized Finances Program, Ministry of Finances (Word Bank project), Maputo, 28 January 2005.

Baltazar, Alfredo Domingos, water supply network worker, Dondo, 18-19 October 2004.

Buana, Pilaure, RENAMO member of the Nacala Municipal Assembly, 15 November 2004.

Bwana, S., member of the Municipal Assembly, Nacala, 15 November 2004.

Carimo, Sheik Abdul, National Islamic Council, Electoral Observatory, Maputo, 27 January 2005.

Carvalho, Jorge de, civil society member and project coordinator, Dondo, 18-19 October 2004.

Chamucha, Momade Abdala, member of the Municipal Forum, Angoche, 18-19 October 2004.

Chicuecue, Noel, (OREC) Organizacao para Resolucao de Conflictos Comunitarios, Electoral Observatory, Maputo, January 2005.

Chilengue, Refinaldo, journalist, *Correio da Manhã*, Maputo, 8 September 2004.

Chimoio, Dom Fransisco, Catholic Church, Electoral Observatory, Maputo, 2 January 2005.

Colquhoun, Marcia, First Secretary, CIDA, Maputo, 27 January 2005.

Conceição, Paulo da, Journalist, *Notícias*, Maputo, 8 September 2004.

Cumbane, João Carlos, Editor, *Conteúdos*, Maputo, 9 September 2004.

Delfim, António, member of the Municipal Assembly, Nacala, 15 November 2004.

Dos Santos, Manuel José, mayor of Nacala, 15 November 2004.

Ferreira, Horacio, civil society activist, Beira, autumn 2004.

Francisco, Valentino, Councillor of Health and Environment Sector, Municipality of Ilha de Moçambique, 17 November 2004.

Gamito, Alfredo, member of Parliament, National Assembly, Maputo, 28 January 2005.

Greva, João Francisco, member of the Municipal Assembly, Nacala, 15 November 2004.

Greva, Joaquim, member of the Municipal Assembly, Dondo, 16 November 2004.

Gonçalves, Dom Jaime, Catholic Church, Electoral Observatory, Beira, 16 November 2004.

Guambe, Manuel, National Director of Local Administration-MAE, Maputo, 28 January 2005.

Idland, Sissel, First Secretary, Development, Embassy of Norway, Maputo, 27 January 2005.

Ilal, Abdul, ex-coordinator of a German Technical Cooperation, decentralization project and a PRODER team member-GTZ, Maputo, 8 September 2004.

Jafar, Jafar Gulamo, lawyer and ex-member of Parliament from Renamo, Maputo, 15 November 2004.

Lourenço, Jalma, ex-candidate (FRELIMO) for mayor in 2003 municipal election, Beira, 9 September 2004.

Lundin, Iraê B., researcher, CEEI-ISRI (Centro de Estudos Estratégicos e Internacionais do Instituto Superior de Realçoes Internacionais), Maputo, 9 September 2004.

Macedo, Iara de, project coordinator, Municipalities Program, AECI, Maputo, 9 September 2004.

Macuane, José Jaime, Consultant, UTRESP (Technical Unit for Public Sector Reform), Government of Mozambique, Maputo, 28 January 2005.

Maduela, Amélia, student, Public Administration Department, UEM, 8 September 2004.

Malhecua, José Carmone, member of the Municipal Assembly, Ilha de Moçambique, 17 November 2004.

Mangade, Luísa Janete, councillor, Health, Woman and Social Action Unit, Nacala, 15 November 2004.

Manhique, Gregório, civil society member and project coordinator, Angoche, 18-19 October 2004.

Mangeira, Omar, National Program Officer, PADEM-SDC (Programme in Support of Decentralization and Local Development of the Swiss Agency for Development and Cooperation), Maputo, 9 September 2004.

Manjate, Marcelo, journalist, *Conteúdos*, Maputo, 8 September 2004.

Marrengula, Ramos, chairman of Association of Workers and Operators of Informal Sector (ASOTSI), Maputo, 13 November 2004.

Matsinhe, Campos, member of the Municipal Forum, Vilankulo, 18-19 October 2004.
Matusse, Angelo, country representative, Awepa, Maputo, 9 September 2004.
Mondlane, Jeremias, journalist, Rádio Moçambique, Maputo, 9 September 2004.
Morais, Barbosa, director, CEPKA (Centro de Pesquisa Konrad Adenauer), Maputo, 9 September 2004.
Mosse, Marcelo, journalist and sociologist, Maputo, 9 September 2004.
Mucarissane, José Abacar, administrator of Ilha de Moçambique, 17 November 2004.
Mucudos, Custódio dos, project coordinator of District Planning and Decentralized Finances Program, Ministry of Finances (Word Bank project), Maputo, 28 January 2005.
Nacir, Josefina M., member of the Municipal Forum, Angoche, 18-19 October 2004.
Polaize, Saúl, Journalist, Rádio Moçambique, Maputo, 8 September 2004.
Priest Pedro, Dondo, 18 November 2004.
Raúl Abacar, member of the Municipal Forum, Angoche, 18-19 October 2004.
Rodrigues, Manuel, National Director of Municipal Development (MAE), Maputo, September 2004.
Roque, Mário, Civil Society Member and project coordinator, Vilankulos, 18-19 October 2004.
Rosário, Domingos de, Electoral Observatory, Maputo, 27 January 2005.
Santos, Manuel José dos, Mayor of Nacala, 15 November 2004.
Silva, Alberto da, program official, CIDA, Maputo, 27 January 2005.
Simango, Daviz, Mayor of Beira, Beira, 16 November 2004.
Simões, Jorge, Civil Society Member and member of the Municipal Assembly, Ilha de Moçambique, 18 November 2004.
Sousa, Arsénio de, member of the Municipal Forum, Vilankulo, 18-19 October 2004.
Taillon, Danyel, development official, Democratic Governance Fund, CIDA, Maputo, 27 January 2005.
Tsamba, Inácio A., journalist, Rádio Moçambique, Maputo, 8 September 2004.
Tembe, Carlos, Mayor of Matola, 28 January 2005.
Tito, Chinai Dique, community leader, Municipality of Dondo, 18-19 October 2004.
Tvete, Berit, Second Secretary, Development Sector, Embassy of Norway, Maputo, 27 January 2005.
Vibe, Maja de, governance adviser, DFID (UK Department for International Development), Maputo, 9 September 2004.
Vilanculo, Mário Fernando, member of the Municipal Forum, Vilankulo, 18-19 October 2004.
Vilanculo, Ricardo, member of the Municipal Forum, Vilankulo, 18-19 October 2004.
White, Maria, member of Municipal Assembly, Dondo, 18-19 October 2004.
Xavier, Celestino, chairman of the Municipal Assembly, Nacala, 15 November 2004.
Yassin, T., member of the Municipal Assembly, Nacala, 15 November 2004.
Yassir, Paíla, member of the Municipal Assembly, Nacala, 15 November 2004.
Zacarias, Maria, member of the Municipal Forum, Vilankulo, 18-19 October 2004.

Chapter 8 (Guatemala: Hauge and Thoresen)
Alvarez, Enrique, Coordinator of Incidencia Democratica, 28 April 2005.
Argueta Villalta, General Victor Manuel, AVEMILGUA (Asociación de Veteranos Militares de Guatemala), 10 May 2005.
Asturias, Rodrigo, former commander of ORPA (Organización Revolucionaria del Pueblo en Armas), 2 May 2005.
Berg, Rolf, ambassador, Norwegian Embassy, 25 April 2005.
Bol Matz, Jorge Mario, former PGT (Partido Guatemalteco de los Trabajadores) combatant, 4 May 2005.
Calderas Teo, Maria Teresa, former EGP (Ejército Guerrillero de los Pobres) combatant, Chimaltenango Community, 30 April 2005.
Chacón Orizabal, Irma Leticia, former ORPA combatant, 4 May 2005.
Corral, Enrique, leader of Fundacion Guillermo Toriello, 29 April 2005.
Escalante, Cesar August, Salvador Fajardo CPR-Petén (Comunidades de Población en Resistencia de Petén), 8 May 2005.

Fajardo, Salvador, Junta Directiva, CPR-Petén, 8 May 2005.

Figueroa, Ana, Salvador Fajardo CPR-Petén, 8 May 2005.

Figueroa, Marisol, former FAR combatant, El Horizonte, 6 May 2005.

Garcia, José Carlos, former EGP combatant, Chimaltenango Community, 30 April 2005.

Herrera Rodriguez, Juan Carlos, Salvador Fajardo CPR-Petén, 8 May 2005.

Hurtado Paz y Paz, Juan José, former guerrilla leader in EGP, 5 May 2005.

Junta Directiva (meeting with), El Horizonte, 6 May 2005.

López Osorio, Carmelita, former EGP combatant, Chimaltenango Community, 30 April 2005.

Maldonado, Alba Estela, former EGP combatant, deputy in the Congress representing the URNG (Unidad Nacional Revolucionaria Guatemalteca), 28 April 2005.

Monsanto, Pablo, commander of FAR, 11 May 2005.

Montes, Cesar, adviser for Encuentros por Guatemala (political party being established), 29 April 2005.

Rosada, Hector, former leader of COPAZ (Comisión Presidencial de la Paz), 11 May 2005.

Saldoval, Vidalia, former FAR combatant, El Horizonte, 6 May 2005.

Soberanis, Catalina, responsible for the OAS Central American program to strengthen the democratic dialogue, 11 May 2005.

Contributors

Gabriel Aguilera Peralta: Dr. Gabriel Aguilera is currently the deputy regional coordinator of the Organization of American States Program to Strengthen Democratic Dialogue in Central America. He is also a board member of the Program for Participation and Democracy (PPD) in Guatemala. PPD focuses on promoting citizen participation in the Development Councils at the local and regional levels. Dr. Aguilera has been a vice-minister of foreign affairs as well as the commissioner for peace, in which capacity he played a key role in coordinating the implementation of the peace accords in Guatemala. Dr. Aguilera also has a distinguished history of scholarly work on issues of war, peace negotiations, and security sector reform in Central America.

Stephen Baranyi: Dr. Stephen Baranyi is the principal researcher on conflict prevention at the North-South Institute (NSI), where he has led the "What Kind of Peace Is Possible" project. NSI has been one of Canada's leading centres of policy research on international development issues since 1976. Before joining the institute, Dr. Baranyi worked with the International Development Research Centre, Foreign Affairs Canada, the Canadian International Development Agency, and several NGOs in Europe. Dr. Baranyi has published on the role of the UN, regional organizations, civil society, and Canada in peacemaking, peacekeeping, and peacebuilding. His PhD is from York University.

Wenche Hauge: Dr. Wenche Hauge is senior researcher at the International Peace Research Institute (PRIO) in Oslo, Norway. PRIO is an independent research institute that conducts research on and teaches about the causes of war, foreign and security policies, as well as conflict resolution and peacebuilding. Dr. Hauge received her PhD in political science from the University of Oslo in 2003. Her dissertation, "Causes and Dynamics of Conflict Escalation: The Role of Economic Development and Environmental Change," is a comparative study of Bangladesh, Guatemala, Haiti, Madagascar, Senegal, and Tunisia.

Carolina Hunguana: Ms. Carolina Hunguana was a researcher at the Centre for the Study of Democracy and Development (CEDE) in Maputo, Mozambique, throughout the WKOP project. CEDE was established in 1999, on the basis of a formative experience with the War-Torn Societies Project during the mid-1990s.

Since then, CEDE has worked extensively on breaking the links between elections and violent conflict, and promoting informed citizen participation in processes of democratic governance at the local and national levels. Ms. Hunguana completed her MA in 2001 at the Institut d'Etudes Politiques de Lyon, Université Lumière 2, in Lyon, France. She has published papers on decentralization, democracy, and peacebuilding and has written papers on East-West social identities.

Hérard Jadotte: In 2006, Professeur Hérard Jadotte completed a term as secretary-general of the Université de Notre Dame d'Haïti. Since returning to Haiti in 1991, Professeur Jadotte has written extensively on the challenges of democratic development in that country. He has also advised several national and international development agencies, including the World Bank. Professeur Jadotte studied law at the Faculty of Law of the Université d'Haïti before completing his MA in anthropology and political science at the Faculty of Social Sciences of the Université de Montréal.

Jane Murphy Thomas: Jane Murphy Thomas is a Canadian social anthropologist and independent consultant who, since 1984, has specialized in Afghanistan, aid and development analysis, community development, and participatory development. Currently she is on contract with a development project in Afghanistan. She obtained her MA from the School of Oriental and African Studies, University of London, UK, and has published numerous papers in her areas of specialization.

Yves-François Pierre: Dr. Yves-François Pierre is a Haitian sociologist and independent consultant. He has worked extensively on issues of democratic development, violence, and rural development for international agencies such as the US Agency for International Development, Transparency International, and the Institute for International Food Policy. He obtained his PhD from Columbia University in 1992, and his dissertation focused on agrarian labour dynamics in Haiti.

Kristiana Powell: Ms. Kristiana Powell is a Program Officer at the UN Department of Peacekeeping Operations in New York. She contributed extensively to the WKOP project through her position as a Researcher in Conflict Prevention at the North-South Institute. In that capacity, she coordinated the WKOP project and initiated work on the Responsibility to Protect and security sector reform in Africa. Before joining NSI, Ms. Powell worked as an analyst at Project Ploughshares, focusing on regional security and small arms issues in Africa. She has published papers on the G8 and conflict prevention in Africa, on the African Union's Standby Force, and on the African Union and the "Responsibility to Protect." Ms. Powell has an MA in international relations and political science from the University of Toronto.

Pamela Scholey: Dr. Pamela Scholey is a Principal with the SecDev Group in Ottawa, Canada. Prior to that she was a senior program specialist in the Peace, Conflict and Development Program Initiative at the International Development Research Centre (IDRC). Before joining IDRC, she headed the Gender and Development Unit at the Management Development Institute of Kanifing, The Gambia. Dr. Scholey obtained her PhD in anthropology from the School of Oriental and African Studies, University of London, where her research was based on return migration to post-Oslo Palestine. She has published several articles on peacebuilding issues in Palestine and internationally.

Khalil Shikaki: Dr. Khalil Shikaki is the director of the Palestinian Center for Policy and Survey Research (PSR). PSR is an independent non-profit institution that conducts policy analysis and academic research. It was founded in 2000, with the goal of advancing scholarship and knowledge on issues of current concern to Palestinians in three areas: domestic politics and government, strategic analysis and foreign policy, and public opinion polls and survey research. PSR also sponsors study groups, task forces, conferences, and briefings on issues of critical importance to Palestinians. It is dedicated to promoting objective research and analysis, and to encouraging a better understanding of the domestic and international factors affecting the Palestinian Occupied Territories, in an atmosphere of open debate. Dr. Shikaki holds a PhD from Columbia University and has published extensively on Palestinian issues, in Arabic and in English-language periodicals such as *Foreign Policy*.

Eduardo Sitoe: Eduardo J. Sitoe has a PhD in government from the University of Essex, UK. Dr. Sitoe's doctoral dissertation is on the comparative politics of democratization in Angola and Mozambique from 1984 to 1994. Dr. Sitoe is currently a senior researcher at the Centre for the Study of Democracy and Development (CEDE) in Maputo, Mozambique. Established in 1999, CEDE now works on breaking the links between elections and violent conflict and promoting citizen participation in processes of democratic governance. Dr. Sitoe deals particularly with the program on democratic decentralization. He is also a senior lecturer of governance and public administration at the Eduardo Mondlane University in Maputo.

Arne Strand: Dr. Arne Strand is senior researcher at the Chr. Michelsen Institute (CMI) in Bergen, Norway. CMI is a private social science foundation conducting research on and teaching about issues of development and human rights, primarily in sub-Saharan Africa, Asia, and the Middle East. Dr. Strand obtained his PhD from the University of York in postwar recovery studies, specializing in the coordination of humanitarian assistance in complex emergencies. He has extensive experience directing Norwegian NGO work in Afghanistan and has been involved in developing the management and professional capacities of many Afghan NGOs. He has led and participated in many commissioned studies on Afghanistan, on aid coordination and peacebuilding, including leading a World Bank-commissioned study on community-driven development.

Beate Thoreson: Ms. Beate Thoresen holds an MA in political science from the University of Oslo, with an emphasis on development and international issues. Fieldwork for her master's thesis was conducted in Chile. Ms. Thoresen has work experience with aid management to Latin America and in conflict areas. She lived in Guatemala for thirteen years and worked with private NGOs in Central America and Mexico. For the last five years, Ms. Thoresen has worked as an independent consultant for project evaluation, investigation, and organizational development, especially in the fields of conflict, DDR, refugees, democratic transition, human rights, and participation of civil society.

Jayadeva Uyangoda: Dr. Jayadeva Uyangoda is a foundation professor and the head of the Department of Political Science and Public Policy at the University of Colombo, Sri Lanka. He is also the editor of *Polity*, a semi-academic journal on contemporary Sri Lanka and South Asian affairs. He has published extensively on Sri Lanka's conflict and peace processes and has advised President Kumaratunga on negotiations with the LTTE. He recently completed a book entitled *Conflicts and Contexts: Explorations into Conflict Dynamics in Sri Lanka*. Dr. Uyangoda is a member of the Social Scientists' Association (SSA), an association of prominent Sri Lankan scholars. Founded in 1977, it has conducted pioneering research on ethnic conflict, agrarian change, class formation, and women's social history. SSA also has a respected history of organizing policy dialogues on key national and regional issues.

Omar Zakhilwal: Dr. Omar Zakhilwal is an Afghan-Canadian economist who is currently the president of the Afghanistan Investment Support Agency. In addition, he has been a member of the Supreme Council of Da Afghanistan Bank (Afghanistan Central Bank) and teaches economics at Kabul University. Since his return to Afghanistan, Dr. Zakhilwal has been part of the two Loya Jirgas that elected the president for the Afghanistan Transitional Government (June 2002) and ratified Afghanistan's Constitution (December 2003), served as an author of Afghanistan's First National Human Development Report, and took part in many other initiatives with respect to rural development. He has a long history of fostering constructive debate on peacebuilding in Afghanistan. He and several colleagues have established the Afghan Centre for Policy and Development Studies to nurture indigenous research capacity in key areas of economic and social development. Dr. Zakhilwal obtained his PhD in economics from Carleton University and has since published many works in national and international journals. Prior to his return to Afghanistan, Dr. Zakhilwal served as a senior research economist and taught economics at Carleton University in Ottawa.

Index

Fundación Guillermo Toriello (FGT), 218, 219, 221

G8, Miyazaki Initiative, 13
G20 (organization), 77
García, Romeo Lucas (General), 214
Gaza Strip. *See* Palestine
gender: Afghanistan, gender-focused aid, 153, 154; Afghanistan, program recommendations, 176; and approaches to peacebuilding, x, 10-11, 28, 29, 313; equality, and sustainable peacebuilding, 16; Guatemala, gender equality among guerrilla fighters, 221; Guatemala, gender issues for female ex-combatants, 233; Guatemala, policy development within FGT, 199; Guatemala, women's issues in peace talks, 36-37, 52, 56; Haiti, gender equity and agricultural committee members, 102-3, 104, 105; Mozambique, and agricultural labour markets, 76; Mozambique, gender inequality addressed through decentralization, 59, 76, 82; Sri Lanka, proposal for gender subcommittee, 199. *See also* women
German Technical Cooperation, 160
Global Partnership for the Prevention of Armed Conflict (GPPAC), 13, 294-95
Gnambe, José Elija, 68
Gonaïves CARE development project, Haiti, 87, 96-99, 104
Gonçalves, Jaime (Archbishop), 73, 80
GPPAC (Global Partnership on the Prevention of Armed Conflict), 13, 294-95
Gros Morne development project, Haiti, 87, 96, 99-101, 104-5
Group of 184 (Haiti), 94
Guatemala: blocks to reform, 309; constitution, 39, 42; decentralization, and peacebuilding, 33; democratization, socioeconomic obstacles to, 231, 234, 309; development councils, 42-48, 50; economic growth, 308; former combatants, and peacebuilding, 210-34; human rights violations, 34; indigenous peoples, participation in civil war, 213, 214-15; Land Fund, 24; local administration of municipal lands, 25; minimal tax reforms, 12; Peace Accords (1996), and DDR of former combatants, 216-18; Peace Accords (1996), implementation assessment, 32, 33, 34-42, 50-55, 298; peacebuilding, 5, 12, 33, 49, 55-56, 296, 297; postwar criminal violence, 298; racism, as issue in civil war, 214; Special Commission for

Reintegration, 218; spoilers, 38; urban and rural development councils, 42-49. *See also* PACs (civil defence patrols), Guatemala; URNG (Guatemalan National Revolutionary Unity)
Guatemalan Communist Party (PGT), 213, 214, 219, 223, 225
Guatemalan military police (PMA), 216, 217, 228
Guatemalan National Revolutionary Unity (URNG). *See* URNG
Guatemalan Republican Front (FRG). *See* FRG (Guatemalan Republican Front)
Guebuza, Armando, 64
Guerrilla Army of the Poor (EGP), Guatemala, 213, 214, 219, 223, 225
Guidelines on Conflict, Peace and Development Co-operation (OECD, 1997), 6

Haiti: anti-government demonstrations, 94; community development projects, 96-104; Constitution (1987), 86, 89-92, 305-6; decentralization, and local governance, 105; democratization efforts, 305-6; economy, 89, 91-93, 95-96, 105-6, 302, 308; elections, 91, 92-93, 107, 302; as fragile state, 15; human rights violations, 85, 94; infrastructure improvement projects, 98-99; local economic development projects, 104-6; peacebuilding efforts, 15, 17, 108-9, 295, 300-3, 313, 314; political history, 85, 87-89; poverty reduction strategy, 107; US military intervention (1994), 6, 92. *See also* Aristide, Jean-Bertrand; Duvalier, François; Duvalier, Jean-Claude
Haitian Armed Forces/Forces armées d'Haiti (FADH), 85, 89
Hamas, Palestine: armed wing, 265; and Cairo Declaration (2005), 266, 285; and DDR, conditions necessary for, 289-91; and DDR efforts, 269, 277, 286; demonization of, by Israeli and Western governments, 282, 285; election to Palestinian parliament (2006), 8, 110, 111, 113, 116, 129, 138-39, 267, 303-4, 331-32; and Izz Eddin al-Qassam Brigades, 267, 269, 271-72, 290; on lack of respect shown by peace negotiators, 287-88; on meaning of armed resistance, 287; and national unity government (2007), 136; opposed to "Road Map for Peace," 112; and Oslo Peace Accords (1993, 1995), 124; political philosophy, 116; and Popular Resistance Committees (PRC), 265, 268, 272;

OAS (Organization of American States), 93, 94, 301

ODA (official development assistance) agencies, 14-15

OECD DAC (Organisation for Economic Co-operation and Development, Development Assistance Committee): Fragile States Group, 15; Guidelines (1997), 13; policy statements on local democratic institutions, 18

OEF (Operation Enduring Freedom), Afghanistan, 155, 240, 247, 249, 303, 311

official development assistance (ODA) agencies, 14-15

Olmert, Ehud, 116

Operation Enduring Freedom (OEF), Afghanistan, 155, 240, 247, 249, 303, 311

Operation Restore Democracy, Haiti, 85

OPL (Organisation politique Lavalas), Haiti, 92

Organisation for Economic Co-operation and Development, Development Assistance Committee (OECD DAC). *See* OECD DAC

Organisation politique Lavalas (OPL), Haiti, 92

Organization of American States (OAS), 93, 94, 301

ORPA (Revolutionary Organization of the People in Arms), Guatemala, 213, 214, 217, 219, 221, 223, 225

Oslo Peace Accords (1993, 1995), Palestine-Israel: constraints on Palestian jurisdiction, 115; DDR not included, 292; Declaration of Principle (1993), 114; expectations by Israelis and Palestinians, 114; failure of, and spoilers, 114, 283; Interim Agreement (1995), 114; loss of legitimacy in view of Palestinians, 111; priority given to Israeli security, 122, 124-25, 132, 264; terms, and difficulty of governing Palestine, 122-25. *See also* PA (Palestinian Authority); Palestine; "Road Map for Peace," Palestine-Israel

Oxfam, 160

PA (Palestinian Authority): and agenda of international donors, 129; as authoritarian regime, 113, 121-22, 131-33; budget, dependent on international donors, 132-33; DDR program, inability to implement, 266-67, 269; establishment of, 114, 117; governing difficulties, and loss of legitimacy, 119; and local government, reform recommendations, 139-43; Oslo Peace Accords, 111, 122-25, 129, 265-66; and PSS (Palestinian security sector), 264-65, 269; reform, recommendations, 133-38. *See also* Oslo Peace Accords (1993, 1995), Palestine-Israel; Palestine; "Road Map for Peace," Palestine-Israel

PACs (civil defence patrols), Guatemala: background, 213; demobilization and reintegration, 215, 217, 227-30, 232, 233; embedded in communities, 216; human rights violations by, 215, 216, 228, 232; role of, 214-15; as signatory to peace accord (1996), 210; as spoilers in peace process, 230

Pakistan, assistance to combatants from Afghanistan, 242-43

Palestine: armed resistance groups, 265, 267-73; arms, sources of, 268-69; Basic Law (constitution) (2002, 2003), 119, 120, 134; Cairo Declaration (2005), 266; DDR, challenges of, 303, 311; democratization efforts, 19, 306; desire for international intervention against Israel, 16, 130-31; economy, 8, 115, 116, 118, 130; elections, 108, 118, 137-38; and Israeli "unilateral separation" policy, 114, 115-16; Law of the Judiciary, 121, 134, 135, 137; local governments, 119, 121, 139-43; national unity government, 267, 288-89; and Oslo Peace Accords, 8, 264-65, 295, 299; peacebuilding, issues of, 7, 110-13, 111, 112, 117-18, 133, 143-46, 288-91; political system, 120-21; president, powers of, 120, 134; public sector salaries, 129, 135; "Road Map for Peace," 112, 114, 131, 135, 267, 280, 289; second intifada (2000), 8, 127-28, 265; security, reform recommendations, 136-37; two-level conflict (state-to-state and intra-state), 110. *See also* Fateh, Palestine; Hamas, Palestine; Oslo Peace Accords (1993, 1995), Palestine-Israel; PA (Palestinian Authority); PIJ (Palestinian Islamic Jihad); PLO (Palestinian Liberation Organization); "Road Map for Peace," Palestine-Israel

Palestinian Authority (PA). *See* PA (Palestinian Authority)

Palestinian Center for Policy and Survey Research (PSR), 8, 133

Palestinian Islamic Jihad (PIJ). *See* PIJ (Palestinian Islamic Jihad)

Palestinian Liberation Organization (PLO). *See* PLO (Palestinian Liberation Organization)

RENAMO (Mozambican National Resistance): decentralization, opposition to,
305; and elections, 64; in municipal
governments, 70, 71, 72; opposition to
Law 3/1994, 66-67; as party derived from
military organization, 65; and peacebuilding, 297; on philosophy of gradualism, 68-69; rivalry with FRELIMO, 61;
signing of Rome Peace Accords (1992),
58; on unbalanced distribution of
resources, 80; viewed as spoiler, 281-82;
youth leaders, 64. *See also* Mozambique
Report on the Prevention of Armed Conflict
(UN Secretary-General, 2001), 13
Responsibility to Protect (R2P): debates
dominated by Northern states, 18; definition, 14; and fragile states, 16; and
lack of credibility of Western countries,
16; Millennium Declaration (2005), 3,
4; report (ICISS, 2001), 14, 16, 131, 132;
and stabilization operations, 313. *See
also* UN Peacebuilding Commission
Revolutionary Organization of the People
in Arms (ORPA), Guatemala, 213, 214,
217, 219, 221, 223, 225
Revolutionary Resistance Front, Haiti, 85
"Road Map for Peace," Palestine-Israel:
avoidance of integration of armed groups
into political process, 131; challenges
of, 267; as internationally negotiated
solution, 131, 280; peacebuilding, and
state building, 112; provisions, 114, 289;
view of prime minister's role, 135. *See
also* Oslo Peace Accords (1993, 1995),
Palestine-Israel; Palestine
Roberts, Nigel, 130
*The Role of United Nations Peacekeeping
in Disarmament, Demobilization and
Reintegration* (2000), 237-38
Rome Peace Accords (1992), Mozambique,
58, 63, 72
rural development: Afghanistan, 26, 159-
73, 176-78; Guatemala, 50, 219, 220,
230; Haiti, 99, 101, 103-4, 105
Rwanda, 6, 13

Salazar, Antonio, 61
Saraya al-Quds, Palestine, 268, 272
SEPAZ (Peace Secretariat), Guatemala,
38
Sharon, Ariel, 114, 115-16, 299
Shia Islam (Afghanistan), 240, 243, 245
Sierra Leone, 212
SIRHN (Subcommittee for Immediate
Rehabilitation and Humanitarian Needs),
Sri Lanka, 199

socioeconomic development: Guatemala,
36, 37, 40-41; Mozambique, 74-76; and
peacebuilding propositions, 29
Special Commission for Reintegration,
Guatemala, 219
Special Consultative Group for the Reconstruction of Central America, 40
spoilers: Afghanistan, 253, 258, 260; definition, 7, 281; denial of socioeconomic
assistance to, 23; emergence of, and
minimalist peace agreements, 299;
Guatemala, 40, 52; motivations, 283;
peace agreement tactics, 283-84; spoiling
as negotiating tactic, 283-84, 285; strategies for addressing, 237. *See also* DDR
(disarmament, demobilization, and reintegration) programs; former combatants
Sri Lanka: ceasefire, signing (2002), 179;
civil war, resumption of, 185, 193-94,
207; DDR, failure of, 187-88; decentralization, limited, 20; democratization,
barriers to, 185-87, 306; economy, 194-
207, 309; ethno-political civil war, 180-
81, 192-94, 202-7; governance, federal
options, 182-85; Muslim ethnic group,
180, 181, 189-91, 202, 205; Oslo Agreement (2002), 184; peacebuilding efforts,
24-25, 31, 181-82, 182-201, 207-9, 295,
314; post-tsunami rebuilding efforts,
200-1; security dilemna, after failure of
DDR, 187-89; Sinhalese ethnic group,
180, 181, 183, 189, 191, 202, 205; "strategic peace," 179; Tamil ethnic group,
180, 181, 189, 190, 202-3, 205. *See also*
LTTE (Liberation Tigers of Tamil Eelam),
Sri Lanka; UNF (United National Front),
Sri Lanka
structural adjustment programs (SAP), 23
Subcommittee for Immediate Rehabilitation and Humanitarian Needs (SIRHN),
Sri Lanka, 199
Sudan, 7
suicide attacks, 270, 272
Sunni Islam, Afghanistan, 240, 243
Swedish Committee for Afghanistan, 160

Tadjik people, Afghanistan, 240, 244
Tadjik Shura-e Nazar, Afghanistan, 236
Take the Guns Away (2004), 236
Taliban, Afghanistan: discouraged opium
growing, 154; estimated numbers, 156;
international intervention against, 26,
149, 150, 235, 236, 241; resurgence of,
155; rise of, 148, 246-47; women, conditions under, 153
Tamil National Alliance (TNA), 186

221, 222, 233, 239; in Guatemalan Peace Accords, 36-37, 52; Haiti, credit assistance, 100-101, 102; Haiti, participation in agricultural communal committees, 102; Haiti, participation in economic development projects, 98-99, 105; Mozambique, economic importance of, 75-76; Palestine, recommendation for participation in local elections, 141. *See also* gender

World Bank: Afghanistan, and NSP (National Solidarity Program), 160; LICUS (Low-Income Countries Under Stress) initiative, 15; Mozambique, decentralization strategy, 21, 69; Palestine, effect of Israeli closure policy on economy, 130; on socioeconomic measures to preventing armed conflict, 23. *See also* donors, international

Set in Stone by Artegraphica Design Co.
Copy editor: Joanne Richardson
Proofreader: Lesley Erickson
Indexer: Annette Lorek

The authorized representative in the EU for product safety and compliance is:
Mare Nostrum Group
B.V Doelen 72
4831 GR Breda
The Netherlands

www.ingramcontent.com/pod-product-compliance
Lightning Source LLC
Chambersburg PA
CBHW030636270326
41929CB00007B/96

The authorized representative in the EU for product safety and compliance is:
Mare Nostrum Group
B.V Doelen 72
4831 GR Breda
The Netherlands

www.ingramcontent.com/pod-product-compliance
Lightning Source LLC
Chambersburg PA
CBHW030636270326
41929CB00007B/96